Emotion and Discourse in L2 Narrative Research

Full details of all our books can be found on http://www.multilingual-matters.com, or by writing to Multilingual Matters, St Nicholas House, 31–34 High Street, Bristol BS1 2AW, UK.

Emotion and Discourse in L2 Narrative Research

Matthew T. Prior

MULTILINGUAL MATTERS
Bristol • Buffalo • Toronto

Library of Congress Cataloging in Publication Data
Prior, Matthew T., author.
Emotion and Discourse in L2 Narrative Research/Matthew T. Prior.
Includes bibliographical references and index.
1. Emotive (Linguistics) 2. Language and emotions. 3. Narration (Rhetoric)—Psychological aspects. 4. Discourse analysis—Psychological aspects. 5. Psycholinguistics. I. Title.
P325.5.E56P75 2016
401'.9–dc23 2015023408

British Library Cataloguing in Publication Data
A catalogue entry for this book is available from the British Library.

ISBN-13: 978-1-78309-443-1 (hbk)
ISBN-13: 978-1-78309-442-4 (pbk)

Multilingual Matters
UK: St Nicholas House, 31–34 High Street, Bristol BS1 2AW, UK.
USA: UTP, 2250 Military Road, Tonawanda, NY 14150, USA.
Canada: UTP, 5201 Dufferin Street, North York, Ontario M3H 5T8, Canada.

Copyright © 2016 Matthew T. Prior.

All rights reserved. No part of this work may be reproduced in any form or by any means without permission in writing from the publisher.

The policy of Multilingual Matters/Channel View Publications is to use papers that are natural, renewable and recyclable products, made from wood grown in sustainable forests. In the manufacturing process of our books, and to further support our policy, preference is given to printers that have FSC and PEFC Chain of Custody certification. The FSC and/or PEFC logos will appear on those books where full certification has been granted to the printer concerned.

Typeset by Techset Composition India (P) Ltd, Bangalore and Chennai, India.

Contents

	Acknowledgments	vii
	Prologue	ix
1	Getting Emotional	1
	A Brief Emotional History	3
	Moving Beyond Narratives and Stories	9
	Taking a Discursive Orientation	10
	The L2 Participants and Data	11
	Summary	24
	Overview of the Chapters	25
	Transcription Conventions	27
2	Constructing Discourse	29
	'Doing' Emotionality	31
	'Reading' Emotionality	32
	A Discursive Constructionist Approach	36
	Getting Contextual	44
	Discursive Construction	48
	Discursive Deconstruction	51
	Summary	52
3	Telling and Remembering	54
	Autobiographical Tellings	55
	Features of Tellings	56
	Launching Tellings in Casual Conversation	61
	Launching Tellings in Institutional Settings	62
	Launching Tellings in L2 Interviews	63
	Expectational Features of Emotional Story Prefaces	74
	Tellings, Memories and Emotional Words	76
	Summary	82
4	Inviting Emotional Tellings	85
	Soliciting Authentic Knowledge and Subjectivity	86

	Considering Competence and Expertise	87
	Questioning in 'Ordinary' and 'Institutional' Interaction	90
	Eliciting and Producing Emotion Talk	93
	Soliciting Emotional Stories	95
	Summary	104
5	Eliciting Feelings	106
	Part 1. 'Feeling' Questions	106
	Feeling Question Sequences	115
	Part 2. Emotion-Implicative Questions	120
	Examples from Other Studies	127
	Summary	130
6	(Re)Formulating Emotionality	132
	L2 Research Interviews and Psychotherapeutic Interaction	133
	Formulation and Reformulation	134
	Summary	152
7	Managing Emotionality and Distress	155
	Problems and Failures	156
	Emotion Management and Emotional Work	157
	Interviewee Distress and Emotion Management	158
	Interviewer's Emotional Work	169
	Emotional Contagion	173
	Emotional Danger	174
	Summary	176
8	Being 'Negative'	179
	Resisting 'Positive' Emotionality	180
	Explaining 'Negativity'	185
	Summary	195
9	Reflecting Back, Moving Forward	197
	Contributions to Research	199
	Contributions to the Study of Emotion	205
	Contributions to Discursive Practices	207
	Moving Ahead	208
	Emotional Well-Being and Regulation	209
	Summary	212
	Final Words	214
	References	216
	Author Index	246
	Subject Index	253

Acknowledgments

This book would not have been possible without the contributions of a great many people. First, I would like to express my deepest appreciation to the individuals who graciously shared their time and experiences over the course of this research. I am sincerely humbled by your generosity and patience. You helped a clumsy researcher learn to listen. *Cả̂m ơn, or-kun, zoi sia* and *salamat* for allowing me into your lives and for forever changing mine.

My evolving interest in and approach to emotion, identity, narrative, qualitative interviewing and discourse analysis have been profoundly shaped by the ideas and writings of scholars who have wrestled with these matters far longer than I have. I am especially indebted to Charles Antaki, Paul Atkinson, Carolyn Baker, Michael Bamberg, Gary Barkhuizen, Richard Bauman, Mike Baynham, Phil Benson, Bethan Benwell, Niko Besnier, Jack Bilmes, David Block, Jan Blommaert, Charles Briggs, Richard Buttny, Lisa Capps, Susan Chase, Elizabeth Couper-Kuhlen, Anna De Fina, Norman Denzin, Jean-Marc Dewaele, Patsy Duff, Derek Edwards, Susan Ehrlich, Alexandra Georgakopoulou, Jaber Gubrium, Paul ten Have, Alexa Hepburn, John Heritage, James Holstein, Ian Hutchby, Gail Jefferson, Yasuko Kanno, Celia Kitzinger, Irene Koshik, Michele Koven, Claire Kramsch, Anthony Liddicoat, Jennifer Mandelbaum, Numa Markee, Douglas Maynard, Julia Menard-Warwick, Elliott Mishler, Bonny Norton, Elinor Ochs, Aneta Pavlenko, Annsi Peräkylä, Jonathan Potter, Timothy Rapley, Keith Richards, Catherine Riessman, Kathy Roulston, Johanna Ruusuvuori, Harvey Sacks, Paul Seedhouse, Emmanuel Schegloff, Jack Sidnell, David Silverman, Susan Speer, Tanya Stivers, Liz Stokoe, Gergana Vitanova, Margaret Wetherell, James Wilce, Sue Wilkinson, Robin Wooffitt and many others whose work continues to inspire and challenge my own.

Additionally, I extend my heartfelt thanks to my community of colleagues, mentors and friends both near and far for their unwavering encouragement. I owe a special debt of gratitude to Diana Eades, Gabi Kasper and Dick Schmidt for their friendship, patience, wisdom and indefatigable intellectual and emotional support throughout my career. They taught me that academic life requires human compassion as well as scholarly rigor. Sarah Benesch, Vai Ramanathan and Stephanie Vandrick deserve acknowledgement for motivating me to write this book and for so generously offering their helpful guidance and advice.

I am especially appreciative of Steven Talmy, a phenomenal *senpai* and applied linguist, for being a critical sounding board and for encouraging me to discover my own voice as a scholar and author.

Among others whom I sincerely admire and who have had a hand in shaping my personal and professional journey, I wish to acknowledge Dwight Atkinson, Chris Casanave, Bee Chamcharatsri, Dorothy Chun, Graham Crookes, Christina Higgins, Mark James, Yasuko Kanno, Ruby Macksoud, Tim McNamara, Aya Matsuda, Paul Matsuda, Liz Miller, Junko Mori, Su Motha, Hanh Nguyen, Amy Ohta, Hanako Okada, Lourdes Ortega, Aek Phakiti, Ellen Rintell, Jeff Siegel, Merrill Swain, Irene Thompson, Manka Varghese, Doris Warriner and Jim Yoshioka. Thanks also go to colleagues and students in the Department of English at Arizona State University, the Department of Second Language Studies at the University of Hawai'i at Mānoa and the National Foreign Language Resource Center (UH Mānoa). To those whom I have failed to acknowledge, I offer my sincere apologies. Please remind me to thank you in person.

I am also grateful to Kim Eggleton, Anna Roderick and the rest of the fantastic Multilingual Matters team for believing in this project and seeing it through to completion.

And finally, my most special thanks go to my mother, Ruth Prior, who has believed in me and supported me all along the way – there are not enough words to express my love and appreciation.

To all those who made this book possible, *Mahalo nui loa.*

Prologue

Reflexivity and 'Violent Acts'

In a book advocating greater reflexivity throughout the life of research and the life of the researcher, it would be conspicuous if I did not acknowledge how my own personal ecology has shaped these chapters. Yet, despite an intellectual commitment to reflexivity, I admit that I find such disclosure personally uncomfortable and even 'unnatural'. As qualitative researchers, our professional activity is largely defined by investigative inquiry. We are accustomed to gathering intimate details on the lives and practices of research participants; we are less forthcoming, however, with the personal histories that propel our own scholarly activities and alignments. This reticence may be due to a desire to carefully craft a veneer of objectivity and analytical rigor as well as to avoid being accused of emotionalism and over-involvement. It may also stem from fear of subjecting ourselves to criticism or of appearing self-congratulatory or even self-indulgent, particularly in this contemporary era where the lines between private and public selves are progressively blurred.

Perhaps a more apt, albeit radical, characterization of this struggle with reflexivity and representation is found in the words of Merleau-Ponty, the phenomenological philosopher, who suggests that personal reflection constitutes a 'violent act which is validated by being performed' (2013: lxxxv). I confess that I have wrestled with doing scholarly 'violence' against self throughout the various stages of this project, indeed my academic career. How much of my own private history and biases do or must bleed (perhaps an apt metaphor for the embodied nature of research) into and out of my professional persona?

Because conversation analysis, at least 'basic' CA (Heritage, 2005b), has largely eschewed data deemed 'non-naturalistic' or 'contrived' (e.g. research interviews), researcher reflexivity has not been a central concern (cf. Housley & Fitzgerald, 2000). However, feminist and critical scholars, whose work is defined by attention to personal and ethical accountability, have long recognized the psychological burden (and cathartic potential) reflexive research engenders. Fine and Weis (1998: 27), for example, speak of the researcher's own 'anxieties ... struggles, passions, and pains' across the process of fieldwork, and Olesen (2011: 135) forcefully writes that reflexivity 'demands steady, uncomfortable assessment' and 'acute awareness' of the influence of the researcher's background on the research. In uncovering our own personal histories and emotional responses, there exists also the hidden danger of finding that 'feelings of guilt and shame evoked by research activity may have deeper roots that go beyond the particular piece of research we are engaged in' (Danchev & Ross, 2014: 22). Perhaps this tension itself can lead to the acceptance that all research and its representation, despite the most compelling intellectual theorizing and empirically grounded claims, remains ineluctably partial and perspectival.

With these admitted caveats and reservations, and in the spirit of reflexivity, I briefly contextualize this project by presenting a version of my own emotional history and how it has shaped the development of my research interests, scholarly focus, theoretical framework, methodological choices and interpretive stances. Rather than slipping into 'self-indulgent' or 'sentimental' posturing (Atkinson, 2015), I purposefully reflect here on these deeply personal components of my own biography to trace their relevance for the trajectory of the research as well as the trajectory of the researcher. As I aim to show, because research never takes place in a social, intellectual, emotional or moral vacuum, the seeds that inspire scholarly inquiry may be planted long before the official study is ever undertaken.

My Emotional History

I suspect my fascination with matters of identity and the various psychological dilemmas tied to language, place and belonging arose from my personal journey with the visible as well as 'hidden identities' (Vandrick, 2009) of my formative years and beyond. I have previously written on the intersection between language and identity (Prior, 2011c), contending that one's multiple identities may not only encounter points of conflict (e.g. *researcher* and *friend*), they may also be perceived and experienced as mutually exclusive (e.g. *gay* and *religious*). From the list of ascribable social categories, I have been identified as *male, son, brother, friend, white, mixed, gay, straight, single, partnered, Christian, academic, colleague, student, musician, factory worker, 'native' speaker, L2 user, foreigner, gaijin* and *haole*, among others. Because of the polysemous and contextually shifting connotations of such labels, they afford differing degrees of psychological and social stability while generating and constraining possibilities for avowal, confirmation, contestation and denial.

In many ways, I consider myself a 'modern nomad' and a cultural 'inbetweener', having moved more times that I can count across the United States, Canada and overseas. A legacy of growing up as a 'PK' (pastor's kid) and the child of parents and grandparents who were themselves rootless, is that dislocation and relocation became part of my 'lifeworld' or habitus (Bourdieu, 1991). Every new locale brought with it new faces, new cultures, new language varieties, new schools and new spaces of (un)belonging. As a child, I was a voracious reader and eager learner, but in the peer-based hierarchies of school, being the newcomer, excessively studious or perceived as 'different' relegated one to the social periphery. Compounded by an introverted temperament and struggles due to undiagnosed stuttering and speech blocking, this brought with it increasing levels of social anxiety and repeated episodes of verbal and even physical bullying. Fortunately, my parents encouraged my musical and artistic endeavors and exposed me to languages such as German, Romansch, French, Chinese, and classical Hebrew and Greek. This ignited my interest in languages and cultures, and I found renewed confidence in my various academic and creative achievements.

After graduating from high school, I continued to move across the US and Canada and found myself in diverse workplaces and communities where I was often in the minority as an Anglo-American man and L1 (first language) English speaker. Kicked out of my home and ostracized at work for being identified as 'gay', for a time I was homeless and saw a side of society that was previously hidden from my comparatively sheltered upbringing. But reflecting on those difficult times, I especially remember my neighbors and co-workers – ethnic minorities and immigrants from Mexico, Central America and Southeast Asia – who took me in and whose values and actions, mundane and consequential, challenged for me the social stereotypes I had unwittingly learned growing up.

Returning to school to pursue my undergraduate studies in Washington State, I became interested in teaching ESL (English as a second language) through volunteer opportunities as a peer advisor who assisted international students' acclimation to life in the US, and then as an English teacher in the local immigrant community. These experiences eventually led me to complete my ESL training and move overseas to teach English in Japan, where I began an extended seven-year sojourn that among much else, bolstered my commitment to the field of English language teaching. My time in Japan also introduced me to the linguistic and sociopolitical challenges and discrimination faced by transnational migrants, particularly those from China, the Philippines, Thailand, Iran, Brazil and Peru. I loved Japan, but many of the migrants and Korean residents I met expressed an ambivalent relationship with Japanese society, ranging from affection and fascination to fear and distrust. These feelings were often expressed with an attitude of fatalism, represented in the ubiquitous Japanese expression *shikata ga nai* ('It can't be helped').

I was also continually reminded that I, too, was an outsider in Japan. Although my multilingual competence and integrative motivation enabled me to lead a relatively comfortable life, in public and in private I was always the *hen na Amerikajin* ('the strange American') – the foreign oddity that was neither Japanese nor quite stereotypically American. On many occasions I recalled the forewarning given to me years earlier by the host mother of one of my Japanese students. Originally from France, she married a Japanese national and they raised several children in the US. As we spoke one day about my efforts to study Japanese language and culture before going to Japan, she took me aside and said, 'No matter how long you live in Japan or how well you know the Japanese language and culture, never forget that you will never belong. You can never, ever become Japanese.' At the time, I thought her jaded outlook a product of a much earlier period in Japanese–US relations. Colored by a mix of youthful optimism and arrogance, I knew better, and I was going to prove her wrong. However, the reality of life in Japan, for all its positive qualities, later confirmed her assertions. Of course, I was also made keenly aware by my interactions with transnational migrants and Japanese citizens that my visible whiteness and gender, American citizenship and status as a native English speaker and language teacher afforded me a socially and economically elevated status. As a result, I have learned how essential it is to recognize that my perspectives are unavoidably filtered through privilege and protection.

Eventually I returned to the US. Intent on furthering my career as a language professional, I pursued graduate studies at the University of Hawai'i at Mānoa. It is there, in one of the most linguistically and culturally diverse environments in the world, that I discovered an intellectual space for advancing my knowledge of second language acquisition (SLA) while teaching and volunteering in local immigrant communities. In Hawai'i, I often heard it said with pride that 'everyone is a minority' and 'everyone is an immigrant'. While this discourse of Hawai'i as a 'rainbow' of ethnic harmony has been perpetuated in tourism and the media (Linnekin, 1997; Talmy, 2010a), it has not gone unchallenged by native Hawaiians and others (e.g. Trask, 2000). I also became aware when working with Vietnamese, Cambodian, Micronesian and other community members that not all minorities and immigrants are afforded equal opportunities for socioeconomic attainment and sociopolitical participation. Individuals forced to migrate and seek physical and political refuge due to war, persecution, exploitation and other upheavals face very different conditions and social circumstances than those who voluntarily elect to relocate from a desire to explore the world or try out new life opportunities. As I observed, the consequences of these conditions were also thoroughly affective, involving quiet resignation and sadness as well as explosive anger and even violence.

Although my early research interests centered on psycholinguistic and cognitive processes in SLA, I became increasingly interested in sociolinguistic explorations of identity and belonging. When I was conducting a series of testing experiments involving L1 Vietnamese speakers recruited from the local community (Chaudron *et al.*, 2006), I noticed between experiments and in background interviews that participants often digressed into telling stories about life back in Vietnam and their present-day challenges in the US. Initially I viewed these digressions as 'verbal clutter' or impediments to the task of collecting the experimental data. As I carried out more experiments with other participants, I continued to observe digressions into storytelling. Eventually, I mentioned to a trusted professor that I found it curious and even frustrating that the research participants kept telling stories. Rather than sympathizing with my frustration, she offered her advice: 'Listen'. So, I did. As it would turn out, this simple suggestion led to a pivotal change in the course of my professional research as well as my own personal trajectory.

By learning to listen (Briggs, 1986), I began to notice various matters that these speakers highlighted and treated as unforgettable, emotional and influential on their lives as immigrants, former refugees, multilingual persons and transcultural citizens. Chief among their concerns were issues of belonging (e.g. social, linguistic, ethnic, national, spiritual) and feelings of anger and shame surrounding limited English abilities and education. I then began to use my academic studies as an opportunity to investigate these various interrelated topics, including immigrant literacy practices, social and participation networks and motivational trajectories.

Among other influential factors that fueled my interest in the experiences of transcultural migrants were the circulating media and social discourses that asserted that immigrants were content to live in ethnic enclaves or ghettos and were unwilling to get beyond their troubled histories and cultural ties to successfully blend into the social fabric of mainstream North American society (Ong, 2003; Portes & Rumbaut, 2014). As another university professor commented, perhaps to offer a challenge, 'Why can't they stop being so tragic and get over it?' Thus it was this growing critical awareness of and interest in better understanding the lived realities of immigrant groups and individuals that prompted me to pursue research exploring their language and literacy practices, family structures, social networks, self-perceptions and personal and community biographies.

I discovered that contrary to societal assertions that immigrants were lazy and uninterested in learning English, those whom I met were deeply concerned with matters of language learning, development, maintenance and even attrition. Moreover, they often stated that they desperately wanted to belong and desired to break through the boundaries of accent, ethnicity, national origin and socioeconomic status. The centrality of autobiographical tellings in their talk led me to become more conscious of both the discursive and the psychological aspects of making sense of and representing or (re)constructing self and experience. To better examine these personal and emergent aspects of second language use and social participation, my research agenda then shifted to a more discursive constructionist and social interactional approach. This book represents part of this journey, including the successes, the failures, the challenges and the dilemmas – but mostly the inescapable emotionality of it all.

1 Getting Emotional

> *Emotions play a crucial part in our lives. The sharing of emotions, whether in face-to-face interactions or through written communications is an important social activity, and the ability to do so helps us maintain physical and mental health.*
> (Dewaele, 2013: 208)

> *Investigations of the role of affect in language cannot proceed without a fine-grained ethnographic inquiry into language use in context ... Ideal contexts for the study of the relationship between language and emotional life are situations in which emotions themselves become the focus of attention ... and the ethnographic interview itself ... can provide rich ethnographic opportunities for such investigations.*
> (Besnier, 1990: 437–438)

Due to its personal and in-depth focus, narrative or autobiographical[1] research (terms used here as shorthand for qualitative, interview-based research involving first-person accounts, tellings, life stories and related talk of memorable episodes, turning points and other personal experiences) is often described as a highly confessional activity (e.g. Atkinson, 1998; Coffey, 2004; Gubrium *et al.*, 2012; Riessman, 2008; Weiss, 1994). It seems only fitting to begin with a confession: this is not really a book about *emotion*. Neither is it centrally about 'feelings', 'moods', 'subjectivities' or whatever other descriptive labels popularly used to refer to affective phenomena.[2] This may appear a contradictory way to introduce a chapter titled 'Getting Emotional' in a book promising 'Emotion and Discourse', but it is crucial for understanding the approach informing these chapters.

What, then, is this book about? The short answer is that it is concerned with the interactional construction and management of *emotionality* in L2 (second language) autobiographical interview research. The distinction made here between emotion and emotionality is more than semantic. Turning attention to emotionality reframes emotions as *social actions* rather than intra-psychological properties or 'thing-like entities' (Sarbin, 2001: 217) waiting to be discovered or measured. This action orientation engages with affective and other putatively 'psychological' components of speakers' identities and experiences by exploring the dynamic, dilemmatic, (in)consistent, multilayered and agentive aspects of their representation. Thus this book contributes to the investigation of emotionality and autobiographical talk by turning the analytical lens on a surprisingly under-examined aspect of scholarly research: our own practices. By advancing a discursive constructionist approach, it offers a timely methodological and interaction-based perspective that examines how emotionality is collaboratively managed as both *topic* and *resource* within the institutional and interpersonal business of qualitative research.

Located in the context of contemporary narrative and ethnographic inquiry on multilingual identities and transcultural flows, this interdisciplinary project weaves together discussions and analyses based on the L1 (first language) and L2 literatures as well as original research I carried out with adult immigrants from Southeast Asia living in the United States and Canada. Although this book addresses issues of relevance for qualitative research practice in general, its primary audience is scholars in *L2 studies* (including the various intersecting fields, domains and disciplines of second and foreign language studies, applied linguistics, TESOL (Teaching English to speakers of other languages) and related bi/multilingualism research). Even within L2 studies, autobiographical interview research is not a unitary program but encompasses a wide range of methodologies, topics, theoretical and philosophical perspectives and approaches to data generation and analysis. Recognizing this diversity, I invite readers to compare the issues explored here with their own sociolinguistic contexts, speakers and data of interest.

I must emphasize that this is *not* a 'how-to' text or manual. It will not present a list of procedures specifying how to conduct autobiographical inquiry or analyze narratives; neither will it offer guidelines stipulating what constitutes a 'good' or a 'bad' narrative or research interview. These chapters open up various interview activities and products for inspection, and readers are invited to co-analyze and develop their own informed conclusions. Because this book attends to research challenges and even 'failures' (Prior, 2014; Roulston, 2014), it may prove largely instructional on what *not* to do. Emotion is omnipresent, but I will nevertheless refrain from laying out a taxonomy of emotion or proposing yet another theory of affect. Herein I advocate approaching emotionality and autobiographical tellings as discursive, social practices, and I aim to show there are compelling grounds for this. However, I do not assert this is the only approach or the final word on such matters. It is also not my intent to elevate stories of hardship over stories of success or 'negative' emotions over 'positive' ones. This investigation opens up just as many questions as it answers. Therefore it embraces and seeks to make visible the inherent tensions and 'messiness' of autobiographical research and qualitative inquiry more broadly.

In the remainder of the chapter I describe in more detail the background, motivations and objectives of this project. I begin with a brief overview of the recent growth of emotion research and the ways in which it intersects with autobiographical inquiry. I then address concerns about researcher reflexivity and implications for exploring the affective interface of research practice. Concluding the Introduction, I describe the L2 research context, the focal participants and the data that inform these chapters.

A Brief Emotional History

Getting emotional in L2 research

There is no doubt we are getting emotional. Across the interdisciplinary field of L2 studies, scholars are increasingly taking a keen interest in investigating the forms and functions of emotion in human language life. Where once there was only a scattered collection of monographs and articles that addressed emotion and affective variables (e.g. Arnold, 1999; Horwitz *et al.*, 1986; Rintell, 1984, 1990; Schumann, 1997; Scovel, 1978), we now have a rapidly expanding library of emotion-relevant scholarship from diverse yet often intersecting perspectives such as *L2 motivation* (e.g. Dörnyei, 2009; Dörnyei & Kubanyiova, 2014; Dörnyei *et al.*, 2014; Dörnyei & Ushioda, 2009, 2011; Murray *et al.*, 2011; Oxford, 2011), *bi/multilingualism* and *cognitive processing* (e.g. Dewaele, 2005, 2006, 2010; Dewaele & Pavlenko, 2002; Koven, 2004; Pavlenko, 2005, 2006); *critical pedagogy* (e.g. Benesch, 2011; Crookes, 2013); *sociocultural approaches* (e.g. Garrett & Young, 2009; Swain *et al.*, 2011; Zuengler & Miller, 2003); *language socialization* (e.g. Baquedano-López, 2004; Garrett & Baquedano-López, 2002; Kanagy, 1999); *language and desire* (e.g. Motha & Lin, 2013; Takahashi, 2013); *L2 writing* (e.g. Chamcharatsri, 2013; Hanauer, 2010); *teacher cognition* and *professional development* (e.g. Akbari, 2007; Borg, 2015; Golombek & Doran, 2014); *language and identity* (e.g. Block, 2007; Golombek & Jordan, 2005; Kanno, 2003; Kramsch, 2009; Mantero, 2007; Motha, 2006; Norton, 2013); and *narrative perspectives* (e.g. Barkhuizen *et al.*, 2014; Baynham & De Fina, 2005; Benson & Nunan, 2005; Kalaja *et al.*, 2008; Menard-Warwick, 2009; Pavlenko, 2005, 2007; Prior, 2011a, 2011b, 2011c; Vitanova, 2013; Warriner, 2013). Recent edited collections further evince this renewed interest in the emotional dimensions of language acquisition and use (Dewaele, 2010; Gabryś-Barker & Bielska, 2013; Pavlenko, 2006; Prior & Kasper, 2016).

Following the recognition that emotion plays an integral part in the lives and practices of L2 users, we are now witnessing a growing shift in the field toward the treatment of emotion as a distinct topic of scholarly inquiry in its own right, not just a peripheral concern or a post-hoc observation by the researcher. This contemporary interest in emotion has been spurred in part by what has been labeled the 'affective' or 'emotional' turn (Clarke & Hoggett, 2009; Clough & Halley, 2007; Greco & Stenner, 2008; Massumi, 2002) that has made its way across the social sciences and humanities (for concise overviews in applied linguistics, see Benesch, 2011; Pavlenko, 2013). This turn, though by no means a uniform program, is characterized by a shared rejection of researcher neutrality; a feminist and postmodern critique of body politics; a re-theorizing of narrative, emotional labor and power; and an intensified commitment to self-reflexivity.

Another factor that has contributed to the recent attention to affective matters in L2 studies is the overwhelming body of evidence that points to the presence and relevance of emotionality within all aspects of our research: in the motivated selection of topics and questions, in the recruitment of participants, in our methods, in the generation of data, in the data fragments that capture our attention, in the decisions to include or reject data and participants, in our analyses and findings, in the ways we report and disseminate our research, in the practical applications and in the ongoing ethical and sociopolitical dilemmas and other challenges that we encounter (Dörnyei, 2007; Heigham & Croker, 2009; Prior, 2014; Richards, 2003; Roulston, 2010; Simpson, 2011; Willig & Stainton-Rogers, 2008).

Facing resistance

The contemporary appreciation of the emotional content and activities of qualitative research does not mean that all have fully embraced this area of inquiry. Dominant 'Western'[3] scientific traditions still view emotion with suspicion (Gilbert, 2001; Jaggar, 1992). Thus when researchers show an interest in 'feelings' and 'affective realities', they may find themselves accused of being 'emotionalist' and giving in to 'romantic' impulses that elevate 'the experiential as the authentic' (Silverman, 2011: 179; also Atkinson, 2015):

> Under emotionalists' exclusive focus on inner feelings and self-reflective confessions, all substantive inquiries about social reality dissolve into self-explorative texts. (Silverman, 2010: 106)

Researchers continue to be reminded in not so subtle ways that 'emotions are seen to be the very antithesis of the detached scientific mind and its quest for "objectivity", "truth" and "wisdom"' (Williams & Bendelow, 1998: xvi). Some scholars have even suggested that emotion research, because it may challenge dominant beliefs and practices, can be professionally risky, particularly for women, minorities and those less established in their careers (see also Blackman, 2007; Boler, 1999):

> However, it is only possible to assert the importance of emotional labor if we challenge the dominance of the Western philosophical tradition wherein emotions are judged to be an anathema to academic production. This is not as easy as may be presumed. Focusing on emotions in social research, especially our own, is problematic in practice, as a concern with emotional issues can result in a Catch-22 situation for women situated as academics. If we focus on emotions, we fit a stigmatized stereotype and may end up positioned below rational cognitive actors in the hierarchy constructed on the basis of dominant conceptions. (Gilbert, 2001: 133)

Despite resistance by some to the explicit engagement with emotion through and within our research, it is becoming clear that L2 researchers (incidentally, a group comprised largely of women, minorities, 'non-Westerners' and L2 users) can no longer claim or feign ignorance of affective phenomena. Emotion scholarship has reached a critical mass and the 'turn' has already been made. We are therefore left with two options: reject emotion (implicitly or explicitly) – by ignoring it or charging it as unscientific and not amenable to serious, scholarly inquiry – or acknowledge and explore it as a topic and resource. Many of us in the field have found emotion and affective phenomena worthy objects of scholarly attention, and we are investigating these matters from increasingly diverse perspectives. The recent rise of emotion-related research in peer-reviewed publications and professional conferences further suggests a growing confidence that a scholarly interest in emotion need not make us automatically guilty of romantic emotionalism or researcher bias. Moreover, as I assert throughout these chapters, neither does taking an active interest in emotion preclude analytical rigor and defensibility.

Getting emotional in autobiographical interview research

As a result of this increased attention to affective domains and practices, L2 researchers are coming to appreciate what sociologists and anthropologists have long acknowledged – namely, that emotionality is not a tangential part of human language, life and experience but is the communicative force that pulls and binds them together:

> Although it seems obvious that studying emotions can help us understand human biology and psychology, it might be less apparent that studying emotions can help us understand basic sociological questions ... Both [social] division and cohesion, and their coexistence as well, are in part the products of patterned and often ritualized *interchanges* of human emotions ... social emotions ... glue us together, albeit in unequal arrangements. (Schmitt & Clark, 2006: 468)

> Social emotions may provide the motivation to form and maintain social bonds, but communicating those feelings enables individuals to reach beyond their private feelings to make social contact. Emotion accomplishes very little in the social world unless it is communicated. (Planalp, 1999: 138)

Perhaps nowhere more visible is this interest in the communicative potential and meaning of emotionality than in L2 narrative inquiry and autobiographical interview research, most notably by scholars aligning themselves with sociocultural and feminist/critical frameworks (e.g. Barkhuizen, 2011; Baynham & De Fina, 2005; Benson & Nunan, 2005; Block, 2007; Kalaja *et al.*, 2008; Kanno, 2003; Koven, 2002, 2004; Menard-Warwick,

2009; Miller, 2003; Motha, 2014; Norton, 2000; Pavlenko & Blackledge, 2004; Swain, 2011; Vitanova, 2004). Through the elicitation and examination of first-person accounts, research itself inspired by the 'narrative' or 'biographic' turn (e.g. Atkinson, 1997; Barkhuizen, 2011, 2013; Barkhuizen *et al.*, 2014; Pavlenko, 2007), this diverse body of work has persuasively articulated the intense *intra*personal and *inter*personal conflict that multilingual groups and individuals face across the life trajectory.

Getting reflexive in autobiographical interview research

Amid the ongoing celebration of autobiographical inquiry, narrative sensemaking and the emotional content and impact of our scholarly research, frequently absent is a careful inspection of the activity of self-representation and a critical, reflexive examination of the institutional and interpersonal frames of the research process itself. This has prompted repeated calls across the human sciences for a more restrained celebration of interviews and other autobiographical inquiry and greater attention to the ways in which they operate as sociocultural and institutional practices (e.g. Atkinson, 2015; Briggs, 1986; De Fina & Georgakopoulou, 2012; De Fina *et al.*, 2006; Gubrium *et al.*, 2012; Hammersley & Atkinson, 2007; Holstein & Gubrium, 1995; Mishler, 1986; Pavlenko, 2007; Rapley, 2001; Riessman, 1993; Talmy, 2010b; Talmy & Richards, 2011):

> The ubiquity of the narrative and its centrality to everyday work are not license simply to privilege those forms ... We need, in other words, to treat them as 'social facts', like any other that is equally conventional, and apply the same canons of methodological skepticism as we would apply to any other acts and social forms. (Atkinson, 1997: 341)

> A reflexive research practice does not conclude with the design and conduct of interviews – it is also very much part of how we analyze and represent others in reports from our studies. Through combining the various reflexive strategies – subjectivity statements, researcher journals, interviews, and analysis of interaction – researchers can explore the particularities of their encounters with others in their examination of research problems, and, in doing so, learn something more about themselves and others. (Roulston, 2010: 127)

Denzin (1992) has criticized 'scientific' inquiry, both qualitative and quantitative, for the failure to consider the discursive and representational history of speakers' lived and felt experiences:

> But, like their empiricist counterparts, they seek 'scientific' accounts of emotionality and contemporary life, which privilege the researcher over

the subject, method over subject matter, and maintain commitments to outmoded conceptions of validity, truth, and generalizability. They refuse to address how the subject's experiences are transformed into textual representations that are only stand-ins for the actual experience being described and analyzed. (20)

Blommaert (2001a) echoes this perspective in his critique of discourse analysis, directed mainly at critical discourse analysis and conversation analysis (CA):

One of the most important methodological problems in discourse analysis in general is the framing of discourse in particular selections of contexts, the relevance of which is established by the researcher but is not made into an object of investigation. (15)

'Critique' thus becomes, too often and too much, a matter of the credibility of the researcher, whose account of power in contextual narratives is offered not for inspection but for belief. (17)

Blommaert is particularly critical of CA for what he describes as its unwillingness 'to recognize even the existence of the entextualizing practices it applies to text' (2001a: 18). Although he does not use the term 'reflexivity', his arguments reiterate the urgent need for researchers to attend more closely to the processes by which research data become *generated* and *represented* (rather than collected) in relation to the research project and its goals.

Reconsidering researcher reflexivity and positionality

Of course, not all researchers have ignored their own influence on the research process. Researcher reflexivity, often treated synonymously with positionality, remains an explicit topic of concern for scholars whose work is in a qualitative or interpretive vein (e.g. Bucholtz, 2003; Duff, 2008; Eckert, 2003; Etherington, 2004; Hesse-Biber & Leavy, 2008; Jones *et al.*, 2006; Marshall & Rossman, 2006; Menard-Warwick, 2009; Ramanathan, 2002, 2005; Roberts, 2001). In qualitative research, it is now axiomatic that researchers' own biographies cannot help but shape their research. How researchers locate themselves in relation to their work, as well as how they are located by others, impacts the research process and leaves an indelible mark on the selection of topic, context, participants and procedures as well as the subsequent representation and dissemination of the research and findings.

For qualitative researchers, there is no theory-free knowledge or value-free research (Denzin & Lincoln, 2011). They also recognize that although objectivity cannot be successfully sustained by either qualitative or quantitative paradigms, there is nevertheless a tendency to perpetuate the 'illusion of objectivity' (Holliday, 2007; Medawar, 1996) through scientific and fact-reporting prose, the presentation of a step-by-step research model (Walford, 1991) and the deletion of the problematic aspects of doing research (but for counter examples, see e.g. Nairn *et al.*, 2005; Prior, 2014; Rapley, 2012; Roulston, 2010). Indeed, many researchers (e.g. Canagarajah, 1996; Denzin, 2001; Denzin & Lincoln, 2011; Mehra, 2001; Norton & Early, 2011; Talmy, 2011), located primarily along the borders of interpretive, constructionist, feminist and 'post' (-modern, -structural, -colonial) traditions, have emphasized the importance of disclosing the researcher's own presence and positionality and encourage reflexivity throughout the various stages of the research process.

> Three interconnected, generic activities define the qualitative research process. They go by a variety of labels, including theory, method, and analysis; or ontology, epistemology, and methodology. Behind these terms stands the personal biography of the researcher, who speaks from a particular class, gendered, racial, and ethnic community perspective. (Denzin & Lincoln, 2011: 11)

Rather than ignoring or dismissing the researcher's voice and biography, these critiques urge a more direct and personal engagement with all aspects of the research process. Moreover, as Herr and Anderson (2005: 30) remind novice scholars, 'the degree to which researchers locate themselves as insiders or outsiders will determine how they frame epistemological, methodological, and ethical issues in the dissertation'. Roberts (2001: 326) speaks also of the 'researcher's personal anthropology' – those aspects of the researcher's background and historical context that contribute both to the particular topics of inquiry as well as the ways in which the studies get framed. Thus, the position taken by many contemporary qualitative researchers is that by attending closely to the influences of these contextual factors in the research process, we become more aware of the presuppositions and predispositions that permeate our methodologies.

Despite repeated recommendations urging researchers to critically (re)examine their *actual* (i.e. in situ, rather than purported or ideal) practices, narrative and autobiographical interview studies continue to flood the field while researcher reflexivity is frequently reduced to revealing one's positionality, glossing one's own personal history, elevating research participants' voices and identifying unequal power relations. These may indeed function as significant components of researcher reflexivity, yet they stop short of a careful inspection of the practices that actively exploit the personal biographies, communicative competences and other resources of interactants within the contexts in which the research material is generated and recorded. Arguing the need for greater reflexivity in L2 qualitative research interviewing, Talmy (2010b; see also Bucholtz, 2003) contends that whatever the conceptual framework, urgently required of the researcher is a conscious engagement with the assumptions underpinning the research and more careful attention to the methods that are employed leading up to, during and after the interviews:

> I would suggest that there is considerable need for heightened reflexivity about the interview methods that applied linguistics researchers use in their studies, on the role of the interviewer in occasioning interview answers, on the subject 'behind' the interviewee, on the status ascribed to interview data, and on how those data are analyzed and represented, regardless of whether one opts to conceive of interviews as research instrument, or research interviews as participation in social practices. (Talmy, 2010b: 143)

Moving Beyond Narratives and Stories

As a means to address these various concerns, this book explores the ways in which emotionality and identity are implicated in methodological, ethical and other closely related matters in L2 autobiographical interview research. It is not just interested in participants' *narratives* or *stories*, the usual 'stars' of qualitative inquiry (Atkinson & Delamont, 2006); it extends its analytical gaze to the surrounding talk and in-between spaces – to make visible the often taken-for-granted or 'seen but unnoticed' (Garfinkel, 1967: 41) work that goes into the production and reception of autobiographical material as well as diverse forms of meta-talk or commentary. Consequently, this analytical stance contrasts sharply with perspectives that elevate the thematic and dramatic content of talk and narrative at the expense of an understanding of the agentive and even contested nature of its representation and interpretation.

It cannot be overstated that despite all the methodological texts on interviewing, and the extraordinary number of interview-based studies published in recent years, the *activity* of interviewing remains greatly under-examined:

> Although there is some work on the dynamics of accounting practices, in real terms we still know very little about the interactional work of qualitative interviews beyond the very basics. (Rapley, 2012: 546)

> [I]nterviewing has been too easy, too obvious, too little studied, and too open to providing a convenient launching pad for poor research. (Potter & Hepburn, 2012: 555)

By giving priority to emic procedures of identity work and meaning-making, this book attends to both the production and reception of emotionality as it is elicited, co-constructed, interpreted and otherwise embedded in the interactional activities of research. Attending also to the researcher's 'emotional labor' (Gilbert, 2001; Hochschild, 1983/2003; Toerien & Kitzinger, 2007), it takes seriously recent calls to engage more closely with activity, theory and analysis in autobiographical interviewing, thereby contributing to what Rapley (2012: 552) has called 'social studies of interview studies' (see also related discussions in Atkinson, 2015; Barkhuizen, 2011; Briggs, 2007; Gubrium *et al.*, 2012; Holstein & Gubrium, 2003; Prior, 2014; Roulston, 2014; Talmy, 2011; Talmy & Richards, 2011).

Taking a Discursive Orientation

Departing from models that view emotions as cognitive or intra-individual constructs and autobiographical interview research as a window into experience and personal psychologies, this book maintains a commitment to the close analysis of interaction and the practices by which speakers mobilize and make visible their discursive and extra-discursive resources and competences. As a means to empirically ground this investigation of emotionality and the representation of self and experience, it advances a discursive constructionist (DC) approach that draws on conversation analysis (CA) (e.g. Hutchby & Wooffitt, 2008), discursive psychology (DP) (e.g. Edwards, 1997, 1999; Potter & Hepburn, 2007), ethnographic methods (Atkinson, 2015; Maynard, 2003), narrative scholarship (e.g. Atkinson & Delamont, 2006; De Fina & Georgakopoulou, 2012; Ochs & Capps, 2001; Riessman, 2008; Sparkes & Smith, 2008) and cognate lines of discourse analysis and linguistic and cultural anthropology (e.g. Besnier, 1990; Buttny, 1993; Lutz & Abu-Lughod, 1990; Wilce, 2009). I outline this approach in more detail in Chapter 2.

Taking into account the 'whats' as well as the 'hows' (Holstein & Gubrium, 1995) of speakers' emotional landscapes, this project also makes visible the dialogic and performative potential of emotionality. For example, individuals struggling with memories of war and disruption use the L2 to mediate and reframe painful experience. Previously told stories are revised to construct an evolving (though not always consistent or cohesive) self, able to move from passivity to anger and action. Those speaking about stigmatization based on accent, lack of formal education and language attrition challenge mistreatment and 'talk back' to others (including the interviewer) in and through their stories and meta-commentary. Describing ethnic hierarchies, social 'othering' and struggles with sexual identity and identification, speakers reframe their liminality by constructing stability based on L1 literacy skills and imagined/desired communities of belonging (Kanno & Norton, 2003). As I will also show, interviewer and interviewee may even collaboratively engage in ad hoc or lay 'psychotherapeutic' work, thus blurring the institutional boundaries between research interviews and therapeutic interaction.

In light of research involving groups and individuals who no longer have a homeland to return to, or who see themselves as 'forever foreigners' (Lo & Reyes, 2004; Talmy, 2004), the implications of this project for insight into long-term well-being become particularly salient. Thus, attending to the active representation and negotiation of emotionality offers an analysis of speakers' personal concerns and experiences as well as their ongoing discursive work to locate themselves in relation to their socio-affective worlds. Another contribution of this book is its attention to immigrant working-class men. Contemporary L2 scholarship has enthusiastically investigated matters of identity, agency, power and access in relation to the experiences of immigrant women (e.g. De Fina, 2003; Goldstein, 1996; Langman, 2004; Menard-Warwick, 2009; Norton, 2000; Pavlenko, 2001; Vitanova, 2004; Warriner, 2004) and immigrant youth (e.g. Stritikus, 2002; Talmy, 2004, 2008), but work on a wider range of identities and contexts is yet needed. By bringing into focus the articulated and interactional realities of adult immigrant men, this project extends scholarship on gendered experiences, masculinities and non-heteronormative identities.

In sum, the stance taken throughout these chapters is that speakers' emotional talk and histories are not simply pre-formed objects waiting to be identified and collected by a conscientious and resourceful researcher: they are occasioned and assembled in response to the research project and the interpersonal and sequential contexts of their production. As a result, this talk is generated within particular interpretive frames (Goffman, 1981) while flexibly constructing and often challenging versions of the social worlds between and around interview interactants (i.e. interviewer and interviewee). Focusing on these interconnected aspects of identity negotiation provides a critical reflection on issues of importance for understanding 'the interactional work' of qualitative interviewing (Rapley, 2012: 546; also Atkinson, 2015; Roulston, 2010) and the mediating role of language in emotion management and interpersonal sensemaking. Thus this project constitutes a critical treatment of emotionality that refuses to reduce it to the *outcome* of experience by instead examining how it is *constitutive* of its organization and interactional relevance.

The L2 Participants and Data

Identifying and being identified

The original L2 data examined in these chapters come from longitudinal research interviews I conducted between 2004 and 2010 for my graduate studies and dissertation work. In those interviews I sought to explore the sociolinguistic trajectories of adult working-class immigrants, all former refugees, living in the US and Canada. I recruited the participants[4] through the process of 'snowball sampling', where one person introduced me to another, and so on. In an effort to protect participants' privacy, I have anonymized names and portions of the data. Because of the potentially sensitive nature of the personal histories and topics of discussion, I first developed a social relationship with each of the participants before inviting them to take part in this study. I also joined in many social events and activities to better familiarize myself with members and their communities and to allow them to get to know me. I introduced myself as a second language educator and researcher and explained my interest in immigrants and their experiences with language and coming to and living in the US and Canada.

I met Kai, one of the first key participants, through a previous research project involving L1 Vietnamese speakers recruited from the local Hawai'i community. Friendly and outgoing, he expressed a desire to share his Vietnamese language and culture with others. I later contacted him for assistance as a cultural contact and informant. He subsequently introduced me to several of his gay friends and acquaintances in the local immigrant community, but he later dropped out of the study when he moved to the US mainland for work. As I soon discovered, Southeast Asian immigrant groups tend to be highly transient. Many relocate for better work opportunities or to be closer to friends, family members or ethnic communities.

I did not request that Kai recruit gay men for me to interview, nor did I even mention or anticipate sexual orientation or related issues as research topics or areas of concern. However, he later explained that these were the people he knew and it would be easier for them to feel comfortable talking to a 'gay'[5] researcher, especially one who is an English teacher and *haole* (a local term in Hawai'i for Caucasians). Because Kai introduced me as his 'new gay friend', initially there was some humorous confusion regarding the exact nature of our relationship and the purpose of the research. This was made even more ambiguous (perhaps intentionally so) since he insisted several of us meet first at a local gay bar (where he said they would feel more comfortable). Kai's friends playfully peppered me with questions, asking if I planned to evaluate their language skills or teach them English, if I was gay or bisexual, if I was single or partnered, if I liked Asians and Asian culture, and some inquiries even more intimate and unexpected.

Navigating stigmatized identities

Though I was initially unprepared for this kind of close 'interrogation' of the researcher, it is not uncommon, particularly in research involving stigmatized identities and histories, and it functions as an important means for establishing a shared ground (Briggs, 1986). Kong *et al.* (2002: 101) point out, '[b]efore being interviewed, many gay men want to know where both the researcher and the teller of that life are coming from, what kind of relationship they are having together, and how intimate details will be used and represented.' This applies not just to studies involving 'gay' or non-heteronormative identities but to any research context involving other 'hidden minorities' or those whose potentially stigmatizable experiences intersect with language, ethnicity, social class, literacy, legal status, (dis)ability, age, religion and so on.

The decision to include attention to non-heteronormative identity matters in this book is not one I have made lightly. In essence, it entails 'coming out' in the data and 'coming out' in academia. I was cautioned early in my career by mentors and colleagues not to make gender or sexuality part of my research (at least not until tenure), since such topics might stigmatize or even tokenize me as an emerging scholar and create difficulties for publication, employment, promotion and research funding (see discussions in LaSala *et al.*, 2008; McNaron, 1997; Mintz & Rothblum, 1997). Despite progressive claims of inclusivity in academia, discrimination and fear stemming from heterosexism, heteronormativity and homophobia remain ever-present concerns. Thus the reality is that GLBTQ (gay, lesbian, bisexual, transgender, questioning) scholars – and their allies – may be inclined to focus on survival by 'covering' (Goffman, 1981; Yoshino, 2011) or minimizing aspects of their personal identities and professional research interests that might negatively impact their career trajectories.

Navigating the 'erotic'

At this point I must comment also on the 'the hidden dimensions of romance, passion, and sexuality' (Kong *et al.*, 2002: 103) that often get left out of published studies. Because of the personal nature of qualitative research and the fact that participants are often recruited to take part in what may be described as 'intimate' encounters, there is a very real possibility for the researcher–participant relationship and data to become entangled with the romantic and even the erotic (Blackman, 2007; Cupples, 2002; Kulick & Willson, 1995; Pini & Pease, 2013), regardless of gender or sexual orientation. Though I consider here these issues in relation to non-heteronormative identities, because that is what is frequently made relevant in my data, this is not meant to stigmatize such identities or imply that these or similar concerns are not relevant to all research interactants and contexts.

While it may be true that shared sexual orientation, gender, class or other social categories may help the researcher and participants establish rapport and overcome asymmetric power relations (Kvale & Brinkmann, 2009; Reinharz & Chase, 2002; Stanley & Wise, 1983), at its core qualitative research involves human beings – complex individuals with diverse expectations, desires, responses and interpersonal boundaries. There nevertheless appears to be a taboo against acknowledging or discussing sexuality and related concerns and dilemmas in our scholarly work. I have read many interview and ethnographic studies, for example, where the sexual subtext between the researcher and the participants, though seemingly obvious, was never addressed. Even L2 studies by 'out' gay and lesbian scholars who explicitly investigate gender, sexuality and non-heteronormative identities in classroom and naturalistic settings (e.g. King, 2008; Nelson, 2009) tend to offer little or no comment on the romantic or the erotic in the research process. It is as if researchers, as ethical paragons, somehow check their sexuality at the research door and are therefore immune to such concerns.

Outside the field of L2 studies, scholars acknowledge that men who interview men – whether 'straight', 'gay', 'bisexual', 'questioning' and so on (labels and cultural scripts that cannot be assumed to be consistently used, understood or shared) – may experience flirtation and attraction in the interview (e.g. Kong *et al.*, 2002). Even hugs and touching can be interpreted as desire or intimate gestures. Walby (2010: 651), in his interview study of same-sex escorts, notes that he was propositioned by his research participants and goes so far as to say that 'any smile or movement of the hand can be interpreted as sexualization in research encounters between men, even if it is not intended to be'. In my interactions with the participants and their friends that I met over the course of the interviews and our social interactions, I consciously avoided giving or reciprocating signals that could be construed as romantic interest. However, due to the often casual nature of our interactions, and increased familiarity over time, playful flirtation and 'gay' banter or 'camp talk' (Cameron & Kulick, 2003) can be found in the data. On those occasions where I was propositioned (one participant, a divorced and partnered man from Cambodia, repeatedly made playful advances), I refocused the topic or used my prepared excuse that I was not allowed to get involved in that way because I was doing university research. Still, these uncomfortable moments forced me to become aware of just how little I had prepared to manage such dilemmas.

I am by no means advocating that we treat the research interview as a hypersexual environment and suspect every word or action as a possible romantic or flirtatious advance; I do contend, however, that these and other intimate research environments necessitate careful preparation of strategies for managing such contingencies. Moreover, greater acknowledgement and transparency of these issues in our presentations and published studies would contribute to a more reflexive, ethical and honest representation and inspection of human research practices.

The L2 data

The larger data corpus consists of over 100 hours of face-to face interviews, conversations and spontaneous storytelling in L2 English. After I explained to potential participants that I was a researcher and teacher interested in learning about their immigration and language-related experiences, some of the men I met agreed to be contacted for follow-up meetings. This led to me identifying and meeting with eight Vietnamese participants and several others from Cambodia, the Philippines, China and Taiwan.

The seven focal participants whose data inform the present study are described in more detail in the following section. After we met at least once or twice, and participants gave oral consent to be recorded and appeared comfortable with me and the recording equipment (some refused to be recorded for privacy reasons, allowing only notetaking), I asked them about topics concerning their experiences coming to and living in the US and Canada. This invited them to talk about their sociolinguistic histories, including their various languages and contexts of use, their learning of English, how they immigrated to North America, their social participation networks and their perspectives on multilingualism. Our recorded meetings took place in locations convenient for them: most often at our homes, in parks or coffee shops, as well as in the context of socializing and mealtimes. We normally began the interviews with small talk about our families, mutual acquaintances, travels and other interests. It is important to note that I was not explicitly seeking to elicit or explore emotion or psychological matters at the time the interviews were conducted. Because participants often commented on sexuality and sexual identity, I later included some attention to those topics as they came up in the interviews.

Autobiographical narratives (Pavlenko, 2007; Riessman, 1993, 2008) were also a large part of the interviews, and although I did not always ask participants for stories, storytelling was encouraged. A later re-analysis of the data – as represented in these chapters – indicates that the research participants and I strongly expected that stories would be produced. Eventually, after recognizing interviews as co-constructed events and sites of data *generation* and *co-construction* rather than data *collection* (Byrne, 2004; Given, 2008), I made an effort to let participants steer the interviews to topics that they viewed as significant to an understanding of themselves and their experiences. At the same time, approaching interviews as conversational encounters (Holstein & Gubrium, 1995, 2003; Potter & Wetherell, 1987), I actively participated by following up various topics and at times even challenging accounts to encourage interviewees to elaborate and to better make visible their accounting practices.

Some non-English (e.g. Vietnamese, Khmer, Visayan/Cebuano, Tagalog, Pidgin/Hawai'i Creole) data were produced but consisted mostly of isolated vocabulary, cultural terms, proverbs or short translations. I acknowledge that only having L2 English data from these speakers offers a limited perspective of their sociolinguistic competences. Pavlenko (2007: 172) writes, 'Many researchers collect stories in one language only, the one most convenient for analysis, without thinking through the implications of this choice.' Concurring with Pavlenko, I take the perspective that in interviews with multilingual participants, the choice to use (and even *not* use) a particular language or languages should be left to the interviewee. Eliciting a more accurate representation and baseline of speakers' own multilingual repertoires also addresses matters of power and agency (objects of concern for many researchers), since

L2 interviews frequently tend to be conducted in one language only, most often the stronger language of the interviewer.

Nevertheless, because I was not a competent speaker of any of my participants' primary or home languages, the interviews were conducted in English (my L1 and participants' L2 or L3). To obtain comparative data, I arranged for L1 Vietnamese and Cambodian researchers to conduct interviews with some of the participants. Despite these plans, each of the participants refused, citing various reasons (e.g. discomfort with a stranger, time constraints). However, the primary reason given was emotion-driven: *fear.* They expressed fear that they would lose their anonymity and fear that their secrets and personal histories would be broadcast to their small, ethnic communities and beyond. There is also some evidence to suggest that participants may have felt more comfortable speaking about their experiences (particularly those concerning uncomfortable and highly emotional topics) in their L2. As multilingualism scholars (e.g. Dewaele, 2010; Pavlenko, 2007) have shown, the L2 may carry less emotional weight and allow for more emotionally detached responses. I also surmise that participants recognized that my status as cultural outsider meant I was unlikely to challenge the authenticity of their claims or undermine their epistemic authority. Because many of the participants frequently lamented their lack of interactions with 'native' English speakers, it is likely that taking part in the interviews afforded them opportunities to use English and perhaps even find a space for self-empowerment by receiving formal recognition as cultural experts and informants.

At the start of data collection, I had intended to compare the experiences of long-term residents with those of recent immigrants, but most of the recent arrivals (residing in the US or Canada less than two years) worked long hours or moved often, making it difficult to find suitable times to meet. Potential participants also expressed concerns about whether the interviews would affect their legal status or relationships in their communities. As noted above, several immigrant men from Cambodia, Vietnam and the Philippines agreed to be interviewed informally and 'off the record', but they did not want to be audio recorded, citing worries about privacy and citizenship status. Their unrecorded interviews provided useful contextual information that enabled me to notice some of the social forces and personal concerns they identified as relevant to understanding their experiences with language, identity and immigration.

Field notes, email correspondence, online chats, as well as solicited and unsolicited interview reflections supplemented the interview data. Observations and conversations were also carried out at mealtimes and various social gatherings and other activities. Additional audio-recorded data include several hours of recordings of some of the participants in group interviews and talk at mealtimes or during home interactions, and 10 hours of bilingual data from heritage language classes. Although the interview data are the focus of this study, the supplemental data and extra-discursive or background material give further evidence that these speakers made use of emotional stories and topics in their interactions with the interviewer and others with whom they interacted.

Focal participants

Biographical data of my seven focal participants are represented in Table 1.1.

Five of the men shared very similar immigration and life experiences. Trang immigrated to Canada, and Jack, Bona, John and Kiet immigrated to the US as refugees in the early and mid-1980s during the second wave of post-war immigration from Vietnam and Cambodia. All had witnessed firsthand the violence of war and experienced displacement as children and had spent two to three years in refugee camps in the Philippines or Thailand. It is remarkable that despite the emotional upheavals and violent histories detailed in their personal accounts and in their ongoing struggles with language, identity and belonging, they have all successfully carved out various sociolinguistic spaces to achieve a sense of stability, albeit often tenuous and constantly managed.

The interviews with Trang and John were the longest and most in-depth, spanning a period over five years. Consequently, their data feature prominently in these chapters. They had been friends for several years before the start of this study and were later introduced to Jack through their mutual acquaintances. Kiet knew John but had only met him a few times. Jack and Bona were well-connected with Cambodian communities in Hawai'i and the mainland US and often took part in festivals, religious ceremonies and other community events. John, although he had a few Vietnamese friends, did not take part in community events, stating that he did not want to be known so well because they might talk about him.[6] Trang lived in Canada but visited Hawai'i every year for two to three months at a time – because, as he said, its tropical environment reminded him of 'home'. For the most part, Trang avoided interactions with Cambodians and Vietnamese because he did not want them to ask about his accent or mixed ethnicity (his father was Cambodian and his mother was Vietnamese).

Rico, an asylum seeker in Canada, did not know any of the other study participants. A local Filipino friend introduced me to Rico after asking about my research project. He told me that Rico, a buddy from his hometown in the Philippines, was planning to file for asylum in Canada, seeking protection from threats made against his life by gang members after he witnessed their illegal activities. We first met through email and then carried out approximately 10 hours of online text and video chats before he left the Philippines. Fortuitously, travel plans took me near to where Rico was living in Canada, so we were able to carry out several face-to-face audio-recorded interviews. Through Rico's introduction, interviews were set up with five other asylum seekers (his co-workers), but all lost their appeals and were deported before we could meet in person.

Table 1.1 Focal interview participants

Name*	Trang	Jack	Bona	John	Kiet	Kim	Rico
Gender	M	M	M	M	M	F	M
Age	40s	40s	40s	40s	30s	30s	30s
Ethnicity***	Vietnamese Khmer Chinese	Cambodian	Cambodian	'Chinese born in Vietnam'	Vietnamese	Vietnamese	Filipino
Languages	Vietnamese English Khmer Thai (Chinese lost to attrition)	Khmer** English Lao	Khmer English (Chinese lost to attrition)	Vietnamese English Chinese	Vietnamese English (Chinese lost to attrition)	Vietnamese English French	Cebuano Tagalog English
Residence and status	Canada (ON) Canadian citizen	US (HI) US citizen	US (HI) US citizen	US (HI) US citizen	US (CA) US citizen	US (HI) US citizen	Canada Refugee
Yrs residence	25 years	25 years	25 years	25 years	12 years	16 years	1 year
Occupation	Manager in the service industry	Factory worker	Taxi driver	service industry	Nail technician	University student	Caregiver, hotel worker, warehouse worker
Formal Education	High school (Canada) Dropped out of English as a second language classes	High school (US)	2-year degree (US)	High school (US)	High school (US)	High school (Vietnam) 4-year degree (US)	2-year nursing certificate (PH)
Hours of Interviews	40	6	5	15	6	6	11

Notes: *Participants' names are pseudonyms. **I use Cambodian and Khmer interchangeably throughout. ***Ethnicity is described using participants' own labels.

Kim was the only woman in these interviews. She arrived in the US in the 1990s from Vietnam and did not know any of the other study participants. We became acquainted when she was a university student. When she learned of my research interests, she asked if I would be interested in her experiences. I decided to include Kim's interviews in the study to see how they compared with those of the men. Her talk contains many of the same concerns (e.g. accent, ethnicity, gender, discrimination, education, family, troubled past and the uncertain future). Her experiences also diverged in significant ways: she was married, a parent to young children, the sole supporter of her family (her husband was unable to find employment), and was working toward an advanced professional degree.

Reflecting on 'uh-oh' and 'aha' moments

At the time I carried out the bulk of the interviews, and in much of the initial analyses, I took what might be described as a typical approach of studies using interviews and narrative inquiry: I summarized the themes, I picked out some representative quotes and excerpts, I gave attention to matters of voice and identity and I strove to get out of the way and let the authenticity and power of the data 'speak for itself' (cf. Willig, 2013). However, the more I dug into the interview and narrative literature from across various disciplines (e.g. L2 studies, anthropology, sociology, psychology, healthcare, social work, human geography), the more it became obvious that my superficial treatment of these data ignored the highly coordinated and agentive work and various sociolinguistic competences of participants in their interviews. I also began to notice that speakers would retell stories, offer contradictory accounts, revise particular claims and otherwise produce material that was both consistent and inconsistent. This eventually prompted me to more closely examine how interviewees actively represented themselves and their experiences in particular ways for the research study and for me in and outside the interviews.

Two incidents

Two specific incidents further contributed to the shift in my conceptualization of interviewing. First, one day as I was asking a participant about something he said in a previous interview, he stopped me and said, 'Actually, it didn't happen that way. I didn't tell you the real story.' He then explained that he decided not to tell me the 'real' story previously because he was afraid it was too sad or too violent for the purposes of the study. At that moment, my tacit assumptions about participant truthfulness and believability were all called into question. If some parts of the interviews were not true, which parts could I then believe? How could I determine what was sincere, what was a lie, or what was changed? As a researcher interested in accurately understanding and portraying participants' lived sociolinguistic experiences, what analytic claims could I make if any part of their accounts – however seemingly 'truthful' in their production – could be in doubt? Moreover, what implications did this have for the validity or trustworthiness of my analytical findings and conclusions? Ochs and Capps (2001: 252) acknowledge that the emotional and traumatic aspects of some stories may prevent them from being told:

> A life episode may be too painful or too distant to put into words; or tellers may perceive a rendering of events to be inappropriate or politically unfeasible for the interlocutors who populate one's surroundings. In these and other circumstances, certain narratives remain untold.

However, in the preceding example, it was not the case of a story *not* being told but of a story being edited and even 'sanitized' for the recipient.

A related encounter occurred soon after, while I was still grappling with how to come to terms with the truthfulness of participants' talk and their sometimes-changing accounts. In an early interview, Kim talked about her difficult school years under communist rule and being forced to memorize and repeat state propaganda. Discussing the one-sided description of history in her school textbooks in Vietnam and the US, she criticized those official versions of historical events while acknowledging that her own stories were themselves versions (I later learned that she sometimes wrote semi-autobiographical stories of her experiences).

In this segment (Excerpt 1.1; see pp. 27–28 for transcription conventions), Kim makes the emotionality of this personal conflict between *truth* and *reality* clearly visible on the interactional surface through her prosodic stress (e.g. line 5: 'ugh'; line 7: 'EXACTLY') and lexical selection (e.g. line 16: 'nightmare'; line 17: 'torture').

(Excerpt 1.1). Kim: 'Real true story'

```
01    K:    I pretty much (.) understand when I (.) taking class
02          or read the paper or you know (.) newspaper or the
03          book, because I know (.) I was there. I been there
04          done that, so whatever they do to me. and now in the
05          book they write something else=an' I say "ugh"
06          ((voiced with disgust)) or some people they write
07          exactly ( ) and I say "EXACTLY" (y'know). but if
08          you never been in (.) you never live in the (.) with
09          communist how do you know. you know only learn it
10          from book. you can learn
11    M:    [mm]
12 →  K:    [but] what is the real (.) true story in there.
13    M:    °mhm°
```

14 →	**K:**	cuz when I write a story I already change something.
15 →		how do you know it a real true story or not. (so)
16		but it was a (.) <u>night</u>mare for me in high school.
17		It was a <u>tor</u>ture for me to live through (what)
18		communist. and <u>finally</u> I say "okay we <u>need</u> to get
19		out." that's all. °we have to get out right?°

Kim's meta-commentary on the contrast between 'truths' and 'realities' held up a mirror to my own analytical struggles as researcher by showing me that interview participants, as ordinary lay people (i.e. non-researchers), are also deeply concerned with the authenticity and changeability of their own and others' stories. A liberating realization, this allowed me to recognize that the onus was not on me as researcher to determine a story's truthfulness; instead, it required that I recognize that every narrative is a representation and a version produced for a particular purpose, audience and occasion (see Chapter 2). This experience confirms Rapley's (2012: 548) observation that closely engaging with interview dilemmas 'can be a therapeutic intervention for researchers, in that they may learn to question or reflect on their own practice'. This is not to suggest that this means simply replacing a *realist* perspective on truth with a *relativist* one. Rather, it entails the acceptance that *truth, believability, honesty, certainty* and other such concepts and their 'psychological relevancies' (Potter & Edwards, 2013) are themselves practical concerns and rhetorical objects and therefore subject to speaker avowals, contrasts and revisions (Stokoe & Edwards, 2006; te Molder & Potter, 2005). In this view, truth is only a problem as long as one insists that there is only one 'real' or accurate version of events. How speakers manage information and their moral states (Atkinson, 2015: 91) is of far greater interest from a discursive constructionist perspective.

Catherine Riessman, a leading narrative scholar, points out that truthfulness of a sort – in the form of 'validity' – is indeed a pressing concern for narrative researchers who must speak to a wider audience:

> Narrative truths are always partial – committed and incomplete. Nevertheless, students in the social sciences have to make their arguments to persuade audiences about the trustworthiness of their data and interpretations – they didn't simply make up the stories they claim to have collected, and they followed a methodical path, guided by ethical considerations and theory, to story their findings. This is all the more reason for students to attend closely to the methods they are using (and developing) for arriving at 'valid' interpretations of the type of narrative data they are collecting. (Riessman, 2008: 186)

As I aim to show in the following chapters, a discursive constructionist approach provides such a 'methodical path' for research on emotionality in L2 autobiographical interview research. Though it is not the only way to carry out this investigation, it is one that provides a thoroughly reflexive and empirically-based approach that makes plain our research objects, practices and claims.

Transcribing and representing talk-in-interaction

The interviews were audio-recorded and initially transcribed fairly loosely and focused on quotes, glosses and thematic summaries (cf. Potter & Hepburn, 2005, 2012; Rapley, 2012; Talmy, 2011). Later, revisiting the data from a more social interactional approach, I re-transcribed, re-examined and re-analyzed the data following CA procedures (Atkinson & Heritage, 1984) that attempt to capture the fine-grained detail of the recorded interaction (depending on analytical purposes, some excerpts are more detailed than others). This detail includes attention to *what* was said (i.e. the words, topics), *where* it was said (i.e. the utterance boundaries and location in the overall talk), *who* said it (i.e. the speakers and their turns), *how* it was said (e.g. linguistic code, intonation, speed, pitch, vocal quality, represented speech), and even what was *not said* or *not responded to* (e.g. pauses, silences, partial or abandoned utterances, uncompleted adjacency pairs). Video-recordings are preferable to audio only as they permit a much richer multimodal, interactional record that allows the analyst to observe gestures, body positions, eye gaze, the physical setting and other nonverbal and environmental cues. However, as I have noted, the participants in this study were unwilling to be video-recorded, expressing concerns over privacy and the personal content of their talk.

Recordings and transcripts are always representations, never the object or event that was recorded. As such, transcripts are always partial, selective, motivated, methodologically driven and an integral part of the analytic process (Hutchby & Wooffitt, 2008; Lazaraton, 2002; Ochs, 1979; Psathas & Anderson, 1990). Transcripts are useful referential tools in the study of recorded interaction, but they do not replace the recordings (Hutchby & Wooffitt, 2008; Wooffitt, 2005). Viewing transcription as a process of observation and noticing (Zimmerman, 1988), after re-transcribing the data, I read the transcripts repeatedly and compared them with the recordings. I then examined them for actions (e.g. blaming, justifying, denying, questioning, answering, storytelling); identity work; structural, sequential and rhetorical organization; co-construction; and 'curious' patterns (Maynard, 2003). Because of the prevalent topicalization of emotions and psychological matters in the interviews, I began to identify and focus on emotionality as an object of analytic attention. In turn, I examined how both interviewer and interviewee actively invoked and managed emotionality in the 'there-and-then' (storyworld) as well as the 'here-and-now' (interactional world) of the telling.

Representing the interviewer

As I have remarked, a criticism that has been made against much of the narrative and interview research literature concerns the glaring absence of the interviewer in data representation and analysis. Although researchers frequently show strong interest in the stories, responses and other material produced by research participants, the conspicuous absence of interviewer questions and other contributions in published studies results in an impoverished understanding of the ways in which data get generated and subsequently represented (Potter & Hepburn, 2005; Prior, 2014; Richards, 2003; Roulston, 2010; Talmy & Richards, 2011). To bring greater attention to these matters, here I examine interviewee *and* interviewer contributions (e.g. questions, responses) in the representation of data as well as in the analyses. This offers a more contextualized perspective that allows insight into the activity of data generation as well as the content.

Another matter also concerns the presence and representation of the researcher in the analysis and discussion. In L2 autobiographical interview research studies where the analyst is also the interviewer/story recipient, it is a prevalent practice to refer to oneself in the first person. Presumably the reasons for this include the researcher's desire to avoid perpetuating the 'illusion of objectivity', to take an explicit reflexive stance toward the material and to avoid privileging the interviewer's epistemic status over the interviewee's. In CA studies, as Bucholtz (2003: 406) notes, 'the researcher often recedes from view altogether, since data that betray awareness of the researcher's presence are often excluded from analysis as "unnatural" or inauthentic'. Such criticisms have been addressed by CA and DP scholars (e.g. Antaki *et al.*, 2007; Potter & Hepburn, 2012) who, though largely eschewing interview data because of its 'contrived' status, nevertheless urge for greater inclusion of the interviewer in the data representation and analysis.

Although I am the interviewer in the L2 data excerpts from my corpus, I follow accepted CA conventions by referring to myself in the third person as 'the interviewer', 'M' or 'Matt'. This does not mean to imply that I am distancing myself from the material as an exercise in objective neutrality or to privilege my analytical perspective. To the contrary, it is highly reflexive and equalizing because it seeks to take in the whole interaction on its own terms rather than proceeding from a one-sided perspective that assumes because I was a participant in the interaction I necessarily have direct insight into what interviewees or I were thinking or feeling at the time (though I will offer such commentary where warranted). Thus, this is foremost an analytic stance that seeks to locate and support its observations and claims in the data as it unfolds. At the same time, it holds up an analysis that is accountable to the reader.

The 'naked' researcher

Finally, I recognize that as a researcher and early-career academic, publicly opening up my own interview practices for inspection is a potentially risky and embarrassing endeavor. It may, and frequently does, reveal my mistakes, my failures, my inadequacies and my methodological naiveté. I still find myself wincing when I listen to my interviews and observe my own practices. It also feels too personal and too exposing. Because I have been socialized, like many in the field, into carefully presenting my professional persona and activities in a positive light, the unflattering lens of re-analysis is humbling (even humiliating) as it is enlightening: it reveals us for what we are – as well as what we are not. However, without greater reflexivity and methodological critique (and self-critique), we can little expect to advance our own professional practices as well as the knowledge-seeking, knowledge-building and knowledge-sharing practices that our disciplinary communities require. It is no wonder that scholars such as Ramanathan (2010: 114) urge greater problematizing of the 'ways in which we qualitative researchers have, on the whole hesitated to speak about local tensions and problems in our researching practices' (see also, Prior, 2014; Rapley, 2012; Roulston, 2010). Because of the pressing need for greater researcher reflexivity and attention to our professional practices, I argue the lasting benefits for the research profession far outweigh any transitory or personal discomforts for the individual researcher.

Summary

This introduction has provided an overview of the background and contributions of this book in its investigation of the representation and management of emotionality in contemporary L2 autobiographical interview research. It has also stressed the urgent need for more rigorous attention to reflexivity throughout the entire research process. In sum, the purpose of this project is three-fold as it addresses a number of gaps and issues in the literature. First, it examines emotion as both a discursive topic and resource, thus including attention to the ways in which emotionality is constituted *by* and constitutive *of* interaction. As a relatively unexplored area of inquiry (at least within L2 studies), a crucial contribution is its close examination of the interactional and semiotic resources that go into the active construction, management and reception of emotionality in talk.

Second, this book explores the links between emotions and the autobiographical representation of experience. In other words, it is interested in what these adult immigrants and transcultural persons make relevant in their talk of language-*in*-use and language-*of*-use (not just language learning) as well as how they locate themselves and others and how those accounts are shaped by the context and interactants. By including attention to the lives of adult immigrant and transcultural men, it expands previous research by shedding light on a wider range of gendered experiences than represented in the present literature. In addition, by considering emotionality and the rhetorical and agentive work speakers carry out within and across their interviews and narratives over time, this project offers potential links for future interdisciplinary research on matters related to acculturation, mental health and social participation.

As I have outlined in this chapter, this project seeks to arrive at local or emic understandings of the representation and organization of emotionality and experience. A distinctive aspect of this approach, in comparison to other work on emotions, autobiographical talk, and L2 and transcultural experiences, is its point of departure. It engages with these matters not by starting with assumptions about power and life conditions and working down but by looking at how speakers themselves make sense of past experience and represent and manage their own and others' emotionality in and through their talk in the present.

A third purpose of this book is that by exposing various activities making up L2 autobiographical interview research, it seeks to address matters of relevance to methodology, analysis and representation – particularly for L2 and multilingual users, topics and settings. Through this methodological and analytical critique, it provides a model and framework to approach L2 autobiographical talk and interaction. Though it advances a discursive constructionist approach, the project of opening up the interview context and activities for inspection offers equally productive insights for other approaches to these topics.

Overview of the Chapters

Launching this investigation of emotionality in the activity of L2 autobiographical interview research, Chapter 2 describes the discursive constructionist framework informing the discussion and analysis. Special attention is given to the key intersecting discursive programs (DP, CA, ethnomethodology and membership categorization analysis) and ethnographic mentality that inform this approach. It also considers matters of 'visible' and 'invisible' contexts and the ways in which a discursive constructionist approach offers an analytically grounded and reflexive means to investigate emotionality and L2 autobiographical narratives and interview talk.

Chapter 3 explores *interviewee* contributions by examining the key conventions and constraints of speakers' tellings, or storied material. It then focuses on ways in which speakers remember, preface and launch their emotional and often complaint-filled tellings and invite their recipient (i.e. the interviewer) to respond accordingly. Chapters 4 and 5 turn to *interviewer* contributions in constructing emotionality in autobiographical talk. Chapter 4 focuses on question sequences that solicit emotional tellings and related meta-commentary. It compares and contrasts casual conversation with institutional talk and shows that interviewees actively produce cognitive displays to show they are selecting an appropriate story for the interviewer. Chapter 5 continues with interviewer question sequences by looking at two types of question formulations that potentially invite talk of feelings and opinions: *explicit feeling questions* ('How do you feel about'; 'How does that feel?') and *emotion implicative questions* ('Was it hard?'; 'Is it easy?').

Chapter 6 explores the intersection between L2 autobiographical interviews and psychotherapeutic interaction. It shows that both interviewer and interviewee use *formulations* and *reformulations* to both take up and resist each other's descriptions and epistemic stances ('scary', 'tough') while carrying out psychological evaluations, showing empathy and progressing the interview talk and interaction.

Chapters 7 and 8 investigate intense or negative emotionality and its management before, during and after the interview. Chapter 7 takes up the ways in which interviewer and interviewee attend to the emotionality of their talk and how they are sensitive to their own and each other's emotionality. It also considers some of the effects of emotional talk, including emotional contagion and emotional danger, and it advocates researchers prepare for possible effects of research on their own and participants' mental health. Chapter 8 addresses the prevalence of negative emotionality in these data and in autobiographical interview research more broadly. It also explicates some of the reasons why speakers sometimes appear to resist 'positive' emotionality. These influences include the features of the interview activity as well as more general matters involving tellability, the nature of trauma and memory, cultural conventions and researchers' ongoing interest in investigating problems that negatively impact human social life well-being.

Chapter 9 critically reflects on the contributions and findings of these chapters. Discussing the implications for theory and methodology, it concludes by pointing to future directions for L2 autobiographical interview research involving and focusing on emotionality and related matters.

Notes

(1) Although the terms 'autobiographical' and 'autobiographic' are both used in the research literature (e.g. Baynham & De Fina, 2005; Pavlenko, 2007), I prefer the former (*-al*) because it highlights the constructed and representational nature of personal experience. In the research interview, what becomes the 'official' version is not necessarily autobiographic (i.e. one's personal history, the 'facts') but autobiographical (i.e. a *version* that is collaboratively assembled and shaped also by the recipient(s) and the context(s) of its production).
(2) Many scholars make distinctions among these various terms and the conscious, unconscious, behavioral, embodied, neurophysiological, etc. phenomena they index. Ochs and Schieffelin (1989: 7), for example, '... take affect to be a broader term than emotion, to include feelings, moods, dispositions, and attitudes associated with

persons and/or situations' (see also discussions in Besnier, 1990; Edwards, 1997; Pastor & De Fina, 2005; Wetherell, 2012; Wilce, 2009). Because this book focuses on *emotionality* (i.e. emotions *in* and *as* interaction), I am less interested in specifying taxonomies than I am in understanding how emotion-related matters get managed. Thus, I use the labels *emotion, affect, feelings* and so on, interchangeably.

(3) As various scholars have asserted (e.g. Atkinson *et al.*, 2003), the *Western/non-Western* binary is itself a problematizable rhetorical trope.

(4) I use the term 'participants' to bring attention to the fact that interviewees are agentive interactants and contributors to the process of research rather than passive 'respondents', 'informants' or 'subjects'.

(5) This co-identification as 'gay' came about due to our mutual acquaintances. Because not all the participants referred to themselves as 'gay' or even 'straight', I refrain from noting or labeling their sexual orientation unless they make it relevant. For example, John, an immigrant from Vietnam, alternatively referred to himself as 'gay', 'straight' and 'no label'. Sang, a Cambodian man, described himself as 'really gay' even though he had been married to a woman. Others used terms such as 'straight', 'gay friendly', 'mostly straight', 'gay', 'macho gay', 'non-girly', 'no label', 'maybe gay' and 'not sure'. A few sometimes used 'mahu', a local Hawaiian word, to refer to themselves or others as gay or 'feminine' guys. This can be a playful or pejorative term, but it is now being reclaimed (much like the label 'queer') by gender-variant community members.

(6) John frequently commented that despite having a same-sex partner, he was not 'out' about his sexuality and did not want to become a topic of gossip in the Vietnamese community.

Transcription Conventions

Adapted from Jefferson (2004)

[ ]	Overlapping talk
=	Contiguous or latched utterances
(0.5)	Silence measured in tenths of seconds
(.)	Untimed micropause
:	Prolongation of the immediately prior sound
↑	A hearably raised pitch in the next sound
↓	A hearably lowered pitch in the next sound
.	Falling or declarative intonation
?	Rising intonation (not necessarily a question)
,	Slightly rising/continuing intonation
.hh	Audible inbreath
hh	Audible outbreath (may also indicate laughter)
word	Speaker emphasis
WORD	Noticeably louder speech
°word°	Noticeably softer or quieter speech
$word$	Produced with 'smiling' or 'laughing' tone
#word#	Produced with a 'creaky' voice

"word"	Represented (i.e. quoted, reported) speech or thought (usually produced in a different 'voice' or set off by pauses and pitch resets)
word-	A restart or sharp cut-off
>word<	Produced more quickly than surrounding talk
<word>	Produced more slowly than surrounding talk
(word)	Unclear fragment/Transcriber's best guess
((description))	Additional transcriber explanations or descriptions
→	Indicates a line of special interest

2 Constructing Discourse

> *Every time we tell a story, we create for ourselves and for others one or more versions of experience. Each version we present brings to life a view of ourselves and others in our world that carries us into the future.*
> (Capps & Ochs, 1995: 175)

> *Just as interview participants tell stories, investigators construct stories from their data.*
> (Riessman, 2008: 4)

A scene at the conclusion of the popular novel *The Life of Pi* (Martel, 2001: 307), the fantastic tale of a young castaway at sea, dramatically illustrates the social fact that all experience is versioned. The protagonist, Pi Patel, when asked by the representatives of the shipping company which tale of survival was true, responds:

'You can't prove which story is true and which is not. You must take my word for it.'

'I guess so.'

'In both stories the ship sinks, my entire family dies, and I suffer.'

'Yes, that's true.'

'So tell me, since it makes no factual difference to you and you can't prove the question either way, which story do you prefer?'

Which story do we prefer? This is a key piece of the emotionality and narrative 'puzzle'. I will suggest that researchers and research participants often prefer the one that is problem-driven and affect-laden. But social research is not just about documenting dramatic stories or emotional responses: it must involve 'systematic, methodical investigations of what people do, as well as what they say or feel' (Atkinson, 2015: 23). It is this perspective, that autobiographical and emotional tellings are empirically analyzable discursive constructions and social actions, which underpins the approach taken in this book. Though often uncritically employed as a convenient and expeditious means of eliciting data, qualitative research interviewing is in reality less a neutral tool for collecting or 'downloading' stories of personal experience than it is a dynamic, collaborative activity where speakers select and (re)present particular tellings, stances (e.g. affective, epistemic, moral), and interpretations for the researcher – and where the researcher solicits and responds to the tellers and their productions.

The constructed nature of speakers' stories is further exemplified by Excerpt 2.1 from an interview with Rico, an asylum seeker from the Philippines:

(Excerpt 2.1). Rico: 'That's my story' (simplified excerpt)

My lawyer advised me to make ... a ... story about ... what would be the reason why I have to get ... I have to apply ... a refugee. So I made a statement I made a story like ... um ... somebody ... um ... uh there's a group who persecute me. That's my story. That's why I'm afraid to go back to the Philippines because ... people persecute me ... somebody.

Like Pi Patel's story, Rico's account of how he came to produce his 'official' statement is itself a version about versions. In it he traces its trajectory (with his lawyer, with the Immigration and Refugee Board, with the researcher) to show how 'the story' was shaped across events and across time. It brings into view that the issue of practical importance is not *which* version is more or less inherently authentic but *how* each particular version is truthful and apposite for its purpose. Without a *logical* story that connects disruptive events in a causal chain leading to legitimate fear of persecution, Rico would not have cause to seek asylum in the first place and the right to claim refugee protection and legal representation. Without an *official* story, put in writing and fitting within the parameters of eligibility defined by refugee law and submitted to the immigration board, his petition would carry no legal weight. Without a *consistent* and *believable* story, built with supporting facts and documents, the authenticity of his claims would be cast into doubt. Without an *emotional* story that convincingly demonstrates his well-founded fear and suffering, the threats of persecution and the danger to his personal safety lose their urgency and even visceral credibility. Therefore, each of these tellings serves important functions in enabling Rico to move forward in his quest to receive political asylum and achieve personal stability.

For us as researchers, this recognition that autobiographical stories are versioned and collaboratively assembled requires that we reflect critically on the circumstances and manner of their production as well as on the content – and the status – of the generated material. To contribute to this reflexive process, in this chapter I outline a theoretical and analytical framework for a discursive constructionist (DC) approach to emotionality in L2 autobiographical interview research. Bringing together the tools and findings of conversation analysis (CA), discursive psychology (DP), ethnography and various lines of supporting interdisciplinary scholarship, I consider some of the potential benefits and challenges of this approach. Namely, I propose that recognizing emotionality as an empirically analyzable interactional and interpersonal resource and topic enables us to extricate ourselves from the definitional quagmire inherent in affective research by advancing scholarly dialogue that contributes to a greater understanding of L2 user experiences, competencies and trajectories – and explicates how speakers actively represent and respond to these matters.

'Doing' Emotionality

Emotions are a ubiquitous part of human social life and communication. We produce and respond to a far-ranging spectrum of affective phenomena: *laughter, crying, joy, grief, loneliness, disgust, surprise, love, anger* and the like. Whatever else emotions may or may not be (and here I leave that debate up to philosophers and neuroscientists), they are a constitutive part of our communicative repertoire and socially shared experiences. The primary means of cultivating and maintaining relationships with others and establishing intersubjective understandings is through the activity of communicating and assigning meaning to particular emotional states, behaviors and stances (Besnier, 1990; Denzin, 1984; Edwards, 1997; Harré, 1986; Ochs & Schieffelin, 1989; Whalen & Zimmerman, 1998).

This is not to say that emotions are *only* discursively constituted. It is impossible to deny the neurophysiological, psychological, cultural and possibly even universal components of emotions (see discussions in Candland, 2003; Edwards, 1997; Kramsch, 2009; Pavlenko, 2005; Röttger-Rössler & Markowitsch, 2009; Ruusuvuori, 2013; Schumann, 1997; Turner & Stets, 2005; Whalen & Zimmerman, 1998; Wierzbicka, 1999; Wilce, 2009). Pointing out the self-imposed limitations of sociological and constructionist inquiry, Turner and Stets (2005: 9) advocate a broader treatment of emotion:

> ... sociological theories and research will always be incomplete, especially approaches that continue to assert that all emotions are socially constructed ... Emotions are the result of a complex interplay among cultural, social structural, cognitive, and neurological forces. The goal should be to figure out how they are interconnected.

I concur with Turner and Stets, that to better understand emotion we must explore more carefully this complex interplay of forces. The relationship between language and emotions likely has 'no single coherent story' (Pavlenko, 2005: 42) but involves multiple interconnected physiological, psychological and semiotic processes that are socioculturally mediated (e.g. facilitated and constrained) and meaningful (e.g. visible and relevant).

Though there may indeed be universal components of emotions, at the social level their distinctiveness lies in the culturally specific 'display rules' that dictate what, when, how and to what degree emotions may be displayed or masked (Ekman, 2003: 4; also Fussell, 2002).

> A study of emotions requires acute attention to differences in culture, social class, race, and gender. The dominant culture applies inconsistent norms and rules to different communities; likewise, each culture reflects their own internal norms and values with respect to emotional rules and expression, and variable modes of resistance to the dominant cultural values. (Boler, 1999: xiii)

This does not mean that all members from a particular community will necessarily produce and respond to emotionality in the same way but that there are norms of behavior into which speakers are socialized and expected to conform. Lutz and Abu-Lughod (1990) have argued that essentialist and universal treatments of emotions make alternative forms of emotion invisible and obscure how emotionality functions as a social practice. In the United States, for example, the emotional (or affective) socialization of young boys into masculine roles involves learning not to cry or look afraid (Eisenberg *et al.*, 1998; Ekman & Friesen, 2003; Galasiński, 2004; Kindlon & Thompson, 2000). Conversely, white, middle-class girls tend to be socialized into using a wider range of affective vocabulary than are boys (Kuebli *et al.*, 1995). For L2 users and others who navigate complex linguistic and cultural borders, *emotional socialization* and *emotional competence* (i.e. the ability to appropriately produce, recognize, respond to and manage emotionality in interaction) may be just as important as linguistic, cognitive and other competences (Dewaele, 2005, 2006, 2010; Kramsch & Whiteside, 2007; Pavlenko, 2005; for other perspectives on emotional competence, see e.g. Galasiński, 2004; Saarni, 1999).

'Reading' Emotionality

Emotionality is always interpreted, albeit with varying degrees of accuracy (Fussell, 2002). It is through our communicative conduct that we encounter emotions as social phenomena and subsequently assess and label the emotional states and emotion-indexing productions and responses of others and ourselves. In other words, despite not having a direct conduit into the minds and feelings of others, we act *as if* we do. Even the socioculturally mediated actions of showing empathy or sympathy (Boler, 1999) are built on the presumption that we can indeed perceive another person's emotional state and somehow identify with and even share in it. To quote Hochschild (2003: 76), 'All of us try to feel, and pretend to feel, but we seldom do so alone. Most often we do it when we exchange gestures of signs of feeling with others.'

Yet as most of us have experienced, showing empathy or sympathy does not always necessitate the naming of specific emotions. More often, interactants invoke a social relationship and show their desire to understand others' emotion*ality* and to understand others emotion*ally*. Following Ruusuvuori (2013: 340), here 'empathy is taken to refer to understanding the other's experience: imagining oneself in the same situation as the other but never losing track of the fact that this experience is not one's own but belongs to the other'. This may include seeking to ameliorate the other person's pain or other unpleasant feelings as well as sharing in events that evoke joy and other 'positive' emotions.

John Austin, regarded as the founder of speech act theory, advanced the perspective that language is used to *do* things (i.e. that all utterances are performative) rather than to simply communicate. As he (Austin, 1962: 78) writes, with no small amount of emphasis, the action potential of language extends also to the communication of emotionality:

> There are numerous cases in human life where the feeling of a certain 'emotion' (save the word!) or 'wish' or the adoption of an attitude is conventionally considered an appropriate or fitting response or reaction to a certain state of affairs, including the performance by someone of a certain act, cases where such a response is natural (or we should like to think so!) In such cases it is, of course, possible and usual actually to feel the emotion or wish in question; and since our emotions or wishes are not readily detectible by others, it is common to wish to inform others that we have them.

Although it may be common to inform others of our emotions through self-avowals (e.g. 'I'm mad', 'I'm so happy for you') or through various embodied displays (e.g. smile, grimace, hug, tears, averted gaze), it is equally common to comment on the apparent emotionality we read off others (e.g. 'Why are you upset?', 'You're certainly in a good mood today!'). Therefore, a primary linguistic means by which people communicate *emotionality* and communicate *emotionally* in daily life is through emotion-indexing descriptions and categories (Buttny, 1993, 2004; Edwards, 1997, 1999; Harré, 1986).

An illustrative example

To illustrate the production and reception of emotionality and the prevalent practice of 'emotional reading', I consider Excerpt 2.2 that I transcribed from a CNN (Cable News Network) television news interview between Don Lemon (news anchor and program host) and Father Pfleger (Catholic priest and activist against gangs and guns). In this excerpt, Lemon is interviewing

Pfleger about the recent deaths of two teens in a gang-related shooting outside Pfleger's church:

(Excerpt 2.2). 'Shot outside church' (CNN, Lemon, 2009)

```
01   DL:    Father Pfleger (.) was, extremely, extremely
02          upset in that video an' you can see him there
03          now live, he joins us now from Chicago, (0.4)
04          .hh a:h (.) you doin' okay sir?
05          (0.5)
06   FP:    .hh much better today Don, u:m (.) than was last
07          night. it was very painful last night, u::m (.)
08          when I- (0.2) heard the gunshots, I ran to the
09          uh (.) gym. (0.9) .hh right inside the doorway I
10          saw (.) two young boys, uh: (.) shot. (0.4) um:
11          one laying there, (.) um (0.2) blood gushing
12          from him an'- (0.3) .hhh (0.2) a:nd, (.)and
13          screaming for help. (0.3) and uh, to see that in
14          the, (0.3) .hhh (0.2) in the entranceway of a
15          building that you've, (0.2) built as a place o'
16          safety and a sanctuary for safety for kids all,
17          (0.2) .hh (.) year round u::m (0.2) was-was
18          hurtful=an' I was angry, an'-an' I was d- .hhh
19          (.) very uh (0.3) very sad by it to see this (.)
20          this reality brought to my door.
21          (0.3)
22   DL:    yeah. an' I can see that you are still hurting,
23          uh:=
24   FP:    =yeah
25          (0.3)
26   DL:    ba- (.) about it right now Father. (.) 'cuz I I
27          know you and, (.) you look upset.
28   FP:    right.
```

Immediately observable in this excerpt are Lemon's characterization of Pfleger's emotional states across time (lines 1–2: 'Father Pfleger was extremely, extremely upset'; line 22: 'I can see you are still hurting'; line 27: 'you look upset') and Pfleger's own emotional avowals (line 7: 'It was very painful'; line 18: 'I was angry'; lines 18–19: 'I was . . . very sad'). In this interaction the interviewer and interviewee are collaboratively describing and affirming the epistemic certitude of emotionality and its relevance to their communicative exchange. Moreover, emotionality is produced as part of a cause and effect chain involving specific people and events. Here, for example, both parties are orienting to emotionality as something that can be read off of events (e.g. lines 13–18: 'to see that ... was hurtful') as well as people (line 22: 'I can see that you are still hurting'; line 27: 'you look upset'). Located within the institutional setting of the news interview, where the interviewer's primary objective is to elicit newsworthy commentary (McHoul & Rapley, 2001), it is Pfleger's emotional reaction to events, not Lemon's, that is treated as relevant. Pfleger also provides an intensely dramatic and affect-laden account that describes how he came across the shooting victims and characterizes his sadness and anger as normal, warranted and a direct consequence of transgressive events and an unexpected break in the moral fabric of society (e.g. lines 18–20: 'an' I was angry, an'-an' I was d- .hhh (.) very uh (0.3) very sad by it to see this (.) this reality brought to my door').

Another important aspect of emotionality that this interaction highlights is *directionality*. In folk psychological perspectives as well as the psychological literature, emotions are not independent phenomena but are tied to objects, people, events and so on. This is reminiscent of Sara Ahmed's (2010) work on affect and *'sticky' objects* (see also Benesch, 2011). Similarly, Edwards (1997: 199) has pointed out that *emotions* can be conceptually distinguished from *moods* 'on the grounds that emotions take "intensional"[1] objects' and moods do not: we are angry *at* things, fearful *of* things, but can be simply jovial or frivolous' (see also, Coulter, 1986; Du Bois, 2007; Parrott, 2001; Rorty, 1980; Ruusuvuori, 2013).

Lemon's description of Pfleger's emotional state not only references the initiators of emotions and their intensional objects but also the intensity (Labov, 1984; Prior, 2016) and duration of those emotions (e.g. 'Father Pfleger was extremely, extremely upset'; 'I can see you are still hurting'). Furthermore, the lexical categorization of the two victims as 'young boys' and 'kids' (rather than *teens, youths, young men, people*) works to foreground their innocence and helplessness and contributes to a reflexive characterization of the heinousness of the tragedy and a corresponding and intensely emotional reaction to their deaths. By collaboratively describing events in emotion-implicative terms, Lemon and Pfleger are constructing the tragic and morally accountable nature of this shooting (and its newsworthiness; see also Chapter 3 on accounts and accounting work), thus locating it within a larger interpretive frame (Goffman, 1981) of public tragedy and thereby supporting Pfleger's activist agenda against urban gang activities, shootings, violence against children and related social problems.

As this example illustrates, though undoubtedly shaped by the news interview practice of soliciting emotional displays as evidence of authentic, first-hand experiences, invoking and accounting for emotionality is a collaborative activity in our social interactions, both intimate and public. Moreover, these matters are not limited to journalistic interviews but are woven into the fabric of all social settings – including, as I explore across these chapters, the institutional and interpersonal contexts of qualitative interview research.

A Discursive Constructionist Approach

As a means to investigate the interactional management of emotionality and emotional life, I draw on an approach informed largely by contemporary discourse analytic work associated with *discursive constructionism* (Potter & Hepburn, 2008) and *discursive psychology*, as developed by Jonathan Potter and Derek Edwards and expanded by their colleagues associated with the 'Loughborough School' of discourse analysis (e.g. Edwards & Stokoe, 2004; Hepburn & Wiggins, 2007; Potter, 2010b; Potter & Hepburn, 2008; Stokoe et al., 2012; te Molder & Potter, 2005; see also Benwell & Stokoe, 2006; Wooffitt, 2005). Like DP, I also make use of the analytical methods and findings of CA (Heritage, 1984; Hutchby & Wooffitt, 2008; Liddicoat, 2011; Sacks, 1992; Sidnell & Stivers, 2013), *ethnomethodology* (Garfinkel, 1967), and *membership categorization analysis* (MCA) (Hester & Eglin, 1997; Sacks, 1992; Schegloff, 2007), sometimes collectively referred to as EMCA,[2] which I will describe in the following section.

This approach is further informed by intersecting lines of *discourse analysis* (Bilmes, 1986; Buttny, 1993, 2004; Couper-Kuhlen, 2012; Goodwin & Goodwin, 2001; Holt & Clift, 2007; Maynard, 2003; Speer, 2005), scholarship on *psychotherapeutic interaction* (Labov & Fanshel, 1977; Pawelczyk, 2011; Peräkylä et al., 2008; Peräkylä & Sorjonen, 2012), *sociological* and *anthropological approaches* (e.g. Bauman, 1986; Bauman & Briggs, 1990; Besnier, 1990; Goffman, 1963, 1981), *personal narratives* (e.g. Becker, 1997; Briggs, 1986, 2007; De Fina & Georgakopoulou, 2012; Mishler, 1986; Riessman, 2008), and *ethnographic methods* (e.g. Atkinson, 2015; Atkinson et al., 2011; Blommaert & Jie, 2010; Bohannan & van der Elst, 1988; Hammersley & Atkinson, 2007; Watson-Gegeo, 1988; Wolcott, 2008).

EMCA

Giving attention to emotion and discourse as part of *talk-and-other-conduct* in interaction (Kasper & Wagner, 2011; Sidnell, 2010a) requires examining how those actions get built by various semiotic resources and, in turn, what kinds of work they enable interactants to accomplish. This entails attending not just to *speakers* and the utterances and actions they produce but also to the intended *recipients* and how they take up and respond to those productions. These various resources may be linguistic (e.g. vocabulary, grammar, metaphor) or embodied (e.g. gestures, facial expression), vocal (e.g. response cries) or paravocal (e.g. prosody, intonation, stress), and explicit (e.g. labels) or implied (e.g. topics, contrasts). In the literature, these features are sometimes referred to as the 'micro-analytic' aspects of interaction, which are then contrasted with 'macro-level' constructs such as *agency* and *power*, concerns traditionally associated with various lines of critical discourse analysis (on micro-macro distinctions, see discussions in Benwell & Stokoe, 2006; Kitzinger, 2000; Kupferberg & Green, 2005; Speer & Stokoe, 2011; Wooffitt, 2005).

Ethnomethodology lies at the heart of the various EMCA projects (on internal diversity and debates, see Clayman & Maynard, 1995; ten Have, 2002; Maynard & Clayman, 1991). Emerging from the sociological work of Harold Garfinkel (Garfinkel, 1967; Heritage, 1984; see also Lynch & Bogen, 1996), ethnomethodology concerns itself with the mundane or taken-for-granted features of human activity. As an inductive or 'bottom-up' approach to social action, 'ethnomethodology seeks to recover social organization as an emergent achievement that results from the concerted efforts of society members acting within local situations' (Maynard & Clayman, 2003: 174). This early pioneering work by Garfinkel, with intellectual ties to Erving Goffman (1956), was later expanded by Harvey Sacks (1992) and associates Emmanuel Schegloff and Gail Jefferson (e.g. Sacks et al., 1974; Schegloff, 2007; Schegloff et al., 1977), eventually influencing the development of CA and its programmatic investigation of the mechanisms (e.g. turn-taking, sequence organization, recipient design) underlying all talk-in-interaction and the institutional function of conversation as the 'primordial site of sociality' (Schegloff, 1992: 1296; for historical overviews, see Heritage, 1984; Hutchby & Wooffitt, 2008; Kasper & Wagner, 2014; Liddicoat, 2011; Psathas, 1995; Sidnell & Stivers, 2013; Wooffitt, 2005). Sacks' MCA, with its focus on membership categories and cultural logic is also a robust (though often underrepresented and contested) analytic project (e.g. Baker, 2004; Fitzgerald & Housley, 2015; Hester & Eglin, 1997; Housley & Fitzgerald, 2002; Jayyusi, 1984; Kasper, 2009; Sacks, 1992; Schegloff, 2007; Stokoe, 2012). DP is a relative latecomer to the intersecting EMCA programs. Because its theoretical and analytical sensibilities guide the approach to emotionality and autobiographical talk taken in these chapters, and it is increasingly coming to the attention of L2 researchers, I will briefly describe its history and philosophical stance in the following section.

Early and contemporary discursive psychology

DP is an interdisciplinary field and approach, not a method (Potter, 2012a, 2012b, 2012c; cf. Hammersley, 2003; Potter, 2003). It investigates 'psychology' as a fundamentally social concern and an interactionally consequential resource in the lives of real people in everyday (rather than experimental) settings. DP arose out of social psychology in the 1980s and 1990s (e.g. Billig, 1996; Billig et al., 1988; Edwards, 1997; Edwards & Potter, 1992; Harré & Stearns, 1995; Potter, 1996; Potter & Wetherell, 1987; Wetherell & Potter, 1992) and has since established itself across the social sciences as a highly influential and prolific line of discourse analytic work. Early DP studies, not always labeled 'discursive psychology' (much of it was labeled 'discourse analysis'), drew on an eclectic mix that included post-structuralist theories, Wittgensteinian language philosophy, discursive rhetoric (Billig, 1996), the sociology of scientific knowledge (Gilbert &

Mulkay, 1984), ethnomethodology and CA. It took aim at mainstream psychology by advocating a thorough respecification of traditionally 'cognitive' topics (e.g. memory, attitudes, perceptions, prejudice, emotions) from a discourse and interaction based perspective. Thus DP was not offering an alternative or complementary approach to mainstream cognitive psychology but a radical reworking of it.

Over the years, DP's diverse lineage has contributed to the development of multiple strands of discourse analytic research labeled as or aligning itself with DP (e.g. Edley, 2001a; Harré & Stearns, 1995; Hook, 2001, 2007; Korobov & Bamberg, 2004; Parker, 1992, 2007), thereby contributing to some of the disciplinary overlap and debates. Historical reviews of DP further underscore the complexity and breadth of the DP project by offering their own perspectives on the various DP strands and their points of convergence and divergence (e.g. Augoustinos & Tileaga, 2012; Edwards, 1997; Hepburn & Wiggins, 2007; Jørgensen & Phillips, 2002; te Molder & Potter, 2005; Potter, 2010a, 2010b, 2012c; Speer, 2005; Wetherell, 2007; Wiggins & Potter, 2008; Wooffitt, 2005).

In a recent survey, Potter (2012b) describes three main strands of DP (Table 2.1). These strands are not linear or discrete in their development but represent intersecting lines of inquiry.

Table 2.1 Three strands of discursive psychology

Strand 1: Interviews and Repertoires

Made frequent use of *open-ended interviews* and gave much attention to *interpretive repertoires*, described by Potter and Wetherell (1987: 138) as 'a lexicon or register of terms and metaphors drawn upon to characterize and evaluate actions and events'. Discourse analysts have used the concept of interpretive repertoires to investigate identity work in relation to scientific inquiry (Gilbert & Mulkay, 1984), gender and sexuality (Edley, 2001a; Wetherell, 1998), racism (Wetherell, 1998; Wetherell & Potter, 1992) and motherhood (Silverman, 1987, 2001), among other topics.

Strand 2: Discursive Psychology and Constructionism

Focused on *naturalistic interaction* (e.g. conversations, newspaper reports, news interviews) and the management of psychological business in the production of accounts (Edwards, 1997; Edwards & Potter, 1992). This includes work on folk psychological categories and the 'psychological thesaurus': 'the situated, occasioned, rhetorical uses of the rich commonsense psychological lexicon or thesaurus: terms such as angry, jealous, know, believe, feel, want, and so on' (Edwards & Potter, 2005: 241).

Strand 3: Discursive Psychology and Sequential Analysis

Distinguished by a convergence with CA methods, principles and research findings (e.g. conversation, corpus materials, institutional settings, linguistic and paralinguistic analysis, membership categorization analysis; Stokoe & Edwards, 2009; Hepburn & Wiggins, 2007; Potter, 2010a, 2010b).

Source: Adapted from Potter (2012b: 121–122).

Further complicating the picture is that the first strand of DP paved the way for related work alternatively described as 'synthetic', 'critical' or 'feminist' DP (see descriptions in Jørgensen & Phillips, 2002; Speer, 2005; Wooffitt, 2005), which combines post-structuralist perspectives on discourse, power and the subject with forms of CA and discourse analysis (e.g. Bamberg, 2004; Edley & Wetherell, 1997, 1999, 2001; Weatherall, 2002; Wetherell, 1998, 2007; Wetherell & Edley, 1999). Some readers may note the similarity between 'interpretive repertoires' in the first strand and the concept of (macro) 'discourses' central to some critical approaches. Though both refer to distinctive ways of talking about the world, discourse (as used by critical discourse analysts) is more closely aligned with Foucauldian perspectives on power and social members as subjects within ideological structures; whereas interpretive repertoires has been used by some 'critical'[3] DP scholars to place more emphasis on human agency (Edley, 2001a: 202).

Contemporary discursive psychology and 'naturalistic' data

In a bit of disciplinary ring fencing that makes a clear separation with older versions of DP, Potter (2010a; Wiggins & Potter, 2008; see also Edwards & Stokoe, 2004) describes 'contemporary DP' (Strand 3) as an empirical study of *naturalistic* interaction (based on audio and video recordings of naturally occurring interaction in everyday conversation as well as institutional settings). This sets DP firmly within a 'sequential' or 'basic' CA tradition. Contemporary DP is further characterized by a continued focus on psychological topics, increased attention to the investigation of institutional interactions (i.e. 'applied' DP) and a rejection of interpretive repertoires and research interviews.

An issue that Potter and colleagues (e.g. Potter & Hepburn, 2005, 2012) repeatedly address, and one that appears to ignore researcher reflexivity, is that research interviews are rejected because they are contrived and therefore not naturalistic (see also Hammersley, 2014a). In principle, there is good cause for treating interview data with caution. Self-reports are inherently fraught with analytic difficulty. How people *report* what they do or feel does not really tell us what they *actually* do or feel. Moreover the interviewer, as a central participant, is unavoidably implicated in the generation of the data. Despite the strong reservations some researchers have about the status of interview data, I am in agreement with Speer (2002, 2005; cf. Potter, 2002), a feminist CA scholar, that there is no need to throw away interview methodology as long as we approach the research process itself as interaction. From this perspective, interviews are neither natural nor unnatural on their own: what is of practical import is what we do with them and the data they generate. Perhaps the inescapable and more pragmatic reality is that the enduring popularity of research interviewing ensures that this methodology is unlikely to lose favor (Atkinson & Silverman, 1997). Therefore, opening up for inspection the various collaborative activities that constitute its institutional and interpersonal frame can enable us to be better researchers and analysts.

At the same time, it is essential that we recognize that this should not license researchers to view interviews as a privileged or convenient method of collecting data. The research interview is but one type of interactional setting, and as a result of its institutional confines offers a correspondingly limited perspective on social phenomena (see discussions in Kasper & Prior, 2015; Potter & Hepburn, 2005, 2012; Rapley, 2012).

Discursive psychology and conversation analysis

Whereas DP has as its key interest the forms and functions of 'psychology' in the context of everyday life, CA, as a sociological project, has shown some reluctance to directly engage with emotions and psychological matters. This is largely due to CA's relatively agnostic and sometimes antagonistic stance toward the 'mental world' and its own primary interest in elucidating the interaction order. This perspective is exemplified by Garfinkel's oft-cited quote claiming, 'there is no reason to look under the skull, for nothing of interest is to be found there but brains' (Garfinkel, 1963, as cited in Bergmann, 2004: 75; see also, Coulter, 2005; Kasper, 2009; te Molder & Potter, 2005).

Over two decades ago, Buttny (1993: 89) pointed out the lack of attention to emotion by CA scholars: 'To my knowledge conversation analysis has virtually ignored the notion of affect, but it has contributed much to social accountability and accounts'. More recently, Couper-Kuhlen (2009: 94) made a similar observation: 'Conversation Analysis (CA) and affect are uneasy bedfellows: classical CA, with only a few exceptions, has shied away from tackling affect and emotion in interaction directly'. Discussing previous work on 'emotion discourse' by DP scholars (e.g. Edwards, 1997, 1999), Couper-Kuhlen further finds that 'it does not allow a study of the actual display of affect in talk-in-interaction, in particular its non-verbal aspects, both vocal and visceral' (2009: 95). Following other CA scholars of emotion (e.g. Goodwin & Goodwin, 2001; Sandlund, 2004; Selting, 1994, 1996), Couper-Kuhlen (2009: 96) proposes a renewed application of CA to the study of affect and emotion that starts from four distinct propositions supported by mainstream CA:

(a) Affect and emotion are performed as *displays* in interaction.
(b) These displays are realized as *embodied practices*.
(c) The practices are *situated* at specific sequential positions within interaction.
(d) The practices are interpreted in a *context-sensitive* fashion.

Though it is largely true that discursive psychologists' early work on emotion discourse tended to focus on lexical and rhetorical devices (e.g. as in the 'psychological thesaurus'; Edwards, 1997, 1999, 2005; Strand 2, Table 2.1, this chapter; see also Bamberg, 1997), it has since evolved, along with CA, to regularly include attention to prosodic and paralinguistic features and embodied actions (e.g. Drew, 1998; Edwards, 2007; Holt & Clift, 2007; Selting, 2010; Stokoe & Edwards, 2007). Moreover, contributions over the past decade have proven that the distinction between CA and DP is increasingly a tenuous one (e.g. Buttny, 2004; Hepburn & Wiggins, 2007; te Molder & Potter, 2005; Peräkylä et al., 2008; Sidnell & Stivers, 2013), such that contemporary DP research and CA studies involving 'psychological' topics (e.g. cognition, prejudice, emotion) are largely synonymous (see also Levinson, 2006, on the misconception that CA is anti-cognitive). Silverman (2011) points out that much of the distinction between CA and DA (referring to Potter and Edward's brand of DA, i.e. DP) is superficial, as it reflects less the methodology and philosophical stances than it does the researcher's own disciplinary affiliation.

Three key issues

Their disciplinary diversity aside, tying CA and DP together is their ethnomethodological sensibility, action orientation and attention to the orderliness of interaction. Antaki and Widdicombe (1998: 1–2) describe this attitude as:

> ... the general ethnomethodological spirit of treating social life [and emotional life] as the business that people conduct with each other, displayed in their everyday practices ... Identity [and emotionality, narrative, memory, etc.] ... ought not be treated as an explanatory 'resource' that we as analysts haul with us to a scene where people are interacting, but as a 'topic' that requires investigation and sweat once we get there.

With this description, Antaki and Widdicombe highlight three overarching issues crucial to the present project: *reflexivity*, *relevance* and *rigor*.

Considering reflexivity (which takes on a special meaning in EMCA), CA scholars note that human activities ('the business of everyday life') are recognizable and subsequently analyzable through the very actions that constitute them (i.e. in a reflexive and recursive relationship; Seedhouse, 2004). For example, interviews are recognizable as 'interviews' because participants do orderly actions that are normatively associated with that activity (e.g. questioning, responding, summarizing, recording). Conversation analysts describe this reflexive or 'doubly contextual' view of communicative action as 'being both *context-shaped* and *context-renewing*' (Heritage, 1984: 242; emphasis in original). Heritage goes on to explain,

Since every 'current' action will itself form the immediate context for some 'next' action in a sequence, it will inevitably contribute to the framework in terms of which the next action will be understood. In this sense, the context of a next action is repeatedly renewed with every current action. (1984: 242)

This order is not pre-formed or inevitable but is collaboratively accomplished (though with varying degrees of success) through interactants' moment-by-moment actions based on their shared sociocultural knowledge and competences. In addition, each action is tied to what came before and what comes next – what CA scholars refer to as the principle of 'nextness' (e.g. Sacks, 1992). Generic means by which this order is collaboratively achieved include turntaking procedures and the recipient designedness of talk (Sacks *et al.*, 1974). In other words, talk is not just produced: it is produced for (and with) specific recipients and on specific occasions.

A second key observation is that analysts must be cautious when assuming or prescribing what is relevant (Schegloff, 1997). At any given moment in an interaction, there are a multitude of identities, categories, emotions, labels, actions, perceptions, experiences and so on that are interactionally available and thereby *potentially* relevant. My biological sex or ethnicity, for example, may be conspicuous and therefore function as salient markers of my identity (what Zimmerman, 1998, refers to as 'transportable' or non-context-specific identities). But whether participants (or I) will observably orient to those categories and make them interactionally relevant is not something that can be assumed or predicted a priori. Thus, from a CA perspective, *potentially* or *probably* relevant is not sufficient to warrant analytical claims: what can only be taken as relevant, and therefore analytically defensible, is what interactants themselves demonstrably *make* relevant. Moreover, as Brouwer (2012: 4) explains, '[t]his means that the researcher does not have to search for the appropriate data to fit a research problem'.

A third important observation regards the rigorous and demanding nature of discursive research. Antaki and Widdicombe (1998: 2) bring attention to the fact that analysis involves 'investigation and sweat'. It requires close and continuous engagement with the data and its treatment, the categories and topics, the identities, the actions, the orientations, the contextual features, the interactional consequences and the evidence on which we base and represent our analytical claims (Antaki *et al.*, 2003).

An illustrative example

To briefly illustrate some of these issues, I consider a segment involving identity and categorization work from an interview with Bona, an immigrant man from Cambodia. In the interaction leading up to the segment shown in Excerpt 2.3, I have asked Bona about the languages he speaks (Khmer, Chinese and English). In the turn shown in line 1, I invite him to evaluate his English skills. In response, he asserts he knows 'half' of what I know and then makes reference to my category status as an 'American', thereby building a contrast with himself (i.e. as *non-American, immigrant, non-English expert*):

(Excerpt 2.3). Bona: 'Fifty percent'

```
01  M:  tsch (.) descri:- okay (.) if I had to say
02      how would you evaluate your English ability
03      ((lines removed))
04  B:  I rate myself about half of what you know.
05  M:  why do you (.) why do you say that?
06  B:  because I think that's about right what you
07      know is consider a hundred percent. what I
08      know is about (.) maybe close to fifty
09      percent of what you know. because you are
10      an American.
11  M:  [so-
12  B:  [you was born here and your mom and dad (.)
13      American?
14  M:  mhm
15  B:  and (.) you learned (.) that's the only
16      language that is taught to you by your mom
17      and dad when you was like (.) born.
```

Not only does Bona provide a warrant here for bringing citizenship and national origin into the analysis, he also creates an interpretive frame for his talk by invoking a folk ideological trope of 'American as monolingual' and 'American as native English speaker by birth' (lines 15–17). Moreover, the topic (L2 English proficiency) and Bona's quantification of our respective English skills are produced as direct responses to the interviewer's prompt (lines 1–2). Although the interviewer can be seen to invite the interviewee's perceptions of his own sociolinguistic history, Bona conducts his own ad hoc analysis (lines 12–13, 15–17) of the interviewer's sociolinguistic background (which the interviewer later contests, not shown here). From a pragmatics perspective, it is also possible that Bona's self-deprecatory response minimizing his English skills was a kind of 'fishing device' (Pomerantz, 1980) to solicit a compliment from the interviewer (which does occur following this fragment).

In sum, this sequence was generated by the interview context, the categories under which the interviewee was recruited (e.g. *immigrant, L2 learner/ user*) and the interviewer's questions. Without resorting to exogenous theories and 'macro' sociological assumptions, even this short spate of talk offers insights into the interview activity, self-assessment of language skills, 'folk' language ideology and the representation of personal history. It shows that through the production and reception of their talk, interactants (i.e. interviewee and interviewer) collaboratively build their own context and demonstrate what is relevant at each moment. It should be apparent that from a CA perspective, when analysts elect to *begin* their analyses by assuming that they know better than the participants what is interactionally relevant (even when – or perhaps, *especially* when – they are part of the data), they make a particularly precarious interpretive leap.

Getting Contextual

'Invisible elephants'

Conversation analysts have repeatedly pointed out the relevance of those instances where a culturally 'expected' or 'preferred' response is delayed or 'officially absent' (Schegloff, 1968: 1083). In such cases, interactants tend to orient to or mark such response delays or absences as 'dispreferred' by using repetition or repair. Speakers also orient to their responses as dispreferred through pauses, hesitation markers or accounts explaining the delayed, absent or inapposite response. Excerpt 2.4, embedded in a larger complaint sequence, offers a case in point. Trang, a Cambodian-Vietnamese immigrant is speaking here about negative social attitudes toward immigrants like him, and he attributes this to people's ignorance.

(Excerpt 2.4). Trang: 'Okay Matt?'

```
01      T:   "ok because you're ignorant because you don't
02           understand .hh (1.0) where they're coming from.
03           that's why you talk like that."
04      M:   °°mm°°
05  →   T:   ri:ght?
06           (5.4)
07  →        °s'okay Matt?°
08           (6.0)
09      M:   no: that's good n-n-no sorry. (.) no-no
10           that's interesting.
11           (1.7)
12           nah I'm just thinking.
```

Following his representation of his personal perspective on such 'ignorant' people (lines 1–3, produced as represented thought), Trang receives only a minimal response from the interviewer (line 4: '°°mm°°'). By means of a sound stretch and rising intonation, Trang then pursues agreement and a stronger affiliative stance (line 5; 'ri:ght?'), which is unsuccessful. He then seeks to identify the trouble source behind the interviewer's absent response (line 7: '°s'okay Matt?°'). After another extended gap of silence, in lines 9–12, the interviewer accounts for his dispreferred (non)responses by apologizing and attributing his silence to his serious consideration of these matters rather than to a disinterest in or a problem with Trang's talk.

What then is to be made of those things that are 'unofficially absent' or not demonstrably oriented to but are nonetheless conspicuous by their absence or ambiguity? Must we not also recognize that 'the significance of what is said depends on what is not said' (Ziff, 1960: 147; see also Bilmes, 1986: 119; Edwards, 1997: 229). For example, what is signified in a personals ad when age or perhaps weight are not specified (e.g. Rapley, 2007)? Deception? How about the withholding of politeness in an institutional encounter (e.g. Bousfield, 2008)? Irritation? What about when a male stranger suggests to a woman that she 'smile' (e.g. Speer, 2005)? Gendered policing? What of those moments where same-sex couples avoid gender reference by using 'partner' rather than 'boyfriend' or 'girlfriend' (Nelson, 2009)? Reinforced heteronormativity or internalized homophobia? All betray *something* by what is absent as well as present. Just what that *something* is may, of course, be difficult to pinpoint and thereby make difficult a warrantable and defensible analysis. Nevertheless, I argue that this difficulty does not make these matters inherently less relevant or less deserving of analytical consideration.

Take for example, the highly politicized and sensitive categories of race, ethnicity, gender or sexuality that have become taboo in various arenas of 'polite' Western society. Though they may not be talked about, they may nevertheless be 'the elephants in the room' (Eckert, 2003) that participants are making efforts not to overtly notice or comment upon. They may also be talked about in ways that naturalize some categories while denaturalizing others by omission (e.g. assuming *nurse* must refer to a woman). To some scholars, CA's insistence on only considering what is 'demonstrably relevant' (Schegloff, 1997: 165) is 'unbearably limiting' (Kitzinger, 2000: 171), methodologically and epistemologically 'naïve' (Billig, 1999a, 1999b) and even socially irresponsible by claiming to conduct an 'emic' analysis while perpetuating invisibility and inequality for marginalized members of society. A number of researchers across the interdisciplinary domain of discourse analysis (e.g. Atkinson, 1988; Blommaert, 2001a; Enfield, 2007; Kitzinger, 2000, 2005; Stokoe & Smithson, 2001; Talmy, 2009; Watson & Seiler, 1992)[4] have sought to address the above concerns by urging CA to expand its analytical focus in various ways.

'Unmotivated' and 'motivated' looking

Not surprisingly, CA scholars such as Schegloff (1997, 2009), sharply dismiss any claims based on what is not demonstrably oriented to precisely because they fail to provide defensible warrants. For Schegloff (2009: 366), 'If the analyst wants to claim that something is real, it must be demonstrably, analyzably real in its consequences *in the interaction*' (emphasis in original). Schegloff's stance is based on a core tenet of basic CA, 'unmotivated looking' (ten Have, 2007; Sacks, 1992), whereby analysts bracket their assumptions and questions to arrive at an inductive, data-driven understanding and analysis of the recorded interaction. However, Talmy (2009) has proposed 'motivated looking', an approach informed by the methods of CA and MCA, as a means to inform 'analytic accountability and warrantability of assertions in critically-situated empirical research' (2009: 206) to investigate topics such as power, racism, sexism, homophobia and classism as interactional phenomena in everyday life (see related discussions in Antaki, 2011; Speer, 2005; Wilkinson & Kitzinger, 2008).

While offering criticisms of both the real and perceived narrow scope of CA, Celia Kitzinger, a feminist CA scholar, contends that basic CA does offer a rigorous method for investigating various 'political' and 'critical' concerns such as gender and sexuality (see also Speer, 2005). She asserts exogenous theories are unnecessary to attend to the 'invisible' and taken-for-granted aspects of interaction. In her work (e.g. 2000, 2005, 2013), Kitzinger has scrutinized the ways in which speakers produce and reproduce a normative heterosexual world precisely by *not* orienting to it (e.g. through introducing and expecting heteronormative topics and relational terms: such as *husband* and *wife*). With the goal of advancing an 'adequate feminist CA', Toerien and Kitzinger (2007: 658) argue that analysis of the moment-by-moment construction of social worlds and the (re)production of local cultures offers a bridge between 'both the mechanics of social action and the socio-political consequences'.

Nevertheless, the analytical reality is that these matters are not always so straightforward. I was further reminded of these 'invisible' issues as I was shopping in a busy supermarket and ran into a gay Vietnamese friend of one of the study participants. We were surprised to see each other outside his friend's home or the local bar (a popular community gathering spot), and we exchanged brief pleasantries. As we talked, I found myself perceiving our interaction was somehow different this time: *Was he acting a little 'butcher'? Was he cautiously avoiding eye contact and being overly selective with his words?* Before we made our goodbyes he said quietly, 'So, have you got one yet?' To anyone else the indexical meaning would likely be lost – but to me, particularly in light of our previous interactions, the meaning was transparent: 'Are you dating anyone?' (a question he regularly asked). At the time, I was struck by the simple fact that the transposition of our familiar interactional frame into another context triggered the use of a covert code and the desire to conceal rather than reveal. It appears we were, as Goffman (1963: 54) describes in his work on stigmatized identities, partitioning our world by 'concealing something shameful' (see also Yoshino, 2011). Though the shadow of what was *not said* (whether one wishes to explain it as a defensive response to heteronormativity, a desire for privacy, etc.) may have been invisible to overhearers and even to ourselves at the time, was it any less relevant to our encounter or any less important for maintaining and furthering our interpersonal relations?

'Ethnographic' mentality and extra-discursive material

To make visible and to explain some of these hidden and ambiguous matters in data generation and analysis, I find that an *ethnographic mentality*, 'a particular mode of looking, listening, and thinking about social phenomena' (Hammersley & Atkinson, 2007: 230), in tandem with the cultural, commonsense and background knowledge of members and analysts (Stokoe & Smithson, 2001), can function as integral resources in the qualitative researcher's analytical toolkit. Though ethnographic or extra-discursive knowledge has not typically been a mainstay of CA/DP methodology, it can enable researchers to identify topics and concerns and fill in analytical gaps when investigating particular phenomena (see also Antaki, 2011; Atkinson, 2015; Atkinson *et al.*, 2011; Holstein & Gubrium, 2011; Maynard, 2003; Moerman, 1988; Mondada, 2013a, 2013b; Prior, 2014; Roulston, 2010; Talmy, 2009). Mondada (2013b: 38), for example, considers ethnography an important component of fieldwork and thus 'a form of *proto-analysis*' that allows researchers to make informed decisions about what to record.

Douglas Maynard (2003) has been a leading proponent of combining CA with ethnography, though in a restrained fashion. Maynard considers ethnography essential to his in-depth analysis of narrative and interview data of 'bad news' tellings, yet he views the relationship between ethnography and CA to be one of 'limited affinity' (i.e. ethnography as resource, subordinate to sequential analysis) rather than 'mutual affinity' (where ethnography and sequential analysis are on equal footing). A particular insight I adopt from Maynard is that ethnographic knowledge offers crucial contextualization resources for the researcher. Ethnography allows the analyst (and reader) to get a better handle on what Maynard terms 'curious patterns' in the data and to better identify what aspects of members' identities are relevant (*especially* when, they may not be demonstrably oriented to).

The labels 'ethnography' and 'ethnographic' are often overused and misappropriated, particularly in relation to qualitative interview studies (see discussions in Atkinson, 2015; O'Reilly, 2012; Ramanathan & Atkinson, 1999; Spradley, 1979; Talmy, 2010a). When I describe my own research as 'ethnographic', I refer to an *ethnographic mentality* that seeks to get at an emically oriented understanding of the context – as well as *ethnographic knowledge* and *extra-discursive insights* garnered from participation and observation over the course of the research. Because this project involves sequential analysis of micro-behaviors and phenomena in context, individual case studies and extra-discursive material that often resist generalization, it bears an affinity with microethnography (Streeck & Mehus, 2005), a research approach concerned with the moment-by-moment analysis of human life as it emerges in interaction.

Whether labeled 'ethnographic' or not, qualitative fieldwork and research practices are in many ways ethnographically-oriented endeavors (Briggs, 1986, 2007; Gubrium *et al.*, 2012; Mishler, 1986). Researchers frequently explore and encounter unfamiliar topics and contexts by developing close relationships with key informants, using open-ended interview techniques, engaging in reflexive practice, carrying out extended observations and making use of interviewees as observers and reporters of their social worlds. Researchers also become participant observers through doing interviews and other shared activities with research participants. Shared interactional histories built with participants over time (in longitudinal studies) also afford researchers an increased sensitivity to categories, terms, previously-told accounts and other components of the interactional chain that are not necessarily overtly referenced but may be suggested or otherwise made available.

Charles Goodwin (2000) makes a forceful argument that when conducting fieldwork in a new setting (even in a familiar language and country), ethnography is essential to access the knowledge necessary to understand the local actions and phenomena that are relevant to participants. One could even make the case that *all* social research is inescapably cross-cultural (even autoethnography explores the relationship between the self and culture; Irvine *et al.*, 2008). Although discourse analysts may often be intent on examining the forms and functions of language, they are, as Moerman (1988: 2) points out, collecting 'cultural artifacts that come mounted in a context that gives them their momentarily enlivened meaning'. Constructs such as *emotionality, identity, narrative, gender* and even *research* are also cultural artifacts. Thus, sequential analysis and ethnographic or extra-discursive insights are not incompatible and may prove essential in providing sufficient context for understanding and analyzing our data: 'close description of the moment-by-moment constitution of social life in talk-in-interaction can both fundamentally enrich and be fundamentally enriched by broad descriptions of social behaviours, norms and values' (Atkinson *et al.*, 2011: 89; see also Atkinson, 2015). This discursive constructionist approach diverges from canonical CA/DP as well as mainstream ethnography, but I contend that the analytical benefits may necessitate such strategic breaks in formal disciplinary alignments.

Discursive Construction

If *discourse* is conceived of here as 'talk-and-other conduct' in (and *as*) interaction, what then is meant by 'construction' or 'constructionism'? In general terms, constructionism is a philosophical and analytical perspective that views 'reality' (or perhaps more accurately, what 'counts as' reality) as something that is socially assembled and therefore open for inspection and revision. Gubrium and Holstein (2012: 4), describing the importance of Berger and Luckmann's (1966) classic constructionist treatise, *The Social Construction of Reality*, state that '[i]t rendered problematic the most common understanding, the "facts" of experiences that heretofore were treated as matters to be straightforwardly discovered, recorded, and analyzed'. Constructionism, then, opens up a space for radical perspectives on both ontology (the nature of reality) as well as epistemology (the nature of knowing).

This is an admittedly crude oversimplification, as not all 'constructionisms' are the same (Benwell & Stokoe, 2006; Burr, 2004; Hibberd, 2005). Gubrium and Holstein (2012: 4–5) further explain that constructionism remains a diverse collection of approaches:

> Constructionism now belongs to everyone and to no one – a highly variegated mosaic of itself ... Just as constructionism belongs to no one and to everyone, the term *constructionism* has come to mean everything and nothing at the same time.

Whereas Berger and Luckmann's (1966) work (see also Harré, 1986) embraced a form of cognitive constructionism and focused more on a phenomenological understanding of individuals' perceptions (Potter, 2012c), a DC approach more in line with contemporary DP takes an agnostic and at times even seemingly *anti*-cognitivist stance. DP, and CA more broadly, has always been acknowledged as a form of constructionist inquiry. Potter and Hepburn (2008), in their chapter for Holstein and Gubrium's (2008) *Handbook of Constructionist Research*, bring DC to the fore while advancing DP's anti-cognitive program and its contemporary interest in mundane epistemics: 'the study of knowledge and understanding as things that are practical and interactional' (Potter & Hepburn, 2008: 285). Potter and Hepburn insist the reflexive nature of DC makes visible participants' concerns:

> Discursive constructionism (DC) is most distinctive in its foregrounding of the epistemic position of both the researcher and what is researched (texts or conversations). It studies a world of descriptions, claims, reports, allegations, and assertions as parts of human practices, and it works to keep these as the central topic of research than trying to move beyond them to the objects or events that seem to be the topic of such discourse. (Potter & Hepburn, 2008: 275)

Because a DC approach allows an analysis of the researcher's contributions and institutional practices, it offers a means to address some of the criticisms that have been made against research methods that tend to privilege the data and participants' voices while ignoring the process by which these materials were generated and treated (Atkinson & Delamont, 2006; Denzin & Lincoln, 2011; Galletta & Cross, 2013). Similarly, I am interested in how, within the context of a particular interactional setting (e.g. research interviews), speakers use their communicative resources to work up and manage accounts and versions of their 'emotions', 'realities', 'truths', 'perceptions', 'identities' and so on for one another:

> In contrast to [social] constructionism, then, the ontological status of the self is of no particular interest in CA/EM. Instead, the focus is on members' orientations to identity *as* (un)stable, (in)consistent, (in)coherent, and so on. (Benwell & Stokoe, 2006: 68)

The ethnomethodological spirit of a DC approach resists positing theories about cognitive processes or the 'ontological status of self' (Benwell & Stokoe, 2006: 68). Maynard and Freese (2012: 94), in their work on news delivery, summarize this perspective in relation to affective matters:

> Certainly there can be 'feelings' or internal states experienced in association with displays (Stets, 2003, p. 310), but our research on bad and good news shares the constructionist commitment to studying displays of emotion in interaction and remaining agnostic about the existence of internal accompaniments to such displays.

Creativity and constraints

As I have discussed, a DC perspective recognizes and even embraces the creative and contradictory nature of talk and self-representation. Conceptualizing 'construction' in this perspective involves recognizing two of its important aspects: discourse as *constructed* (i.e. how it is built by the various linguistic and paralinguistic resources) and discourse as *constructive* (i.e. how it builds and stabilizes particular versions of the world, actions, events and identities) (Potter & Hepburn, 2008: 277). Instead of assuming talk is representative of underlying cognitive processes or a window into experience, a constructionist perspective recognizes that '[p]roblems have no independent existence apart from humans' versions and evaluations of them' (Buttny, 2004: 5).

Another crucial point to bear in mind is that the constructed nature of discourse does not mean that speakers can produce talk and interaction in any way they please. Though the generative and dynamic nature of language allows a multitude of ways in which something *can* be expressed, there are also significant constraints that shape what *cannot* be expressed and how talk *cannot* unfold:

> At the same time, as we continue to orient to the agency of storytellers, we are not suggesting that narrative composition is haphazard. Not just anything goes in the work of composing a story. If there is improvisation in narrative composition, there are also discernible patterns, formats, and circumstantial constraints on story formation. (Gubrium & Holstein, 2009)

Therefore, because construction is social in nature, it does not support 'anything goes' relativism (Edwards *et al.*, 1995). The constraints on how talk can and cannot be assembled and produced are themselves socially shaped and subject to enforcement and censure as well as open to resistance and contestation.

Discursive Deconstruction

From the preceding sections, it should be apparent that though DC is concerned with the *construction* or formulation of talk, action, social order and interactional objects, it is just as interested in their *deconstruction*. The first sense in which DC is deconstructionist is through the ways that its close data analysis allows researchers to explicate the abstract or context-free resources (i.e. the generic methods and procedures) that are part or all human talk-in-interaction but that get deployed for context-specific purposes and to carry out locally-relevant actions. This attention builds scholarly knowledge by explicating the dynamic nature of human interaction and the extensive semiotic possibilities for making (and remaking) meaning across various settings.

A second and related sense of deconstruction is found in the ways that interlocutors conduct their own ad hoc analyses in the midst of their ongoing interactions. Participants in a given setting are not passive recipients of talk but actively contribute to its progression and interpretation through the responses they produce as well as those they withhold. This may involve actions such as *(dis)agreeing, (dis)aligning, resisting, challenging, supporting* and even *undermining* particular constructions and accounts (Potter, 1996).

A third important way in which DC is a deconstructionist project is that it offers a reflexive, analytically grounded inspection of the research process. For researchers, exposing their professional (and even unprofessional) practices to scrutiny can be an intimidating proposition. But for CA and related social interactional approaches, a form of reflexivity is built into their analytic procedures as well as the practice of making transcripts and recorded data available for subsequent and alternative analysis by others. Because the researcher is not exempt from this analytical scrutiny, DC is an equalizing approach *par excellence*. Potter's (1996) own book is a model of reflexive practice at work. Speaking of 'an element of self-destruction', Potter (1996: 9) notes, 'At the end of the book the ideal reader should be able to turn their gaze back on the book itself and decompose the techniques and tropes that it draws on so freely.' Thus the processes and rhetoric undergirding our analyses and their representations also become objects for deconstruction (or even 'destruction', following Potter). To turn a phrase from the well-known 'turtle's back' myth about the earth's cosmological origins, we might say that a DC approach reveals the ways in which talk-in-interaction as well as the processes and practices of research are supported by rhetoric 'all the way down'.

Summary

In this chapter, I have described a DC approach as a means to investigate the representation and active management of emotionality in L2 autobiographical interview research. Drawing on the methods and findings of CA and cognate perspectives, it entails a commitment to an empirically grounded analysis set in the unfolding sequence and structure of the recorded interaction. A systematic, data-centered approach, DC refuses to remove the researcher from the analysis. Though the DC approach advocated here supports basing analytical claims on what can be warranted and substantiated in the data, it diverges from canonical CA by explicitly making use of extra-discursive insights, including participants' and the researcher's own cultural knowledge and interactional histories. This offers an eminently critical perspective and radical challenge to assumptions about social and emotional life and its significance. As a result, it counters dominant narrative-centered and thematic approaches in L2 interview-based studies by shifting the usual focus from content to construction and action. It embraces creativity and variability of self-representation, and it makes visible speakers' agentive work and their various interactional competences.

As I have indicated, when I use psychological terms such as 'emotion', 'emotionality', 'cognition' etc., no claims are being made either supporting or rejecting them as internal or intra-individual processes. Nor am I attempting to triangulate[5] or otherwise determine the veracity of speakers' talk and perceptions. Rather, I am interested in the ways in which speakers represent and manage such matters (i.e. as 'ways of talking'; Edwards, 1999) and what they achieve by it. An advantage of a DC approach is that it promotes a healthy skepticism toward our taken-for-granted understandings of emotion, identity, interviewing, research, the world and so on. A DC approach can therefore contribute to both the study of emotion and to understanding research practices where emotionality and related matters are invoked and even pursued.

In the following chapters I examine in more detail how emotionality is displayed and managed in the activity of autobiographical interview research. Chapter 3 begins by examining story prefaces, a device that allows speakers to project and launch emotion-related tellings in the ongoing interview interaction.

Notes

(1) Following Edwards (1997) and Button *et al.* (1995), I use 'intensional', a term associated with linguistics and philosophy (Crane, 2003; Searle, 1983), to refer to the *relationship* that emotions and putative 'mental attitudes' (Kenny, 2003) have with their objects (i.e. the 'what' that emotions such as *joy, anger, fear,* etc. are associated with, directed at, or about). This is not to be confused with 'intentional', a cognitive construct, which refers to *mental planning*. Because of its agnostic stance toward speakers'

(1) intra-psychological states and mental processes, the discursive constructionist approach taken here has little to say about intentionality. When it does speak of 'intention', it refers to intentionality as a rhetorical device: 'a *way of talking* rather than a referential term for a mental state' (Potter, 2006: 135; emphasis in original).
(2) Despite some significant internal differences, EMCA is used here to refer to these individual approaches as well as affiliated talk-in-interaction scholarship. Because 'contemporary' or 'sequential' DP is virtually indistinguishable from CA, I subsume it under the EMCA/talk-in-interaction program.
(3) I use scare quotes here to bring attention to the fact that 'critical' is itself a rhetorical device. In addition, feminist and other critical scholars (e.g. Speer, 2005; Talmy, 2009; Wilkinson & Kitzinger, 2008) have shown that sequential CA can contribute to critical and 'motivated' social research agendas.
(4) For further reading on these matters, see some of the various debates within CA and DP: e.g. the Speer-Edley debate (Edley, 2001b; Speer, 2001a, 2001b); the Billig-Wetherell-Schegloff debate (Billig, 1999a, 1999b; Schegloff, 1997, 1998, 1999; Wetherell, 1998); and the Cresswell debate and commentary (Buttny, 2012; Cresswell, 2012; Cresswell & Smith, 2012; Demuth, 2012; Larraín & Haye, 2012; Matusov & von Duyke, 2012; Potter, 2012c).
(5) Ethnographic material, multiple tellings and even historical documents or other information sources can help to further contextualize data analyses, particularly in pointing out and explaining curious phenomena and patterns. This is not the same as *triangulation*, a method that seeks to validate research and minimize researcher bias (Flick, 2004). Silverman (2011: 45) states that triangulation is not compatible with a constructionist approach, since there is no singular phenomenon waiting to be specified by multiple sets of data. There are, however, various ways to reconsider triangulation in discourse analysis. Markee (2000: 60), for example, writes that CA uses an emic form of triangulation involving 'different kinds of text-internal, convergent evidence to establish the credibility of an analysis'. Text-internal triangulation may include a comparison of utterances, a collection of prototypical examples or cases and so on. For other perspectives on triangulation (e.g. getting research participants' feedback on the data, employing multiple researchers), see Denzin and Lincoln (2011) and Maynard (2003).

3 Telling and Remembering

> *In our desire to tell a story in the first place, we resort to certain standard storytelling devices...*
> *This means, in effect, that one has to lie. Nothing in life naturally occurs as a culturally coherent story.*
> *In order to construct such a story, we must leave out the details that don't fit, and invent some that make things work better.*
> (Schank & Abelson, 1995: 34)

> *And e-even if I went- I went back home I- my father and I have a little...argument too. Did I tell you- tell a story Matt? My father and I? Did I tell you- tell you a story?*
> (Trang, study participant)

To extend an analysis of autobiographical tellings that includes attention to the interactional and social contexts in which they are collaboratively produced, this chapter focuses on the interconnected activities of telling and remembering. It has two primary goals: (a) to outline some of the key features of autobiographical tellings, and (b) to examine how emotionality functions as a central part of the process whereby a speaker (i.e. the research participant) *remembers*, *projects* and *collaboratively produces* a telling or sequence of tellings for and with an intended recipient (i.e. the researcher). The discursive constructionist (DC) approach employed here, while taking into account Holstein and Gubrium's (1995) injunction that researchers consider both the 'whats' and the 'hows' of interview talk, also considers the 'whos' and the 'wheres' – that is, the participants and the interactional junctures involved in making emotionality recognizable and relevant.

Drawing on findings from the social interactional literature, I begin by discussing some key storytelling conventions and constraints. I then consider the *story preface* as a device enabling tellers to carry out a number of essential activities: to project the nature of the talk that will follow, to indicate its tellability and relevance within the ongoing interaction, to set the affective tone of the story, and to prepare the recipient to listen, respond appropriately and recognize when the story is complete. The chapter concludes by discussing also the role of memory claims and denials in the storying of experience.

Autobiographical Tellings

In qualitative research, participants are routinely invited to offer commentary on the particular topics of interest identified by the researcher (e.g. identities, attitudes, motivations, linguistic practices, participation networks). A natural and even predictable outcome of this activity is talk describing first-person perceptions and experiences (Briggs, 1986; Denzin & Lincoln, 2011; Mandelbaum, 2013; Mishler, 1986, 1991; Schiffrin *et al.*, 2010). The stories, meta-commentary and related material elicited and produced in the course of research have been the objects of much scholarly attention, often subjected to linguistic, structural, thematic, content and various other analyses (see discussions in Andrews *et al.*, 2013; Barkhuizen *et al.*, 2014; De Fina & Georgakopoulou, 2012; Georgakopoulou, 2007; Kasper & Prior, 2015; Pavlenko, 2007; Riessman, 2008; Roulston, 2010; Talmy & Richards, 2011). Comparatively less attention has been given to the surrounding interactional sequences and the ways in which these tellings get introduced or fitted into the ongoing conversational, interpersonal and institutional trajectory. The present DC approach is therefore distinguished by its action-oriented focus on *tellings* as well as its attention to their *embeddedness* in a larger (temporal, spatial, interpersonal, cultural) context.

Defining Tellings

I use 'tellings', along with 'stories', 'narratives', 'accounts' and related terms interchangeably to refer to the autobiographical material speakers (i.e. the story 'tellers') produce *for* and even *with* (as in co-told stories) other people (i.e. the story 'recipients'). However, I prefer the term *telling* to acknowledge the action-oriented and embedded nature of this material. For my purposes, material counts as an *autobiographical telling* if it: (a) involves the teller (centrally or peripherally), (b) represents (directly or indirectly) a chain of sequence and consequence (linear, nonlinear, past, present, future, real or hypothetical), (c) is embedded in an ongoing interactional sequence (in the present or extended over time), and (d) is produced for an intended recipient (e.g. the researcher) who is usually assumed not to have equal independent epistemic access to the event(s), version(s) and/or perspective(s) represented (Antaki, 1994; De Fina & Georgakopoulou, 2012; Liddicoat, 2011; Mandelbaum, 2013; Ochs & Capps, 2001; Sacks, 1992; Sidnell, 2010a).

I am not interested in verifying the truthfulness or authenticity of speakers' talk or determining intentionality (i.e. if they *really* mean what they are saying; if they are *purposely* seeking to elicit a particular response; if they *know* they are changing the order of events). Neither am I concerned with typological matters, such as whether speakers produce *fully-formed* or *partial*, *canonical* or *non-canonical, prototypical* or *atypical* narratives, or if their tellings are *big* or *small* stories (e.g. Bamberg & Georgakopoulou, 2008; Barkhuizen, 2011; Baynham & De Fina, 2005; Freeman, 2006; cf. Talmy & Prior, 2015).

What matters is profoundly practical and interactional: what tellers and recipients show and recognize themselves to be doing by means of and in relation to these autobiographical tellings.

Features of Tellings

In this section, I briefly consider some of the conventional features of autobiographical tellings, attending to issues of *embeddedness, accounting work, stance, subject-object relations, tellability* and *repetition* (see also Ochs & Capps, 2001, for related perspectives). I argue that an examination of how this material gets assembled and managed offers an opportunity to enhance our understanding of speakers' emotional and communicative repertoires in everyday life as well as in the research context.

Embeddedness

Tellings are bounded material. That is, they do not usually appear randomly in interaction (though that is possible) or without any contextual or interpretive framing (also possible, but they would likely be treated as interpretive 'puzzles' by recipients). Most frequently, tellings are prefaced and/or followed by various explicit and implicit cues that signal to the teller and the recipient that a telling is relevant and that it is being *invited, offered, prefaced, launched, in progress, brought to a close, commented upon* and so forth. Interactants may or may not explicitly signal those boundaries or label the material as 'tellings' or 'stories' (i.e. 'I am going to tell you a story now'), but non-lexical ('oh', 'hey'), prosodic (e.g. pauses, pitch shifts, sighs), nonverbal (facial expression) or other cues can signal a transition space in the ongoing interaction where a telling could be inserted. Therefore, to better understand *what* and *how* tellings get produced, and the various indexical meanings and relevancies attached to speakers' autobiographical material, it is crucial to attend also to the surrounding environment in which this talk gets embedded.

Accounting and stancetaking

An examination of tellings also requires acknowledgement of their function as *accounts*. The concept of accounts has a long history in the literature (for overviews, see Antaki, 1994; Buttny, 1993; Drew, 1998; Garfinkel, 1967; Scott & Lyman, 1968). Although accounts are sometimes treated synonymously with stories or narratives, they are foremost explanatory devices that describe ruptures in the social order and speakers' attitudes toward and role in those events – as well as their representation in the 'here-and-now':

> By an account, then, we mean a statement made by a social actor to explain unanticipated or untoward behavior – whether that behavior is his own or

that of others, and whether the proximate cause for the statement arises from the actor himself or from someone else. (Scott & Lyman, 1968: 46)

The accounts in the present corpus were often built as *troubles tellings* and *complaints* about others' conduct or justifications for the speaker's own; that is, they functioned as offensive and defensive descriptions (see Potter, 1996, on offensive and defensive rhetoric). Many scholars have commented upon the presence of emotionality in stories of complaints, transgressions, misconduct, trauma and troubles (e.g. Becker, 1997; Buttny, 1993; Drew, 1998; Edwards, 2005; Günthner, 1997a, 1997b; Jefferson, 1988; Jefferson *et al*., 2015; Prior, 2011a, 2011b, 2011c). When faced with transgressions or breaches in social norms, people commonly respond with anger, surprise or other strong emotional reactions (e.g. as found in breaching experiments; Garfinkel, 1967).

An integral part of self-representation and accounting is stancetaking work. Edwards (2005) observes that in complaint talk, as in news telling in general, speakers may include an announcement to project the teller's stance or attitude. These announcements often consist of an explicit or implied affective stance or emotional description. Defining stance is not without challenge (for overviews, see Englebretson, 2007; Jaffe, 2009; Ochs, 1996; Ochs & Capps, 2001), as it overlaps with work on *footing* (Goffman, 1981; Goodwin, 2007), *positioning* (Davies & Harré, 1990; Harré & van Langenhove, 1999), and *alignment* and *affiliation* (Steensig & Drew, 2008; Stivers, 2008).

In broad terms, stancetaking involves 'taking up a position with respect to the form or the content of one's utterance' (Jaffe, 2009: 3). Du Bois (2007: 169) offers a more comprehensive description of stance as:

> [A] public act by a social actor, achieved dialogically through overt communicative means (language, gesture, and other symbolic forms), through which social actors simultaneously evaluate objects, position subjects (themselves and others), and align with other subjects, with respect to any salient dimension of value in the sociocultural field.

Thus stance may be intraperspectival (i.e. individual) and interperspectival (i.e. shared), explicit and implicit, verbal and nonverbal. Moreover, evaluation can be found in the reception (i.e. listener-side responses) of talk as well as its production (i.e. speaker-side utterances). The aspects of stancetaking that are pertinent to the present discussion are: its role in assessing talk, people, events, ideas, etc.; its function as a public act of going 'on the record'; its expression of the speaker's relationship with the listener (*interpersonal stance*); its indexing of the speaker's emotionality (*affective stance*) and knowledge and certainty claims (*epistemic stance*); and its attitudes toward normative or accountable conduct (*moral stance*) (Clift, 2006; Englebretson; 2007; Jaffe, 2009; Kärkkäinen, 2003; Ochs, 1996; Stivers *et al*., 2011). Moreover, as Coupland (2003: 426) suggests, because *stance* and *role* are tied to social *identification* (i.e. actions) rather than static identities (i.e. labels), analyzing their use enables us to examine speakers' own concerns and performative work in the midst of their communicative activities.

Subject-object relations

Because tellings are necessarily produced from a particular point of view and therefore convey a speaker's subjective stance or personal orientation toward events, they can also imbue talk with an 'objective' quality due to conventionalized constraints surrounding what is tellable and plausible. It is not the case that *any* scenario will make sense. As speakers shape their talk for recipients (Sacks *et al.*, 1974) they draw on commonsense knowledge of the world, shared or assumed knowledge between interactants, and features of the present conversational context (Maynard, 2003; Schegloff, 1988) to create a recognizable and believable version of reality. This order is not inherent to the data but is 'assembled by participants using their commonsense members' resources' (Baker, 2003: 792). In this way, speakers display sensitivity to their talk as both subjective and objective. These *subject-object* or *mind-world* relations have been topics of interest in discursive psychology (DP) (e.g. Edwards, 1997, 2005, 2006). By producing tellings, speakers index their purported feelings, thoughts, personal stances and reactions (i.e. the 'subject' or speaker-dependent side) as well as the nature of the social reality or things being talked about (i.e. the 'object' or speaker-independent side).

Tellability and newsworthiness

Whether solicited or spontaneous, a built-in requirement of autobiographical talk, stories and news in general, is that the subject matter be *tell-worthy* or *noteworthy* (Labov, 1972; Norrick, 2005; Ochs & Capps, 2001; Prior, 2011a; Sacks, 1992; Taylor, 2006; Thornborrow & Coates, 2005). There must be something that enables it to be told as well as heard (Bourdieu, 1991; Miller, 2003). A normative expectation is that speakers (usually) should not tell story recipients what they already know or what they can be reasonably expected to already know (Sacks, 1992; Schegloff, 2007; Sidnell, 2010a; also Grice, 1975). Most people have undoubtedly had the experience where they or someone else initiated a telling only to have the intended recipient interject, 'You already told me that' or 'I heard that one'.

Tellers also self-monitor the production and reception of their utterances and often preempt trouble or interruptions by immediately confirming the newsworthiness or relevance of their talk. This allows them to successfully produce their telling and avoid appearing forgetful or inadequate interactional partners. Some examples from my data where speakers self-monitor and comment on the tellability and novelty of their autobiographical material include:

- 'I've never told anyone this before.'
- 'I always keep it to myself.'

- 'Actually, this is how it happened.'
- 'I tell you the true story now.'
- 'I probably shouldn't say this but...'
- 'Did I tell you the story about my first job?'

It may also be evident from these examples that speakers are doing at least two other things in addition to claiming tellability. First, they are prefacing or projecting a tellable. That is, they are not just claiming to have a story or a noteworthy piece of information – they are offering or initiating a sequence to produce it in the 'here-and-now'. Second, they are displaying sensitivity to the interviewer-interviewee relationship (conveyed here through the almost 'confessional' quality concerning matters of secrecy, privacy, honesty and so on).

Repetition and familiarity

While *noteworthiness* (or *newsworthiness*, *newness*, etc.) is commonly a requirement ensuring that stories are tell-worthy and listen-worthy, material (e.g. people, events) already known to the recipient can also be relevant and tellable. Repeated stories have been shown to serve as robust interactional resources for doing self-presentation and social commentary (e.g. Koven, 2002; Norrick, 1998; Ochs & Capps, 2001; Prior, 2011a; Schiffrin, 2006). Taking a psycho-cognitive perspective, some scholars observe that repetition of stories ensures 'they are better remembered and remain coherent representations of experience', making the repeated story an important survival tool for humanity by reminding us of what we have learned and should not forget (Kottler, 2015: 16). Schank and Abelson (1995) go so far as to claim that storytelling is essential for long-term memory recall. That is, without repeated telling, mundane and repeated events (e.g. a trip to the grocery store) often disappear from memory precisely because they do not get told and then get replaced by similar sorts of commonplace events. Schank and Abelson further suggest personally significant (i.e. strongly emotional) events, whether repeated or not, are usually *not* forgotten because they deviate from the norm and are less likely to get replaced in the mental index of that story held in memory (see also Ochs & Capps, 2001). As I will show, regardless of their cognitive antecedents, repetition and memory claims are also ways of talking.

Although speakers may abandon a previously-told story when the intended recipient rejects it or interrupts its progress, I have also observed that they often proceed with the telling because, new or shared, it advances their goals in the present interaction. This may involve the speaker explicitly describing (often in the prefatory material) how this story is now relevant, repackaged or otherwise different from what is already known by the recipient. Alternatively, the speaker may just proceed with the telling and place the burden on the recipient to decipher its relevance. Produced as a kind of 'interactional puzzle' (Maynard, 2003), this can be an effective speaker strategy – even one that recalibrates unequal power dynamics to ensure that the story recipient is an engaged listener in the interaction and the story teller remains the expert or epistemic authority on the material discussed (Prior, 2014).

Just how and where repeated stories occur in L1 and L2 interaction, and for what specific purposes, is an empirical question worthy of future comparative research. In my L2 data, I have found repeated stories appear frequently, though they can be separated by minutes, hours, weeks, months or even years. Speakers also recognize and comment on these tellings as repeated:

- 'I think I told you already. (1.0) and this woman (.) I-I keep waiting and...'
- 'Suddenly (2.0) I think I told you this story. (0.7) and suddenly (.) he-they put me on hold for a while.'
- 'I told you already (.) but I tell you again. (.) but little bit different.'
- 'I tell you last time (.) I think so. Little more this time, okay?'
- 'I know I tell before (.) my life no happy here. Not happy so I go back Vietnam. One year, (.) two year later.'

This is not to suggest in any way that a repeated telling, whether in an L1 or L2, necessarily reflects a lack of linguistic resources or functions as a compensatory strategy for memory lapses. It must also be acknowledged that in studies involving a large data set and multiple participants over time, it may be challenging for both interviewer and interviewee to remember exactly what was said previously (and to whom) – yet another reason why recordings and field notes are essential in longitudinal, ethnographically grounded research (Emerson *et al.*, 2011).

Repeated tellings may take on various forms and functions. Even what is ostensibly the 'same' story can be (re)produced in a multitude of ways. It can be told in the speakers' various language varieties and registers, at different intellectual and knowledge levels (e.g. for children, adults, novices, experts), with different degrees of detail, with different intensities of emotional expression, and variously performed through embodied presentation and represented speech[1] (Holt & Clift, 2007; Norrick, 1998; Prior, 2011a; Prior & Kasper, 2016; Schank & Abelson, 1995). In examining the complaint stories and troubles tellings which make up much of my L2 data, I have found retellings allowed speakers to represent the recurrent and intense nature of their mistreatment by others and to build a justification for and a cohesive account of the lasting psychological and other consequences of that mistreatment for the speaker (e.g. quitting school; leaving a job; relocating; fighting back; avoiding social interactions; developing physical, mental and even spiritual health complaints).

For example, in an analysis of an L2 English 'anger narrative' told two years apart (Prior, 2011a), I discovered how the speaker (Trang, a

Cambodian-Vietnamese immigrant to Canada) achieved different rhetorical representations of self through his versions. In one, he represented external events as forcing him to become angry and agentive; whereas the other version allowed him to construct a more general moral stance toward the transgressive conduct of others. In that analysis I suggested that stories may be repeated not because of memory failings or a lack of linguistic competence but because they are flexible and available resources in the L2 users' interactional 'toolkit':

> Telling a story multiple times, as Trang did, undoubtedly made it all the more a readily accessible resource in his communicative repertoire. Moreover, consistency of self-presentation is an important means by which speakers make themselves understandable, sensible, and rational to their listeners. (Prior, 2011a: 64)

Similarly, repeated (i.e. previously shared) stories may allow story tellers and story recipients to make visible and re-experience their shared knowledge of the represented events and their outcomes by commiserating and bonding in the present (i.e. 'here-and-now') through their shared affective and moral stances toward the people and events described in the storyworld (i.e. 'there-and-then'). Ochs and Capps (2001: 8; also Besnier, 2009) point out in their work on narrative, that 'commiserating, gossiping, philosophizing, exchanging advice, and other informal discourse interlaces lives and builds common ways of acting, thinking, feeling and otherwise being in the world'.

Launching Tellings in Casual Conversation

Having identified some key characteristics of autobiographical tellings, I will now consider in more detail how speakers launch and insert this material into the ongoing interactional activity. Ordinary or spontaneous tellings, though depending on length, are often produced within extended turns maintained by a primary speaker (or by multiple speakers, in the case of co-told stories; Lerner, 1992; Ochs & Capps, 2001; Thornborrow & Coates, 2005). Among the challenges tellers face in ordinary conversation are (a) how and where to secure a slot within the ongoing activity to initiate the telling, (b) how to maintain and relinquish the interactional floor as storyteller, and (c) how to demonstrate the immediate relevance of that telling within and for the present occasion.

Story prefaces

Recognizing that talk (even 'self-talk') is always recipient designed, scholars of talk-in-interaction (e.g. Buttny, 2004; Cuff & Francis, 1978; Edwards, 2005; Liddicoat, 2011; Sacks, 1992; Schegloff, 2007; Sidnell, 2010a) have observed that speakers routinely preface conversational tellings to prepare the

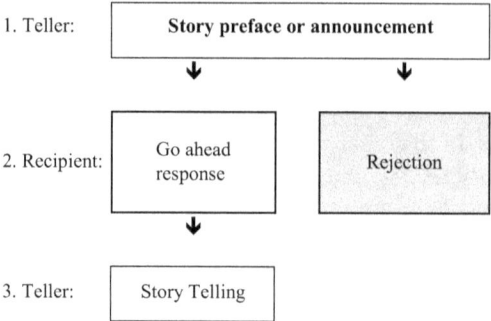

Figure 3.1 Typical story preface sequences

recipient to recognize and receive it. As Sacks (1992: 226–227) points out, tellings are often initiated or rejected by the sequences shown in Figure 3.1.

As an announcement and 'interest arouser' (Sacks, 1992: 226), the story preface works as a methodic device to suspend the normal turn-taking operations so that speakers can take and hold an extended turn, solicit a listening audience, produce a story that is interesting and project its completion:

> Characteristically stories begin with something we call a 'story preface' which contains varieties of information and does a range of businesses, of which a perfectly prototypical instance is 'Something really weird happened to me on the way to work this morning.' That announces more or less that I want to tell a story, and it tells various things about the story relevant to listening to the story. For example, it tells how to listen to the story to find out when it will have been over; where, say, the term 'weird' as a characterizing adjective in the story preface gives a listener something with which to monitor the story so as to see, when something 'weird' has been told, then that's what the teller was intending to tell as the 'story', and until then the story isn't finished. (Sacks, 1992: 530)

This prefatory work is important because it enables the teller to project, take and maintain an extended conversational turn *and* cue the recipient to the relevance of the story. Yet, it is not enough that an extended utterance is heard as a story once it is completed; it must be made recognizable as a story *before* it is completed so that recipients can monitor its progress (Sidnell, 2010a) and, in turn, align their responses appropriately.

Launching Tellings in Institutional Settings

Interviewing is a dialogic activity and therefore may appear in many ways like ordinary conversation. In practice it is a hybrid or 'quasi-conversational' activity (Freed & Ehrlich, 2010; He, 1998; Heritage & Greatbatch, 1989) that draws on features of both casual, spontaneous conversation and formal question-answer-response sequences found across various institutional settings and genres. In other institutional encounters, such as medical and psychotherapeutic settings, patients routinely produce stories to give an account of their reasons for the medical visit (Halkowski, 2006; Heritage & Robinson, 2006a, 2006b), to show how they discovered or are working through various health concerns, and to invite empathy and professional diagnoses. These stories and accounts are often invited by the health care provider (e.g. 'What brings you in today?'), but they may also be self-initiated by the patients to demonstrate their own lay diagnostic efforts and to indicate the seriousness of their concerns (and thereby offer a suitable warrant for their visit). In an analysis of TV talk shows, an institutional setting somewhat akin to research interviews, Thornborrow (2001, 2010) finds that one of the primary goals of this genre is to elicit life stories and talk of personal experiences from participants by asking questions such as 'What happened?' or 'Has it ever happened to you?'

Most previous social interactional research on pre-announcements and announcement sequences has shown concern with spontaneous tellings (i.e. stories presumably of the speaker's own initiative) in conversational settings, not on those elicited by design, touched off by, or produced as storied responses to an interview question or other prompt (see Chapters 4–5 for further discussion on interviewer prompts). When stories are solicited, as in research interviews, the teller is normally allocated a slot for an extended turn and the researcher aligns as story recipient. But interviewers do not always ask for or expect stories, and stories may be produced as responses to many kinds of utterances and other interactional events. Whether a story is solicited or not, in producing a telling the teller must still select and organize material that fulfills its requirement as a relevant next action within the interview activity and that will make sense to the recipient (i.e. the interviewer, and perhaps even a research team or anticipated future audience).

Launching Tellings in L2 Interviews

In keeping with previous research on complaints and troubles tellings (typically about a non-present third party; e.g. Drew, 1998; Jefferson, 1988; Selting, 2010), interviewees in my corpus regularly invoked emotionality through story prefaces and memory claims, immediately before they launched into a telling or a description of an affect-laden episode. This prefatory work and the stories it launched functioned to topicalize and embody the teller's complaints and concerns about various people and events as well as personal difficulties with language, culture, ethnicity, social belonging and related matters. A distinguishing feature of this prefatory work in my data is its function in characterizing the emotionality of events (usually transgressive or problem-centered) and/or tellers' emotional reactions to them. Often these prefaces used explicit emotion terms (e.g. 'angry', 'mad', 'shame') to project an emotional story. Tellers also made emotionality inferentially available through their vocal delivery (e.g. intonation, emphasis, laughter, tone) and description of the episode as unforgettable and/or personally difficult.

The following selected excerpts demonstrate how L2 interviewees prefaced and projected emotionality in their tellings. Again, the emphasis here is on action, not only content or form. Excerpts are represented along with their surrounding sequences to better show the context and trajectory of their production. An exhaustive analysis of these sequences is not possible in this limited space. Therefore, I invite the reader to join in analyzing the emotional content and production of these excerpts. It is my hope that this discussion and analysis will lead to a deeper appreciation of the complex and dynamic activity of producing and responding to interactional tellings, leading even to 'naturalistic' generalization – 'a process where readers gain insight by reflecting on the details and descriptions ... that resonate with their own experiences' (Melrose, 2010: 599).

Discrimination in the workplace

The following two tellings from this corpus (Excerpts 3.1a, 3.1b) come from an interview with Kim, a young woman from Vietnam. As a touched-off 'second story' (Sacks, 1992), 3.1b follows a previous account (3.1a) of Kim's intense encounter with rude customers in her job as a department store clerk. In that first story, she describes how a mother and daughter became 'very angry' and 'very upset' and accused her of discriminating against them by refusing to provide customer service. Using indirect represented speech (lines 4–7), Kim describes their complaint went so far as to claim that she was unable to speak English (thus making claims about her language proficiency as well as her professional conduct and personal disposition). She then describes how Mary, her (L1 English-speaking) manager, came to her defense. I include the closing segment of the 'mother-daughter discrimination' story to better illustrate how prior emotion-laden material may lead into emotional story prefaces and subsequent story tellings.

(Excerpt 3.1a). Kim: 'Discrimination'

```
01      K:      so when Mary she come down (.) and (.) the
02              mother and daughter happened to be Caucasian (.)
03   →          so they-they-they t-talked to Mary and they very
04   →          angry and they're very upset. they said that I
05   →          refuse to-to give them customer service and I
06   →          don't speak English. they don't understand what
07   →          I'm saying.
```

08	**M:**	mm.
09		(0.5)
10	**K:**	so (.) Mary said. Mary asked her °"if she
11		doesn't speak English, how do you know (that)
12		she refused?"°
13	**M:**	heh
14	**K:**	and that's <u>first</u>. and ↑sec↓ond (.) Mary said (.)
15		°"Kim's work here long time. we never have any
16		complaint about she (.) her-her English. so I
17		don't think it's right that you bring it out
18		that this discrimination."°
19	**M:**	hm
20	**K:**	and Mary she just step back and she say "you
21		know what? °that- that is what we call
22		discrimination."°
23		(3.3)
24		°°that's another (thing).°°
25		(0.6)
26	**M:**	and what'd <u>they</u> do.
27		(1.5)
28	**K:**	°°they quiet°°
29		(2.7)
30	**M:**	<u>wow</u>
31		(1.5)

By inserting the ethnicity of the customers as a casual aside (lines 1–2: 'the mother and daughter happened to be Caucasian'), Kim activates a race-related frame (Caucasian-Asian) for understanding this account (as an example of discrimination) while representing herself as unbiased toward such matters. Another observation is that Kim produces Mary's talk as direct represented speech, an evidential device used to *demonstrate* rather than *describe* the authenticity of the speaker's claims (Holt & Clift, 2007). This allows Kim to effectively vitiate the customers' complaint while ostensibly allowing someone else (Mary) to do it for her. First, in the 'storyworld', Mary challenges the customers' complaint on logical grounds (lines 10–12: 'if she doesn't speak English, how do you know (that) she refused?') and then with institutional evidence (lines 15–16: 'Kim's work here long time. we never have any complaint about she (.) her-her English'). Performing Mary's rebuttal and counter complaint on her behalf, produced in a calm, but stern and authoritative voice, Kim creates a sharp contrast against the intensely emotional claims of the 'very angry' and 'very upset' customers. Mary's talk also counters and makes explicit the prejudicial nature of the customers' claims by repeatedly characterizing it as 'discrimination' (lines 18, 22).

The way this telling unfolds, particularly through repair, offers evidence of the care Kim takes to produce this version of events for the researcher. For example in line 10, the repair of the quotative 'Mary said' to 'Mary asked' reformulates Mary's speech act from a statement to a question, thereby holding the customers accountable for their verbal and cognitive conduct (i.e. assumptions, discriminatory logic). Because this is produced in the context of a customer service encounter (elsewhere Kim notes that the store's philosophy was, 'The customer is always right'), the action of a store representative (Mary) demanding such a response from customers further highlights how egregious (and thereby complaint-worthy) their conduct was toward Kim. In line 16, Kim's pronominal self-repair (a frequent L2 English error) of 'complaint about *she' to 'complaint about her' shows her attention to the accuracy of her account and confirms Mary's status as an L1 speaker and thus reinforces her authority to assess Kim's English and communicative competence.

As this segment comes to a close, Kim is vindicated and her morally superior status is confirmed by the customers' silence. Through her storytelling work incorporating the represented speech of her manager, Kim is able to label the customers' talk as a 'complaint' and an instance of 'discrimination' without having to do it herself. This allows her to present the story to the interviewer as objective, factual evidence rather than a self-interested version (on *stake inoculation*, see Potter, 1996; Potter & Hepburn, 2012) and maintain a consistent identity in the 'there-and-then' storyworld and in the 'here-and-now' of the telling as polite, non-aggressive and even a victim deserving of sympathy. Moreover, Kim uses her dramatic telling to resist and 'fight back' against these L2 speaker 'deficit' stereotypes without coming across as aggressive or overreactive herself.

After completing her story, and receiving a *response cry* (Goffman, 1978) from the researcher (line 30: 'wow') that displays shock and an affiliative or empathic response (Couper-Kuhlen, 2012; Heritage, 2011; Selting, 2010) to these events, Kim produces a story preface (3.1b, lines 32–33) projecting the emotionality and unforgettable nature of another set of related events at work involving discrimination from another Caucasian, L1 English-speaking customer.[2] In this hearably more intense second story, an American man outraged by the perceived lack of attentiveness from Kim and her Korean co-worker, berates both women and tells them that they should work in a bar, not in a department store.

(Excerpt 3.1b). Kim: 'You guys should work in the bar'

```
32   →   K:   but- (.) ONE-ONE more (.) that's the one thing I
33   →        can never forget.
34            one night we- (.) we closing. mm (.) and so we
35            work in fine jewelry we have to do a lot of
36            inventory (.) (you know) we count,
```

37	**M:**	right
38	**K:**	ma-ma-the merchandise. and this man he pass by.
39		an' (.) for- for me as a sale person, I <u>want</u> the
40		customer (.) have time (.) to look (.) through.
41		I cannot just run an' an' an' grab him.
42	**M:**	right.
43	**K:**	you know you-you give customer moment to walk,
44	**M:**	right.
45	**K:**	and enjoy shopping right? and he said that (.) uh (.)
46		he-he-he really loud, he talk really loud. he said
47		something that we don't want to
48		serve him? we don't think that he have <u>money</u>? he
49		s-spent a <u>lot</u> of money in this store, he buy a
50		<u>lot</u> of thing. ex<u>pen</u>sive thing. and he look at me
51		and my friend her name is Okee. she Korean (.)
52		an' he said, (.) "YOU ORIENTAL GIRL. YOU GUYS
53		SHOULD WORK IN THE BAR (.) instead of working
54		over here."
55	**M:**	mm
56	**K:**	no, she- he didn't say Oriental girl. he said
57		<u>A</u>sian (.) Asian.
58	**M:**	mhm
		((K continues story about the rude customer))

There is much that could be said about Excerpt 3.1b, particularly in terms of Kim's self-presentation work, but I will comment on a few strategic features that allow her to construct these events as memorable and tellable. To characterize the transgressive nature of these events, Kim describes the routine nature of her work and her conscientious and commonsense conduct toward the store (e.g. protecting its financial interests by taking inventory on fine jewelry at closing time) and the customers (e.g. not aggressively seeking to make a sale; looking out for their emotional well-being by giving them time to look around and enjoy their shopping experience). However, in sharp contrast with Kim's thoughtful actions as a salesperson, the customer is shown to take offense and yell at the two women with comments that are racist and misogynistic (lines 52–54). Kim bolsters the authenticity of her account by providing accompanying details (e.g. the time of day, her coworker's name, the represented talk of the customer). She even self-repairs 'Oriental' to 'Asian' (lines 56–57), which indicates her attention to the factualness of her claims and displays her resistance to overplaying her description of events. In much of the United States, 'Oriental', used as a person reference term, is hearably more of a pejorative than 'Asian' and would strengthen her characterization of the customer as racist. In this respect, by repairing and downgrading the ethnic label that was 'actually' uttered (while making use of the racist perspective it indexes), Kim represents her story as truthful and herself as a believable witness to these events. This also supports her earlier implied racially-neutral perspective in Excerpt 3.1a, where she noted that the rude customers 'happened to be Caucasian' (line 2). Thus, throughout these tellings, Kim maintains herself as unbiased and longsuffering even within emotionally intense and racially charged events.

Here is another place where extra-situational information and comparative data are invaluable to a more nuanced understanding of the context of this telling. In Hawai'i and other contexts with large immigrant populations, there is a pervasive social stereotype that Asian women often work in hostess bars and the sex industry (Ehrenreich & Hochschild, 2003). Alluding to this stigma, Kim stated in another interview that she was employed as a server in a nightclub for a short time (see Excerpt 3.6, this chapter, and Excerpt 6.8 in Chapter 6) but did not tell any of her friends or family where she worked out of fear and shame that they would get the wrong idea about her. Seen in the context of Kim's meta-narrative history and societal ideologies surrounding Asian women, this rude customer story takes on added layers of meaning and memorability by illustrating how it intersects with gender, hypersexualization, L2 speaker status, the immigrant experience and other stigmatized aspects of identity.

Shame and language use

To further examine the dynamic work of telling and remembering, I now examine in more detail an extended segment where another interviewee also launches one in a series of tellings. Excerpt 3.2 comes from an early interview with John, an immigrant from Vietnam. Here he has just finished producing two stories about his experiences being bullied in high school soon after arriving in the US. One story was about problems with an American boy (see Kasper & Prior, 2015, for a related story), and the other was about a disastrous experience in gym class where the teacher forced him to play football for the first time.

While the interviewer checks the recorder, John displays his work to come up with a relevant story (lines 1, 12, 15–18). After John produces a story preface in lines 12–18, the interviewer then prompts him to continue (line 19: 'why is that?'). This results in John producing an emotion-relevant story about the 'shame' he and other refugees felt in the past when learning English in the refugee camp in the Philippines, and he contrasts it with a telling set in the present day, where young children and relatives in Vietnam also experience shame when speaking English. However, in characterizing his personal journey, he indicates that he is no longer the fearful boy of the storyworld but a man who has learned to set his shame aside and talk. In turn, he describes his efforts to model that transformation by encouraging his young nephews and nieces to overcome their own shame by 'speaking up'.

(Excerpt 3.2). John: 'You shame'

```
01  → J:   .hhh (0.9) anyway so what else (.) what else?
02            (1.4)
03     M:   °second (0.5) check this.
04            (1.0)
05          this is working (.) testing testing° ((M is
06          checking the audiorecorder and the microphone))
07            (1.5)
08          okay
09            (1.2)
10          say something
11            (1.3)
12  → J:   OH (0.3) OH then=
13     M:   =>°oh there we go okay°<((M finishes setting up
14          the microphone))=
15  → J:   =remember, (9.5) remember like (0.5) how sh::ame
16  →      we-we not try to speak English in Philippines
17  →      because we like (0.7) ashamed to open my-my- our
18  →      mouth?=
19     M:   =why is that?
20            (0.5)
21     J:   I dunno I guess because like=
22     M:   =mean [in ] the class with Canadian teacher?=
23     J:         [uh-]
24     M:   =with=
25     J:   =YEAH even in the cla:ss or, (0.6)
26          [an' then outside    ] you always have all=
27     M:   [with Filipino people?]
28     J:   =the Vietnamese people around you s[o  ] y-you=
29     M:                                      [oh]
30     J:   =don't open your mouth (by them) (.) in the
31          class you kinda like, (1.5) you shame like you-
32          when you speak up you might say something wro:ng
33          or, (.) somebody might laugh at you. cuz that's
34          ho- (.) uh that's how all the kid in Vietnam
35          like that=even now my-my nieces and nephew in
36          Vietnam when I went to see them? and I ask (0.9)
37          I told 'em "speak up" (.) I mean (.) "can you
38          guys say something °English?°" and they shame
39          °yeah° and that's how I was.
40            (0.9)
41          how I used to be.
42            (1.0)
```

```
43              an' then when I was in high school here (0.4)
44              an' I realize that like (0.6) "oh you gotta open
45              your mouth otherwi' you never (.) be able to
46              speak.
47              (1.0)
48              so (0.5) I just open my mouth one day an' start
49              talking? talking, (0.7) talking to English
50              [to-
51       M:     [in high school?
52              (0.4)
53       J:     yeah, even- (.) I know I said wrong I have to
54              say it=
55       M:     =uhuh
56              (0.4)
57              but how did you do that?
                ((J goes on to give examples of how he made himself speak
                up in English))
```

Pre-preface material

Throughout these chapters, I emphasize that emotionality is embedded in the interview agenda and activity. In Excerpt 3.2, John's prefatory material situates him, the interviewer, the interview context and the emotional content of his autobiographical talk. Lines 1–10 are particularly salient for showing how this emotional talk gets established or selected (Chapter 6 will consider emotion formulations and selection in more detail). In line 1 of Excerpt 3.2, John displays a cognitive search that aligns with the interviewer's agenda ('.hhh (0.9) anyway so what else (.) what else?'), showing his understanding that he is expected to recall and produce talk of autobiographical experience. It is unclear whether John's audible topic search is meant as self-talk or an indirect clarification request. Because it is said aloud and followed by a 1.4-second pause, it is potentially hearable as a request. Instead of responding by giving John examples of suitable topics, the interviewer focuses his attention on the recording device (lines 3–10) and momentarily defers John's topic search, essentially putting John and the 'on the record' activity (i.e. interview, data-generation) on hold. In line 8, with a change of state token 'okay' (Heritage, 1984), the interviewer signals a shift in the present activity or a 'state of readiness for moving to next-positioned matters' (Beach, 1995: 143). This shift offers evidence that the interviewer's goal is not casual or spontaneous conversation but the elicitation of recordable research data.

After initiating a new activity, the interviewer confirms that the recorder is working and then in line 10 instructs John to 'say something' – signaling a return to the on-the-record activity of interviewing. The interviewer's instruction could potentially be taken by John in one of two ways: (a) say something so the interviewer can check the recording levels, or (b) say something relevant to the interview agenda (i.e. continue telling a story or producing talk of personal experience). After a 1.3-second pause in line 11, John provides two emphatic (through louder volume) tokens (line 12: 'OH (0.3) OH') that show an epistemic shift from a state of not knowing to a state of knowing (i.e. from being unsure about an appropriate topic to now having remembered and selected one). In line 13, through a softer and rapid utterance, the interviewer latches onto John's talk to indicate that the recorder is set and now they can continue on the record ('>°oh there we go okay°<'). Only after they both transition from peripheral or 'off-the-record talk' (e.g. what to talk about, setting up the recording device), does John produce his story preface (lines 15–18).

Emotional story preface

In this segment, John progresses the interview activity by prefacing his currently projected story with a reference to a previous telling where he talked about the shame he and other refugees felt when speaking English in the refugee camps in the Philippines:

```
15   J:   =remember, (9.5) remember like (0.5) how sh::ame
16        we-we not try to speak English in Philippines
17        because we like (0.7) ashamed to open my-my- our
18        mouth?
```

As many scholars have observed, stories often appear in clusters and series – with one touching off and leading into another (Edwards, 1997; Georgakopoulou, 2007; Jefferson, 1978; Koven, 2004; Prior, 2011a; Ryave, 1978; Sacks, 1992; Sidnell, 2010). Second (and subsequent) stories display intersubjectivity (shared understanding) because they function as receipts of and responses to previous stories by doing such things as continuing the topic, commenting on the same characters and events, and reasserting or challenging particular stances (Edwards, 1997; Sacks, 1992; Silverman, 1998). However, in this interview setting, it is a single speaker producing a series of stories. In the institutional context of research interviews, interviewers seldom produce stories.

A common pattern in the telling of second stories is that speaker A produces a story and then speaker B latches onto features of that story to tell a related story (see also Sacks, 1992, on tying techniques as ways that speakers build links between turns of talk). Alternatively, a single speaker may tell a series of stories, linking one to another. Speakers may also co-tell a shared story (e.g. Lerner, 1992). John's explicit reference to a previously shared telling (line 15: 'remember (9.5) remember like') and his lexical description of 'shame' in this emotional story preface (lines 15–17: 'how sh::ame ... ashamed') together create an interpretive frame (Goffman, 1981) around this specific emotion for the interviewer to hear and respond to this projected story. John directly links these feelings of shame with speaking English in the Philippines, and his pronominal use represents these emotions as personal as well as collectively shared experiences (lines 16–18: 'we-we not try'; 'ashamed to open my-my- our mouth'). By characterizing shame surrounding L2 learning and use as a shared, community emotion, John bolsters the factuality of his claims and naturalizes his emotional response. Moreover, by linking this emotional story preface with his almost 10-second display of 'remembering' (line 15) and appeals to shared knowledge based on his interactional history with the interviewer, John is also invoking the emotionality of those previous tellings (e.g. as 'shame') as well as reinforcing the consistency of his characterization of himself and those events across time.

Excerpt 3.2 also demonstrates that emotion talk on its own may not always be self-explanatory to recipients – particularly when the recipient is an interviewer engaged in the activity of soliciting emotional and subjective talk of experience. By orienting to emotion talk and emotion state claims as interpretive puzzles, recipients may require the speaker to account for them, potentially even occasioning further affective displays. More importantly, requesting an account likely results in the generation of more data, the primary goal of the research interview. Here, after John provides his story preface, the interviewer requests an account from John to explain why he and the other members in the refugee camp were ashamed (line 19: 'why is that?'). This initially results in brief interactional trouble, where John prefaces his response with hesitation and uncertainty (line 21: 'I dunno I guess because like'). Epistemic uncertainty markers such as 'I don't know' and 'I dunno' are frequently used in response to questioning. They can also be ways of handling the speaker's stake or interest in the building of a particular description (Edwards, 2005; Potter, 1998). The use of 'dunno' or 'I don't know' may also suggest that the speaker does not know how to respond or is taking an oppositional stance toward the question (Widdicombe & Wooffitt, 1995; Wooffitt, 2005). It is not clear if John, by his 'I dunno'-prefaced response is attending to matters of stake and interest, indicating an inability to respond or even resisting or rejecting the interviewer's question.

Speculation aside, what becomes evident is that the interviewer treats John's unsure and tentative 'I dunno'-prefaced response not as stake inoculation or resistance but as a display of uncertainty about which story to select and tell. The interviewer's latched clarification question ('mean in the class with Canadian teacher?') in line 22 offers a candidate formulation based on material from a previous interview, where John talked about learning English in the refugee camp in the Philippines (presumably what John is referring to in line 15). Though John's story preface in lines 15–18 projected a broader issue of shame experienced by John and other refugees in relation to English learning and use, the interviewer's question here centers on a specific learning context (i.e. the English class taught by a Canadian teacher in the refugee camp). In response, John offers an emphatic confirmation in line 25 ('YEAH even in the cla:ss or,'). A closer look at John's use of the adverbial 'even' and conjunction 'or' suggests that while he is acquiescing to the force of the interviewer's formulation, the telling he was initially projecting was perhaps heading in a different direction. Thus, by moving beyond the content of the talk (i.e. 'shame' surrounding English) to examine also the interactional context of its production, analysis shows that even innocent questions and other contributions by the interviewer shape how the interview unfolds and what gets topicalized and foregrounded. Here, for example, the interviewer's question in line 25 brings up 'the class', which may not have been mentioned otherwise. Tracing the interview trajectory further shows that talk of 'the class' eventually leads into subsequent tellings about 'school' (line 43).

In terms of responsibility, this description of events attributes the unwillingness or failure of John and the other refugees to speak English in the camp to feelings of 'shame' rather than to lack of linguistic knowledge, aptitude or opportunity. Shame here gets characterized by John not as an emotion inherent in the activity of speaking but a result of social stigma arising from making mistakes and being laughed at by others – especially by members of his own community (lines 28–33). This claim is naturalized even further as John extends this example of himself and the other members in that refugee camp to include 'all the kid in Vietnam' (line 34). He then offers up a personal example based on his young family members in present-day Vietnam to exemplify the generic emotional strain of language learning and to strengthen his claims. He also projects a possible completion point (as a coda) for his story by making a distinction between how he was in the past with how he is now.

In Excerpt 3.2, not only has John provided the interviewer with an emotion-rich story, he has also provided one related to language learning, language use and his personal experiences across time – thereby displaying his understanding of their relevant identities (i.e. John as immigrant and L2 English user; the interviewer as English teacher and L2 researcher) and fulfilling his role as interviewee by providing suitable talk of autobiographical experience. Moreover, analysis of these data shows how interview interaction is intimately co-constructed through the material that interviewees project and produce as well as the various ways in which interviewers' questions and responses formulate and shape what gets talked about and oriented to as relevant.

Post-story material

At a possible completion point (and transition relevant place or TRP) in John's telling in lines 39–41 ('that's how I was. (0.9) how I used to be.'), the interviewer has an available slot to take a turn to respond to John's previous talk with, for example, an acknowledgement (e.g. 'I see') or affiliative response (e.g. 'yeah, you've come a long way'). After a one-second pause and no contribution is forthcoming from the interviewer, John adds an increment to his story (Liddicoat, 2011) by making a link from the past to the present and his psychological change (by means of represented talk or thought to show his cognitive state): 'an' then when I was in high school <u>here</u> (0.4) an' I realize that like (0.6) 'oh you gotta open your mouth otherwi' you never (.) be able to speak'. This represents another potential completion point and TRP, but still there is no uptake from the interviewer after a one-second pause, so John continues by adding another increment (lines 48–49: 'so (0.5) I just open my mouth one day an' start <u>talk</u>ing? <u>talk</u>ing, (0.7) talking to English to-'). The interviewer then produces an overlapping question pursuing confirmation of the place/time setting for these events (line 51: 'in high school?'), arguably touched off by the interviewer's earlier introduction of talk of 'the class' (line 22). After a short pause, John provides a confirmation with another possible completion point (lines 53–54: 'yeah, even- (.) I know I said wrong I have to say it'). Latched onto John's utterance, the interviewer gives a minimal acknowledgement token (line 55: 'uhuh') and, after a short pause, initiates a new sequence with a question (line 57: 'but how did you <u>do</u> that?'). The contrastive marker 'but', while demonstrating the interviewer's understanding of John's talk, orients to it as insufficiently explanatory. The prosodic stress on the verb '<u>do</u>' further makes clear that the interviewer is not concerned about the content and quality of talk that John produced after deciding to 'speak up'; rather, he is interested in what enabled John to undergo an agentive shift. This gives evidence of the interviewer's work to bring John back to the topic of his personal sociolinguistic trajectory and significant turning points.

Expectational Features of Emotional Story Prefaces

As discussed in the preceding section, interviewees preface and produce their tellings while demonstrating sensitivity to the conversational and institutional context (i.e. that their talk 'fits' the researcher's expectations and aims). The presence, absence, manner or type of recipient responses from the interviewer also have an impact on what and how tellings get produced and in what detail. For example, the interviewer may orient to the relevance or meaning of story prefaces by asking for further clarification (e.g. Excerpt 3.2, line 19: 'why is that?') to explicate the causes and contexts surrounding these descriptions. Tellers also orient to the emotionality of events as a reason for having a story to tell and for telling it.

Excerpt 3.3, from an interview with Trang, a Vietnamese-Cambodian immigrant, also illustrates these matters. In this segment the speaker invokes emotionality and makes it explicit that he expects this to lead to an extended account:

(Excerpt 3.3). Trang: 'Ask me'

```
01      T:      I don't belong to Vietnamese community.
02              I don't belong to Cambodian community because
03              they always talk about me. why?
```

```
04            (2.0)
05    →       ask me?
06            (2.0)
07    → M:    why?
              ((T tells story of discrimination))
```

In line 1, Trang makes an emotion-implicative claim about not belonging to Vietnamese or Cambodian communities because they talk about him.[3] Although he does not use explicit emotion labels (e.g. 'mad', 'shame', 'anger') at this point, it is hearable as an emotion-indexing story preface by virtue of its 'complaining' tone and topic (i.e. social un-belonging, being talked about by others). This emotionality is further brought off by the way Trang orients to what knowledge is shared and not shared with the interviewer (i.e. what is 'news'). In his turn, Trang formulates himself as belonging neither to the Vietnamese nor the Cambodian communities. By not giving an account of why he should be expected to be a part of those communities, he is proceeding from the understanding that membership in those communities would normatively be assumed (e.g. because of his ethnic background, language ability and other biographical details). Produced through syntactic parallelism (e.g. 'I don't belong to X,' 'I don't belong to Y'), his claims of *not belonging* therefore create a dramatic counter-normative rhetorical contrast to what might be expected of a bi-cultural individual.

As a hearable extreme case formulation (Pomerantz, 1986), 'they *always* talk about me' (line 3) characterizes the gossip or other talk about Trang as a recurrent activity of members of those ethnic communities. In addition, by claiming category exclusion from the Vietnamese and Cambodian communities, Trang rhetorically locates himself in an unnamed, 'in-between' space. By not labeling any other space 'belonging' (e.g. 'Canadian community', 'American community', 'immigrant community'), he creates un-belonging by default. Thus, as these claims of not belonging are worked up as hearably extreme and disruptive for the speaker, they are also made hearably emotion implicative and empathy worthy for the recipient.

Even as Trang portrays the nature of his experience as emotional and undesirable, he also orients to an interactional expectation that these present claims require explanatory work to be properly understood (line 3: 'why?'). This expectation aligns with the conventional three-part story-preface sequence described previously (Figure 3.1). When Trang's announcement prompt is not met with the desired response from the interviewer, even after a comparatively long two-second gap of silence. Trang then makes the required response explicit through an imperative utterance and rising intonation (line 5: 'ask me?'). By taking direction of the interview as questioner, Trang now has subverted the typical interview frame and the roles of interviewer and interviewee (see also Prior, 2014). The subsequent two-second silence may therefore be an orientation by the interviewer to this unexpected frame switch. It can further be observed that Trang does not continue his story until the interviewer has provided the second-pair part to his request (line 7: 'why?') – confirming this as the aligning response necessary to allow the story to unfold.

Tellings, Memories and Emotional Words

Throughout the corpus, research participants regularly commented on memorable and emotion-indexing episodes that involved learning a word or being called a name. These words or names were frequently implicated in psychological stress connected with speakers' interpersonal relations (e.g. 'fuck', 'I hate you', 'get away'), (stigmatized) social identity labels (e.g. 'FOB', 'refugee', 'queer', 'gay', 'fag', 'bitch'), personal survival (e.g. 'rice', 'water', 'help', 'fire', 'hungry', 'asylum', 'refugee'), or experiences with finding and keeping employment (e.g. 'account', 'application', 'scarf', 'napkin', 'mop', 'server', 'receipt'). The following selected excerpts illustrate the emotionality and memorability of these vocabulary-learning episodes. I will not go into a detailed analysis of these excerpts, but it is clear that speakers link the emotional context of these words to their memorability.

In Excerpt 3.4, Jack, an immigrant from Cambodia, describes how after he arrived in the US from the refugee camp in Thailand, American students repeatedly called him and other immigrants names and swore at them (he later gave an example of one of these words: 'fuck'; see also analysis in Chapter 7, Excerpt 7.4).

(Excerpt 3.4). Jack: 'A bad word'

```
01  J:    well? (0.6) (I) remember like s- (.) mos' people
02        (they) say bad word we don't know nothing
03  M:    uh[uh
04  J:       [we just say "yes", (.) yeah we smiling?=
05  M:    =uh[uh
06  J:       [EHAHAHAHA .hhh $after we know we say like
07        "oh like THIS guy BA:(H)D"$ ((claps hands))
```

Here Jack describes how he (and other immigrants like him) went from a state of friendly innocence and not knowing (line 2) to a state of knowing and not recognizing this 'bad word' (line 6). His inapposite and naively friendly response in the face of such discrimination is characterized as reasons for the memorability of these events and his subsequent anger toward those American students.

John, an immigrant from Vietnam, said he learned and used his first English word ('rice') from a Vietnamese woman after their boat was rescued at sea by foreign soldiers. He stated that he remembered this event vividly because his first attempt at using the word failed (Excerpt 3.5).

(Excerpt 3.5). *John: 'Rice'*

```
01  J:    so I- so I-I asked the lady="oh how do you say
02        that?" she said "oh just go (.) ask for rice."
03        (0.8)
04        so I gave, (.) I gave the soldier my little
05        container (0.8) I say "rice rice" (.) an' uh he
06        came in (0.7) he took my container he went
07        inside, (.) he came out with a B:IG container of
08        $water.$
09        (1.0)
10  M:    [heh heh
11  J:    [heh heh heh
12        I thought "oh ↑NO:::"
13        ((lines removed))
14  J:    and then later on (0.7) my brother went try. my
15        brother get- (.) get uh somehow they gave him uh
16        a container of rice with w-w-w plus uh like uh
17        bitter melon=I remember it was like bitter melon
18        inside. OH my god that was the first meal we-
19        (.) like was so delicious that we share with the
20        family.
```

Although this telling was associated with a larger sequence of talk about escape, death and survival, John transforms and dramatically packages it as a highly detailed and entertaining performance by means of dynamic prosody, represented talk and thought (lines 1–2, 5, 12), subverted goals, and a range of strong emotionality – from extreme disappointment (12: 'oh ↑NO:::') to extreme joy (18–19: 'OH my god ... was so delicious').

Kim, whose department store experiences were examined previously (Excerpts 3.1a, 3.1b), produced several semi-humorous tellings about her efforts to figure out various vocabulary items. In one telling, she described that when asked by her boss' wife in the bar where she worked to pass a 'napkin', she unsuccessfully tried making up for her lack of knowledge by selecting several items until she finally got the right one (Excerpt 3.6).

(Excerpt 3.6). *Kim: 'Napkin'*

```
01  K:    so she asked me (.) "pass me the napkin"=and in
02        Vietnam we don't learn napkin.
03  M:    uhuh
04  K:    an' we so napkin is not in my dictionary so I
05        don't know which one is napkin.
06        (0.5)
07        so I picked a lot of thing on the table. >an'
```

```
08            she say< "NO not that one. The OTHER one." an' I
09            say which one. $so I picked another one. so
10            whatever on the table you name it. I gave it to
11            her.$
12     M:     heh heh
13     K:     so finally she said "THAT's the one."
```

On another occasion, Kim gave an account of working in the women's handbag section of a department store when a man came by and asked for a scarf. Although she had conscientiously memorized various vocabulary related to her section, she was not prepared to answer a question about scarves. After walking around, Kim said the man came back and shoved the scarf in her face and shouted at her, giving her an unexpected and unpleasant vocabulary lesson (Excerpt 3.7).

(Excerpt 3.7). Kim: 'Scarf'

```
01         K:   h-he walking around and he came back
02              and he pick up the scarf and he said "THIS. IS.
03              SCARF." (.) I said, (.) "oh ↑sor↓ry." ( )
04              ((sweetly embarrassed tone))
05         M:   heh. uh-oh
06         K:   ha ha ha
07   →     M:   $I bet you remembered it$
08   →     K:   $until NOW?$ heh heh heh
09         M:   ha ha
10         K:   because he like almost shove it into my face.
11         M:   uhuh
12         K:   "°this is what you call scarf°"
```

Even though the customer's actions are described in line 10 as face-threatening (pragmatically, and even physically), Kim's naively innocent response to the customer after her failure produces an affective contrast between his explosive anger and her subsequent embarrassment. The interviewer's laughter and exclamatory 'uh-oh' orient to this contrast and the tension between the aggressive customer on the one hand and the perplexed store employee on the other. After Kim joins in the laughter, affiliating with the interviewer by confirming that this is indeed a humorous telling, the interviewer characterizes as obvious the memorability of this episode (line 7: 'I bet you remembered it'). While confirming the interviewer's assertion, Kim emphatically asserts epistemic ownership (Heritage & Raymond, 2005) over her experienced events by upgrading the interviewer's assessment to 'until NOW' and adding further details that indicate the customer's transgressive actions escalated to physical aggression (line 10). She then closes her telling with a fading, softly-produced restatement of the customer's angry words: '°this is what you call scarf°' (line 12).

As the preceding excerpts indicate, though the memorability of these words was linked with stressful and transgressive experiences involving discrimination against immigrants, L2 speakers and ethnic or other minorities, they were largely reframed through humor. Transforming unpleasant and painful events from the past into humorous tellings in the present is one way that speakers displayed their ability to effectively cope with their troubles (Glenn, 2003; Jefferson, 1984; Maynard, 2003) while collaboratively constructing funny and witty stories with the interviewer. I suggest humor is a way that speakers may mitigate the severity of past events and avoid burdening the interviewer with overly emotional and negative content. In my role as interviewer, orienting to and commenting on the humorous aspects of events was also a way that I sought to lessen the emotional intensity and potential negative effects of the interview topics and tellings. As I will discuss in detail in Chapter 7, this emotional management (of the emotionality of self and others) is central to the activity of research interviewing.

Inability to recall or tell

In addition to characterizing emotional events as memorable and recallable, speakers may also make contrasts with what is *not* recallable or tellable. Trang often brought up the topic of hostility between Vietnamese and Cambodians in his interviews and group interactions. In an individual interview, he again described the hostile relations between Cambodians and Vietnamese in his explanation about why he quit ESL class and never went back. To provide context for the interviewer, Trang drew parallels with the historically situated wartime animosity of the US toward the Japanese and French.[4] At the time of this interview in 2004, the US's anti-French sentiment (e.g. as exemplified by the widely publicized and largely unsuccessful bid by some US officials to rename 'French fries' to 'freedom fries') tied to France's lack of support for the Iraq War made this selection particularly salient. It is also important to note that Trang repeatedly represented himself as knowledgeable about French language and culture (his partner was French and they had traveled to France together several times). As shown here in Excerpt 3.8, he links emotionality with what is and is not recallable:

(Excerpt 3.8). Trang: 'I don't remember'

```
01      T:    I have a classmate in X ((city in Canada))
02            call me names.
03      M:    like what?
04      T:    he called me (.) for example, (5.0) what do
05            Americans call French when they're angry?
06            (2.0)
```

```
07               they call them frogs. if the American during
08               the wartime between American and Japanese
09               American have war with Japanese (.) they say
10               Jap. when you (.) have war with another
11               country you give each one a name.
12               for example in Cambodia (.) they call
13               Vietnamese a name (.) a bad name. I didn't
14               expect to hear that in my face. especially
15               from a classmate. I'm just a young man
16               trying to grow up in North America (.)
17               trying to go on with my life. I met a
18               Cambodian classmate. we get along ok. but
19    →          later on (.) we disagree about something. I
20    →          don't remember (.) but I just remember he
21    →          called me a name (.) a name I didn't expect
22               to hear. so I didn't want to associate as
23               much with some of them. I have to be
24               selective. 'cuz I don't want to hear any
25               negative toward me again.
```

In this version of events, Trang describes what is memorable (e.g. meeting a Cambodian classmate, getting along, having a disagreement, being called a name) in contrast to what is not memorable (e.g. the specifics of his disagreement with his classmate). A question that arises is: What do speakers achieve by making claims of remembering and forgetting?

Discursive psychologists have given much attention to the function of memory claims and terms in interaction. They have found that claims of what is remembered or forgotten can shape the details of autobiographical talk as well as the self-presentation work that the talk achieves:

> Inability to recall certain details may also provide a way of implying that those details were not worth remembering. This can imply that, despite the significance they might obtain later ... they did not have that significance at the time for the person now remembering, and this in turn can signal an innocent involvement in those events. (Edwards, 1997: 285)

As I have discussed, claims of the memorability of events characterizes their strong impact upon and personal significance for the speaker. By providing details about represented events, speakers demonstrate to their recipients that their stories are based on their first-person knowledge. This enables them to claim that their story constitutes an objective, factual record for the researcher. However, in the case of highly emotional and personally traumatic events, the absence of details can also establish authenticity. Even neurological research has shown that in stressful and traumatic situations, the 'flight-or-fight response' of the sympathetic nervous system can inhibit memory formation (see Chapter 8). As a result, storytellers may remember only fragments of an event (Christianson, 1992; Ochs & Capps, 2001).

Memory or attentional failure is not just a cognitive explanation; it also functions as a discursive resource – that is, a way of talking about and accounting for events. Claims of forgetting or not remembering are also devices for suggesting that events are not important enough to recall or that some specific details were overshadowed by more significant matters. Thus memory failures also have a pragmatic function in that they are a means by which speakers may attempt to avoid blame or other negative assessments, particularly when called to provide details 'for the record' – such as in courtroom settings (e.g. Coulter, 1985; Lynch & Bogen, 1996, 2005), counseling sessions (e.g. Edwards, 1997), and even, I suggest, in research interviews. By claiming not to remember, witnesses to events are neither confirming nor denying the objective or subjective aspects of events but are indicating their 'practical unavailability' (Lynch & Bogen, 1996: 184) and are thus able to resist the force of interrogation (Ekman, 1985). In Excerpt 3.8, by claiming an inability to recall the disagreement, Trang makes that disagreement unavailable for scrutiny by the interviewer and avoids having to defend against any implications of wrongdoing or overreaction on his part.

Characterizing the ordinariness of his own actions (lines 15–16: 'I'm just a young man trying to grow up in North America (.) trying to go on with my life'), Trang makes use of a generic device commonly used when describing memories of traumatic events: 'I was just doing X . . . when Y' (Wooffitt, 1992). As he describes, *he was just* going about his business as an ordinary immigrant working hard to make a life in a new country *when* his classmate called him a name. This attributes the unexpected and traumatic nature of these events to the personal betrayal by a friend. Whatever the exact nature of the disagreement was, by not naming it, he foregrounds the outcome of that conflict, rather than the conflict itself, as significant. In contrast with his memory failure, Trang's memory claims (lines 20–22: 'but I just remember he called me a name (.) a name I didn't expect to hear') shows what he treats as important and relevant within this particular telling: that he was called a hurtful name and that it was a name he did not expect to hear in North America (i.e. that he expected freedom from racial discrimination in North America). In other interviews, Trang stated that this experience in his ESL class was so traumatic that he never went back, which permanently ended his formal education.

Even when asked by the interviewer, Trang resisted saying 'the name' he was called. Avoiding producing the name therefore constructed it as traumatic and hurtful by making it 'unsayable'. It may also be that the interviewer was not familiar enough with Vietnamese or Cambodian languages to make the *actual* name relevant or meaningful.[5] However, on one occasion, Trang did mention a name that he said Vietnamese called him, which was part of a derogatory rhyme used to insult Amerasian children (this was a curious claim, since Trang was Cambodian-Vietnamese, not Amerasian): *Mỹ lai mười hai lỗ đít, đít lo nhay xi lo kia* ['Amerasians have twelve assholes. If you plug one, gas and shit come out from the others'] (DeBonis, 1995: 6). A result of Trang's discursive work to show what is memorable and relevant within the ongoing interview activity is that his traumatic experience and subsequent decisions to give up his formal ESL studies and avoid the Vietnamese and Cambodian communities come off as natural and understandable reactions to cumulative mistreatment, rather than overreactions.

Summary

This chapter has examined the dynamic interactional and discursive work involved in selecting and producing a telling that is interesting and relevant for the interview context and goals. A close analysis of this activity reveals that speakers are doing much more than simply recalling stories: they are setting them up, launching them, closing them down, shaping how they are interpreted and helping the story recipient to recognize the relevance of these tellings and their emotionality for understanding the tellers in the 'there-and-then' past of the storyworld and in the 'here-and-now' of the present telling. At the same time, the ways in which speakers produce their tellings characterize their personal perspectives or evaluative stances toward the events and people described. As this work projects the nature of the talk that will follow, it indicates the relevance of the story within the ongoing interaction and invites the listener to take up the role of story recipient, to align with and respond to the teller, and to recognize when the story is complete.

Giving attention to story prefaces and how they have been theorized and examined in the research literature, I considered how they function as devices that allow speakers to denote and affirm the tellability and newsworthy nature of their autobiographical material. As multi-functional devices, story prefaces, like speakers' other semiotic resources, enable interactants to attend to (and display their attention to) the interviewer-interviewee relationship and matters of tellability, stance, subject-object relations and memory. I also showed that emotionality need not be explicitly labeled (e.g. 'mad,' 'funny') to be made relevant; prefaces may use implicit and implicative features of talk to make emotionality hearable, empathy worthy and significant for an understanding of the tellings that speakers produce.

Analysis also demonstrates that participants orient to the activity of the interview (and the interviewer's agenda) and show that they are attending to the relevance, quantity and quality of their talk (Grice, 1975). That is, speakers do not just recall memories but use memory claims as a resource to demonstrate that they are fulfilling their obligations as interviewees.

The interviewer is also implicated in these tellings by orienting to speakers' epistemic authority and responding (or in some cases, not responding; i.e. lack of affiliative uptake) to the empathy-worthy aspects of their talk. Moreover, I have found that story prefaces may be treated as interpretive puzzles that need to make sense and thus may require some explanatory work by interview interactants. In fact, interviewees can be found to orient to an expectation that they would be asked – and in some cases, *must* be asked – by the interviewer to account for the emotionality of their talk.

Although this study is focused on the discursive construction and management of emotionality in autobiographical interview research, an additional observation concerns the content of speakers' prefaces and stories. Much of their talk centered on topics such as discrimination, bullying, mistreatment, complaints and other affect-laden matters linked to language use, identity, immigration and social participation. Based on these tellings, a picture emerges of these immigrants' experiences as highly emotional and filled with struggle. I will address the matter of negative emotionality in more detail in Chapter 8. Of relevance to the present chapter is that although giving attention to speakers' stories is an important step in analysis, ignoring the embeddedness of those stories and the processes by which they get launched and collaboratively produced potentially results in an impoverished perspective on the interactional competences speakers bring to bear in their active storytelling and emotional work. In Chapter 4, I continue the topic of emotional tellings by examining how they are produced in response to the interviewer's questions.

Notes

(1) I refer to constructed dialogue (Tannen, 1989) or quotatives as 'represented' speech rather than 'reported' speech to emphasize the fact that it is a version or representation rather than an unmediated reproduction or transparent report.

(2) The L1 and the ethnicity of the customer are implied. This is part of a series of tellings about memorable experiences with English, and Kim contrasted herself (as an L2 English user) with American customers (as L1 English users). She also consistently referred throughout her interviews to non-Caucasians by their ethnicity. For example, in Excerpt 3.1b, Kim refers to her co-worker as 'Korean'. In other tellings, she refers to 'Vietnamese from Vietnam', 'Vietnamese born in the US', 'Filipino', etc. She therefore appears to orient to *Caucasian* (or *haole*) *Americans* as a default category. This is another example attesting to the usefulness of having baseline data for comparison when examining individual episodes.

(3) As the content of the transcripts suggests, and substantiated in the interviews and social observations, Cambodian and Vietnamese interviewees reported that because of the historical enmity between their countries, they generally avoided interactions with members of the other group. During the influx of immigration from Southeast Asia in the 1980s and 1990s, the majority of Vietnamese were from US-supported South Vietnam. Cambodian immigrants fled after the overthrow of the Khmer Rouge regime and the subsequent invasion and occupation by the Vietnamese military. Because of contentious political divisions, it was (and still is) common for members of both communities to view immigrants from their own or the other country

with suspicion and to try to determine a person's regional origin and political affiliations by their accent and place of birth. Because Trang was of Vietnamese-Cambodian inheritance, he reported that he was constantly vigilant when interacting with members of those communities. For a few months, I took part in a Khmer language and writing class attended mainly by heritage speakers and taught by native Khmer speakers. Although Trang generally avoided interactions with Cambodians, he asked to join me and came for one lesson. However, he abruptly left and never went back after some of the community participants (born in Cambodia) made comments about his Cambodian accent and questioned him about his birthplace and family. Later Trang said to me, 'See how it is? They always come to me like that. That's why I try to keep my distance.'

(4) 'Frog' and 'Jap' are well-known pejoratives for French and Japanese people. A recurrent phenomenon that I found in the talk of these immigrant and (linguistic, ethnic, sexual) minority speakers is that they often contextualized their own experiences by referring to the experiences of more visible minority groups (e.g. African-Americans, Asians, Chinese, Japanese). See also Excerpt 7.3 in Chapter 7, where John uses a joke about African-Americans to represent his own struggles as a gay Asian man. I surmise that this allowed speakers to legitimate their stories by showing how their negative experiences were part of a larger societal pattern of discrimination against all minorities. Here, Trang's reference to Japanese likely indexes his knowledge of my experiences in Japan as well as the fact that we were in Hawai'i (where Japanese ethnicity and culture are highly visible and valued). His reference to French also displays his expert knowledge of French culture (as I have noted, he has been to France several times, and his partner was French).

(5) On other occasions, Trang did mention one name with which I was familiar: *bụi đò'i* ['dust of life'], an epithet often used against Amerasian children in Vietnam. It may have been a 'safer' term to bring up as it carried less emotional weight for him (see Dewaele, 2004, on the emotional force of swearwords and related words in the L2). Incidentally, he may have assumed that I was familiar with this particular label because of the popularity of the song *Bui-Doi* from the roadway musical *Miss Saigon*, which we had both mentioned seeing.

4 Inviting Emotional Tellings

> *I also often ask participants to tell me a story about what they are discussing. In a sense, everything said in an interview is a story.*
> (Seidman, 2013: 89)

> *Unlike traditional research, where feelings and private realms of experience are avoided, interactive interviews assume that emotions and personal meanings are legitimate topics of research.*
> (Ellis & Berger, 2003: 470)

In Chapter 3, I examined how participants in qualitative research interviews select, project and launch interactional tellings to represent their sociolinguistic trajectories and personal experiences. These frequently consisted of accounts of mistreatment and other talk of personal troubles. As mentioned previously, my stance on such stories is not that interviewees produce this talk *simply because* they have had numerous difficult and emotional experiences as L2 users, immigrants, transcultural persons, minority group members and so on.[1] Instead, I contend that specific features of the dialogic activity of the interview itself also play important roles in eliciting, foregrounding and maintaining a focus on emotionality and empathy-worthy tellings. Such features include, but are not limited to: the interview format; the institutional agenda; the identities/categories under which participants are recruited; the topics, identities and experiences that are expected and made relevant; the ways in which those topics, identities and experiences are (not) taken up and (not) responded to; and the activity of organizing autobiographical experience.

In this and the subsequent chapter, I shall be concerned with interviewer-initiated sequences that occasion and support emotional tellings and responses. Based on an analysis of data from the research literature, and drawing on my own L2 interview corpus, I seek here to explicate how the activity of questioning (i.e. the solicitation and elicitation of interviewee responses) within the research interview context contributes in significant ways to the affective nature of the tellings and other material that are collaboratively generated.

Soliciting Authentic Knowledge and Subjectivity

Within the diverse literature on the practices and procedures of qualitative interviewing, researchers are frequently encouraged to ask participants about their experiences, perceptions and opinions – or to at least pursue them as topics for further exploration once they are made relevant. A fundamental assumption informing such methodological prescriptions is that interviewees have privileged access to 'inner world' psychologies and 'outer world' experiences that the interviewer does not; the interviewee *is* being interviewed for a particular reason, after all. What the interviewer in such cases is pursuing is often referred to in the literature as 'B-events' (Heritage, 1985; Labov, 1972; Labov & Fanshel, 1977), that is, 'characterizations of what the recipients know, feel, or believe or, alternatively, what they have done or said' (Sidnell, 2010b: 25). As I have noted, instead of asking only about objective events (i.e. 'what happened'), qualitative researchers are primarily interested in investigating the personal or 'deep' meanings and understandings of those events for the individual. Despite the tacit acknowledgement of identities and experiences as socially (and discursively) constructed, there nevertheless remains a desire to elicit and reveal the 'imagined subject behind the interview respondent' (Holstein & Gubrium, 1995: 7) and to gain access to speakers' *authentic* lives as expressed in their own *true* voices:

> ... we were challenged to focus our research agenda and structure our interviews *to reveal the authentic experiences of the informants*. (Ovando & Locke, 2011: 237, emphasis added)

> Narrative inquirers are interested in inclusion in research *to enable authentic stories and observations*, often those of marginalized populations, to be revealed by participants themselves – the telling of their own stories. (Lewis & Adeney, 2014: 165–166, emphasis added)

The widespread interest of academics and laypersons in revealing individuals' authentic voices and truths resonates with Gubrium and Holstein's (2012: 31) profound observation: '[t]he interview society, it seems, is the province of subjects harboring deep inner meanings, selves and sentiments, whose stories retain the truths of the matters in question' (see also Atkinson, 2015; Atkinson & Silverman, 1997; Foley, 2012). Challenging these assumptions, Gubrium and Holstein urge caution, arguing that truth, emotion and so on, are themselves interactional phenomena – not simply signals of deeper, authentic truths:

> Authenticity itself is a methodically constructed product of communicative practice ... Recognizable signs of emotional expression and scenic

practices such as direct eye contact and intimate gestures are widely taken to reveal deep truths about individual experience... We 'do' deep, authentic experiences as much as we 'do' opinion offering in the course of the interview. (Holstein & Gubrium, 2012: 31)

In the field of sociolinguistics, similar concerns have been expressed regarding assumptions that researchers' 'special methods' (Eckert, 2003: 394), including interviews and participant-observation, allow unmediated access to speakers' languages, cultures, minds and feelings in their natural, authentic states.

Taking a stance on the 'truthfulness' and 'authenticity' of autobiographical material as constructed or generated rather than revealed is not to suggest that researchers must suspect participants are dishonest or deliberately manipulative (i.e. that they are trying to 'get one over on' the interviewer). Neither should we naively assume that participants (or researchers) are incapable of purposefully editing, exaggerating, misinforming or being inconsistent and even deceitful. All social research involves human beings and therefore gives rise to a range of actions and behaviors. Rather than subscribing to the extremes of either suspicion or uncritical acceptance, I suggest that a more balanced (and less paranoid) perspective entails reminding ourselves that *all* talk is social action. As I commented in Chapter 1, for the researcher/analyst, this approach is profoundly liberating. It relieves us from the impossible task of trying to be 'truth' or 'BS' detectors and allows us to focus on the knowledge and representations that are generated in relation to the goals and activities at hand. Applying this perspective to autobiographical interview research and storytelling, Kasper and Prior (2015: 229) argue that it offers much-needed attention to speakers 'interactional' realities, not just their 'lived' realities:

> In order for us as researchers to understand storytelling, we must focus attention on the practices by which the participants make their activity understandable to themselves and to each other as they produce it. Although autobiographic stories have been utilized as rich resources for understanding the lived realities of groups and individuals, a detailed analysis of how these stories take shape in the course of their production offers insight into the co-participants' interactional realities.

Considering Competence and Expertise

Despite widespread recognition that questions figure centrally in the activity of interviewing and play an important part in establishing the interviewer's agenda (Clayman & Heritage, 2002) and generating data, the matter of how the institutional activity of *questioning* in research interviews is carried out has received relatively little attention (but see discussions in Briggs, 1986; Mishler, 1991; Prior, 2011a, 2014; Roulston, 2010; Wang & Yan, 2012). Mishler (1991: 7), in addressing the unproblematized use of interviews in qualitative research, describes interviewing as a form of dyadic discourse between speakers, rather than simply a means of data collection:

> Questioning and answering are *ways of speaking* that are grounded in and depend on culturally shared and often tacit assumptions about how to express and understand beliefs, experiences, feelings, and intentions. I have referred to this knowledge as *ordinary language competence*. (emphasis added)

Like Mishler (1991: 7), who speaks of the 'ordinary language competence' involved in carrying out question-answer sequences, Briggs cites 'rhetorical competence' (1986: 88) as an important aspect of pragmatic effectiveness in interviews (e.g. making one's talk relevant, cohesive and culturally appropriate). Atkinson (2015: 86), in a related critique of ethnographic inquiry, argues the need to examine 'the performative competences' and management of appearances and identities. In applied linguistics, Pavlenko (2007: 181) has similarly urged scholars to recognize that an analysis of narratives must attend to their 'discursive, linguistic, rhetorical, and interactional properties' as well as the contexts and conditions of their productions. Again, this echoes Holstein and Gubrium's (1995) insistence that researchers consider the 'whats' as well as the 'hows' of interview talk. By focusing only upon interviewees' responses and excluding how that talk is also occasioned by and assembled for the interviewer, we miss the dynamic linguistic, interactional, rhetorical, cultural and other resources and competences that go into organizing talk and experience for others (including the 'successes' and 'failures').

Researcher as insider/outsider

The matter of the researcher's status as cultural insider/outsider has been a point of concern for many scholars (e.g. Briggs, 1986; Gubrium & Holstein, 2002; Gubrium *et al.*, 2012; Liamputtong, 2010; Mehra, 2001; Merchant & Willis, 2001; Messerschmidt, 1981; Olesen, 2011; Trimble & Fisher, 2006; Voloder & Kirpitchenko, 2014; see also ten Have, 2002, on ethnomethodological perspectives). Some researchers take the position that cultural insiders have better access, superior cultural knowledge and sensitivity and therefore a greater ability to understand participants on (and in) their own terms. Researchers also recognize that though the researcher may claim or reject particular roles or membership statuses in the interview, it does not guarantee that participants will align themselves accordingly. Even 'insiders' can be treated as 'outsiders', and vice versa. Interviewees may resist and even challenge the interviewer's own presumed status and authority (Carter & Bolden, 2012; Prior, 2014; Roulston, 2014; Wang & Yan, 2012).

At the heart of research practice is discursive action. Therefore this requires of the analyst close attention to the ways in which interactants' (interviewer's and interviewee's) salient identities are worked up and occasioned in situ (rather than pre-existing as static categories). These identities and roles are thus *wholly contingent* on the interaction that shapes the ways that they are foregrounded and renegotiated as well as how they stabilize and become cohesive over the course of the interview(s) and the research project. To better contextualize speakers and their utterances, it is therefore important to attend to the membership categories speakers invoke to better understand *to whom* they are speaking (e.g. insider, outsider, friend, researcher) as well as *for* and *as whom* they are speaking (e.g. self, community).

Zimmerman's (1998) three-part framework offers a useful means for explicating how speakers-in-interaction categorize their *situated* or situation-specific identities (e.g. interviewer, interviewee), *discourse* or moment-by-moment *identities* (e.g. story teller, story recipient, questioner, answerer) and *transportable* or latent (physical or sociocultural) identities (e.g. man, immigrant, Asian, youth). In my own experience as researcher-analyst, I have found qualitative interviewing and subsequent data analysis require continuous monitoring of the transitions between, for example, the activities of casual conversation and interview 'business' as well as interactants' *personal* and *professional* identities (e.g. friend, expert, novice, insider, outsider). Making analysis even more challenging is the fact that researcher-participant relationships often become intertwined over the course of longitudinal research (on researcher identities and roles in prolonged ethnographic fieldwork, see Atkinson *et al.*, 2003).

We would also do well to recognize that the greater the gap between interviewer and interviewee in terms of shared sociocultural and linguistic knowledge (as is common in L2 research), the greater the need for access to contextual information (e.g. when I interview people about their experiences with immigration or asylum seeking I must rely on their guidance into those unfamiliar worlds). When more must be made explicit for the researcher, it may occasion detailed explanations and extended tellings. Thus, for the researcher interested in examining accounting practices and generating research material, outsider status may even be facilitative, rather than simply an obstacle to overcome (cf. Spradley, 1979). In my research interviews with individuals discussing personal struggles with language, identity, sociocultural belonging and other experiences, I have also found that they cited my cultural outsider status as a factor that allowed them anonymity and the opportunity to discuss these issues. Of course, when researchers are outsiders and novices in a community, they are also tasked with learning ethical and culturally appropriate ways of asking, interacting and knowing in that setting (Briggs, 1986).

Regardless of how much or how little background knowledge is shared between interviewer and interviewee, it must not be forgotten that the interactional setting and the interpersonal dynamics always shape *what* and *how* material gets pursued, generated, treated as (ir)relevant and even avoided. In addition, interviewees and interviewers – no matter how familiar they may be with the concept of interviewing – always face the task of learning and confirming the expectations and procedures of *this* interview activity with *this* person, on *this* topic, at *this* time, in *this* context and so on. As Atkinson (2015: 95) notes, '[i]n many contexts, there are preferred kinds of questions and preferred kinds of answers'. Just what these preferred forms are may not always be known in advance. This means that the questions and pacing of the interview, the management of interviewee-interviewer roles and expectations as well as the goals and foci of the larger study are all things that must be carefully worked out in the interview, and in many cases, even before it takes place.

I have discussed in this section that the activities of eliciting and producing talk of personal experience involve highly-coordinated interactional competence. Because this collaborative work tends to go off relatively smoothly, it is easy to overlook the fact that interview interactants depend on a wide range of linguistic and sociocultural resources and knowledge to carry out this activity. Just as importantly, these various competences intersect with interactants' identities and roles in ways that invoke and reinforce the normative and conventional features of the setting (whether casual conversation or institutional talk), while allowing room for resistance and challenge. In the following sections, I consider in more detail how the activity of questioning functions as a central interviewing device for eliciting autobiographical tellings and related affect-laden material.

Questioning in 'Ordinary' and 'Institutional' Interaction

In scholarship exploring other institutional settings where various interview components can be found (e.g. doctor-patient interaction, counseling sessions, news interviews, classrooms, courtrooms), question-answer sequences have been an ongoing topic of interest (e.g. Freed & Ehrlich, 2010; Lindström & Lindholm, 2009; Seedhouse, 2004; Steensig & Drew, 2008). In contrast to the workings of casual (i.e. spontaneous) conversation, one of the key findings of discursive research on institutional interaction is that turns may be pre-allocated because of interactants' institutional roles and asymmetric distribution of rights and responsibilities (Atkinson & Drew, 1979; Drew & Heritage, 1992; Frankel, 1984). For example, in health care settings, physicians' utterances consist primarily of questions that limit the scope of the information exchange (Francis & Hester, 2004; Frankel, 1984). In the courtroom, the lawyer holds the right to ask questions, not the witness (Atkinson & Drew, 1979; Eades, 2008; Heritage & Clayman, 2010). In police-citizen encounters, citizens are largely limited to responses (Heritage & Clayman, 2010; Stokoe & Edwards, 2010). Similarly, in journalistic and other investigative interviews, the interaction is largely constrained by interviewer-led question and answer sequences (Clayman & Heritage, 2002).

Although there are occasional exceptions to the norm (e.g. interviewees may resist particular lines of questioning and even challenge the interviewer's agenda and expertise; Harris, 1991; Heritage, 1985; Prior, 2014), the qualitative interview trajectory is nonetheless collaboratively built by the questions as well as the responses produced (and withheld) by both interviewer and interviewee and the ways in which they orient to their respective utterances (e.g. as sufficient, relevant, needing clarification, out of character). Furthermore, questioning sequences, whether in formal or semi-structured interviews, are constructed in accordance with the analytic interests of the researcher as well as prospective research audiences (Gubrium & Holstein, 2002; Heritage, 1985; Wooffitt, 2005). These questioning sequences exhibit institution-specific features – what Heritage and Clayman (2010: 18) have called the institution's 'unique "fingerprint" of practices' such as turntaking structures, lexical choices, sentence patterns, question types and preferred responses. For example, although acknowledging an answer to a question with 'oh' or an assessment (e.g. 'that's great!') may be commonplace in ordinary conversation, it has been shown to be comparatively rare in many institutional contexts (Heritage & Clayman, 2010: 18). This appears especially so for news interviews (e.g. Greatbatch, 1988, 1992; Heritage, 1985; Schegloff, 1992), where interviewers treat the overhearing audience, rather than the interviewer/host, as the primary addressee. This may be true also in research interviews, particularly when the recording device is an ever-present reminder of future analysis, representation, sharing and even re-entextualization of data (Blommaert, 2001).

Despite the body of empirical evidence attesting to some of the unique aspects of institutional interaction (e.g. Antaki, 2011; Heritage & Clayman, 2010), the boundaries between institutional talk and ordinary, spontaneous conversation are not always clearly delineated (Drew & Heritage, 1992). As noted in previous chapters, practices of ordinary conversation (e.g. small talk) can be found in institutional settings; conversely, features of institutional-like talk (e.g. explicit teaching) can be found in conversation – making many settings (e.g. health care visits, teacher-student meetings) 'quasi-conversational' (Freed & Ehrlich, 2010; He, 1998; Heritage & Greatbatch, 1989). Heritage (2005b: 108) explains '[t]he relationship between "ordinary conversation" and "institutional talk" can be understood as that between a "master institution" and its more restricted local variants'. For the individual and society, the *institution* of ordinary conversation is relatively stable. Institutional talk, in contrast, is relatively recent and involves a great deal of change.

Because conversation is the bedrock of social life (Heritage & Clayman, 2010; Schegloff, 1987a, 1987b, 1995) and thus enables the functioning of institutions such as 'the economy, the polity, the family, socialization, and so on' (Schegloff, 1995: 187), a continued topic of debate is the warrantability of analytical claims about the 'institutionality of institutional interaction' (Kasper, 2009: 15). For Schegloff (1992: 127), the analyst's focus should not be overly restricted to questions such as 'how are they now doing interview?' but should include more open attention to the organizational and interactional details of the setting.

> If the form of inquiry is the organization of conduct, the details of action, the practices of talk, then every opportunity should be pressed to enhance our understanding of any available detail about those topics. Invoking social structure or the setting of the talk at the outset can systematically distract from, even blind us to, details of those domains of events in the world. (Schegloff, 1992: 127)

Aligning with conversation analysis' (CA) contextually grounded perspective, the discursive constructionist approach employed here starts with actions and practices – for it is they that give form and meaning to the activities, identities, emotions and other social constructs that then become identified as research phenomena and components of institutional practices.

Defining questions

A question is often identifiable through its interrogative form (e.g. by means of inversion or a *wh*-element) and/or rising intonation (Crystal, 2011). But defining questions is not always so straightforward (Tsui, 2013). Sidnell (2010b: 21) specifies *question* as 'both a practice and a category implicated in members' own reflection upon, descriptions of, and ideas about their practice'. In other words, what 'counts as' a question is sequentially and retrospectively determined by the interactants themselves. Put simply, if participants orient to an utterance as a question, it is a question. Freed and Ehrlich (2010: 6), adopting a broad definition based on functional and sequential characteristics, view questions as utterances that (a) solicit or are treated by the recipient as soliciting information, confirmation or action, and (b) are delivered in a way that creates a slot for the recipient to produce a responsive turn. This action-orientation to questioning informs the present chapter.

In my discussion on the prefacing and launching of story prefaces in Chapter 3, I showed that they may be self-initiated by the interviewee as well as produced in response to the interviewer's questions and comments.

I also noted that much of the qualitative research interview literature recognizes, if not encourages, the elicitation of emotionality, regardless of the topic of inquiry:

> Investigations of emotions such as anger in interview contexts may lead to emotional responses in researchers and also in the participants. In addition, the method of interviewing itself, which often involves participants sharing personal aspects of their lives with researchers, can elicit emotional responses whether or not the interview focuses on a topic of emotions. (deMarrais & Tisdale, 2002: 116)

Despite the recognition that emotions are elicited and made relevant in qualitative interviews, few researchers have addressed the matter of how interviewers and interviewees make emotions explicitly accountable (i.e. tellable, hearable, relevant) through their questioning practices. In the remainder of the chapter I will examine interviewer question sequences that invite tellings or otherwise make relevant the production of emotional responses.

Eliciting and Producing Emotion Talk

As I noted in the preceding chapter, much of the research literature on storytelling sequences has focused on those initiated by the storyteller (Hutchby & Wooffitt, 2008; Sacks, 1992; Sidnell, 2010a), particularly in everyday conversational settings. However, stories may also be prompted, invited or otherwise solicited by others (e.g. Cuff & Francis, 1978; Labov & Waletzky, 1967, 1997; Lerner, 1992; Sidnell, 2010a):

(Excerpt 4.1). From Lerner (1992: 251)

L: Oh you haftuh tell'm about yer typewriter honey,

(Excerpt 4.2). From Lerner (1992: 255)

M: 'Member the wah- guy we saw?

In both of these examples from multi-party conversations given in Excerpts 4.1 and 4.2, one speaker is prompting another to tell other co-present members a story that is shared by the prompter and the projected storyteller, but not the other listeners.

Some researchers also recognize that storytelling may be an invited or normative practice in institutional settings (e.g. Cuff & Francis, 1978; Hall *et al.*, 1997; Liddicoat, 2011; Lynch & Bogen, 1996; Wooffitt, 1992), and may even be used in research interviews as a data elicitation technique (e.g. Chase, 2008; Labov & Waletzky, 1967, 1997). The interactional organization of storytelling in institutional settings has received relatively little attention, as much research has centered on conversational storytelling (e.g. Hutchby & Wooffitt, 2008; Liddicoat, 2011; Norrick, 2000; Sacks, 1992; Sidnell, 2010a). However, a number of researchers have investigated related practices such as accounting (Buttny, 2004; Garfinkel, 1967), blaming (Edwards & Potter, 1992), complaining (Buttny, 2004; Drew, 1998; Günthner, 1997a; Prior, 2011a), assessing (Heath, 1992; Speer, 2005), aligning (Boden & Zimmerman, 1991; Speer, 2005), managing epistemic status (Drew & Heritage, 1992; Edwards & Potter, 2005) and making memory claims (Lynch & Bogen, 1996, 2005; Wooffitt, 2005). Nevertheless, how stories are occasioned in research interviews remains an understudied topic of research.

Unlike storytelling in casual conversation, where the storyteller is tasked with securing and maintaining an extended turn within the ongoing interaction to tell a story, settings in which self-selected story recipients solicit or invite storytelling sequences provide that space by design. The key functions of story prefaces (see Chapter 3) in both self-initiated and other-initiated stories are similar: namely, to align participants to the activity of storytelling and to project what kind of telling(s) will follow (Heritage, 2011; Hutchby & Wooffitt, 2008). Bringing interactants into alignment is essential in enabling recipients to know when the telling is complete and what kinds of responses are appropriate (Sacks, 1992).

Cuff and Francis' (1978) examination of sociological interviews on marriage breakdowns is one of the few studies to directly address the topic of solicited stories. In their study, Cuff and Francis note that although the interviewees were not faced with the difficulty of locating a slot to tell their stories within the ongoing interaction, they were still challenged with various other issues when invited to produce particular stories, such as complying with the invitation, determining how to begin, knowing what to tell and how much to tell and identifying the story recipient(s) (e.g. the immediate listener(s), a subsequent audience who will hear the recording). Similar sorts of interviewer dilemmas are present also in L2 autobiographical interview research.

Lynch and Bogen (1996), in their ethnomethodological investigation of the testimonies of witnesses in the Reagan era Iran-Contra hearings, observed that not only do questioners routinely occasion the telling of particular stories (e.g. Excerpt 4.3), they 'often collaborate in the telling of the witness's story by making specific claims about what the witness already knows' (Lynch & Bogen, 1996: 161), as in Excerpt 4.4:

(Excerpt 4.3). From Lynch and Bogen (1996: 161, emphasis added)

Nields: Would you simply pick up the story of the Hawk shipment, starting with that call that you received from the Israeli official, and *tell us in your own words what you remember.*

(Excerpt 4.4). From Lynch and Bogen (1996: 161, emphasis added)

Nields: Uh- well, in fact Colonel North, *you believed* that the Soviets were aware of our sale of arms to Iran, weren't you.

An additional aspect of stories solicited in various institutional settings (e.g. court hearings, news reports, research interviews) is that, as they are 'on the record' accounts, speakers may be held accountable to 'the accumulating record of the events' (Lynch & Bogen, 1996: 162) they are asked to describe. For publicly solicited stories, these records may include official institutional documents as well as previous testimony and eyewitness accounts. In autobiographical interviewing, the audio and video recordings, written transcripts, research notes, presentation and publication of the data, shared interactional history between the interviewer and interviewees, documented socio-historical events (e.g. the Vietnam War, diasporic migration) that are brought up as topics, and even 'commonsense' cultural knowledge, potentially serve as records by which to hold tellers (and researchers) accountable. As shown in many of the excerpts throughout these chapters, speakers display a sensitivity to the accountability of their talk by giving a historical and contextual frame and evidence to support the epistemic and affective validity (i.e. 'authenticity') of their tellings and versions of events.

Soliciting Emotional Stories

Both *self*-initiated and *other*-initiated stories often make use of story prefaces to align the interactants toward the activity and topic of storytelling. Based on an informal review of the published literature and my own interview corpus, I find that interviewer-initiated story prefaces appear to occur more often than interviewee-initiated story prefaces. As these stories are told in response to an invitation or request for a telling, they point to an underlying institutional agenda within the interview setting. More specifically, I have found that emotional story solicitation by the interviewer is a prevalent practice that encourages the production of extended stories detailing experienced events. In the following section I will consider how interviewers actively solicit and contribute to the shaping of emotional story prefaces by the interviewees and the emotional material they project.

I have noted that interviewers often invite stories from interviewees. These story invitations involve both explicit story requests as well as requests for elaboration (e.g. 'tell me about ...'). Some of these story invitations employ extreme case formulations (Pomerantz, 1986; e.g. *happiest, funniest, craziest*), employing a well-known sociolinguistic research strategy of eliciting 'spontaneous' material, by asking about extraordinary and emotionally charged topics (e.g. Labov & Waletzky, 1967, 1997; Milroy, 1987). Again, I take the stance that whether stories and emotion talk and emotion displays are interviewer-initiated or interviewee-initiated, *all* interview talk must be treated as interactional accounts rather than 'more' or 'less' truthful representations of experience.

By way of illustration, I now consider examples of interviewer questioning sequences that initiate storytelling in my data corpus. All are from one-on-one interviews and involve the interviewer inviting the interviewees to supply autobiographical stories tied to experiences and emotional episodes. Only brief excerpts are shown here to illustrate some of their general features, but I locate them in the unfolding interactional sequences.

Some general features of story invitations

Story invitations, like other interactional sequences such as requests, complaints and adjacency pairs (the most basic units of interaction) are all bounded units. That is, they are embedded in a larger interactional structure and topical organization. These sequences have beginnings and endings and alternative ways in which they could potentially occur. Of importance from a social interactional perspective is not how these sequences are pre-structured (i.e. existing in memory as free-standing stories) but how participants in their 'practices of talking accomplish recognizable beginnings and endings' (Schegloff, 1996: 120).

One way in which story invitations are bounded is by the interviewer producing a question that explicitly invites a story, particularly one involving strong, emotional and memorable experiences. Three illustrative cases are shown in Excerpts 4.5–4.7. The first excerpt is from my second interview with Jack (J), an immigrant from Cambodia, and takes place at his apartment (see Prior, 2014, for an extended analysis). While the interviewer (M) and Jack are both waiting for Bona (another immigrant from Cambodia recently introduced to the interviewer by Jack) to arrive for an interview, Jack asks about the interview agenda. After the interviewer explains that he will ask Bona about his experiences, Jack then announces that he also has more stories, making inferable that the interviewer should ask about them. The interviewer then follows up Jack's invitation by producing a story request (Excerpt 4.5).

(Excerpt 4.5). Jack: 'Interesting stories'

```
01  →   M:   so, do you have any interesting stories for me:?
02  →        °heh heh°
03      J:   what stories. ((flat, but surprised tone))
04  →   M:   abou::t (.) your life. your happiest experience.
05  →        your funniest experience. your craziest
06  →        experience. °heh heh° (.)
```

```
07          ((S turns on TV, searches for something and then
08          inserts a Cambodian music video into the DVD
09          player))
10          (33.0)
11          ((Cambodian music starts))
12          (40.0)
13    J:    you can read English in there. ((nods head
14          toward TV screen))
15          ((lines removed))
16          they say the same word.
17          (0.7)
18          say khmao you say khmao too.
19          (0.5)
20          on the bottom.
21          ((lines removed))
22          I can translate for you.
23    M:    °oh°
24    J:    you can know how to speak.
25          (2.7)
26          all the word say the same thing.
27    M:    °°m°°
28    J:    say khmao mean black skin (.) I can teach
29          ( ) the rest later.
```

Initiating a change in activity with a disjunctive *so*-preface that also ties the interviewer's utterance, a direct consequence of Jack's previous claim of having more stories, the interviewer makes an open-ended request to Jack for a particular category of stories: interesting stories (line 1: 'so, do you have any interesting stories for me?'). Instead of providing a story or asking for elaboration on the kind of story that is being requested, Jack orients to the story request as problematic and even surprising (through his tone) by initiating a repair in line 3 ('what stories'). Reformulating his request, the interviewer lists several types of stories that fit within the category 'interesting': stories about Jack's life, and extreme case formulations such as his 'happiest', 'funniest' and 'craziest' experiences. The interviewer follows his initial and reformulated story descriptions with laughter (lines 2 and 6) and takes a humorous stance toward his own questions. It is possible that the interviewer may be orienting to the potential of these intense kinds of story requests to elicit sensitive material (e.g. laughter can be a signal of a face threatening act; Jefferson *et al.*, 1976). He may also be working to mitigate the possible seriousness and overt institutionality of his questions and the activity of interviewing since this interaction is taking place not in a neutral setting but in Jack's home, where the interviewer is an invited guest as well as a friend.

Although Excerpt 4.5 shows an interviewer's explicit story request, it does not appear to represent a successful story elicitation. Instead of providing a story or even an acknowledgement, Jack instead inserts a music video in his DVD player and spends the next 30 minutes directing the interviewer to watch Khmer music videos and teaching him Khmer vocabulary and culture (e.g. *khmao* ['black'], *chiet mun* ['reincarnation']). I initially assessed this interview as a 'failure'; however, in a later reanalysis, I found that both language teaching and storytelling were occurring, though not in ways recognizable to me at the time (see discussion in Prior, 2014).

Excerpts 4.6 and 4.7 come from interviews with Kim (K), and also show interviewer story requests for intense or emotional experiences.

(Excerpt 4.6). Kim: 'Strong experiences'

```
01  →   M:   do you have any like (.) really (.) strong
02  →        experiences or-or something you re-remember
03  →        about (.) learning English? or, maybe after you
04  →        came here using English, some (.) funny
05  →        experience, or (.) crazy experience, something
06  →        happened?
07      K:   when I come here?
08      M:   yeah. sure. about English.
09      K:   I guess it ((English)) not helping in-in
10           Vietnam. it not helping in Vietnam, but it help
11           to be here. you have to be here. I- (.) my first
12           job? (.) yeah?
13           (2.0)
14           is uh (2.0) bartender helper.
15      M:   oh okay
16      K:   I work in a nightclub
17      M:   okay.
18      K:   and so funny (.) one cust- (.) not customer.
19           it's my (.) boss sister
             ((K tells humorous story about learning a new
             word))
```

Excerpt 4.6 is similar to Excerpt 4.5 in that the interviewer explicitly requests talk about 'strong', 'funny' and 'crazy' experiences. Although these particular story solicitations do not use extreme case formulations, they do invite stories that involve not ordinary events but those that are memorable and tied specifically to Kim's experiences using and learning English. The interviewer then reformulates the scope of experiences from which to choose – tied to place (in Vietnam or the United States), time (before and after coming to the US) and language proficiency (while learning English and after using English).

(Excerpt 4.7). Kim: 'Extreme'

```
01  →  M:  mmm. did you have any like (3.0) I don't know
02  →      like (.) really- (.)
03  →  K:  extreme?
04  →  M:  nah (.) I'm just kinda won-wondering what kind
05  →      of experiences you had [with English.
06     K:                         [I have many.
07         (.)
08         umm. as I work longer (.) with the company at
09         XX ((store name)) (.) I know most of the (.)
10         merchandise.
11     M:  °mhm°
12     K:  I know how the procedure (.) i-it true (the
13         action) that I learned
14     M:  oh
15     K:  you learn more and more every day. (1.6) so I
16         get to the point to (.) I move and I also move
17         from one department to another=
18     M:  oh
19         ((lines ommitted. Kim goes into detail about her
20     K:  job and co-workers))
21         so one day I have the mother and daughter they
22         came and (.) they try to (.) return a (.)
23         handbag.
           ((K continues with a story about rude
           customers))
```

In contrast, in Excerpt 4.7, from a separate interview, the interviewer produces another story request (lines 1–2: 'did you have any like (3.0) I don't know like (.) really- (.)'). As in the previous excerpt, he incrementally forms the question with hesitation markers and incomplete utterances, pausing after each possible completion point:

do you have any like (3.0)
I don't know like (.)
really (.)

As shown in Excerpt 4.5, from the interview with Jack, the interviewer self-completes his question with 'interesting'; but in Excerpt 4.7, Kim anticipates the 'affective tilt' of the interviewer's story request by suggesting 'extreme?' (projected as a logical completion of his use of 'really'). By completing the interviewer's question, Kim is displaying her understanding that, like in her previous interview, the interview agenda is aimed at eliciting 'strong' rather than ordinary experiences. The hesitant production of the interviewer's story request further suggests his orientation to the sensitive nature of the talk that it invites and expects. Although neither the interviewer nor Kim specifies in lines 1–3 the topical object (e.g. stories, experiences), both are orienting to a shared understanding that 'any' in line 1 indexes stories. Because Kim's description makes visible her assumption of the interviewer's aim for 'extreme' material, the interviewer now moves to neutralize the strongly affective tilt of his questioning by producing a weak rejection (line 4: 'nah') of Kim's question completer. He then reformulates his question with hesitations and mitigators as he abandons 'really' and downgrades and respecifies the object and the scope of the autobiographical talk he is requesting (lines 4–5: 'I'm just kinda won-wondering what kind of experiences you had with English'). In overlap with the interviewer in line 5, Kim anticipates the question completion and responds with 'I have many' (line 6). Her response here is supplied in relation to 'experiences' (rather than 'experiences with English') and it again displays her understanding of the type of experiences the interviewer is requesting (i.e. strong experiences).

Some story invitations may be focused not just on eliciting specific types of stories (e.g. strong, emotional, autobiographical) but also specific episodes. In Excerpt 4.8, which I introduced at the beginning of Chapter 2, Rico (R), an asylum seeker from the Philippines, is telling the interviewer about his interview with immigration officials in Canada regarding his application for refugee status. The topic here centers on the telling of 'the' story (i.e. the specific, authoritative version), rather than 'a' story. In lines 1–10, Rico tells the interviewer about his recent immigration interview and gives an abstract of the story that he told officials to explain why he was seeking refugee status and why he should be allowed to stay in Canada.

(Excerpt 4.8). Rico: 'Can you tell me the story?'

```
01      R:   so:, I had my interview? um l-last December, (.)
02           eight. but before that uh my:: my lawyer advised
03           me to make (.) a, (.) story about, (.) what
04           would be the reason why I have to get (.) I have
05           to apply: a refugee. so I made a statement=I
06           made a story like, (.) um, somebody (.) um (2.0)
07           uh there's a group who persecute me. >that's my
08           story.< that's why I'm afraid to go back to the
09           Philippines because, peopl:e persecute me,
10           °somebody°.
11   →  M:   so, can you tell me the story?
```

```
12                  (1.8)
13      →           so what is the story you told immigration.
14         R:       okay um (.) tsch [the story was,]
15         M:                        [so,            ] oh sorry (.)
16                  go ahead
17         R:       um (1.4) I-I met a guy and then:: (.) this guy
18                  um:: introduces himself (.) and he wanted me to-
19                  to be his friend. so:: (.)
                    ((continues story about meeting terrorists and
                    having his life threatened))
```

Although I refer to these excerpts as 'tellings' or 'stories', these labels are for the analyst and the reader. It is important to remember that what talk and related material 'count as' and function as (e.g. *story, complaint, question, answer, truth, memory*) to the tellers, recipients, gatekeepers, etc. is an important aspect of the activity of organizing experience for others. For example, Rico's story here is treated as a *story*, a *legal reason* for a refugee application and a *statement* produced to officials. Rico's talk also shows how a particular version may transform from being 'a' story to officially becoming 'the' story (see also work on asylum seeker stories and the processes of entextualization by Blommaert, 2001a, 2001b; Maryns & Blommaert, 2001). The interviewer then asks Rico if he is willing to produce the story in the present interview (line 11: 'so, can you tell me the story?'), a *yes-no* (polar) question that pragmatically functions as an implicit story request. After a 1.8-second pause and no response is forthcoming from Rico, the interviewer self-repairs his question as a direct request (line 13: 'so what is the story you told immigration'). The imperative-like sentence-final falling intonation stands in contrast to the previous request made with rising intonation.

Four-turn questioning structure

The pattern of question-pause-question occurs frequently in questioning sequences. Gardner (2004) found that extended question sequences often consist of a four-turn structure (see also Kasper & Ross, 2007):

A: asks a question
B: [gap (answer unfilled)]
A: rephrases question (e.g. paraphrase, increment, modification, or expansion)
B: answer (usually a dispreferred response)

This four-turn sequence was also found throughout my interview data. In Excerpt 4.8, Rico prefaces his response with an agreement and hesitation markers (line 14: 'okay um (.) tsch the story was'), suggesting a dispreferred response (following Gardner's model) as he produces the requested story.

Rico's prefatory comment, 'the story was', indicates that he is not referring to the story as an objective episode (i.e. as something that 'happened'), but to the story that he told to the immigration officials (i.e. as a telling about a telling). As this suggests, a consideration of stories as activities, rather than simply objects for content analysis, is also a concern for interviewees, not only the interviewer/analyst (see also Stokoe & Edwards, 2006).

In Excerpts 4.9 and 4.10, rather than asking interviewees to provide a strong (e.g. *emotional, funny, crazy*, etc.) story or requesting that they retell specific episodes, the interviewer requests a story that links back to a description previously provided by the interviewee. The first example (Excerpt 4.9) comes from an interview with Trang. This is located in a larger sequence where he speaks of his anger at rude people and verbal confrontations with others:

(Excerpt 4.9). Trang: 'Like what?'

```
01      T:   s-some people yeah pe-people might say something
02           t'other people not nice. I say it. I tell them.
03  →   M:   like what?
04           (3.7)
05  →        can you think of an example?
06      T:   okay
07           (0.7)
08           example when one time one Chinese gir::l from
09           China, sh::e:s-she new worker an' she (0.5) .hh
10           she work there an' (.) this- (.) in my work so
11           many Sri Lankan people work-working there.
12      M:   Sri Lankan?
13      T:   yeah and everyone tried to tease her an' joke
14           with her: .hhand sometime very rude joke.
15           (1.4)
             ((T continues with story about scolding his
             workers for teasing their Chinese coworker and
             making her cry))
```

Following up his previous talk about rude people and confronting others, Trang's utterance in lines 1–2 is a defensive account that makes a morally justified claim that his actions are predicated on the wrong behavior of others. He also characterizes his response as appropriate by keeping it at the verbal level ('I say it'; 'I tell them') rather than escalating to physical violence (e.g. he hits them; he threatens to hurt them). However, this story later leads into talk of threats of physical violence. In a four-turn extended question sequence, the interviewer then invites Trang to elaborate on his preceding talk (line 3: 'like what?') by providing an account to explain what it is that he actually 'says' and 'tells' rude people. After a 3.7-second gap of silence and no response from T, the interviewer reformulates his previous utterance as an explicit story request (line 5: 'can you think of an example?'). Trang then produces an acceptance token (line 6: 'okay') and projects a relevant story by labeling it as an exemplar of a larger pattern of transgressive behavior (line 8: 'example when one time ...'), and produces a story for the interviewer.

A similar request for an example story based on an interviewee's previous talk of general experience is shown in Excerpt 4.10. In this interview segment, John is speaking about his time in high school, right after he immigrated to California from the Vietnamese refugee camp in the Philippines.

(Excerpt 4.10). John: 'Can you think of experience?'

```
01      J:   when you hear- when your accent I guess some
02           people like, (1.2) "oh, where you from?" right
03           away
04           (0.5)
05   →  M:   can you think of experience °°or-°°?²
06           (0.8)
07      J:   the experience? uh: (1.9) uh:: (1.4) oh like
08           high school? maybe high school=I got picked-
09           (1.7) °is that (like)[I-°
10      M:                        [you got picked on?
11      J:   I got picked on by the 'merican kid?
12      M:   °why°
13      J:   becau' I guess they think I'm different?
             ((J tells story about a confrontational
             encounter with an American classmate))
```

At the beginning of this segment, John, like Trang in Excerpt 4.9, brings up accent and the issue of origin and belonging – potentially hearable as an emotion-relevant topic. In terms of story elicitation, line 5 ('can you think of experience °°or-°°?') shows the interviewer's explicit request to John to provide talk of an experience relevant to his previous utterance in lines 1–3 (i.e. an example of accent and belonging). In light of these data, the interviewer's story requests in this study sought three interrelated kinds of explicit and emotion-implicative stories: (a) those of strong, extreme and memorable experiences (Excerpts 4.5–4.6); (b) those dealing with specific episodes (e.g. Excerpt 4.8); and (c) those serving as examples of more general experiences (e.g. Excerpts 4.7, 4.9–4.10).

Cognitive displays

Another feature of story request sequences is that they may occasion cognitive displays by the interviewees as they formulate their responses. Heritage

(2005a: 188) notes, '[c]ognitive process is not something which speakers simply report, it is also something which they embody in talk-in-interaction'. In their responses to the story requests, interviewees in my data produced their stories while displaying their active selection, remembering processes and attention to the relevance of their talk. These cognitive processes were displayed, for example, through discourse and hesitation markers (e.g. *um-* and *oh-*prefaces, pauses, restarts: e.g. Excerpts 4.6, 4.7, 4.8, 4.10), prosodic cues (e.g. rising intonation, sound stretches: e.g. Excerpts 4.6, 4.10), confirmation checks (e.g. 'Yeah?'), and provision of contextual information (e.g. time, place, people: e.g. Excerpts 4.6, 4.7, 4.8, 4.9, 4.10). In Excerpt 4.10, for example, John, in his response (lines 7–9) to the interviewer's request, displays his active work to select an appropriate story – through his repetition of the operative lexical item (line 7: 'the experience?') and use of hesitation markers ('uh:') and pauses. John then narrows this search and offers up a candidate story (lines 7–8: '<u>oh</u> like high school? maybe high school=I got picked-'). As an embodiment or epistemic stance marker of cognitive activities such as 'remembering', this *oh*-prefaced utterance (Heritage, 1998, 2005a) also indicates John's primary and independent access to the story being projected thereby signaling it as talk relevant to the interviewer's story invitation.

As interview and storytelling devices, *oh*-prefaces are multi-functional devices. For example, they display a change in state, indicate a cognitive search and make a primary claim to personal knowledge. In Excerpt 4.10, with no confirmation from the interviewer after the *oh*-prefaced response, John then produces a tentative confirmation check (line 9: 'is that (like)') to confirm whether this specific story fits the interviewer's story request or agenda. In line 10, after a 1.7-second pause and confirmation request from John, the interviewer immediately follows up with an understanding check ('you got picked on?'), now requiring John to respond with either a confirmation or further expansion. In line 11, John reformulates his story preface with more details ('I got picked on by 'merican kid?'), as an abstract (Labov, 1972) to his projected story. Just as I showed occurs in emotional story prefaces (Chapter 3), this preface is also followed up by a 'why?' question continuer from the interviewer and subsequently leads into the production of more interview material.

Summary

In this chapter I have sought to illuminate some of the bounded and highly coordinated ways that interviewer questioning sequences invite and result in storytelling by interviewees. Examining my own interview corpus, I found these tellings were often elicited by questions or requests that explicitly asked for personally impactful stories, specific episodes or illustrative examples that continued the previous topic of talk, thereby aligning with the interviewer's agenda and interest in newsworthy (and 'research-worthy') tellings. A central assumption behind these kinds of probing questions is that interviewees have unmediated access to and the ability to explain particular topics of interest, events and their meanings. I can neither confirm nor deny the authenticity of interviewees' accounts and their emotion-implicative outcomes; however, I maintain that verifiability is a concept at odds with a focus on discursive construction and epistemic accountability (Clift, 2006).

These interviewer questioning sequences and the tellings they occasion and shape are highly coordinated activities. As a result, this discursive work involves a range of linguistic, rhetorical, sociocultural and interpersonal resources and competences that often go unnoticed precisely because they are successful in generating the desired research data. A close inspection of these resources as they are mobilized in interaction also makes visible how speakers' personal and institutional identities get locally assembled and managed. Even though interactants may come to an interview setting with various identities (e.g. *immigrant, man, researcher*) and expectations (e.g. to ask/answer questions, to make a friend, to have conversation), the particular identities and roles that are locally (i.e. interactionally, interpersonally) relevant – even 'interviewer' and 'interviewee' – cannot be separated from the actions that constitute the context and are constituted by it.

With few exceptions, I found that questioning sequences in which the interviewer invited or solicited emotional tellings resulted in the generation of emotion-implicative material by the interviewees. This material and the process by which it is produced and performed are treated by both the interviewee and interviewer as relevant to the ongoing talk and interview activity. I also showed that story request sequences frequently occasioned cognitive displays by which interviewees indicated that they were selecting, recalling and producing for the interviewer an experience fitting the story solicitation. In the following chapter, I extend this analysis by examining interviewer questioning sequences that elicit emotion talk by asking about *feelings* or by implying emotionality.

Notes

(1) In taking this position, I am in no way denying the authenticity of participants' experiences; rather, I am urging for greater recognition and appreciation of the ways in which the *representation* (rather than *reporting*) of personal experience is occasioned and organized within the activity and for the explicit purpose of the interview.
(2) Through re-transcribing and re-examining the data, I have found a few instances where dropped articles appear to indicate that I was modifying my speech. This code-switch could be considered a type of speech accommodation or 'foreigner talk'. Foreigner talk can be seen as an orientation to the non-native status of the addressee, it has also been considered as a kind of linguistic modification to aid in repair and better communication (see also Hatch, 1992; Snow *et al.*, 1981). Because most of these interviews took place in the Hawai'i context, this could also be seen as 'Pidgin' (Hawai'i Creole), the local language variety that we sometimes used.

5 Eliciting Feelings

> *In the interview situation ... the main questions should normally be in a descriptive form: 'What happened and how did it happen?' 'How did you feel then?' 'What did you experience' and the like. The aim is to elicit spontaneous descriptions from the subjects rather than to get their own, more or less speculative explanations of why something took place.*
> (Kvale & Brinkmann, 2009: 133)

> *Most helpful questions would be those that guide the storytelling toward the feeling level ... Questions such as, 'How did that feel to you?' Or comments such as, 'You seem to be saying ...,' coupled with a sincere, endearing sense of wonderment and appreciation at what is being revealed to you, will go a long way in assisting the storyteller to share his or her deep story.*
> (Atkinson, 1998: 41)

In the previous chapter, I attended to the ways in which interviewer question sequences solicit emotionality from interviewees by inviting personal tellings and other meta-commentary. Analysis showed that interviewees respond to interviewer prompts and responses by actively selecting topically tell-worthy (and listen-worthy) material. In this chapter, I continue the focus on questioning sequences by examining how *feeling*, *thinking* and *implying* are bound up in this emotion-related work. I begin by reviewing how *feeling questions* have been used and theorized in the qualitative research literature and then attend to their interpretive and productive ambiguity. I then examine how feeling questions are used to collaboratively shape recipient responses in my own L2 interview data. Particular attention is given to the ways the interviewer incrementally builds these elicitation devices in ways that prefer and orient to particular recipient responses. In the second part of the chapter, I examine *emotion-implicative questions*, interviewer formulations that invite emotion-related talk without explicitly labeling it as such. I conclude by considering examples from the L2 literature that confirm feeling questions are a common, yet often unnoticed and unexamined, part of autobiographical research interviews.

Part 1. 'Feeling' Questions

A common research practice that yields emotion-related talk (at least ostensibly) involves 'feeling' questions: interactional sequences inviting talk of interviewees' feelings, emotional states or personal stances toward specific topics and events (e.g. 'How does ... feel?'; 'How do you feel about ...?'; 'What does that feel like?'). As a point of clarification, I make a distinction here between feeling questions such as 'How do you feel today?', that are produced as general greetings or interaction openers, and questions such as 'How do you feel about ...' and 'How did you feel when ...', that are produced for the purpose of eliciting personal opinions or views on particular topics, people, objects or events. Though both question types can potentially make emotionality relevant, it is the latter that concerns the present chapter.

'Feeling' questions in qualitative research

The research literature is replete with examples of questions that invite respondents to go on spoken and written record with their personal viewpoints. In survey research, for example, feeling questions are commonly used to elicit opinions from respondents (emphasis added):

Course Evaluation Survey (Brown, 2005: 287)
Q. *How do you feel about* the objectives?

Teacher Surveys (O'Donoghue, 2006: 81)
Q. *What do you feel about* the experience of teaching online?

Telephone Survey (Fink *et al.*, 2003: 105)
Q. *How do you feel about* congressional proposals for stimulating the economy?

Basic Needs Survey (Sirgy & Samli, 1995: 184)
Q. *How do you feel about* the income you and your household have?

Social Indicators Research (Andrews & Withey, 1976: 87)
Q. *How do you feel about* your life as a whole?

Despite the prevalence of feeling questions in survey and interview research, some scholars (e.g. Fink, 2008; Schwalbe & Wolkomir, 2001) advise that formulations such as 'How do you feel about ...', because they enter personal and emotionally-charged territory, may potentially offend or put off some interviewees and should therefore be avoided or used with caution. This warning has been extended especially to interviews with men, based on the cultural ('Western' and 'Anglocentric') and gendered assumptions that men tend to be uncomfortable discussing feelings. Schwalbe and Wolkomir (2001: 211) suggest framing the question as 'How *did* you feel *when* ...' rather than 'How *do* you feel *about* ...' is a more effective elicitation technique because, 'It may be easier for many men to report emotion that arose in the past than to give a report that implies an "emotional self" in the present'. Offering additional advice on conducting emotion-related research with men, they recommend researchers ask about *thoughts* before delving into *feelings* to avoid threats to participants' masculinity:

> Ask about thoughts, not feelings, then work back to feelings. Asking, 'How do you feel about ____ ?' can pose a threat to the masculine self. Asking, 'What do you think about ____ ?' can, in contrast, seem to offer an opportunity to signify masculinity. But then, as the subject expounds, the interviewer must be ready to probe: 'It sounds like ____ makes you feel a bit [sad/angry/embarrassed/happy/etc.].' Once men feel that they have justified themselves – by saying what they think – they may be more willing to talk about what they feel. (Schwalbe & Wolkomir, 2001: 211)

While acknowledging these admonitions against producing potentially face-threatening feeling questions, we must recognize that just because the interviewer asks interviewees how they *feel* about something does not necessarily make emotionality or talk of feelings the default response. Some scholars (e.g. Patton, 1990) have pointed out questions such as 'how did you feel about ...?' can be treated by recipients as general opinion, stance, value solicitation or 'perspective display' (Maynard, 1991) requests. Similarly, asking someone what they *think* about a topic neither guarantees a mental claim nor precludes an emotion-indexing response. As I will also show, questions that are *not* formatted as 'feeling questions' can and frequently do produce accounts of feelings and emotionality. This again offers an important reminder that advancing (or following) methodological prescriptions apart from contextual and empirical analysis ignores how the research interview functions as a social practice (Talmy, 2010b).

Representing and invoking stances

Defining overlapping terms and constructs is an ever-present challenge for the researcher, but it is an essential component of all scholarly inquiry and its presentation. In the interdisciplinary literature on interviewing it is unclear, for example, just how *opinions, views, stances, sentiments,* etc., differ from one another, as they tend to be treated interchangeably (e.g. Gubrium *et al.*, 2012; van den Berg *et al.*, 2003):

> Both Clayman (1987) and Greatbatch (1988) document a predominant turn-taking organization in which interviewers refrain from stating

opinions, and ask questions of interviewees who, in answering, are
allowed long turns in which to express their views. (Maynard, 1988:
324–325)

One of the key issues addressed by analysts stems from the fact that, in
their role as questioners, interviewers are required to avoid stating their
views or opinions on the news. Rather, their task is to elicit the stance,
opinion, or account of the one being questioned, but to do so at least
technically without bias or prejudice. (Hutchby, 2005: 444)

Though the two preceding quotes concern turntaking activities within broadcast news interviews, they are indicative of 'default' or naturalized theories of interview prevalent in other interview contexts such as autobiographical or narrative research. For present purposes, I consider opinions, perspective displays, accounts, and the like, as stancetaking actions (see Chapter 3) by the interviewee in response to interviewer prompts inviting stories and commentary on specific topics, events, people and so on. I also note that opinions and other presumably 'cognitively'-driven responses can be constructed as emotional by using emotion labels ('What really *irritates* me is ...'), by embodied emotion displays (e.g. smiling, frowning, crying, shaking) and by prosodic or vocal cues (e.g. changes in pitch or volume, response cries such as 'wow' or 'gosh').

As previous chapters have demonstrated, speakers need not always use explicit resources to represent emotion. The auspices under which people are recruited for the research project (e.g. as members of particular social categories; as speakers with memorable and tellworthy histories and narratives) can frame and 'expect' emotionally charged tellings. Speakers can also do emotion-implicative work through topic selection (e.g. discrimination, trauma, complaints) and implying cause and effect. For example, a research participant's utterance such as, 'I was arrested the first time I tried to escape my country' is indexing emotionality through the topic, its memorability for the teller, its tellability and its accompanying prosodic cues – even without labeling specific emotions. Based on commonsense understandings, the recipient (i.e. the interviewer) can reasonably assume that being arrested is an unwanted and traumatic experience. Likewise, talking about 'escape' implies the existence of something dangerous or fear-inducing that the speaker was trying to avoid. Claims of escaping from one's *country* further characterize the scale of the danger as so severe that the speaker must flee their homeland (and abandon family, friends, birthplace, property, etc.). Flat affect (i.e. *'non-emotionality'*) can also be an important stancetaking device by its contrast with any surrounding emotional talk. For example, in complaints and troubles tellings, speakers may intensify the characterization of someone else's emotional outburst as irrational by representing and performing their own contrastively self-controlled and calmer or emotionally-neutral response (e.g.

Chapter 3, Excerpt 3.1a). All of the interviewees in my corpus produced stories about mistreatment by others. In fact, this was an unanticipated but defining feature of much of my study data.

Feeling questions in face-to-face interviews

Feeling questions can be found across many interview research contexts, as shown in the following worked examples from the literature. Excerpt 5.3 comes from Margaret Wetherell's (2003) study of race talk in New Zealand. In her analysis, Wetherell focused on how interviews with majority *Pakeha* (Caucasian) group members made visible speakers' prejudices toward the minority Maori people. In this sequence, the interviewer (I) is asking a Pakeha New Zealander (R) about personal responses to the social tensions surrounding the revival of the indigenous Maori culture and language. The interviewer uses questions with both 'think' and 'feel' to successfully elicit a topic-relevant response from the interviewee:

(Excerpt 5.3). Adapted from Wetherell (2003: 16)

```
01  I:   Do you think in general that's been (0.4) constructive or
02       (1.4) what do you feel about the way things are going
03       (0.2) on that front? (2.0)
04  R:   I think they'll end up having Maori w:ars if they carry on
05       the way [they have I mean no it'll be a=
06  I:           [((laugh))
07  R    =Pakeha war
08  I:   Yes
09  R:   U::hm (1.6) they're ma:king New Zealand a racist cu-
10       country uhm but ya'know you usually feel (.) think that
11       racism is uhm (1.4) putting th- putting ([.)=
12  I:                                            [Yes
13  R:   =the darker people down
14  R:   [but really they're doing it (.) the other way around
15  I:   [( )
16  I:   A sort [or reverse [racism
17  R:          [I feel     [yes
18  I:   Yeah
```

Another example, Excerpt 5.4, from Holstein and Gubrium (1995), comes from an open-ended interview with an adult daughter who is the primary caregiver of her mother suffering from dementia. In this context, the interviewer is asking the daughter how she manages taking care of her mother while working part-time and sharing the household with her husband and two sons. The interviewer (I) begins by asking a *feeling* question that invites the daughter (R) to talk about the psychological (i.e. emotional and mental) impact of the present circumstances:

(Excerpt 5.4). Adapted from Holstein and Gubrium (1995: 35)

```
01  I:   How do you feel about it in your situation?
02  R:   Oh, I don't know. Sometimes I think I'm being a bit
03       selfish because I gripe about having to keep an eye on
04       Mother all the time. If you let down your guard, she
05       wanders off into the backyard or goes out the door and
06       down the street. That's no fun when your hubby wants your
07       attention too. Norm works the second shift and he's home
08       during the day a lot. I manage to get in a few hours of
09       work, but he doesn't like it. I have pretty mixed feelings
10       about it.
11  I:   What do you mean?
12  R:   Well, I'd say as a daughter, I feel pretty guilty about
13       how I feel sometimes. It can get pretty bad, like wishing
14       that Mother were just gone, you know what I mean? She's
15       been a wonderful mother and I love her very much, but if
16       you ask me how I feel as a wife and mother, that's another
17       matter.
```

In Excerpts 5.3 and 5.4, the interviewers' feeling questions were designed to elicit interviewees' talk about their personal views and opinions. The questions were all successful in eliciting further talk and commentary that described interviewees' feelings and mental processes in relation to these topics. I now consider in more detail the feeling questions in these excerpts and the talk that is produced in response to them.

In the segment represented in Excerpt 5.3, immediately noticeable is the alternation between question types as well as talk of *thinking* and *feeling*. In lines 1–2, the interviewer makes use of both 'think' and 'feel' through a split or alternative question structure (Clayman & Heritage, 2002; Sidnell, 2010b). The interviewer's incremental and hesitant production of the question creates slots for the interviewee to collaboratively complete the utterance. Produced as a *thought*-prefaced alternative *yes-no* question ('Do you think in general that's been (0.4) constructive or ...'), the interviewee is invited to produce a relevant response. The space after 'do you think in general that's been (0.4)' projects a relevant transition relevant place (TRP) by means of a pause and a *designedly incomplete utterance* (Koshik, 2002) for the interviewee to insert a descriptive term. Sacks *et al.* (1974: 715) observe that if a pause is an intra-turn silence, it is *not* a TRP and 'not to be talked in by others'. However, intra-turn silences and pre-completion positions (Schegloff, 1996) may be equally available for opportunistic completion (Lerner, 1996: 261).

Continuing in line 2 of Excerpt 5.3, after a potential transition-relevant pause where the interviewee could offer a response, the interviewer repairs the preceding utterance by reformulating the subjective state/opinion marker from 'think' to 'feel' (line 2: 'what do you feel about ...'). By reformulating the previous closed question to an open, 'feeling' question type, the interviewer recalibrates the question sequence to invite a broader and more personal or subjective response, which the interviewee subsequently provides.

At first glance, the interviewer (line 2: 'what do you feel about ...') appears to be inviting the interviewee to frame a response to cultural politics in New Zealand by expressing an affective stance. However, taking advantage of the potential interpretive ambiguity of this question, the interviewee responds to the interviewer's question not with an emotion-related response (e.g. 'I feel ...') but with a *thought*-prefaced opinion ('I think ...'). In contrast, in line 10, the interviewee begins with a generalized feeling claim and then self-repairs it to 'think' ('you usually feel (.) think that ...'). In practice, both *thought* and *feeling* formulations can function to elicit the interviewee's subjective opinion or perspective. A closer inspection of this segment makes visible a parallelism between the interviewer's *think/feel* questions (lines 1–2) and the interviewee's *think/feel* answers (lines 4, 10, 17). This further underscores the ways in which interview questions and responses are co-constructed as interactants work toward achieving an intersubjective understanding of the goals of the interview activity and the meaning(s) of the described events.

Feeling and thought questions and the responses they occasion appear to be used similarly in the interview segment (e.g. to solicit subjective responses) shown in Excerpt 5.3, but their location in the talk suggests subtle differences in their function. Though these are only brief excerpts from longer sequences, there is some indication here that *thought* formulations are used by this interviewee when representing more specific opinions and *feeling* formulations are used for more general or less certain claims. For example, in line 1, 'Do you think ...' is used by the interviewer to elicit a general opinion about specific features of the Maori movement (i.e. whether it has been 'constructive' or otherwise). When the interviewer reformulates the question, 'what do you feel about ...' is used to elicit an open-ended response. In the following turn (line 4), the interviewee uses 'I think ...' to offer a specific opinion about potential Maori wars. In line 10, although the interviewee begins with 'you usually feel ...', it is quickly reformulated to 'think ...' to preface a specific opinion statement (i.e. that racism is about putting the darker people down). The speaker then negates this by a contrastive reality claim that the 'darker people' are actually putting whites down.

In Excerpt 5.3, the interviewee's use of 'I feel' in line 17 (note that the speaker shifts from the generic 'you feel' to a more personal, opinion claim 'I feel') cannot be seen as a response to the interviewer's formulation of 'reverse racism' (line 16), as it is produced in overlap. It may therefore be a mitigation move, to downgrade the potentially sensitive claims that Maoris are racist. In following, the first part of the interviewer's utterance in line 16 ('A sort') claims a weaker epistemic stance begun by that description. Thus, although both *thought* and *feeling* questions may work in similar ways to elicit subjective opinions and perspective displays, they may be used to convey different strengths of epistemic authority and certainty. Attending to questioning and response patterns using *think/feel* may be a productive area for future research examining interviewing as a social and interactional practice.

Thought-feeling alternation can also be seen in Excerpt 5.4, after the interviewer presents a feeling question to the interviewee. In the published transcript, the researchers have not provided interactional details (e.g. pauses, restarts, prosodic cues), but there are still a number of subtle insights that can be gathered. The interviewer here makes use of a feeling question to elicit a response from the interviewee (line 1: 'How do you feel about it in your situation?'). The interviewee then prefaces her response with a change of state token ('Oh') and an epistemic uncertainty marker ('I don't know'), orienting to the topic as sensitive as well as displaying her cognitive processing (Heritage, 2005a) of the question and her response. Heritage (1998: 286) observes that *oh*-prefaced responses are common in the second position of an adjacency pair and can 'indicate that the inquiry being responded to is problematic as to its relevance, presuppositions, or context' or can otherwise show the interviewees' reluctance to advance the conversational topic.

As I discussed in Chapter 4, epistemic uncertainty markers such as 'I don't know' and 'I dunno' are also frequently produced in response to questioning; because they are resources for managing sensitive topics and possible negative interpretations of responses, they can be used to hedge the speaker's opinion and even resist the force of the question. The interviewee's use of 'I don't know' here offers a stake inoculation (Potter, 1996) (i.e. that she has not given much thought to her own feelings; that she does not want to sound selfish) that precedes her account of 'griping' (line 3) about having to watch her mother while neglecting her husband.

Similar to Excerpt 5.3, the interviewee in Excerpt 5.4 uses 'think', rather than 'feel', in her response to the interviewer's question (line 2: 'Sometimes I think I'm being a bit selfish ...'). In Excerpt 5.3, the speaker used *thought*-prefaced responses before describing a general opinion or stance. In Excerpt 5.4, although the speaker is talking about herself and her actions (and the actions of others), the rhetorical structure of her account (e.g. coordinate and subordinate conjunctions, cause-effect relations), the use of the generic 'you' and the listing of the facts work together as an objective account (Chapter 3) to highlight the conditions of her situation, imply its emotionality and assess and give an account of her actions and their consequences rather than describing how she personally feels (which was earlier set up by her use of the stake inoculation device in line 2).

In lines 9–10, after describing her situation in hearably objective terms, the interviewee formulates the upshot of her account ('I have pretty mixed feelings about it'), bringing her response to a possible turn completion (similar to Excerpt 5.3, line 17). Summary assessments and utterances that present an 'emotional take on what has preceded' (Schegloff, 2007: 186) have been shown to function as moves by the speaker to close a sequence or the topic-in-progress. Again, although the interviewee formulates her summary in general emotion-indexing terms ('mixed feelings'), she does not explicitly label any of those feelings – which, by not labeling them, further indexes them as dilemmatic and difficult to specify.

Instead of accepting the interviewee's response as adequate, the interviewer orients to the problem of ambiguity or the specificity of her response (see also Schegloff, 2000, on the problem of granularity) and produces a next turn repair initiator (NTRI) in line 11 ('What do you mean?'). Launching a repair, the interviewee begins with a tentative *well*-preface. When following questions and NTRIs, *well*-prefaced turns indicate to the recipient that a non-straightforward response (projecting topical or interactional trouble) is forthcoming (Schegloff & Lerner, 2009). After her *well*-preface, the interviewee then formulates her response with 'feel', recycling this particular lexical item from the interviewer's original question in line 1 (a tying move that shows the speaker's understanding of the topic focus) to now give a personal (by consistently using the first-person pronoun) and explicitly emotion-indexing response (lines 12–13: 'I feel pretty guilty about how I feel sometimes').

Relatedly, in terms of categorial consequence, Excerpt 5.4 also indicates that feeling questions such as 'How do you feel about …' may occasion responses that make directly relevant a number of membership categories and their category-bound emotions. In lines 12–17, the interviewee invokes the categories of *daughter*, *wife* and *mother*, and the category-bound obligations and differential emotions that attach to those membership categories. For example, 'guilt' and 'love' are bound to the category of daughter, but the categories of *mother* and *wife* occasion different yet unnamed emotions. In not naming those emotions, the interviewee makes hearable the dilemmatic nature of her situation and the contrast between her caregiver identity in the mother-daughter relationship and that as a wife and mother who is possibly neglecting her own family.

In this section, I briefly reexamined data excerpts from the published literature to consider how interviewer questioning sequences may occasion particular emotion-implicative responses from interviewees. Though the original published analyses did not examine in detail the question sequences or emotionality, reanalysis offers new insights for understanding interviewing as a social and affective practice. This suggests that being transparent about the activity of data generation and making data transcripts available for others to analyze should be more widely encouraged – and practiced (see also Goodwin, 2012; Wästerfors *et al.*, 2014). Wetherell (2003: 26), for example, welcomes reanalysis, commenting, 'One of the most intriguing things is having one's own discourse analyzed.'

Feeling Question Sequences

Turning now to my L2 data, feeling questions were found to elicit and directly lead to emotional responses and descriptions from the research participants. There is also evidence that the interviewer invited emotionality when it was not immediately forthcoming, and interviewees even pursued emotive involvement from the interviewer when it was missing. Before I continue with the analysis, I must acknowledge how affectively and interpersonally powerful these data are within the context of the interactional history between the interviewer and interviewee as well as in relation to the speakers' sociolinguistic trajectories. As the following data excerpts indicate, these are highly personal, morally implicative and affect-laden admissions (e.g. of abuse, psychological turmoil), not casual or neutral tellings. Because this material is collaboratively and contextually constructed, it necessitates an analysis that foregrounds *how* the emotionality and its interpersonal impact are built into the production and reception of this material by both interviewer and interviewee.

'Did you feel better?'

Excerpt 5.5 is from an interview with Trang (T). Leading up to this particular segment, Trang told the interviewer (M) a story about his recent experience returning to Cambodia and Vietnam to visit his father and other relatives. Trang often brought up the topic of the emotional, mental and even physical abuse he received from his father and other authority figures and institutions (e.g. police, soldiers, lawyers, banks, classrooms), and this became a recurrent theme throughout much of his talk within and outside the interviews. This particular segment was located at the end of a telling where Trang describes how he finally confronted his father about the continued abuse. After the confrontation, he reported that his father refused to speak to him for a week.

(Excerpt 5.5). Trang: 'I feel better'

```
01        T:   suddenly I realize I don't want ((him)) to
02             mistreat ((me)) like that. so I told him.
03             a whole week he got mad at me. wouldn't talk to
04             me. heh heh
05    →   M:   did you feel better?
06        T:   I feel better.
07    →   M:   I mean after telling him.
08        T:   I feel relieved. you know I got it off my chest
09             for a change. for a:ll 25 years later. I become a
10             man now. I'm not a boy anymore. you cannot talk
11             to me like that. heh heh
```

In his description of events in first position, Trang makes use of contrasting *objective* and *subjective* stances (see Chapter 3) to categorize *father* and *son* in terms of the (im)morality and (ir)rationality of their respective mental states (e.g. attitudes, dispositions) and actions. He characterizes his conscious (i.e. rational) psychological realization and decision to act against mistreatment. In contrast, he describes his father's emotion-driven response whereby he got 'mad' (rather than 'sad', 'ashamed', etc.) and would not talk to Trang for 'a whole week' – an extreme case formulation (Pomerantz, 1986) that adds descriptive weight to Trang's description of his father as unstable and unrepentant.

In relation to these serious matters, Trang's laughter in lines 4 and 11 represents a typical display of resistance to troubles talk. As I have mentioned, tellers often insert laughter to indicate to their listeners that they are coping and bravely dealing with their troubles instead of overreacting or taking them too seriously. Recipients of troubles talk, however, generally avoid producing or joining in the laughter; instead, they tend to treat the trouble seriously to exhibit 'trouble receptiveness' (Jefferson, 1984: 351). As shown in this excerpt, although Trang initiates the laughter, thereby puncturing the 'abusive' and heavy affective frame of this talk, the interviewer takes a serious and empathic stance toward these represented events by not laughing along or otherwise treating the story lightheartedly. The interviewer then displays concern with the emotional upshot of these events for Trang by means of a feeling question (line 5: 'did you feel better?'). This question trades on psychological inferences by leading with the presumption that after confronting someone about abuse or mistreatment, one should normatively be expected to respond with positive feelings (e.g. relief, satisfaction). Moreover, the grammatical construction of the question prefers a confirmatory response (Heritage, 2010), and Trang confirms that confronting his father did lead to a positive psychological outcome (line 6: 'I feel better').

Because the interviewer's question inquired about Trang's emotional state in the past, Trang's response in the grammatical *present* tense makes it unclear whether he is talking about how he feels *now* or how he felt *then*. This ambiguity touches off a repair sequence (line 6) where the interviewer orients to the trouble source (in first position), not with a repetition or explicit attention to the grammatical past tense (e.g. 'I mean, did you feel better?') but by respecifying his question in relation to the temporal sequence of events in the storyworld (line 7: 'I mean after telling him'). As a repair initiator in second position, the interviewer's question occasions Trang's repair (rather than a repetition) of 'I feel better' (line 6) to 'I feel relieved' (line 8) in third position and results in an extended account. This repair also involves an emotion state formulation in the present tense ('I feel relieved') instead of the expected past tense 'I felt better' or 'I felt relieved'. This may be attributable to Trang's sometimes idiosyncratic control of English past tense (e.g. he produces 'got' in lines 3 and 8 but not 'realized' or 'became' in lines 1 and 9). In terms of emotionality, 'relieved' reformulates 'better' into a more explicit and personal affective state description, a type of reformulation or lexical substitution also commonly found in therapeutic discourse (e.g. Bercelli *et al.*, 2008; Rae, 2008; see also Chapter 7 for a more detailed discussion and analysis of emotion reformulations).

'And how does that feel?'

Another example of an interviewer-initiated feeling question in these data comes from an interview with John, where he constructs a metaphorical description of himself as 'split in pieces' from being pulled back and forth between his various identities (e.g. *Chinese, gay, straight*). Like Excerpt 5.5, here the interviewee produces talk of serious, personal turmoil in the past and characterizes its heavy affective and psychological weight carried into the present (see also Prior, 2011c).

(Excerpt 5.6). John: 'I split myself in pieces'

```
01      J:    so if the wind blow me a gay direction, >I can go
02            to °gay°. but if it blow me to a straight
03            direction< °I can go straight direction.°
04      M:    °hm°
05      J:    so (.) I can yeah (.) go to (.) yeah (.)
06            basically (.) I split myself in pieces.
07            (0.7)
08  →   M:    UH: (.) and how does that feel?
09            (1.4)
10      J:    it not good sometime bu:t, (2.0) like I say (0.8)
11            I have to live with all these lie and it- (.) it
12            feel (.) not too good.
13            (1.3)
14            but then, (.) hopefully it not be continue going
15            °but- (.) I-° (.) HOPEfully it not continue going
16            but I don't know when
17            [(.) i ]t could stop (.) unless I tell (.)
18      M:    [oh: ]
19      J:    come out (.)and tell everybody. I still don't
20            have the nerve.
```

As John formulates an emotional description and psychological diagnosis of himself as 'split in pieces' (line 6), his pauses and hesitant production of his utterance (lines 5–6) display his situated 'thought' process (Heritage, 2005a)

– showing his work to organize and summarize the upshot of this affect-laden talk for the interviewer. The interviewer responds to John's psychological formulation at a TRP, and treats it as emotion-implicative and characterizable in affective terms (line 8: 'UH: (.) and how does that feel?'), based on the assumption that the precipitating conditions and state of being 'split in pieces' result in a tell-worthy emotional account.

By formulating the upshot of John's talk as a description of feelings toward events, the interviewer is building an assumption into this talk (i.e. that one would likely have a 'feeling' about such things). The interviewer's *uh*-prefaced question is produced here with many of the same features (e.g. increased volume, sound stretch, pause) found in the use of other possible disjunctive topic shift markers such as 'anyway' and 'oh' (see also Drew, 1997: 76). However, by continuing with 'and' and using the demonstrative 'that' as a deictic/indexical (line 8: 'and how does that feel?'), the interviewer links the present topic of talk to John's previous mention of identity troubles – thereby furthering the previous topic rather than starting a new one.[1] In Jefferson's terms, the interviewer's work here 'potentiates further talk by the troubles recipient' (Jefferson, 1984: 202).

An examination of John's extended response to the interviewer's 'feeling' question highlights several matters central to an understanding of these data and their generation. First, John aligns with the affective tilt of the interviewer's question by formulating his responses as emotion-implicative (line 10: 'it not good'; lines 11–12: 'it feel (.) not too good'). This maintains across the turns a shared focus on the personal and emotional consequences of John's experience. Second, although John could have formulated his response to the interviewer's feeling question (line 8: 'how does that feel?') along the lines of, 'I feel not good sometimes' or 'I don't know when I could stop', his consistent use of deictic reference displays his recognition that they both share the same topic focus; that is, John responds with a consistent use of 'it' to refer to the 'emotional object' (i.e. the cause of the imputed emotion or the object toward which the emotion is directed) specified by the interviewer's question:

Line 8:	**M:**	**how does that feel?**
Line 10:	**J:**	it not good sometime
Lines 11–12:		it feel (.) not too good
Line 14:		hopefully it not be continue going
Line 15:		HOPEfully it not continue going
Lines 16–17:		I don't know when (.) it could stop

Eliciting Feelings 119

In contrast, John consistently uses the first person pronoun to describe his *actions* (or inactions), not his *feelings* or *desires*:

Line 10:   Like ⟦I⟧ say

Line 11:   ⟦I⟧ have to live with all these lie

Line 16:   ⟦I⟧ don't know when

Line 17:   unless ⟦I⟧ tell

Lines 19–20:   ⟦I⟧ still don't have the nerve*

(*Although *'have the nerve'* indexes emotionality, it also projects an inability to carry out an action)

Another illustration of the interviewer's question shaping the interviewee's response is found in a comparison of Excerpt 5.5 (Trang) with Excerpt 5.6 (John). A similar consistency between the form of the feeling question and the form of the feeling response is immediately apparent (see also Chapter 6 on formulations).

Line 5:   M: did ⟦you feel⟧ better?

Line 6:   T: ⟦I feel⟧ better

Line 8:   ⟦I feel⟧ relieved

Lines 8–9:   ⟦I got it⟧ off my chest for a change

Lines 9–10:   ⟦I become⟧ a man now

Lines 10–11:   You cannot ⟦talk to me⟧ like that

Just as the interviewer's use of 'that' in Excerpt 5.6 occasioned the interviewee using 'it' in his response, here, responding to 'did you feel better?' (line 5), the interviewee recycles part of the interviewer's question ('feel') and produces the first-person pronoun, thereby keeping consistent the emotional subject (i.e. the person experiencing the putative emotions). Similarly, in Excerpt 5.6, John uses the first-person pronoun to highlight his individuality within these emotional events. Paying analytic attention to this discursive work underscores the point that these linguistic devices are just some of the many semiotic resources that interviewees marshal to produce such devastating accounts of emotional and psychological trauma.

Part 2. Emotion-Implicative Questions

'Was it hard for you sometimes?'

Not all interviewer-initiated question sequences soliciting emotion talk in my L2 interview corpus used descriptive terms such as 'feel' and 'feelings'. Emotionality was also brought out by emotion-implicative assessments and questions. An analysis of an interview with Jack (J), an immigrant from Cambodia, provides an illustrative case of the interviewer (M) soliciting talk of experience, negative experience in particular.

Leading up to this excerpt (5.7a), Jack spoke about some of his difficulties (e.g. learning English, being picked on by 'American' and 'Asian' students) in high school in the Midwest. Upon the interviewer and interviewee discovering they had both lived in the same Midwestern city, they joked about the short summers and cold winters (occasioning the laughter in lines 1 and 3). After the shared laughter, the interviewer abruptly transitions to a more serious tone and initiates a new sequence:

(Excerpt 5.7a). Jack: 'Was it hard for you sometimes'

```
01        M:  heh heh heh
02            (1.0)
03        J:  heh
04            (0.6)
05        M:  ((sniff))
06            (0.3)
07        M:  yea::h
08            (2.0)
09   →        was it hard for you sometimes to talk to
10   →        American people?
11        J:  °oh yeah lot of time yeah. uh (.) I don't have
12            (.0) I don't have (any:- (.) any more) friend
13            with American people so I- (.) my English is
14            bad (that time).°=
15   →    M:  =>did you have< (.) you had no friends?
16            (0.5)
17        J:  °no friend at all that time°=
18   →    M:  [only the pastor?]
19        J:  [only only       ] Lao. Lao people.
20        M:  oh
21            (0.8)
22        J:  yeah (.)°Lao people are my friend.°
```

The laughter (lines 1 and 3), gaps (lines 2, 4, 6, 8), and vowel stretch (line 7: 'yea::h') work together to jointly initiate closure of the current sequence

(Chafe, 2007; Glenn, 1992; Holt, 1999, 2010; Liddicoat, 2011). After a two-second silence in line 8, the interviewer initiates a new topic sequence with a question to Jack inquiring about past language troubles (lines 9–10: 'was it hard for you sometimes to talk to American people?'). Although the interviewer's question is not requesting talk of a specific episode, the lexical stress on 'hard' and 'talk' (instead of on 'was', 'sometimes', 'American people', etc.) makes relevant the interviewer's interest in matters involving communicative difficulty. Moreover, this positive polarity or grammatically affirmative question (Quirk et al., 1985: 808), along with the quantificational adverbial (Binnick, 2012) 'sometimes' (which denotes even a small relative frequency), expects or 'prefers' a confirmatory answer from the interviewee (i.e. 'yes it was hard').

Responding with the second pair part to the interviewer's question, Jack offers an emphatic agreement with an *oh*-prefaced epistemic marker in line 11 ('°oh yeah lot of time yeah°'). This *oh*-preface serves as a recognizable display of remembering and an epistemic claim to personal experience similar to that found across previous excerpts. Instead of simply offering a confirmation (e.g. 'yes', 'yeah', 'uhuh', 'that's right'), Jack continues with a strong agreement through repetition and word stress on 'yeah' (line 11), upgrades the interviewer's time formulation from 'sometimes' to 'lot of time', and gives an account that explains why it was hard (e.g., he didn't have American friends, his English was bad). After Jack describes his English as 'bad' at that time, the interviewer immediately follows up with a question (line 15) that orients to Jack's extreme claim ('you had no friends?') and the corresponding *intensity* of his experiences, not his language skills as pursued previously.

This segment gives further evidence of some of the ways that the formulation of interviewer questions may structurally prefer particular interviewee responses. In line 15 ('did you have'), the interviewer begins his utterance with a positive polarity repair initiator favoring a 'yes' response and then abruptly repairs it to a negatively polarized question ('you had no friends?') that favors a 'no' response (Heritage, 2010). Following the conversational preference for agreement, Jack responds to the interviewer's question with an upgraded reformulation by claiming that his lack of 'any' friends (lines 12–13) extended from having no American friends to having no friends at all (line 17: '°no friend at all that time°'). Orienting again to the extreme nature of the claim that Jack had 'no friend at all', the interviewer initiates a repair (line 18: 'only the pastor?') that challenges Jack's version of events. In overlap, Jack self-repairs by downgrading his claim of having 'no friend at all' to state he only had Lao[2] friends (members of another stigmatized Southeast Asian immigrant group at his school). As this shows, interviewer pursuits and responses strongly influence the shape of interviewees' talk and the details they provide and revise.

'Is it easy?'

Later in the interaction (Excerpt 5.7b), the interviewer contrasts Jack's talk about the past with the present (lines 23–24):

(Excerpt 5.7b). Jack: 'Is it easy for you?'

```
23  →  M:  how about now? is it (.) easy for you to talk
24  →      to American people or,
25     J:  (now-)now it's okay
26     M:  now no problem?
27         (1.0)
28     J:  °yeah I s-sometime I have problem too but (.)
29         it's ok I can (.) let them explain and I can
30         understand.°
31         (0.7)
32     M:  oh
33     J:  $°but before when I- (.) they explain I still
34         don't understand°.$
35     M:  oh really?
           ((S tells a story about how he learned swear
           words in school and became angry when he
           learned what other students were calling him))
```

In an analysis of Excerpt 5.7a (a sequence focused on Jack's *past* experiences), it was found that the interviewer's questions made use of the conversational preference for agreement to elicit confirmatory responses. Each of those responses confirmed that the interviewee had problems interacting with others. In Excerpt 5.7b (a sequence focused on Jack's *present* experiences) the interviewer's question in lines 23–24 ('how about now? is it (.) easy for you to talk to American people or,'), produced with a continuing intonation contour, creates an alternative or split question (Clayman & Heritage, 2002). The first part of the question invites agreement (i.e. that it is *easy* for Jack now to talk to American people). The contrasting response projected by the disjunctive marker 'or' (i.e. that Jack still experiences some difficulties talking with American people) leaves room for Jack to contradict the propositional content of the interviewer's question. Instead of responding with a claim of difficulty, in line 25 the interviewee aligns with the interviewer's initial time description ('now') and the proposition that communicating with Americans has become easier for Jack: 'now it's okay'.

Although Jack has confirmed that he has no problems talking with American people, the interviewer does not treat this response as sufficient by offering an acknowledgement token (e.g. 'I see', 'Okay', 'Oh').[3] Instead, in his turn as a third position repair, he responds with a negative polarity question (line 26: 'now no problem?') that favors, as before, an aligning negative response (e.g. 'no problem'). The interviewer's rising intonation and interrogative structure possibly indicate a request for clarification or elaboration, a pursuit of 'problem' talk, or even an invitation to reformulate (see Chapter 6) Jack's description of 'okay' into more explicit terms (i.e. as 'problem') to occasion a complaint story. The interviewer's code-switch to a simplified register[4] (line 26: 'now no problem?'), by reducing the focus of the question to time and the matter of 'no problem', also functions as a repair or a rephrasing of Jack's prior turn. Rather than providing a negative response, after a one-second pause (potentially an embodied display of thinking), Jack responds with '°yeah I s-sometime I have problem too but (.) it's ok I can (.) let them explain and I can understand°' (lines 28–30). Thus, Jack appears to orient to this as a dispreferred response as he provides an account to explain that even when he does experience problems he has effective strategies to work around them (compare with Excerpt 5.9).

Further evidence of the interviewer's agenda to elicit 'problem' talk is found in the next line when he replies to Jack with a minimal response (line 32: 'oh') made up of a simple news receipt (Heritage, 1984; Wilkinson & Kitzinger, 2006) rather than an expression of surprise. In contrast, when Jack produces a laughter-filled comment about some trouble in the past, the interviewer's response becomes a more emphatic expression of surprise (line 34: 'oh really?'). As multi-functional devices, *oh*-prefaced responses can indicate surprise by upgrading the change of state display (Liddicoat, 2011). Wilkinson and Kitzinger (2006) found that *oh*-prefaced surprise tokens can also display affect (particularly through prosody) as well as affiliation toward the speaker.

In retrospect, I cannot say whether I was intentionally seeking to elicit more intense tellings from Jack. My questions and responses do appear to indicate that was indeed happening. Jack also had a tendency in his everyday conversations with others to produce utterances that veered away from the main topic of discussion. Although this suggested he sometimes had difficulty following the topic of talk, based on my observations of Jack in other settings I suspect he may have had some mild hearing loss. Another issue, as I have commented previously, is that Jack's talk was sometimes interspersed with flirtation and sexual innuendos, which I found humorous but sometimes uncomfortable and at odds with the goals of the interview project. For example, a few times he insisted on teaching me Khmer words that turned out to have sexual connotations.[5] He was later admonished by Bona and Trang who told him that it was not proper to teach me such words. It is possible, then, that producing more emphatic responses to his talk about language-related issues was a strategy I used to steer the conversation away from topics I found uncomfortable and to keep him on task with the interview activity.

'How do you deal with things like that?'

The following illustration of interviewer-elicited emotionality is from the middle of a second interview with Kim (K), an immigrant woman from Vietnam. The interview took place in the interviewer's (M) office. Excerpt 5.8 follows her previous talk about an angry and rude customer who complained about customer service and told Kim and another female co-worker that they should work in a bar (Chapter 3, Excerpt 3.1b). Immediately prior to this sequence, the interviewer was called away to the phone for a few minutes and has now returned:

(Excerpt 5.8). Kim: 'How do you deal with things like that?'

```
01        M:   ((M hangs up the phone and returns to his
02             chair))
03        K:   [do I talk too much?]
04        M:   [°testing.          ] ((checking the mic))
05             >no no no no no no no< no. testing. testing.
06             ((checking the mic))
07        K:   heh heh
08        M:   yeah I can hear it.
09             ((phone call. 12 minutes omitted))
10             umm (.) no but you said something (.) you said
11             (.) people- (.) because you have an accent,
12             because you're a non-native speaker=
13        K:   =mhm
14        M:   people can do that (.) or people do that or
15             something. I'm wondering, (3.4) as a nonnative
16             speaker (.) >whatever that means.< and having
17   →        an accent (.) >whatever that means.< how do
18   →        you deal with things like that
19             (2.5)
20   →        I mean **do you** (.) **get angry** or do you just say
21   →        "oh there's nothing I can do about i:t or-"
22        K:   I-I-I guess. it depends also on my mood of the
23             day.
24        M:   heh heh heh
25        K:   so sometime if you're in a good mood you
26             tolerate? and sometime (.) you cannot
27             tolerate. especially that (.) very insulting
28             the way he s- (.) you know that how he sound?
29        M:   mhm
30        K:   like- (.) "oh, you should (.) work in the
31             bar." and I look at him and I say, "an:: (.)
32             who are you? I mean (.) w-what do you think?
```

```
33              (.) that I'm deserve that and and the way you
34              speak like that(.) what category that you fit
35              in? You know are you some kind of a (.) a (.)
36              doctor? lawyer? teacher? or just a low class
37              (.) ↑spea↓ker that I have to pay attention
38              to."
39        M:   you said that to him?
40        K:   no, [I said that in my-my [mind, right?
41        M:        [Oh                    [oh
42        K:   that's what I'm thinking. if-if you insulting
43              me, in that way. I can insulted him also too
44              (.) but (.) I don't want to do that. if- I
45              don't want to level with him to begin with.
46        M:   °mhm°
```

I will focus attention on the segment beginning in line 10. The interviewer initiates a change in activity by means of an extended turn with a disjunctive preface (line 10: 'umm (.)'). In lines 10–15, by formulating Kim's previous talk of difficulties and mistreatment linked to her status as an L2 speaker, the interviewer directly invokes their shared interactional history and displays his understanding of the gist of her talk as well as the matters that he is treating as relevant to the present interview. Embedded within these formulations is the projection of an upcoming sequence. When asking questions, particularly on potentially sensitive topics, speakers often project their question through a pre-question sequence (Schegloff, 1980, 2007). These preliminary sequences signal to the listener that a particular sequence is coming and prepares them to respond to it. In questioning contexts, these pre-sequences are often initiated by a question announcement (e.g. 'Can I ask you a question?').

In lines 10–15, the interviewer projects a question sequence by producing a pre-sequence as well as *pre*-pre-sequence (Schegloff, 2007). First, through a pre-pre-sequence that reports what Kim said (through indirect represented speech), he is putting her talk 'on display' and treating it as accountable – thereby projecting that in the next step of this sequence he will make clear its relevance. Next, the interviewer produces a pre-question (line 15: 'I'm wondering,') followed by a long pause (potentially displaying his stance toward the projected question as delicate or requiring careful, deliberate wording; Lerner, 2013). The interviewer then begins an insertion (lines 15–17: 'as a nonnative speaker (.) >whatever that means< and having an accent (.) >whatever that means.<'), produced as a 'rush through' (Schegloff, 1982) that extends and holds his turn and shows Kim that he is leading up to a question. This also allows the interviewer to manage the delicate nature of the talk, which categorizes Kim as a 'nonnative' speaker of English. At the same time, he goes on record that these are labels open to challenge.

126 Emotion and Discourse in L2 Narrative Research

Having projected and prefaced his question, the interviewer now begins to formulate his question (produced as a four-turn sequence). This extended questioning sequence is represented below. I label these segments to show the progressivity of the interaction and how it incrementally occasions particular responses:

10	**M:**	umm (.)	New topic initiator
10–15	**M:**	no but you said something (.) you said (.) people- (.) because you have an accent, because you're a non-native speaker=	*Pre*-pre
	K:	=mhm	
	M:	people can do that (.) or people do that or something.	
15	**M:**	I'm wondering, (3.4)	Pre-question
15–16	**M:**	as a nonnative speaker (.) >whatever that means.< and having an accent (.) >whatever that means.<	Insertion
17–18	**M:**	how do you deal with things like that?	Question 1
19		(2.5)	Gap (non-response)
20–21	**M:**	I mean do you (.) get angry or do you just say "oh there's nothing I can do about i:t or-"	Question 2
22–23	**K:**	I-I-I guess. it depends also on my mood of the day.	Dispreferred response

Just as sequence organization is normative and thereby exercises a moral imperative, so is categorization-in-sequence (Baker, 2004; Jayyusi, 1984, 1991; Sacks, 1992; Schegloff, 1988). That is, by the interviewer asking a question that ascribes an identity category, the interviewee is called upon to respond as a member of that category – though a category which can also be resisted (Day, 1998; Prior, 2014; Talmy, 2009). Of all the potential categories or identities that Kim could have been called upon to speak as (e.g. *woman, mother, wife, store clerk, immigrant, Asian, Vietnamese, second language user, student*), she is identified here by the interviewer as a 'nonnative speaker' and a victim of mistreatment. 'How do you deal with things like that?' (lines 17–18) stands to elicit an answer to a wider problem (mistreatment in general) not just the rude customer incident; thus, Kim is asked to speak not just as a clerk, but also from a wider range of categories (i.e. 'mistreated person') of which *clerk, female, Asian,* etc. are all potential membership subcategories with their associated experiences and responses.

Because the formulation of the interviewer's question opens up the potential for Kim to respond from multiple identity categories, it also allows for a range of possible affective responses (e.g. anger, laughter, exasperation). After a 2.5-second silence, a possible TRP for Kim to respond to the question, the interviewer reformulates the question to invite a more specific response (lines 20–21: 'I mean do you (.) get angry or do you just say 'oh there's nothing I can do about i:t or-'). The *alternative question* structure narrows her response to comment on two courses of action: (a) an angry, escalating response that could potentially result in action (+agency), or (b) a quiet resignation that deescalates the situation and results in no action (-agency). The interviewer's use of direct represented talk/thought characterizes one possible reaction and invites Kim to respond with a description of her interior psychological world.

Kim's initial response to the interviewer's disjunctive question is produced with tentative agreement and hesitation (line 22: 'I-I-I guess'). Again, this is a dispreferred response in Gardner's (2004) four-turn model. Kim's following qualification of her response in lines 22–23 ('It depends also on my mood of the day.') resists the interviewer's candidate responses by offering up a third option based on mood. She now constructs her own emotionality (as *mood*) as something that is context-bound, situated and occasioned. Initiated by the interviewer, emotion talk in this segment becomes a resource for Kim to explain her actions and responses to events in a morally accountably way. Her account, 'it depends also on my mood of the day?' (lines 22–23) prefaces the conditions that generate particular transient emotion responses: i.e. a good mood allows her to tolerate abuse, but insulting behavior prevents her from being tolerant (lines 25–28). By qualifying her response in this way, Kim progresses the conversation by linking back to the previously shared story of the rude customer (see Chapter 3, Excerpt 3.1) as well as creating an emotional story preface (or a pre-expansion; Liddicoat, 2011; Sacks, 1992; Schegloff, 2007) that signals an upcoming story.

Through direct and indirect emotion-indexing terms and inferences (e.g. *anger, helplessness, mood, good mood, tolerate*), a story preface and attendant affective stances provide interactional cues that a telling of an emotional nature will follow. By accepting the request to produce a telling, Kim makes visible their respective situational and discourse identities (Zimmerman, 1998; e.g. Kim as interviewee and storyteller, and Matt as the interviewer and story recipient).

Examples from Other Studies

Question sequences soliciting talk of feelings and emotions can also be found in other interview-based studies. An example comes from Miller's

(2011) research interviews with adult immigrant learners of English. In Excerpt 5.9, Miller (I), is interviewing Peng (P), a Chinese-born immigrant to the US about his experiences. Leading up to this excerpt, Peng has produced a narrative about his trouble at the post office when the clerk did not understand the number of stamps Peng wanted to buy. Miller leads this sequence with a 'feeling' question:

(Excerpt 5.9). Adapted from Miller (2011: 6)

```
01  →   I:   Has- have y- has anyo:ne (.) made you feel
02  →        bad? (.) Have you had someone sometimes make
03  →        you feel bad because you couldn't speak or
04  →        you couldn't understand?=
05      P:   =>Yeah yeah yes.<
06      I:   What- what happened?
07           (1.0)
08      P:   Mmmmmmmm
09  →   I:   Did they say some[thing bad o::r]
10      P:                    [sssss          ]
11           U:::h i- if if uh very important, for
12           example, if my my my workplace.
13      I:   Yeah
14      P:   If uh really important, uh the cowork uh wri-
15           write the paper for me,
16      I:   Mmhmm
17      P:   And and use from dictionary.
18      I:   Mmhmm
19      P:   And sometimes- some the guy if just talking,
20           if I didn't understand, and they talking
21           again,
22      I:   Yeah
23      P:   But if not understand, uh, o(hh)h that's
24           okay, that's jus- that's okay.
25      I:   Yeah
26      P:   The the speak the other uh subject.
27      I:   Yeah.
28      P:   Yeah.
```

At the start of this sequence, the interviewer produces two positive polarity 'feeling' questions that take advantage of the conversational preference for agreement:

(1) Has- have y- has anyo:ne (.) made you feel bad?
(2) Have you had someone sometimes make you feel bad because you couldn't speak or you couldn't understand?

As might be expected, following preference norms, P responds with an agreement – produced here as an emphatic agreement (line 5: '=>Yeah yeah yes.<'). This is followed by a story solicitation (line 6). When P does not respond right away and produces an extended hesitation or search-marker (line 8: 'Mmmmmmmm'), the interviewer produces a question in line 9 that makes use of a negative emotion-implicative structure ('... something bad') as well as a split or alternative question structure ('... o::r') that expects a response with a negative emotion description. Although this example illustrates how the interviewer's questioning may lead the talk, it also shows that the interviewees may resist or misunderstand that agenda. In Excerpt 5.9, while P confirms that he has felt bad because of his language-related difficulties (line 5), in lines 11–26, his account avoids attaching blame to his coworkers. Instead, he describes the collaborative strategies they employ to resolve language difficulties (e.g. writing things down, repeating, changing the subject). It is also possible that he was addressing the matter of 'understanding' made relevant by the last part of the interviewer's question (lines 3–4: '... you couldn't speak or you couldn't understand?') rather than the emotionality of language difficulty suggested by the first part of the question.

Another example comes from Norton's (2000) study of immigrant women in Canada. In Excerpt 5.10, Norton is interviewing Eva, a Polish immigrant, about her feelings of oppression at work.

(Excerpt 5.10). Adapted from Norton (2000: 65)

```
01      E:   When I'm at the cash – when somebody goes for
02           summer – I take the order but the manager she
03           comes and she listens and then I feel like –
04           she's watching my mistakes and I already do
05           some mistakes when I say something.
06   →  B:   You mean that **makes it worse**? You think that
07   →       **makes you nervous**?
08      E:   Mm–hmm.
```

After Eva describes how her manager keeps a watchful eye on her when she works as cashier, Norton offers up two successive descriptions that formulate (i.e. summarize or give an interpretation; Drew, 2003; Heritage & Watson, 1979) the gist of Eva's story and assess its psychological import. In the first description, the interviewer employs a common formulation ('you mean...') to offer her candidate understanding of Eva's talk, while assessing its emotional upshot ('You mean that makes it worse?'). In the second, the interviewer formulates not the meaning of Eva's talk but her internal mental processes so that she can conduct a psychological self-diagnosis ('You think that makes you nervous?'). Drew (2003) also notes formulations may be lexically realized differently in various institutional settings. For example, he states that 'you mean' formulations are common in psychotherapy (see also

Peräkylä *et al.*, 2008) but 'what you're saying is' is found in call-in programs. Chapter 6 will take up (re)formulations in more detail.

I have argued here that the topics and content of the interview and interviewer-initiated questioning sequences (e.g. using questions such as 'How does that make you feel?') steer the interview toward emotion-related and psychological talk. However, 'How does that make you feel?', although preferring an emotional response, is an open-ended question that allows the interviewee to select from alternative descriptions. In contrast, formulations such as 'You mean that makes it worse?' and 'You think that makes you nervous?' – as positive polarity questions – make agreement the preferred response. Again, like Excerpt 5.9 and the data in my corpus, in Excerpt 5.10 the interviewer steers the topic and affective frame of the talk toward emotional and psychological matters.

Summary

This chapter investigated the role of interviewer question sequences in the solicitation and elicitation of emotional responses. I showed that questioning is a normative interview practice that enables the interviewer to establish the interview agenda and obtain talk on particular topics of interest to the research project. Focusing on two specific question sequence types, *feeling questions* and *emotion-implicative questions*, I examined how they can be used to steer the interview toward emotional matters. Feeling questions, because they seek subjective responses, may elicit both talk of opinions and emotionality. Emotion-implicative questions, while not necessarily requesting talk of feelings or emotions, make emotionality relevant by their use of assessment terms such as 'good,' 'bad', 'easy' and 'hard' – terms that invite interviewees to respond to or from a particular affective stance. Also, as I noted at the start of the chapter, just because a question seeks (or does not seek) an emotion-related response does not automatically mean it will (or will not) get it. These matters cannot be prespecified or predicted but are worked out in the interview activity itself. This again reinforces the need to attend to the analysis of empirical data – the questions that are produced and the responses that are occasioned.

The various sequences discussed throughout this and preceding chapters should not be thought of as rare or deviant cases. They are very common and can be found with little effort in interview-based studies that provide detailed transcripts. Unfortunately, emotion-eliciting question sequences may have received little attention in the L1 and L2 literature due in part to the absence of extended transcripts and the tendency of researchers to focus mainly upon interviewee responses and less upon interviewer prompts that were responsible for eliciting the tellings and shaping the surrounding material.

Finally, in this chapter I have described how interviewer questioning sequences expect and collaboratively produce interviewee responses. The central point here is that particular kinds of questions often occasion particular kinds of answers and other talk involving intense emotions and talk of emotional experiences (e.g. through preference organization, affective framing, repair, the use of emotion-implicative words). Interviewees orient to the normative nature of these sequences and the interview context by providing emotional responses relevant to the interviewer's questions. It further confirms that by attending to the influence of questioning sequences upon the content and trajectory of interview talk, we can better understand the interview as a dynamic site of social action and identity construction.

Notes

(1) See Sacks (1992) on related topic tying techniques.
(2) Jack reported that his family and several other immigrant families were sponsored by local church groups. Also, as some of the transcripts suggest, and substantiated in the interviews and social observations, the Cambodian and Vietnamese interviewees reported that because of the historical enmity between the two countries, they generally avoided interactions with members of the other group.
(3) It is possible that Jack may be hinting that he does have some problems in the present – as evidenced by his downgrade of M's description of 'easy' (line 23) to 'okay' (line 25).
(4) On code-switches and possible 'foreigner talk' or Pidgin in these interviews, see Chapter 4, endnote (2).
(5) Many of Jack's friends commented that his language (Khmer and English) was a little coarse or immature. According to them (and Jack, himself), even though he had lived in the United States for over 20 years, he was still 'very Cambodian' and 'FOB-ish'. FOB (Fresh Off the Boat) is a derogatory term often directed at Asian immigrants and refugees (though also used by immigrants, themselves). See Talmy (2009) for an insightful discussion on the social and discursive construction of this label in institutional settings.

6 (Re)Formulating Emotionality

> *Another complexity inherent in seeking the essence of the lived experience of participants is that our access to lived experience is primarily though language: the words we use to guide the participant and the words they use to respond.*
> (Seidman, 2013: 18)

> *... in general, as an interviewer you should acknowledge and if necessary try to verbalise, the emotions you observe (e.g. 'does this make you sad?'). You should not ignore such emotions ... Emotional life is an essential part of our experience and therefore will be an integral part of the interview process.*
> (King & Horrocks, 2010: 115–116)

In Chapter 3, I examined *interviewee*-side work to produce autobiographical tellings for the researcher. Chapters 4 and 5 focused on *interviewer*-side questioning practices and how they invited and expected emotional tellings and other talk. This chapter continues with the analysis of emotionality and its management by investigating the ways in which autobiographical interviews become sites for 'getting psychological' and even doing 'therapy-like' work[1] through speakers' descriptions. The following excerpts from Vitanova's (2004) published interviews with East European couples (Excerpt 6.1), and an interview from my L2 corpus (Excerpt 6.2), illustrate how speakers selectively label or formulate the emotionality of their experiences:

(Excerpt 6.1). Adapted from Vitanova (2004: 268–269)

Sylvia: I am *afraid*
Boris: I no *feel guilty*
Sylvia: I am *afraid* all the time
Boris: I no *feel guilty*. American people / all American people / was / immigrate. Live a few people / now / English. A few [...] Why not for me?
Sylvia: (Sighs.)
Boris: Why / I / must / be *guilty*? Why?

(Excerpt 6.2). Trang: 'Anxiety' (simplified excerpt)

T: I'm become *fear* see? B-right now ... become *fear*?
M: Uhuh
T: *Fearful?* and then ... *panicking?* No ... *anxiety?*
M: Uhuh?
T: *Anxiety* that the *worse.*
M: That's the *worst?*
T: Yeah that's the *worse. Anxiety?*

In Excerpts 6.1 and 6.2, speakers describe their emotional and psychological states through specific lexical descriptions (e.g. *afraid, guilty, fear, anxiety*) that orient to the (un)desirability of particular emotions as well as the contrast between one emotion and others. Taking up these issues, in this chapter I am concerned with the description and use of emotion and emotion-implicative categories within the process of data generation (Roulston, 2010). Henceforth, I will refer to this activity as *emotion (re)formulation*. I shall consider the ways in which interview interactants topicalize, and otherwise discursively manage emotion and its psychological import in the storyworld as well as in the interactional world of the interview. I begin with an overview of how formulation and reformulation have been theorized in conversation analysis (CA) and related traditions and extended to psychotherapeutic settings. I then identify and analyze emotion reformulations from my own L2 interview corpus for insight into how they were selected, generated, organized, confirmed and even resisted in the ongoing interview talk and interaction. Through this investigation I aim to reveal how emotion-indexing descriptions get selected and negotiated within the interview activity.

L2 Research Interviews and Psychotherapeutic Interaction

At first blush, L2 narrative interviews (and qualitative interviewing in general) and psychotherapy share little in common. The primary purpose of L2 research interviewing is to elicit insider accounts of multilingual lives and to make visible the various trajectories of L2 learning and use. This includes issues of attrition, motivation, acculturation, socialization and social participation (e.g. Baynham & De Fina, 2005; Benson & Nunan, 2005; Block, 2008; De Fina & Georgakopoulou, 2012; Koven, 2004; Menard-Warwick, 2009; Miller, 2011; Norton, 2000; Norton-Peirce, 1995). Employing one of the most widely used methods of data collection and generation, interview studies have contributed greatly to our understandings of individual learner differences, hybrid identities and the social and psychological processes involved in L2 acquisition and use across time and place. In contrast, in psychotherapeutic settings, clients seek out the expertise of a trained therapist who will then intervene to help the person in distress achieve and regulate a state of optimal mental and emotional health and well-being. Thus, in L2 research, interviewees are seen as the experts of their own lives, and autobiographical talk is viewed as a vehicle for informing the researcher's understandings of speakers' sociolinguistic experiences and perceptions. In psychotherapeutic settings, where the therapist's expert role is to facilitate the 'talking cure' (Stevens, 2012), the client is expected to take an active part in the process of self-discovery and personal change.

Nevertheless, despite their divergent agendas and location of expert knowledge, these two institutional settings share a number of key features: both seek to get at members' representations of their social worlds in their own words; both involve introspection and retrospective accounts; both make use of question and answer sequences; both involve some form of analysis; and, explicitly or otherwise, both actively solicit and ratify interviewees' talk of thoughts and feelings to further the ongoing interaction. Although researchers across the social sciences (e.g. Atkinson, 1998; Gubrium & Holstein, 2012; Seidman, 2013; Weiss, 1994) have noted areas of convergence between research interviewing and psychotherapeutic interaction – largely in terms of their intimate, confessional nature and the potential of interviews to lead to increased self-awareness and personal transformation – the ways in which research interviews, particularly those involving multilingual speakers and their sociolinguistic histories, may also function as an activity for generating psychological talk has received little attention (but see Prior, 2011a, 2011b, 2011c, 2014, for recent contributions). As I will argue in this chapter, not only are interviewees' psychological states and perceptions central topics of discussion in L2 research interviews, they are also fundamental resources for constructing and representing experience and identity as well as the interview activity.

Formulation and Reformulation

In its most general definition, formulation is synonymous with *representation* or *description* (Antaki, 2008) and encompasses 'speaker choices in style and content of expression, including categorization' (Bilmes, 2011).[2] In another use of the term, formulation – or more accurately, *re*-formulation – refers to recipients' comments about a previous utterance (Schwartz, 1976) or 'descriptions of where-we-both-are-in-the-conversation' (Antaki, 2008: 31). Garfinkel and Sacks (1970) observed that in an interaction listeners at any point can offer up a 'gloss' or a retrospective formulation (i.e. 're-formulation') of another speaker's talk to display their understanding of the situation so far. This activity of commenting on a prior utterance is an important resource by which interactants keep track of the ongoing interaction, to show they are listening, to indicate what matters are treated as significant (or not) and to project what next actions are relevant.

The glossing of prior talk is a general device found across both casual and institutional settings. In research interviews, where the goal of the interviewer is to elicit extended accounts in answer to particular questions and topics, it is not surprising that reformulation is a recurrent practice. Moreover, in contexts where interactants have little or no shared interactional history and may even orient to their differential linguistic and cultural knowledge and expertise (as is common in L2 research), the need to explicitly keep track of the ongoing talk may be even more acute. As a case in point, in Excerpt 6.2 from the study corpus, the interviewer summarizes commentary made by Trang, a biracial Vietnamese-Cambodian immigrant, about his family, his languages, his immigration experience and his decision to quit ESL (English as a Second Language) classes due to discrimination by classmates:

(Excerpt 6.2). Trang: 'Nasty word'

```
01        M:   and you said your father tongue, (0.5)
02             and you talked about your mother °t-°
03             (2.0)
04             an' then you tol' me how you ( )
05             stopped (0.8) speaking Cambodian
06             (1.4)
07             because (0.3) when you went to school?
08             (1.1)
09             some (.) Cambodian?=
10        T:   =yeah=
11   →    M:   =said some nasty word to [you              formulation
12   →    T:                            [°yeah yeah°     confirmation
```

The interviewer's institutional objective of eliciting research material from the interviewee's language-learning history is clearly visible through the gloss in lines 1–11. By offering a chronological and topical summary of the interviewee's talk from the previous interview, these reformulations characterize for the interviewee the content of the previous interview that is treated as relevant and newsworthy (Hutchby, 2005). This gloss is also produced to elicit from the interviewee confirmation and clarification (and more study data), as evidenced by the gaps of interviewer silence (lines 3, 6, 8), the incrementally produced and designedly incomplete utterances (Koshik, 2002) in lines 5, 7 and 9, and the rising interrogative contour of lines 7 and 9. Moreover, the lexical formulation of 'nasty word' in line 11, and its accompanying prosodic emphasis, convey the interviewer's shared negatively-valenced assessment of and affective stance toward the interviewee's painful

ESL experiences and invites him to comment on his psychological world where the name-calling incident caused him to abandon his formal English studies (see Chapter 3, Excerpt 3.8).

Reformulation as editorializing

As formulation scholarship has matured, led in large part by the institutionally-oriented work of Heritage and Watson (1979, 1980), it has come to refer to the ways in which speakers editorialize upon an interactant's previous utterance (Antaki, 2008). Here, the speaker is not simply glossing a prior utterance but is transforming and even repairing it. In their work, Heritage and Watson refined the concept to encompass a narrow adjacency pair structure:

A: Utterance
B: Formulation of A's previous utterance
A: Confirmation

Formulations in this sense consist of two types: *gist* and *upshot*. Summarizing the gist of what has been said so far is essentially to paraphrase and summarize, while preserving and highlighting relevant features and recasting or transforming others. Formulating the upshot, on the other hand, involves arriving at a logical presupposition or conclusion. Excerpt 6.3, from the study corpus, contains both types.

In the interaction represented in Excerpt 6.3, Bona, an immigrant from Cambodia, is describing his previous job and the decision to quit and move to a new state before receiving his five-year bonus. After Bona preemptively rejects the potential inference by the interviewer that he needed or cared about the five-hundred dollar bonus, the interviewer requests and receives an explanatory account by means of a 'why' question (Sidnell, 2004).

(Excerpt 6.3). Bona: 'Five hundred dollar is nothing'

```
01      B:   every five years they give uh (.) like
02           a bonus. and I'm not waiting for that.
03           I don't want to use the word 'I don't
04           care' but (1.0) I don't need it.
05      M:   why?
06      B:   five hundred dollar is nothing. ah-
07           each year (.) they give give you(.)
08           five hundred dollar. if you work
09           there ten year you get a thousand
10           dollar (.) if you work the:re what
11           uh (.) twenty year?(.) you get (.) I
12           mean fifteen year you get one thousand
```

```
13              five hundred. twenty year you get two
14              thousand? twenty five year (.) every
15              five years. twenty five year you get
16              two thousand five hundred. thirty years
17              (.) you get uh::: three thousand
18              dollar.
19    →   M:    so money's not important to you=        gist formulation
20    →   B:    =no=                                    confirmation
21    →   M:    =cuz you're rich?                       upshot formulation
22    →   B:    yeah (.) that's right. that's right.    confirmation
```

In his extended turn in response to the interviewer's account request, the interviewee describes and calculates the future bonuses that he knowingly gave up. By offering these details, he portrays his decision to move as carefully weighed, not a result of a whim or lack of maturity. In the beat of the next turn, the interviewer offers a *so*-prefaced (Drew, 2003) gist formulation (19: 'so money's not important to you'), which claims shared understanding of the interviewee's personally-held value system. Bona then immediately confirms with a preferred, type-conforming response (20: 'no'). *So*-prefaces and similar formulations (e.g. 'you're saying ...') have been shown to occur infrequently in casual conversation but appear often in institutional settings such as broadcast news interviews, workplace meetings and psychotherapeutic interaction (e.g. Antaki et al., 2005; Drew, 2003; Hutchby, 2005). They are also important devices by which the interviewer marks particular material as newsworthy and comment-worthy. *So*-prefaced formulations regularly appear in my L2 interview corpus, suggesting, as one would expect, an orientation by the interactants to the institutional activity of interview.

Immediately latched onto the confirmation, the interviewer produces a playful upshot formulation offering an explanation why money is not important to the interviewee (21: 'cuz you're rich?'). The interviewee then sarcastically agrees with the interviewer's formulation through a po-faced confirmatory 'yeah' followed by a sequence-closing summative repetition ('that's right. that's right.'). Although these interviewer-produced formulations are not explicitly emotion-indexing, they do tread into psychological territory by describing mental or putatively 'interior' states and processes. As evidenced in other reformulation sequences in the corpus, a repeated confirmation is a means by which interviewees ratify the interviewer's description while asserting epistemic superiority over their own perspectives and experiences (Heritage, 2011; Heritage & Raymond, 2005; Raymond & Heritage, 2006).

Reformulations in psychotherapy

One institutional context where reformulation has received much attention is in psychotherapeutic settings, where it has been shown to be a pervasive practice for displaying intersubjectivity and allowing the therapist to cast the client's talk toward a psychologically-oriented agenda (e.g. Antaki *et al.*, 2007; Davis, 1986; Gale, 1991; Goss *et al.*, 2010; Peräkylä, 2005; Peräkylä *et al.*, 2008; Rae, 2008). Bercelli *et al.* (2008: 46) define therapist reformulations as 'something that was implicitly meant by the client, so claiming that they are still offering a candidate reading of the perspective expressed by the client'.[3] These reformulations often take the form of 'you mean ...', 'so you're saying ...', and similar expressions. However, in therapeutic settings, reformulations are not simply verbatim or gist repetitions; they are selective and partial, frequently focusing on the client's emotional state and making use of lexical changes and secondary descriptions that narrow or otherwise reshape the meaning of an utterance as well as the way in which it should be interpreted toward resolution and personal change (Bercelli *et al.*, 2008; Peräkylä *et al.*, 2008; Rae, 2008) – the primary goals of therapy.

Discursive and rhetorical psychologists have long noted that all descriptions are performative, rhetorically organized, produced within particular interactional sequences and entail the selection among potential and even contrasting alternatives (e.g. Billig, 1996; Edwards, 1997; Edwards & Potter, 2005):

> [T]he fact that formulations allow the current speaker to select some parts of the prior speaker's words, ignore others, add spin, and present the package in a form that projects agreement makes them a powerful discursive tool. (Antaki *et al.*, 2007: 168)

> Moreover, by producing one descriptive utterance from a range of potentially usable items, speakers 'bracket in' or index certain particulars of the referent of the description, and, at the same time, 'bracket out' other aspects of the referent. Thus, any description is a selection which brings to the recipient's attention specific particulars of the state of affairs being described. (Wooffitt, 1992: 15)

Located within the activity of psychotherapy, Rae (2008) refers to these alternative and subsequent reformulations as proposing a *redescription*. Rae further points out *lexical substitution*[4] as a subtype of reformulation (and repair). In lexical substitution, the therapist, while ostensibly offering up the gist of what was said, inserts specific terms toward therapeutic ends. For example, in Excerpt 6.4, from a counseling session, the therapist explicitly reformulates the client's own emotion state formulation from '*a little* uncomfortable' to '*a lot* uncomfortable', and this upgrade is taken up by the client:

(Excerpt 6.4). Adapted from Rae (2008: 64)

01   **CL:**   I am **surviving** and I am
02 → **TH:**   But it **feels** (.) **doesn't feel right**

03	**CL:**	It **feels** a **little uncomfortable**
04 →	**TH:**	Or **a lot uncomfortable**.
05	**CL:**	It **feels a l(hoh)ot unc(huh)omfortable** actually

Note: **bold** = emotion-indexing (re)formulations; **boldbox** = (re)formulations that are taken up in subsequent turns.

In his analysis, Rae notes that the therapist's reformulation reproduces part of the client's utterance ('uncomfortable'), but through the contrastive marker 'or' and substitution of 'a lot' for 'a little', constructs an alternative description that proposes, for therapeutic purposes, 'a freer expression of feeling' (2008: 64). This also shows that after the client uses 'I am surviving' (line 1) as a general psychological self-assessment, the therapist reformulates it with the affective state verb 'feel' and the description 'uncomfortable' to highlight negative feelings and to turn the focus from survival (i.e. as a state of maintenance) to a need for conflict resolution. These reformulations/lexical substitutions are successful in leading the client to provide a more personal description of feelings and conflict, which the therapist can then seek to resolve.

Another example of redescriptive psychological reformulation in therapeutic talk is shown in Excerpt 6.5 from Rae (2008), this time between a client (CL) mourning her husband's death, and the therapist (TH) working to help her come to terms with her loss.

(Excerpt 6.5). Adapted from Rae (2008: 66)

12	**CL:**	It's **hard** talking about this Michael
13	**TH:**	Yeah I can s:ee: that (.) w- when you say **har:d**
14 →		I think you mean **painful**
15	**CL:**	Yeh it's **painful** talking about this it's actually
16		**painful**

In this excerpt, the client initially describes the current activity of talking about her husband as 'hard'. The therapist, displaying his expertise on such matters, offers a candidate repair that claims to represent a more truthful description: line 14: 'I think you mean painful'. In light of the therapist's institutional role, Rae (2008: 66) suggests that the therapist is proposing 'painful' as a more suitable alternative that 'describes affect more explicitly'.

In sum, previous research demonstrates that reformulations operate not only as periodic summaries of what was said (i.e. as intersubjective 'checks'); they can also function to recast or *re-describe* speakers' talk to align with the institutional language and goals of the setting. Thus, the ways in which particular utterances are oriented to, reformulated and taken up (and rejected) have direct consequences on interactants' participation frameworks and their perceptions of the activity and its expected outcomes. In therapeutic settings, for example, reformulations narrow the focus of the previous utterance toward therapy-centered topics (e.g. emotions, feelings, memories) and resolution; nevertheless, they are still ostensibly treating the therapist's reformulation as what the client truly means or feels. Excerpts from my interview corpus as well as the available published literature show similar types of interactional work. Because reformulations enable individuals to arrive at intersubjective understandings, I suggest they are also particularly robust resources for managing psychological business outside of therapy settings.

In the following section, I focus on selected excerpts from the present corpus to examine in more detail the use of emotion (re)formulations by the interviewer and interviewees. A close examination of how the interaction unfolds offers a more nuanced understanding of how interviewer and interviewee collaboratively manage emotionality as both topic and resource.

Reformulations in L2 research interviews

It is important to emphasize that the reformulations in this corpus were not just initiated by the interviewer acting as a kind of 'quasi-therapist'. As the analysis will show, interview participants also described, maintained and rejected particular emotion reformulations within and across utterances.[5] They also adjusted their talk to pursue an affiliative (Stivers, 2008), empathic (Heritage, 2011), or stance-sharing response from the interviewer when it was not forthcoming. The first two extended Excerpts (6.6a, 6.6b) are from an interview sequence with Rico, an asylum seeker from the Philippines. He speaks here about the personal stress and risks involved in being an illegal worker in Canada.

Repeating reformulations and pursuing affiliation

Immediately prior to this segment, Rico reported that he had just learned that two other asylum-seeking friends were about to be deported. Here Rico speaks about his night job in a warehouse where he loads boxes onto delivery trucks. He expresses his fear that if the police or immigration officials find out he is working illegally, he could go to jail or be deported before his upcoming asylum hearing.

(Excerpt 6.6a). Rico: 'Scary' and 'Dangerous'

```
01   R:    °it's really hard,°
02         (1.1)
03         °that's why I'm-I'm- I'm stress:.°
04         (1.5)
```

```
05          ((drinks tea))
06          (1.2)
07        * ((cup hits saucer loudly))
08          (0.9)
09          °'s very tough[:°
10    M:                  °[that's scary.°
11    R:    °|scared.|°
12          (1.4)
13    M:    so if they come to your work, (0.4)
14          they can, (1.1) take- (.) send you
15          home?
16          (1.0)
17    R:    ↑YE:A↓H.
18          (0.5)
19          ~probably.~
20          (1.7)
21          H↑YE↑↑:↓AH.
22          (0.8)
23    M:    °dange[rous°
24    R:          [it's a big risk
25          (0.7)
26          that's true=
27    M:    =why you °do that?°
28          (0.5)
29    R:    .hh
30          (0.8)
31          because your-you want to earn.
32          (1.3)
33    M:    °|dangerous.|°
34          (0.7)
35    R:    |dangerous|. ↑rea↓lly.
36          (1.7)
37          <.hhhhh> >AN' EVERY< TIM::E=I work at
38          night, (1.5)
            ((R continues with a story about
            loading boxes and worrying about being
            caught by the police))
```

Beginning the sequence in Excerpt 6.6a, Rico produces a meta-comment describing his present situation (line 1: 'it's really hard') and then formulates the upshot in terms of the negative psychological consequences (line 3: '°that's why I'm-I'm stress.°'). After gaps (lines 2, 4–8), where the interviewer passes up opportunities to provide an affiliative response to display his understanding of Rico's stress-inducing situation, Rico restarts with 'it's *very tough'*, a semantic equivalent to 'it's really hard'. This reformulation and self-repair succeeds in eliciting a response from the interviewer, who now offers up his own emotion-implicative assessment. Similar to Excerpts 6.4 and 6.5 from therapeutic settings, the interviewer here reformulates Rico's description of his situation from ''s very tough' (line 9) to 'that's scary' (line 10). Although this assessment is affiliative in meaning (i.e. by its empathetic characterization of Rico's situation), its neutral prosodic delivery conveys detachment. Following the lack of sufficient affiliative uptake from the interviewer, Rico then produces a lexical substitution (line 11: 'scared'). Despite the morphological similarity with the interviewer's reformulation, there is an important difference. 'Scary' describes external events as fear-inducing; however, 'scared' indexes the speaker's own emotional response, thereby asserting an epistemic stance (i.e. knowledge and ownership of his own psychological states) as well as an affective stance. In the same way that in Excerpt 6.5 reformulating 'hard' to 'painful' creates a more emotionally focused and subjectively experienced description within the therapeutic setting, the reformulation of 'tough' to 'scary' in this research interview also expects the interviewee to respond with a more personal, psychological description – one that even solicits empathy.

As the interview continues, the interviewer provides an upshot formulation (lines 13–15: 'so if they come to your work, they can (.) take- send you home?') that invites further recorded material by seeking confirmation of the lifeworld source of Rico's psychological conflict. In his response slot following a one-second gap, Rico first produces an epistemically robust confirmation (17: '↑YE:A↓H.') characterized by a steep, hearably affect-laden prosodic rise and fall. CA scholars have repeatedly observed that a gap of silence following a first-pair part often signals disagreement or other dispreferred response (Pomerantz, 1984). Silence may also function to indicate an embodied or visceral response to extraordinary events (Wilkinson & Kitzinger, 2006). In this context, Rico's response following the gap is hearable as an emotional response cry (Goffman, 1978) triggered by the interviewer's hypothetical (yet very likely) deportation scenario. This, in turn, is followed by two self-repairs. Following the first gap of silence in line 16, Rico produces an epistemically weaker and prosodically flatter, though 'wobbly' or tremulous, epistemic downgrade (17: '~probably.~'). Following a 1.7-second gap in line 20, he produces an epistemic upgrade ('H↑YE↑↑:↓AH.') by means of a lexical repetition of line 17 and a marked steep prosodic rise and fall that displays certainty and a heightened state of emotional arousal.

Reformulation, because it involves transforming and editing the words of another, entails risk in relation to interactants' epistemic rights and entitlements (Heritage, 2011; Heritage & Raymond, 2005; Raymond & Heritage, 2006). Activities such as offering up a description of how someone else presumably feels; making an assessment of an event that you, yourself, did not witness; and repairing another's utterance are all interactionally risky propositions because they involve treading onto someone else's *epistemic* and *affective* domains. Responding to Rico's three-part confirmation sequence, the interviewer offers up another reformulation (line 23: 'dangerous') to display his candidate understanding of Rico's situation (in sharp contrast to the earlier lack of affiliative responses in lines 2–8). In overlap with the interviewer's production of 'dangerous', Rico, rather than taking up the exact lexical reformulation offered by the interviewer, reformulates it as 'a big risk' (line 24). This reformulation may be hearable as a semantic equivalent to 'dangerous'; however, 'it's a big risk' (consistent with the stance projected by 'very tough' in line 9 and 'scared' in line 11) implies that it is a risk for someone (i.e. highlighting the risk Rico is taking by working illegally), thus narrowing the characterization to a more personal level, possibly even aimed at soliciting an empathic response.

Pursuing affiliation

This does not mean that empathy solicitation is always successful. Following Rico's utterance in line 24, the interviewer (as in lines 2–8) passes up an opportunity to display a shared perspective. In pursuit of an affiliative response, Rico then reaffirms the factualness of his lifeworld claims ('that's true') and his epistemic authority. Instead of affiliation, this is met with another account-soliciting question from the interviewer ('why you °do that?°') in line 27. Heritage (2011), Jefferson (1984), and others refer to these non-affiliative questions as ancillary questions – questions that raise a related matter at a point where an empathic response would be expected. The subsequent pauses and in-breath can be heard as Rico orienting to the lack of affiliative uptake as well as a display of thinking as he prepares to provide the second-pair part to the interviewer's question. After Rico cites the urgent need to earn money for survival (line 31), the interviewer again pursues the lexical selection of 'dangerous'. Following a short gap of silence, Rico adopts the interviewer's stance by recycling 'dangerous' (line 35). However, by following it with an emphatic confirmation punctuated with a steep prosodic rise and fall ('↑rea↓lly.'),[6] which might be glossed in vernacular speech as 'tell me something I don't know', Rico again asserts primary epistemic and affective rights over the events being discussed and assessed.

At the time, I considered myself empathetic to Rico's plight and emotional stress. I thought I was showing compassion in our interviews and other interactions by being a friendly and supportive listener. Our mutual acquaintances confirmed Rico was worried about these issues, and we were hopeful that he would be successful in his asylum petition. Adding to his stress as an illegal worker was that he could not talk to many people about his present situation for fear of being reported and then deported before his asylum hearing – and he expressed these fears throughout our interactions. However, I also see now that interviewer contributions that might be analyzed as 'empathic moments' (Heritage, 2011), 'affiliation' (Stivers, 2008), or 'emotive involvement' (Selting, 2010) can also be implicated in the subtle struggles over epistemic and affective rights to characterize one's own personal experiences. The epistemic struggles that are now visible in the reanalysis of this interview suggest that the teller's ownership over his autobiographical telling is something over which he sought to exert control. In this and other chapters, I have noted that speakers may use their tellings as agentive devices allowing them to 'talk back' to people and events in the storyworld. Re-analysis of this story also produced an important reminder that speakers may use their tellings, even in subtle ways, to 'talk back' and resist the epistemic and interpretive force of the talk of their story recipients (i.e. the interviewer) in the present.

Affective reframing

At this point in Rico's telling, the interactional mood can be described as somewhat somber. After a 1.7-second gap, Rico reframes the affective key (Ochs & Schieffelin, 1989) by launching into a telling that characterizes the 'dangerous' nature of his work while imbuing it with a wry, humorous tone. I have noted throughout these chapters that following talk of complaints and troubles talk, speakers frequently make use of laughter and humorous tellings to make light of their troubles (Jefferson, 1984) as well as to talk back to or criticize the trouble-source people and events (Kasper & Prior, 2015; Prior, 2011a).

Continuing his story (Excerpt 6.6b), Rico describes through an extended represented speech segment (lines 53–74) how the company owner and manager told him if the police or immigration showed up unexpectedly and saw him loading boxes, he should pretend he is just a curious tourist and not a warehouse worker. As the interaction develops, the emotion reformulations 'scary' and 'dangerous' are again brought up by the interviewer.

(Excerpt 6.6b). Rico: 'That's crazy'

```
53      R:    an:d .hh my manager also in the eh- in-
54            in the warehouse.=IF- (0.5) .hh
55            °f- (u-u-)° the immigration, (0.7)
56            will visit there?=and .hhhh if for
57            example, (1.2) they will ask me, (0.5)
58            and (0.6) I will tell them I am juS:
59            s::eeing (0.5) $aro(h)und (.)°hehe°$
60            (1.0)
61            .hh $seeing around. >hh-< and- (.) I-I
62            ask her,$ .hh what if she caught me
63            and and hoh- .hh $I am lifting boxes?$
64            °.hh hh°((stifled laughter))=
65            =$an' an' she-she told me- >an' he told
```

```
66              me,<$ (0.3) .hh um: you are curious.
67              ((mock serious tone))
68              (0.5)
69              you-you lifting, (0.3) boxes because
70              you are curious=y-y-you want to (sell-)
71              t'see something inside the box.
72              >°hehehe°<
73              (1.2)
74              .hhh=
75    →   M:    =$that's cra[zy.$]
76    →   R:               [.hh ]=$ that's crazy? $
77              (0.3)
78              .hh
79              (2.5)
80              so:: th-they have a false alarm now.
81              (1.9)
82        M:    false alarm,
83              (1.6)
84        R:    I ↑mean, (1.4) not to get in trouble.
85              (0.8)
86        M:    °oh°
87              (3.0)
88    →   R:    °°.hh ↑↑ mh°° ((whimper))
89              (3.0)
90    →   M:    °scary.°
91    →   R:    # scared #
92              (1.2)
93    →   M:    °dan↑ger↓ous° ((sing-song voice))
94              (0.2)
95    →   R:    da::ngerous ((dramatic tone)) that's
96              °(right)°=
97        M:    => so whaddya gonna do?<
98              (2.2)
99        M:    [(    )
100       R:    [°°#(whatever)#°°
                ((talk continues))
```

Rico's extended laughter-filled enactment of the dialog with the owner and manager provides an affective frame through which the interviewer is expected to understand the represented events. After Rico punctuates his utterance with a laughter-filled coda in line 72 ('>°hehehe°<'), the interviewer formulates an affiliative assessment or empathic response (75: 'that's crazy.') that comments on the absurdity of the manager's and owner's instructions. This coordinated activity allows Rico to recalibrate his status in both the storyworld and the lifeworld. Because the story and the interviewer's affiliative response mark Rico's workplace superiors as objects of ridicule, Rico is able to contrastively come off as logical and hypervigilant, not just a victim (or lawbreaker).

Rico then repeats the interviewer's assessment with an exact lexical repetition (line 76: 'that's crazy?') that confirms the interviewer's formulation as accurate and, as before (Excerpt 5a, lines 26, 35), reaffirms his epistemic authority over his account. Although 'crazy' is not an explicit emotion state description like 'angry', 'sad' or 'scared', it does express empathy with Rico by offering up the recipient's (i.e. the interviewer) independent psychological interpretation of these events. The interviewer's assessment is produced with declarative intonation (indexing epistemic certainty), and the interrogative shape of Rico's utterance both confirms the interviewer's assessment while inviting further affiliative commentary.[7]

As the interaction continues, in lines 90–95, the interviewer and Rico repeat the exact reformulations and sequential order of lines 10–11 and 33–35:

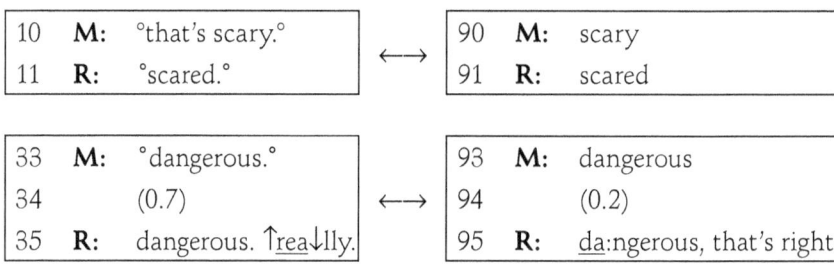

In this interactional sequence, each time the interviewer offers up an emotion-indexing description (e.g. *scary, dangerous*) of the events and concerns mentioned, the interviewee takes up those reformulations and produces a confirmation that reaffirms his own epistemic authority. When the interviewer formulates events as 'scary', the interviewee reformulates it to 'scared', a more personal and empathy soliciting representation of his emotional state. Although not shown here, as the interaction continues, both parties continue to recycle the terms *scary, scared* and *dangerous*.

I have commented that interview participants may confirm the interviewer's reformulation by offering up a semantic equivalent and reinforcing their epistemic ownership over their own stories. I also showed that the interviewer may even repeat or pursue a particular reformulation when it is not taken up or otherwise confirmed by the interviewee (Excerpts 6.6a, 6.6b). Thus, in the same way that a counselor may reformulate and shape the clients' psychological descriptions in psychotherapeutic settings, in talk produced in these L2 research interviews, the interviewer is also active in reformulating talk in psychological terms and can be seen to pursue a psychological agenda. However, as the following sequence will show, the interviewer's agenda is not always accepted, and it may even be actively resisted.

Resisting reformulations and pursuing affiliation

In another interview sequence from the corpus, Jack, an immigrant from Cambodia, described his early high school years in the US. Jack stated that when he first arrived in the late 1980s, he did not speak any English. His stories frequently spoke of his difficulties in understanding teachers, students and co-workers. In the sequence represented here (Excerpt 6.7), a number of emotion-implicative reformulations are produced by the interviewer and the interviewee, but only some are pursued and confirmed. Thus, this sequence demonstrates some of the tensions that arise when interviewer and interviewee are at odds over which particular reformulations are appropriate or accurate.

(Excerpt 6.7). Jack: 'Hard', 'Difficult' and 'Tough'

```
01   M:   was it difficult learning English:? (.)
02        >in the beginning?<=
03   J:   =↑yea:↓:h
04        (0.4)
05        °a lot°
06        (0.3)
07        °yeah.°
08   M:   did you have BAD experience or good
09        experience?=
10   J:   I- (1.0) thi::nk, (0.8) the first when I
11        learn English °I thi:nk (oh:) it's uh REAlly
12        hard.
13        (0.7)
14   M:   °mhm°
15        (0.3)
16   J:   very hard y'know?
17        (3.0)
18   M:   what was most [dif]ficult ?
19   J:                 [( )]
20        (0.3)
21   M:   [OH] (.) go ahead I'm sorry
22   J:   [( )]
          ((Lines omitted. S produces a story about
          being picked on by other kids and not doing
          homework because he couldn't understand
          English.))
99   M:   that's ↑tough
```

148 Emotion and Discourse in L2 Narrative Research

```
100         (0.4)
101  J:     yea::h (0.2) ⌞hard⌟ °y'know?°
102         (0.2)
103         °°(I mean that)°°
104         (0.4)
105         °°uh°°
106         (0.5)
107  M:     °mhm°
108         (0.3)
109  J:     an' um, (1.5) well like, (1.7) when we
110         ((refugees)) came they put- (0.2) put us in
111         high school right?
112         (0.3)
113         °⌞ha:rd⌟ in high school.°
114         (0.3)
115  M:     °mhm°
116         (0.8)
117         was that ⌞tough⌟?
118         (0.5)
119  J:     °yea:h°
            ((talk continues about school))
```

This sequence begins with the interviewer soliciting trouble or emotion-implicative talk from Jack (line 1: 'was it difficult learning English?'). Troubles talk and its solicitation is a prominent feature of psychotherapeutic interaction (Miller & Silverman, 1995) and has been found to occur in L2 research interviews as well (e.g. Kasper & Prior, 2015; Prior, 2011a, 2011b, 2011c, 2014). Jack thrice confirms 'difficult' as an appropriate formulation (lines 3–7). His first confirmation ('↑yea:↓:h'), produced without mitigation and with a high pitch onset and elongated vowel, makes hearable an emotional, visceral reaction and his epistemic certainty based on personal experience. In contrast, the prosodically downgraded second and third confirmations ('°a lot°' and '°yeah°'), suggest a more reflective and even slightly 'sorrowful' response. Together, these reproduce the interviewer's perspective of learning English as a difficult, emotional and readily memorable experience.

Continuing this topic of inquiry, in lines 8–9, the interviewer offers up an alternative or split *either-or* question that restricts talk of Jack's L2 experience to two psychological outcomes: talk of *bad* ESL experiences or talk of *good* ESL experiences. Because Jack has already confirmed the experience was difficult, the interviewer's question 'expects' a response about bad experiences (the louder production on 'BAD' also supports this analysis). In his second pair part of the question-answer adjacency pair, Jack does not repeat the previous descriptions 'bad', 'good' or even 'difficult'. He does, however, produce a topically coherent response that narrates his psychological process. In lines 11–12, his thought-prefaced response indicates his state of mind at the time, and his description 'the first' displays his understanding of the specific chronological point in his personal language-learning history specified in line 2: 'in the beginning'. Jack's represented self-talk in lines 11–12 (('oh:) it's uh REAlly hard'), produced with louder volume and emphatic stress, reproduces his emotional and mental response to learning English in the past. This receives only minimal acknowledgement from the interviewer (14: '°mhm°'), and the brief gap of silence in line 15 suggests the interviewer was waiting for Jack to provide a response expansion. Jack then characterizes those events as 'very hard' (line 16), a semantic reformulation of his description in lines 11–12.

Instead of taking up Jack's lexical reformulation or offering an affiliative response, the interviewer pursues a specific story. He produces an exact lexical repetition of his previous reformulation ('difficult'), but upgrades it to 'most difficult', an extreme case formulation (Pomerantz, 1986). As noted in previous chapters, within active interviews (Holstein & Gubrium, 1995), extreme case formulation can be a powerful device to elicit extended talk from participants (Prior, 2014; see also Labov & Waletzky, 1967, 1977, on soliciting emotional narratives of near-death experiences). This succeeds in eliciting a story from Jack about being made fun of by his classmates for his poor English skills and inability to do his homework. After Jack completes his story, the interviewer offers his own assessment of the described events: 'that's tough' (line 99). Although Jack confirms the interviewer's reformulation (line 101: 'yeah'), he continues with 'hard y'know', which recycles his own previous reformulation ('hard') from lines 12 and 16. This again can be heard to solicit an affiliative response from the interviewer, but none is forthcoming. In lines 102–106 and 108, Jack's increment ('I mean that') as well as pauses and perturbations suggest his orientation to an absent affiliative response from the interviewer – who only offers a minimal response in line 107 ('°mhm°'), as he did earlier (line 14). Jack then again pursues an affiliative response through his expansion in lines 109–111 and 113. Once more, he is met with a minimal response (line 115:'°mhm°') from the interviewer.

Analysis of the interviewer's and interviewee's contributions in this interaction makes visible their conflict over competing reformulations and epistemic rights. Following Jack's production of 'really hard' (lines 11–12), 'very hard' (line 16) and 'hard' (lines 101, 113), there is only a minimal response token and gaps of silence. In line 117, the interviewer returns to the reformulation he used in line 99 ('tough'), but this time he inserts it in a question ('was that tough?') – arguably a stronger reformulation that solicits a polar or type-conforming 'yes or no' response. The confirmation the interviewer receives to his formulations in lines 101 and 119 is a prosodically flat 'yeah' (there is a sound stretch, but it is not accompanied by other prosodic emphasis), which contrasts with the emphatic response in line 3 ('↑yea:↓:h'), which did not follow a rejection of the interviewee's formulations. In the sequence illustrated by Excerpt 6.7, both parties produce various reformulations, and each

150 Emotion and Discourse in L2 Narrative Research

repeats the particular ones they have used. However, the interviewer pursues confirmation of his own reformulations (e.g. 'difficult' and 'tough') through questions and prompts (lines 1–2, 18, 99, 117), but the interviewee does not seek confirmation to the same degree (the tag 'y'know' in lines 16 and 101 does invite affiliation, but it does not make the lexical formulation the focus).

In this corpus, interviewer reformulations, often using explicit emotion-indexing lexical terms, steered the interview toward talk of an emotional nature. Contrary to the metaphor of the interview as a 'window' or 'inner view' to speakers' psychologies, these data show that the emotionality produced in these L2 research interviews and the specific descriptions that interactants use are directly shaped by the interview questions and reformulations. It can also be seen that, in keeping with previous CA research on institutional talk (e.g. Heritage & Watson, 1979), speakers orient to the conversational preference to provide a confirmation after a reformulation. This may stem from the basic interactional need for speakers to intersubjectively and economically arrive at a shared understanding of the topic, content and meaning of talk and its relation to the ongoing interaction, the social relationships of those involved and their lifeworld concerns (Mishler, 1986).

Collaboratively completed reformulations

Although confirmations after reformulations retrospectively treat them as shared understandings of prior talk, speakers may also show concurrent intersubjectivity in their overlaps. I have a few instances in the data that show the interviewer and the interviewee collaboratively completing an emotion reformulation.

In the following interview segment, Kim (K) is telling a story about how she initially broke up with her boyfriend (who later became her husband) in Vietnam before she immigrated to the United States. After she arrived, her first job was in a bar as a cocktail waitress.

(Excerpt 6.8). Kim: 'Ashamed'

01		K:	so we break apart.
02		M:	cuz you came here.
03		K:	and then I came here. and when I came here I
04	→		(.) **disconnected** with (.) people in Vietnam.
05	→		**I feel like I'm (.) lost.**
06		M:	°why?°
07		K:	to me (.) if I have to work in the bar **that**
08	→		**look really bad.**
09		M:	°oh°

10	**K:**	that (.) I (.) I cannot tell people "oh, I
11		came to the United State to work in the bar"
12		(.) people they do not know what that mean.
13		they only think that term is (.) **a bad place (.)**
14		to begin with. why should I go th-there
15		to work.
16	**M:**	so you cut off contact with people in Vietnam
17 →		cuz you're (.) [**ashamed**
18 →	**K:**	[**shamed.** but mostly I don't
19		have time. I work from two to two. and
20		then I try to take one class. back and forth. I
21		don't have car. I drive- I take the bus.
22		right? an' by the time I get home I am really
23		tired already an' I have nothing to talk
24		about.

In lines 3–5, Kim describes feeling 'disconnected' and 'lost' after arriving in the US. The interviewer then invites her to account for those feelings. Again, this indicates the interviewer's pursuit of emotional and personal accounts. In her response, Kim attributes these feelings to working in a bar and the negative associations typically attached to that kind of work (see also Chapter 3, Excerpt 3.1b and Chapter 5, Excerpt 5.8). In lines 16–17, the interviewer offers up an upshot formulation (i.e. the reason Kim cut off contact with people in Vietnam was because she worked in a bar) via a designedly incomplete utterance (Koshik, 2002). After a micropause, the interviewer and Kim simultaneously produce the emotion reformulations 'ashamed' and 'shamed' in a collaborative completion (Lerner, 2004), thus displaying their intersubjectively shared understandings of why Kim cut off contact with people in Vietnam. In this corpus, once a particular emotion state claim was put out in conversation, it was often explained and accounted for by the person to whom it was ascribed. In lines 18–24, Kim downgrades the claim of shame by giving other explanations for not contacting her friends in Vietnam: she did not have time, she had class, she was tired, and as a result, she did not have anything to talk about. Taken together, Kim's explanations form a device that might be called 'objective practical exigencies of everyday life' and thus enable her to manage her account of being ashamed.

Idiosyncratic interviewing?

Because the present L2 corpus features the same interviewer engaged in longitudinal interviews with these research participants, it is possible to attribute the psychological focus of the data to his idiosyncratic interviewing style, his interactional history or relationship with the research participants and his own interest in psychological matters. In retrospect, I cannot be certain *why* I kept asking questions implicating emotionality. Analysis of the data shows that participants' own orientations and talk display such a concern and focus (I discuss some possible reasons for this in Chapter 8). I know that I was interested in understanding participants' sociolinguistic trajectories and their differential outcomes. It may also be that our mutual life histories and shared interests in stories, languages, cross-cultural politics and identity dilemmas intersected in such a way that made emotionality the communicative hinge upon which our institutional and interpersonal relationships developed.

Published data for comparison is sparse, due to the fact that interview-based studies rarely provide detailed transcripts or even the questions or other contributions of the interviewer. However, in the few published studies that do include interactional details, similar kinds of psychological work can readily be found – as in the examples from Miller (2011) and Norton (2000)[8] discussed in the previous chapter:

Adapted from Miller (2011: 6)

Interviewer: Has- have y- has anyo:ne (.) made you *feel bad*?
Interviewer: Have you had someone sometimes make you *feel bad* because you couldn't speak or you couldn't understand?

Adapted from Norton (2000: 65)

Interviewer: You mean that makes it *worse*?
Interviewer: You think that makes you *nervous*?

These are just two examples, but they are indicative of the types of emotional solicitation and reformulation work that frequently take place in L2 research interviews. It is apparent that researchers, rather than simply discovering the psychological impact of speakers' experiences with and through their languages, are profoundly implicated in the active construction of how those experiences and their psychological outcomes are represented – and contested.

Summary

In this chapter, I considered how (re)formulation, a prominent feature of psychotherapeutic discourse, is also a recurrent device in L2 research interviews. Interviewees took up and confirmed emotion state reformulations through at least four procedures: (a) through an *exact lexical repetition* of all or part of a previous formulation, (b) through an *explicit confirmation* (e.g. 'that's right'), (c) by offering a *semantic equivalent* (e.g. 'it's dangerous' → 'It's a big risk') and (d) by lexically or prosodically *upgrading* or *intensifying* (occasionally downgrading) the reformulation (e.g. 'hard' → 'very hard').[9] Although rare, interactants also collaboratively completed a reformulation at a relevant turn constructional unit (Sacks *et al.*, 1974). These findings emphasize that the pursuit and confirmation of particular reformulations directly influence the emotional trajectories that are pursued as well as those that are abandoned. Ultimately, *what* gets talked about in interviews and *how* that talk is understood is directly tied into the specific formulations and reformulations that are used and treated as relevant.

The majority of interviewer-initiated reformulations received confirmations, but not all interviewer-produced emotion reformulations were taken up by the interviewees. In those cases, two patterns emerged: (a) the interviewee used a different lexical formulation but gave an account for it, or (b) the interviewer pursued a particular lexical formulation until it was confirmed. Although qualitative interviews are often 'confessional' or 'therapy-like', therapy is not their explicit or institutional purpose (Weiss, 1994). Therefore, it is not surprising that contrary to CA findings on therapeutic interaction (e.g. Bercelli *et al.*, 2008), *reinterpretations* – reformulations expressed from the *interviewer's own perspective* – were not present in these data. Even when the interviewer pursued particular emotion reformulations, they were shaped as the interviewee's own perspective. Moreover, they functioned to highlight the emotionality of events and to explain speakers' decisions within and in reaction to their sociolinguistic trajectories.

Finally, as the quote from Seidman (2013: 18) at the preface to this chapter reminds, the language and words used to access and represent experience in research interviews is a 'complexity inherent' in the method. The stance taken here is that this complexity is not something to be ignored or avoided (if indeed that were possible). Rather, I contend that this very complexity requires us to attend to the research interview as a rich site for psychological and sociolinguistic analysis and thus offers us an opportunity to carry out a thoroughly reflexive inspection of our methods.

Notes

(1) When I initially shared data from this corpus in data sessions, listeners offered a prescient observation by commenting that they thought the recordings were from counseling sessions.
(2) Jack Bilmes (2011), personal communication. Bilmes notes that Harvey Sacks most often used 'formulation' in this broad sense. This is the sense in which it is often applied to a number of utterance types, including *extreme case formulations* (e.g. Edwards, 2000; Pomerantz, 1986), *person reference formulations* (e.g. Enfield & Stivers, 2007; Sacks & Schegloff, 1979), *place formulations* (e.g. Sacks, 1992; Schegloff, 1972), *time formulations* (Button, 1990), *memory formulations* (e.g. Edwards & Potter, 1992; Lynch & Bogen, 1996; Wooffitt, 1992), *story formulations* (e.g. Stokoe & Edwards,

2006), and *script formulations* (e.g. Edwards, 1997). Formulation as description also informs my use of the term *emotion (re)formulations* (see also Edwards, 1999).

(3) Bercelli *et al.* (2008: 47) also examined *reinterpretations*: 'something that, though grounded in what the client has said, is caught and expressed from the *therapist's own perspective* – therefore something possibly different, and ostensibly so, from what the client meant' (emphasis added). Examples of reinterpretations were not found in the present study, indicating the fundamental difference between the institutional settings of therapy and autobiographical research interviews: the object of research interviews is 'eliciting information useful to a study' and the object of therapy is the 'functioning of the patient' (Weiss, 1994: 134). Nevertheless, I suggest that interviewing and 'folk therapy' may often be intertwined.

(4) Antaki (2008) and Bercelli *et al.* (2008) consider what I refer to here as *emotion* or *psychological* reformulations, however Rae (2008) attends more directly to their alternative selections.

(5) Although researchers have primarily studied formulations produced by institutional agents (e.g. therapists, broadcast interviewers), a few studies (e.g. Drew, 2003) have also examined formulations produced by respondents (e.g. clients, interviewees).

(6) On possible instances of 'foreigner talk' or Pidgin (i.e. Hawai'i Creole), see Chapter 4, endnote (2).

(7) Based on the rising final intonation of Rico's response in line 76 (indicated by a question mark on the transcript), it may appear that he is possibly challenging the interviewer's assessment in line 75. However, its fall-rise contour suggests it is produced as a prosodic tag-question (Arndt & Janney, 1987; i.e. 'that's crazy, right?').

(8) Again, no criticism of these scholars is intended. I am simply using them as examples to illustrate that emotion reformulations and emotion management are prevalent throughout L2 interview research and to point out the need for scholars to include the researcher's contributions in data representation and analysis.

(9) Upgrading was found to be much more prevalent than downgrading in the corpus.

7 Managing Emotionality and Distress

> *The interviewer's emotions affect what he or she can hear and understand. If the interviewer is anxious, it may be difficult to really hear what interviewees are saying; if the interviewer is angry at what is being said, he or she may change the direction of the questions or fail to hear positive things about the research question.*
> (Rubin & Rubin, 2005: 26)

> *Clearly, research interviews can and do have strong resonances on interviewees' lives (and others in their lives) and can remain strong in people's memories. And clearly, discussing some topics can raise distinct issues for both interviewees and interviewers. However, those resonances are routinely of a different order and play out in radically different contexts. For us, as researchers, the resonances are never just 'personal' or 'emotional' per se; they are also deeply analytic.*
> (Rapley, 2012: 552)

What I want to consider in the present chapter are some of the 'seen but unnoticed features' (Garfinkel, 1967: 41) of interview-based research and the active work through which participants evoke and manage their own and each other's emotionality. In the preceding chapters, I have suggested that there is sometimes an 'unnatural'[1] tendency within qualitative research training and practice to elevate the positive and successful outcomes of personal inquiry and the investigative and socially embedded nature of this work at the expense of attending also to the dilemmatic and the distressing. However, as the various data and discussions thus far indicate, autobiographical narrative research, as an intimate and highly relational activity, has the potential to expose researchers as well as research participants to a great deal of emotionality associated with storyworld events as well as their (re)production and reception in the present. This emotionality, rather than just an epiphenomenal effect of the processes of research, is regularly found to be the nexus around which the questions, responses, stories and other components of the talk-in-interaction intersect. Indeed, it is central to the creative forces that underlie the research and that shape its interpretive outcomes. Because emotionality unavoidably seeps into and out of research as it unfolds, it may, and often does, result in intrapersonal and interpersonal dilemmas, both subtle and profound, for individuals who find themselves interconnected over the life of the research.

Problems and Failures

In the qualitative methods literature, much has been written on the need for researcher mindfulness and preparation, particularly to better negotiate sensitive topics and identities, to recognize and negotiate power dynamics, and to anticipate possible problems (e.g. Arksey & Knight, 1999; Briggs, 1986; Denzin & Lincoln, 2011; Gubrium *et al.*, 2012; Kirsch, 1999; Kvale & Brinkmann, 2009; Mishler, 1986; Riessman, 2008; Roulston, 2010; Weiss, 1994; Wengraf, 2001). As part of conducting scholarly research, we follow ethical and human-centered protocols by obtaining approval from our institutional review board (IRB), seeking informed consent,[2] preparing our interview questions and working to establish rapport and as non-threatening an interactional environment as possible.

Though introductory research methods courses and texts are essential and unquestionably instructive for novice interview researchers, repeated rehearsal and 'hands-on' experience are perhaps the two most important tools for learning the mindset and skills required of the professional 'craft of interviewing' (Kvale & Brinkmann, 2009). When problems do arise over the course of data generation, they are frequently minor, often attributable to unexpected equipment malfunctions, ambient noise, an over-ambitious investigative scope, ambiguously worded questions, privacy concerns, nervousness or even miscommunication over the goals and procedures of the study. On those rare occasions where we encounter difficulties a bit more serious and unexpected, we may turn to our more seasoned colleagues and the research literature for guidance.

Even for the most novice of interviewers, due to (or perhaps even despite) our conscientious efforts, our interviews and interactions with our research participants go well and we successfully obtain the target data to answer our research questions, thereby allowing us to carry out our particular methods of analyses, representation and dissemination. Because of researchers' and laypersons' familiarity with the generic format that constitutes the public and private activity of interviewing, as well as the apparent ease with which interviews get accomplished, it is not surprising that it is a method taken for granted – even by those whose scholarly careers have come to rely on it (see discussions in Atkinson & Silverman, 1997; Potter & Hepburn, 2012; Rapley, 2012). However, despite increased calls across the academic disciplines for greater reflexivity and rigor in interview research, it remains puzzling how little visible impact there has yet been on researcher training and practice.

For these reasons, I hope that we fail more often and that we fail in unexpected ways. I also hope that we choose to examine and report these failures rather than hide them. It is not until researchers come face to face with situations where their control, competence and confidence are challenged that they become aware of just how dynamic and demanding the activity of interviewing is (Richards, 2009; Roulston, 2010, 2011, 2012). I suggest here that this need for greater self-awareness within research extends also to a greater recognition and closer examination of the emotional work that goes on in the activities of research, especially the interactions between the researcher and research participants.

Emotion Management and Emotional Work

The 'affective turn' that has swept across the social sciences and humanities over recent decades has resulted in much attention to the work of Arlene Hochschild (1979, 1983/2003) and her conceptualization of *emotional labor*. This has led to something of an affective 'bandwagon' (Bolton, 2005), where the term has since lost much of its original focus on customer service encounters and the exchange of services in order to carry out the duties of one's job. Hochschild (1983/2003) distinguishes between *emotional labor* in the workplace (where emotion has an 'exchange value') and *emotion work* or *emotion management* in private contexts (e.g. the home) where it has a 'use value', but these distinctions have been criticized (for a concise review and application of emotional labor to interaction analysis, see Toerien & Kitzinger, 2007; also Benesch, 2011, on emotion work in the field of English language teaching). It should also be acknowledged that Hochschild's work was highly anecdotal and relied largely on self-report data. Toerien and Kitzinger (2007) comment there has been almost no interaction-based analyses of emotional labor.

Because interviews are in many ways a blend of the public and private, as well as the institutional and the conversational, my use of the terms *emotion management* and *emotional work* is informed by Hochschild's observation that emotional labor involves 'management of feeling to create a publicly observable facial and bodily display' (2003: 7) and 'the act of trying to change in degree or quality an emotion or feeling' (1979: 561). I find the concepts 'labor' or 'work' useful because *emotionality* (i.e. emotions *in* and *as* interaction) involves both intrapersonal as well as interpersonal effort (including, e.g. production, reception, interpretation, avoidance, intensification, minimization). This also acknowledges Atkinson's important reminder that fieldwork is also mental, physical *and* emotional work (2015: 4).

My conceptualization of emotion management is also informed by scholarship on emotional regulation, which 'refers to shaping which emotions one has, when one has them, and how one experiences or expresses these emotions' (Gross, 2014b: 6; see also Philippot & Feldman, 2004). Whereas Hochschild's (1979, 1983/2003) work has tended to focus more on individuals' management and displays of their own emotions (i.e. *self*-regulation), I am interested also in *other*-regulation (i.e. the ways in which we display our recognition of others' emotions and our work to shape others' emotions). Because the present project concerns the discursive construction and management of emotion, I have little to say on *actual* emotional states, underlying cognitive processes, explanatory pathologies or the *(un)conscious* nature of this work. Rather, the emotional labor and emotion management I am concerned with involves the interactional and discursive monitoring and shaping of emotionality as it gets foregrounded and backgrounded or otherwise oriented to and not oriented to in various ways in the course of research.

Interviewee Distress and Emotion Management

Because qualitative research involves social beings whose experiences, personalities and subjective understandings and responses are often dynamic and contradictory, personal distress is an inevitable part of the research process. Distress may not always rise to the interactional surface where it is immediately recognizable. It may appear as subtle hints: as pauses, reticence, shifts in energy levels, nonverbal cues (e.g. grimaces, tapping, twitching, averted gaze, crying, nervous laughter), and defensiveness. Distress may also be manifested verbally through explicit statements ('I need a moment', 'can we change the topic?') and vocally through prosodic shifts (e.g. jitter and shimmer – changes in frequency and amplitude).

When research participants project and produce their personal stories, particularly those that concern distressing events in the past (or hypothetical events of the future) or that induce distress for the teller (or the recipient) in the present, researchers may take it upon themselves to neutralize the distressing talk and reestablish a safe and comfortable environment. Anticipating such instances of personal trouble, King (2010: 113), for example, offers some practical advice on how to turn things around when participants exhibit distress:

> You should still always take participant-distress seriously, but the best response is to give them a moment to compose themselves and then offer them choices as to what to do next. You might say something like: 'I can see you find this upsetting. Would you like to take a break now, or move on to a different topic? We can always come back to this point later if you feel like it. If you want to stop the interview altogether that's fine too.' My experience is that people very rarely choose to terminate the interview entirely because of emotional upset – most often they choose to have a short break and then carry on.

Letherby (2000: 101), a feminist researcher, shares a similar experience as she notes '[w]hen women cried I always offered to turn off the tape but only once did an interview end early because a respondent was distressed'. As these and many other researchers observe, even when interviews do give rise to emotionally challenging moments, interviewees are generally able to recompose themselves, thereby allowing the interview to continue. Wengraf (2001: 128), offers a different tack by advising that if strong emotions do come up, the interviewer should mirror and acknowledge them (e.g. 'That makes you sad when you think about it') in 'an empathetic and non-judgmental way' rather than changing the topic or rushing to rescue interviewees. This lets them know that you accept and are not bothered by their emotions:

> If they express feelings of anger, you might say 'You feel angry about it' to show that you understand what the emotion is that they are expressing, in such a way that they can stay with the emotion or emerge from it in their own time. (Wengraf, 2001: 128)

In the course of my own research, I have sometimes encountered occasions where it became apparent that the topic or activity of talk was creating distress for interviewees. In such cases, we changed the topic, took a short break before continuing, or stopped the interview for that day. I consider an example of this below. It bears repeating that throughout this research, I was not intentionally soliciting emotional stories or responses from participants to test them or otherwise provoke emotional episodes.

'Can we stop?'

In one particularly affect-laden interview (Excerpt 7.1), Trang, an immigrant from Cambodia and Vietnam, talked at length about his difficult life experiences. Over the course of the interview, the emotional intensity continued to palpably escalate as he described in detail his failure to be happy, his inability to forget the bad memories and his overwhelming feelings of shame, guilt, sadness and social rejection. Finally, after producing an extended monologic utterance, he asked if we could stop, and I turned off the recorder.

(Excerpt 7.1). Trang: 'Can we stop?'

```
01    T:    I try an' try an' I-I get- (0.3) I we- I went
02          through such emotionally. .hhh (0.5) not
03          physically but emotionally, (.) I- (0.7)
04          emotionally I'm-I'm wreck (0.2) I'm- (0.5) I'm
05          in pieces.
06          ((several lines removed))
07          it different kind of °struggling but still
08          struggling.°
09          (1.2)
10    →     I don't want to: m-make you sad but true, (0.5)
```

```
11              because I knew myself >I'm-I'm-I-I'm so use',<
12              (0.5) I'm so use' to it
13              ((several lines removed))
14              seem like uh: I cannot relax.
15              (1.0)
16              °°you kno:w,°° (0.2) see, like I never feel
17              satisfied and relax=because, (0.7) I have
18              guilt,=I have- (1.5) sadness, (2.6) anxiety?
19              (1.3)
20              >everything,< (0.6) >so many thing (at) that-
21              that< haunted me.
22              ((several lines removed. Trang talks about
23              rejection by Cambodians and other groups))
24              it affect me so much that's why I feel like
25              that.
26              (0.6)
27              >but I shouldn't feel anymore=I know I shouldn't
28              uh-I should just get over it an move o:n. I know
29              that.< .hhhh >but sometime jus- (0.6) when you-
30              when you feel so much< inside become part of
31              you: (.) hard to °forget°.
32              (1.3)
33              °°y'know°°
34              (0.5)
35              because some people if they abuse so much they
36              become just >take it-take it-take it.<
37              (0.7)
38   →          .hh >°'kay Matt can we stop Matt?°<
39              (0.4)
40   →   M:     °°wow°°
41              (1.0)
42   →          tired?
43              (1.0)
44   →   T:     I'm not tired but I'm a little but uh: (0.5)
45   →          sad?
46              (0.5)
47       M:     °yeah that's okay.°
                ((M turns off recorder))
```

Plainly visible here is the intensely descriptive and almost poetic characterization (Blommaert, 2006) by Trang of his personal psychological state (e.g. 'I'm a wreck', 'I'm in pieces', 'struggling', 'haunted', 'I cannot relax', 'I have guilt') and his claims to intimate self-knowledge of such matters (e.g. 'because I knew myself'; 'I'm so use to it'). His descriptions hint at the complexity of this struggle (lines 7–8) and the inability to 'relax' (lines 14, 16–17) or find a place of peace. Incidentally, his characterization of being 'in pieces' (lines 4–5) bears striking resemblance to John's own self-description of his identity struggles described in Chapter 5, Excerpt 5.6: 'I can yeah (.) go to (.) yeah (.) basically (.) I split myself in pieces', and suggests that this fragmentation is as much a way of talking about and embodying emotionality as it is a psychological outcome of experience.[3] Thus, the false starts, perturbations, prosodic stress and other embodied actions constitute discursive artifacts that perform and index through their production the speaker's affective claims of 'being in pieces'.

In keeping with the findings of previous chapters, conspicuously absent here are the interviewer's responses at various relevant points (e.g. lines 9, 15, 19, 26, 32, 34, 37) where he could offer an empathic response (Heritage, 2011) or ask Trang if he wanted to continue or even stop the interview. I have noted that throughout this corpus speakers could be seen to orient to such missing affiliative responses. Thus the escalating emotionality of Trang's story could also be suggestive of his aim to elicit the affiliative responses the interviewer is noticeably failing to provide. Evidence supporting this interpretation is that after each point where the interviewer's response is not forthcoming, Trang incrementally elaborates and escalates his account to the point that he finally asks the interviewer explicitly to stop, which suggests he is orienting to the interviewer's implacable silence as an implicit request to continue. Of course, without video data, it is unclear what facial and other nonverbal cues may also have contributed to this interaction.

This episode is also a reminder of the fact that emotion management is an integral part of interviewees' discursive productions: they actively reflect on, describe, represent, account for, manage, intensify and minimize their own emotionality – in the story and 'internal' (i.e. *intra*-psychological) worlds as well as in the interactional and 'external' (i.e. *inter*-psychological, relational) worlds of the telling. Moreover, as shown in line 10, Trang also orients to this emotion management as he articulates his 'layperson's' analysis and personal concern that his talk here could have a negative effect on the interviewer: 'I don't want to: m-make you sad but true'. He then goes on to describe the long-term psychological effects of mistreatment, ultimately culminating in a request to stop the interview and an explicit self-avowal of his present emotional state (line 45: 'sad').

Following the juncture where Trang requests to stop the interview, the interviewer does give a muted response cry (line 40: '°°wow°°') that suggests he is overwhelmed by the emotionality of these matters. However, rather than explicitly acknowledging this emotionality, he offers a somatic explanation by asking if Trang is 'tired' (line 42). Trang then rejects this as the reason for stopping the interview by giving a tentative, but explicitly psychological or emotional explanation (lines 44–45: 'I'm a little but uh: (0.5) sad?'). Even though the interviewee has confirmed that it is his *emotional* state that is at issue here, the interviewer's softly-produced response ("°yeah that's okay.°") is vague in whether it is comforting (or excusing) Trang for being 'sad' or for stopping the interview.

But I'm a researcher, not a therapist!

This is perhaps one of the most emotional extended productions across Trang's interviews. Consequently, the intense emotionality of it and the psychological distress represented by Trang made me increasingly uncomfortable. Not only was I directly implicated in its collaborative production (e.g. due to my questions, responses, research agenda), I was faced with the predicament of how to manage this highly emotionally-charged outcome of the research project. Although I recall wanting to bring the interview to a close before it reached its emotional zenith, it presented a number of professional and personal dilemmas. I feared that interrupting his talk might possibly damage our interview relationship and his willingness to be forthcoming in the future. As his friend (at least from my perspective), I felt I also had a responsibility to share that burden as listener. It is possible, then, that by withholding an empathic response or emotive involvement (Heritage, 2011; Selting, 2010), I was subtly signaling my discomfort and my detachment from his extended monologue. This also possibly displays my recognition of the interviewee's own apparent discomfort. At the very least, my actions here indicate that I was not explicitly encouraging or sympathizing with this talk.

I was quite certain at the time the interviews and accompanying data were generated for my initial research into the sociolinguistic experiences and language-learning histories of the participants, that I gave little conscious attention to emotionality or emotion management. However, looking back now at these data, and reading through my notes, I see that emotionality was something that I had indeed noticed. I found several times I had noted my puzzlement over why there was so much anger and profound sadness in the tellings produced in the interviews, yet these same speakers often appeared outgoing, playful and carefree in their other social interactions. I also was reminded of questions I had about why some of the participants seemed like they came through their experiences 'better' adjusted (i.e. 'happier') than others.

Trang and John: An emotional comparison

A particularly obvious emotional and discursive contrast was that between Trang and John, whose interviews were the longest and the most in-depth in my data set. They were friends with each other before the start of the study and frequently commented on their longstanding friendship. Each identified as 'gay' (though John presented himself as 'straight' with co-workers and family) and were in long-term relationships with men outside their ethnic communities. Trang and John spoke Vietnamese and English with each other, and they had very similar immigration and life experiences. Although both men were sociable and enjoyable interactants, Trang's stories and his personality were at times overshadowed when anger and sadness came to the surface (as shown previously), which he remarked upon often.

In contrast, John's stories and experiences, though often filled with sadness and some anger, were largely tempered by humor (as previous chapters attest). I discovered in my notes that I had written, 'Why is John so different from Trang?' Reviewing some of the recorded data (shown as Excerpts 7.2a–7.2c), I even found that Trang had explicitly commented on the differences between himself and John in an interview where he details how he was able to leave the refugee camp in Thailand and immigrate to Canada by helping government workers. After describing his personal anger and anxiety in an extended sequence, he then shifts footing (Goffman, 1981), through the use of generic pronominal 'you', to describe the struggles that immigrants face and how others (non-immigrants) respond by labeling them 'uptight' and 'serious'. This again serves as evidence that he understood 'immigrant' as the relevant category under which he was recruited for this study, and that he was expected to give insight into patterns of immigrant experiences as well as his own personal experiences.

(Excerpt 7.2a). Trang: 'Why you so uptight?'

```
01  T:   so you haf- you hafto >struggle each
02       every< day:.
03       (1.7)
04       you know. an' (1.9) sometime you try so
05       hard. s::ome people say "why you so
06       uptight? why you so serious."
07       (1.0)
08       °y'see?°
09       (2.0)
10       "why you so serio- why you so uptight?"
```

Trang then produces a list of various other emotions that immigrants feel (including fear and anxiety) and explicitly describes the sources of those negative emotions and the pressures behind the struggle to contribute and belong to society: language barriers, skin color and educational limitations (Excerpt 7.2b).

(Excerpt 7.2b)

```
27  T:   l-language (0.4) barrier (0.7) because
28       the- (0.6) because (0.6) because the color
```

```
29       of your skin different? because (.) you
30       have problem with English?
31       (1.4)
32       because (0.8) you don't have any (.)
33       degree or bachelor ((degree)). you don't
34       have MUCH to offer. you have MUCH to uh
35       (1.5) to uh to prove that you better.
36       (1.7)
37       °you know?°
38       (4.9)
```

After a conspicuous, almost five-second gap of silence (line 38), Trang switches from characterizing a common immigrant experience to pointing out that the *feelings* toward those experiences may differ among individuals. He then uses John as a contrastive example with himself (Excerpt 7.2c)

(Excerpt 7.2c)

```
39   T:  but you know. each individual. each every
40       person feel different. John (0.7) John
41       might feel different. John might feel,
42       (1.8) oh he's fine. he happy.
43       (1.0)
44       but I feel different.
45       (2.0)
46       Jo- (0.3) John he like where he work.
47       (1.6)
48       XX ((place name in Hawai'i)) like that
49       so simple (.) °right?° so simple. deal with
50       local people making clothes?
51       (2.5)
52       in a way it's good for him.
53       (1.8)
54       but (3.5) people like me. >because I live
55       on the mainland. big city like XX ((city
56       in Canada)).<
57       (1.0)
58       so many people and sometime it's a
59       challenge. t- to deal with all kind of
60       people. ((slaps leg))
61       (0.7)
62       challenge
63   M:  °mm°
```

As this extended sequence illustrates, Trang aligns himself other immigrants (i.e. refugees) in terms of their shared experiences with social, linguistic and educational struggles. However, he also orients to his own emotionality described by unnamed others in negative terms ('uptight', 'anxious', 'serious'), and shows that he recognizes that other immigrants' experiences may differ from his own. Here he explicitly contrasts himself with John (lines 40–42: 'John might feel different.' 'oh he's fine.' 'he happy'), in a lighthearted, even 'naïve' tone, suggesting that an individual's job and social environment (dealing with local, small-town people versus big-city people and crowded social spaces) can have a significant effect on emotional well-being. This also functions as a kind of defensive account, as it assigns the origins of his and other immigrants' negative emotions and psychological struggles not with their individual coping strategies but with their social circumstances and surrounding environments.

I would again like to point out something here that is conspicuous to Trang by its absence: the interviewer's verbal responses to him. In the above excerpts, Trang has repeatedly invited an affiliative or stance-endorsing response from the interviewer through various means: *lexical* and *prosodic tags* (e.g. line 8: 'y'see?'; line 30: 'English?'; line 37: 'you know?', line 50: 'making clothes?'), repetition and inversion (lines 5–6, 10: 'so uptight' and 'so serious'; lines 59, 62: 'challenge'), and numerous *pauses* at key junctures (lines 3, 7, 9, 31, 36, 38, 43, 45, 47, 51, 53, 57, 61). Similar to the previous excerpt (Excerpt 7.1), and perhaps suggestive of the interviewer's discomfort, is that there is only *one* place in this interview sequence where the interviewer responds audibly (63: '°mm°'), and this is a comparatively weak and neutral response that withholds affiliation (see also Ruusuvuori, 2007, on minimal, non-affiliative responses).

As the previous excerpts show, Trang's talk was highly affect-laden. In selecting and organizing his descriptions, he managed that emotionality for himself and for the interviewer. He actively pursued (but often did not receive) affiliative responses from the interviewer, and he made a number of psychological assessments and characterizations regarding the emotional experiences of immigrants, himself and his friend John. I should note that I later discovered that Trang had previously been in professional counseling for his anger and depression issues. This no doubt contributed to his familiarity with the interview context, his orientation to it as a kind of quasi-therapeutic activity and the ways he organized his various experiences for the interviewer. In fact, all of the participants, because of their histories as immigrants and/or refugees, were familiar with producing stories in institutional contexts as they had all told various versions of their experiences to United Nations' workers in the refugee camps and other government officials in order to seek residency and eventually citizenship (see also, Baynham & De Fina, 2005; Maryns & Blommaert, 2001).

In the following section, I consider John's version of his own emotionality as I examine some of his emotional work in our interviews and in other social interactions. This comparison allows insight into some of the similarities and differences between Trang and John, and allows me to reflect back on the question of why these two men were so different. However, from a discursive constructionist perspective, perhaps the more answerable question is '*How* were they so different?'

John: 'Gay or Asian?'

In Chapter 3, I noted that storytelling frequently involves humor and laughter, and even jokes are often narrative-like in their performance (see Norrick, 2000, on narrative jokes in conversation). Whether produced as serious or humorous tellings, stories allow speakers to put their psychological work and worldviews on display and invite affiliative responses and commentary from story recipients. Moreover, by putting a humorous spin on events, particularly those that could be viewed as serious or troubling, speakers show they are not overreacting to the described events or taking things overly seriously (Drew, 1998; Edwards, 2005; Glenn, 2003; Jefferson, 1984, 1988).

I found speakers also used humor to indirectly convey their serious concerns and to represent their current perspective on their experiences. John, an immigrant from Vietnam (but who refers to himself as 'Chinese born in Vietnam'; see Prior, 2011c), regularly infused his talk with humor – for which I was increasingly grateful, due to the plenitude of negative and depressing accounts from other participants. In fact, humor was one of John's sociodiscursive strengths, and something that many of his friends commented upon favorably (just as Trang described him as 'fine' and 'happy' above). Although John's stories offered some of the most disturbing accounts of the experiences of the Vietnamese boat people (some of which I cannot yet bring myself to re-listen to), I found his ability to defuse even the darkest story with humor was a rare talent.

John's pronunciation and grammar marked him as an L2 speaker – a fact he said still bothered him, and a reason why he preferred interacting with 'Local' Pidgin speakers and other L2 English users rather than L1 English speakers (which he equated with *haoles*, or 'Caucasians'), people from the mainland or others whom he viewed as judgmental about a person's language and origin. It is possible that because we had developed a friendship and I was not part of his ethnic or work community, and because we both identified as gay men, the interviews afforded him a relatively safe and neutral space for discussing these matters without fear of gossip or reprisal. As I have noted, John's facility with subtleties of English humor and his ability to interact with others through jokes, puns and song lyrics, often giving them his own entertaining twist, afforded him an important form of social capital. I found this fascinating from my personal and professional interests in L2 development and discourse. Moreover, it served as an important reminder for me that there are many kinds of sociolinguistic and interactional resources and competences that enable speakers to successfully navigate their daily lives and relationships in all the languages they use.

In truth, John is the only person I know who could successfully temper the heavy emotional weight of an account about death and survival by singing, 'At first I was afraid, I was petrified...' (the opening verse of the 1970s disco song and gay anthem *I will Survive* by Gloria Gaynor) and 'Ah, ah, ah, ah, stayin' ali-i-i-ive' from the chorus of *Stayin' Alive* (another 1970s disco hit, by the Bee Gees; see also Excerpt 3.5 in Chapter 3 for another example).[4] On a separate occasion, as he was selecting a story to tell, he began with, 'Have I...Have I told you...' and then launched into a rendition of *Have I Told You Lately That I Love You?*, the 1989 Van Morrison ballad. That was the kind of interviewee and person John was with me: spontaneous, playful and worry-free on the surface of his social interactions but one who repeatedly expressed sadness at his life – specifically his lack of formal education, L2 speaker status and his shame at hiding his sexuality while being fearful of 'coming out'.

The following brief interaction took place at an open community potluck that John, several of our mutual acquaintances and I regularly attended every few months. John sometimes came with his boyfriend and sometimes alone. As a rule, John self-identified, in his words, as 'gay' in private but 'straight' or 'normal' in public. Due to his public compartmentalization of his identities, he was also extremely selective about the personal information he shared with others. Because GLBTQ (gay, lesbian, bisexual, transgender, questioning) and straight (i.e. 'gay friendly') community members and visitors attended this potluck, it was common for participants to speculate amongst themselves about the sexual orientation of those who attended. Although many of the participants sat at mixed gender tables, John preferred to sit with one or two men he already knew (he explained that he was not comfortable with 'straight ladies' or lesbians, but freely admitted this was an irrational fear).

As he did on other occasions, John used the time when it was just the two of us to talk about his life and various personal concerns. While we watched people slowly join the gathering, he spoke about his feelings of shame from having to hide his gay identity and American boyfriend from his family and co-workers (see also Prior, 2011c). He then turned toward me, and in a somewhat melancholic tone, remarked that he usually goes to public events alone. I was unsure how to respond to his statement (e.g. with sympathy or encouragement) – as I did not want to say anything to dampen his party mood or suggest he was having problems with his partner (of which there were rumors), so I kept quiet. After a gap of silence, perhaps orienting to the mismatch between his serious tone and the festive party atmosphere, he produced the following joke (Excerpt 7.3):

(Excerpt 7.3). John: 'Gay or Asian?' (from field notes)

J: It's like they say, 'Would you rather be gay or Asian?' ((laughing))
M: I don't know. ((smiling))
J: Asian. Because you don't have to tell your parents. ((laughter))
Well, that was originally about black people, but it's true. Yeah, it's true. That's me. I don't think I could ever come out. ((serious tone))

Here John makes use of a joke that was circulated in the popular culture at the time. True to his penchant for wordplay and funny stories, he modifies it (satisfying the newness and tellability criterion (Chapter 3) to represent and put a humorous spin on his own identity struggles. Although produced as a lighthearted comment on identity-related conflicts tied to ethnicity, family and sexuality, it nevertheless underscores a serious personal concern that he and other gay Asian men brought up repeatedly throughout our interviews and other interactions: the mutual incompatibility of being gay and being a good, traditional son (see Sullivan & Jackson, 2007, on gay Asian identities and filial piety). In John's case, he suspected that his family on the US mainland possibly knew he was gay, since he was in his forties, had never been married, and lived with a male 'roommate'. But officially coming out to them as 'gay' (which, for his traditional family, he said was tantamount to him announcing he wanted to become a woman) would mean turning his back on his family and cultural heritage.[5] Thus, he could never come out to them unless they somehow 'found out naturally'. He did express some optimism that perhaps someday his nephews and nieces, because they grew up in the US, would be more open and potentially able to act as buffers with his family if they found out he was gay. As these and other data confirm, John also recognized his own emotional work in his daily life as he worked to alternatively hide or claim a 'gay' identity.

Although both Trang and John often discussed struggles and stress related to their traumatic experiences in the past (e.g. their ongoing challenges in their interactions with others within and outside their ethnic and sociolinguistic communities, their perceived difficulties due to their non-native speaker status, and their lack of higher education), the ways they represented and managed the emotionality of their experiences was quite different. Perhaps the most obvious difference between the two men was John's use of jokes and spontaneous musical performances to reframe his experiences in a humorous light, while Trang was generally more serious and commented often on his anger and depression. This is not to say that Trang never joked or was 'pathologically tragic' (as one colleague put it). He joked and did find ways to enjoy life and be social with a select group of people, but anger and depression were issues with which he claimed to continually struggle.[6]

Interviewer's Emotional Work

Although I have focused on interviewees' emotional work, the interviewer is also actively involved in managing emotionality in the course of research. As I have discussed throughout these chapters, in our interviews and other interactions with research participants, we constantly manage the emotionality of the activities, the topics and the relationships in which we are involved. Recognizing this interconnectedness, Davis (2001: 59) asserts, '[u]ltimately, we need to recognize the constant interplay between the personal, the emotional, and the intellectual work of the ethnographer in the field'. Researchers frequently engage in emotional labor (Gilbert, 2001; Lillrank, 2012; Toerien & Kitzinger, 2007) in the research setting as they locate themselves along a continuum of emotional affiliation and detachment within the activities of observing, asking, listening and responding.

Talk of troubles and complaints comprise much of my data. Reflecting back, I often found it emotionally draining (see also Chapter 8) to listen to speakers' repeated talk of anger, sadness, violence, death, struggle, discrimination and the overall unjustness of life. It is one thing to go into a study expecting to investigate speakers' sociolinguistic histories by asking about their experiences learning and using languages – it is another to be repeatedly exposed to (and unprepared for) sad and traumatic tellings and complaints of troubles and injustices. I noted in the discussion of previous excerpts that participants managed their own emotionality in relation to the interview activity and their interpersonal relationship with me as interviewer and perhaps even as a friend; however, my own empathetic responses were frequently missing or relatively neutral. Again, these are things that I did not take notice of at the time. It is only by looking back now with a more careful, contextually sensitive and discursive analytic perspective that I see how much I missed beneath the surface and at the surface of the interview interactions.

One specific issue I became more aware of is how my own initial discomfort with addressing and engaging with negative emotionality and disturbing topics influenced my own emotional work to shape the data trajectory as well as my own emotions and those of the research participants. In the following section, I consider one of these episodes.

Jack: 'A bad word'

Leading up to the following excerpt (Excerpt 7.4), Jack, an immigrant from Cambodia, had made some general statements about how he did not speak any English when he first came to the US from the refugee camp in Thailand. Similar to other study participants who arrived as refugees in their teens, Jack reported that he found high school a place of intense struggle and growth. Not only did he face learning a new language and culture in an unfamiliar social environment, he also had to learn new academic content and genres while navigating the highly complex and confusing web of teenage angst and social relationships. Like most of the other study participants, he had repeated experiences with verbal and physical bullying by American (i.e. 'white') kids (see Kasper & Prior, 2015, for a related story), particularly the first few years after he arrived. He reported that he made his first friends through church groups (his first friend was the pastor)[7] that sponsored local refugee families and other immigrant schoolmates. However, most of his early same-age friends were Lao, whose language, culture and experiences bore general similarities to his own.

In my institutional role as interviewer, I then followed up Jack's talk about his school days by asking if he could think of any particular experiences related to learning English that he might share with me. When no immediate response was forthcoming, I produced an emotion-indexing prompt (lines 1–2) stating that another interviewee had mentioned a 'funny experience' (see Chapters 5 and 6 on interviewer-prompted tellings). Although self-disclosure on the interviewer's part can be a way to enact intimacy and elicit interviewee responses (Rapley, 2012), I have found that other-disclosure (as I do here superficially by sharing some material from a non-present party) can also be an effective elicitation device. Here I used it to frame speakers' tellings as part of a larger collection of immigrant experiences. Though I did not give it much thought at the time, the fact that I specifically used the description 'funny experience' displayed my emotional work to shape our interview talk toward humorous or pleasant events.

It is at this point that Jack follows my prompt by producing an emotion-indexing story preface (lines 6–7; see Chapter 3) leading into what could be characterized as a humorous account of how American students called him an unknown word at school and how he later got mad when he found out it was a 'bad word' (Excerpt 7.4). As mentioned in Chapter 3, all participants commented on at least one memorable, emotion-laden episode that led to them learning and never forgetting a particular word.

(Excerpt 7.4). Jack: 'A bad word'

```
01        M:   an' then he told me, (0.7) about that experience.
02             it was kind of a funny experience.
03             (1.3)
04        J:   u:::m
05             (2.7)
06   →         well? (0.6) (I) remember like s- (.) mos' people
07   →         (they) say bad word we don't know nothing
08             (.)
09        M:   uh[uh
10        J:      [we just say "ye:s", (.) yeah we smiling?=
```

```
11      M:    =uh[uh
12      J:       [EHAHAHAHA .hhh $after we know we say
13            like "oh like THIS guy BA:(H)D"$ ((claps hands))
14      M:    oh (.) like (.) that happened here?
15            (0.8)
16            in,
17      J:    $°in United Sta[te°$              ]°°uhu:h°°=
18      M:                   [>in the United State]s?<
19      J:    °in Indiana this the firs' state I come here°
20      M:    OH Indiana?
21            (0.5)
22      J:    °yeah°
23            (1.3)
24      M:    so what happened
25            (1.2)
26      J:    so (I was) y'know I feel uh awww=now I know
27            that- (.)$that one you cannot say that word
28            anymo(h):r(h)e$ heheheh
29      M:    oh- like students were saying to you?=
30      J:    $°yeah°$         [°yeah][yeah (thas right)°
31      M:    =like classmates at [       ][school?
32            (1.0)
33  →   J:    °that "we're gonna fuck you" or something=I
34  →         don't know that guy ( ) did they "fuck you
35  →         you" $"OKA::::Y$ [I (love) you" (.) smiling
36      M:                    [>eheh eheh eheh<
37      J:    >(I know I [do        ]that)<
38                       [((J slaps leg))]
39            (0.5)
40            when I know that word °(that's when) I get mad
41            [#uh#°
42      M:    [oh
43            (1.8)
44            was it difficult learning English?
              ((S talks about learning English in high school))
```

When I examined these interview data, I gradually became aware of several things about it that made me uncomfortable – at the time it was generated and in later reflection. Earlier in this interaction, Jack and I discovered that we had both gone to school in the same city, though at different schools and at different times. Because this was fresh in my mind, Jack's talk about being bullied by American students made me recall my own similar memories of junior high and the unpleasant emotions attached to them. Because we had built up a friendship over our various interactions,

I struggled with whether or not to share my own stories with him or not. In the end, I decided not to inject my own experiences into the interview because the primary purpose of our interviews was to understand his experiences, not mine.

I also recall feeling some discomfort at the time of this interview because the mood of all our previous interactions had been relatively lighthearted, which may have been another reason for me expecting or inviting a 'funny' story from him. Like John, Jack stood out from other participants because of his outgoing personality and his ability to manage talk of traumatic events and present challenges through humor and playful jokes. By re-examining these data, I can see that I attempted to lighten the mood through my story prompt (line 2: 'It was kind of a funny experience'). My responses to his telling are also comparatively subdued, consisting mainly of neutral continuers (lines 9, 11: 'uhuh'; line 24: 'so what happened'), and confirmation requests (line 14: 'oh (.) like (.) that happened here?'; line 20: 'OH Indiana'; line 29: 'oh- like students were saying to you?'). My strongest response in this sequence was at the emotional highpoint or punch line of his story (line 35), where I produce repeated and affiliative laughter in overlap with his smiling reply to the bullies ('I (love) you').

As I noted previously, another point of tension I faced on occasion with Jack was that his humor often had a sexual undertone, and he often playfully flirted with and propositioned me and other male friends. For this reason, I was often on guard to avoid responding to his innuendos either positively or negatively. Though Jack's marked English production here makes a clear analysis difficult, lines 33–35 could be heard as a kind of sexualized double entendre (i.e. a threat of bullying and/or talk of a sexual experience). Because my impression of his talk is unavoidably framed by our prior interactions,[8] it may be that I am misattributing meaning to this utterance. After all, even Freud is said to have remarked that 'a cigar is sometimes just a cigar' (Faragher & Heiman, 1954: 656). But I am also reminded of Hochschild's statement that 'Freud generally found sexual stories beneath social ones, but there are social stories beneath sexual ones' (2003: 183). Perhaps this story was doing multiple things – producing an autobiographical and entertaining telling while imbuing it with sexual innuendo, which would be in keeping with much of his other talk.

Regardless of what Jack's intentions may or may not have been, his inapt and humorously emphatic response to their threats (line 35: '$'OKA::::Y$ I (love) you') punctured the tension in the 'there-and-then' storyworld and in the 'here-and-now' interview world, which may also explain my enthusiastic laughter-filled response (line 36). The previous humorous stance then suddenly dissipates as Jack shifts into a more somber tone in line 40 as he recharacterizes the 'humorous encounter' as a serious and threatening event, because that is when he got 'mad'. Though I could have followed up his talk about getting *mad*, after a gap of silence (line 43), I explicitly refocus the topic by producing a polar (yes-no) question, produced in a neutral tone: 'was it difficult learning English?' In this way, I essentially ignored the emotionality of the previous telling, the possible sexual or violent undertones, the profanity and the more serious, anger-inducing peer conflict (i.e. those things that made *me* uncomfortable). Instead, I changed the topic to ancillary matters (Heritage, 1998) involving generic difficulty with language learning, thus reducing the emotional intensity of his talk and narrowing the parameters of his possible response.

Emotional Contagion

Thus far, I have commented on the ways in which interviewees and interviewers work to manage their own emotionality as well as the emotionality of their interlocutors. I now consider another aspect of emotional work. For researchers involved in investigating topics and contexts that involve highly emotional content and interaction, there is invariably a risk that emotionality connected to their research topic and data, their relationships with the research participants and even their own responses can spill over into their personal lives (Kleinman & Copp, 1993; Lee-Treweek & Linkogle, 2000). This is an aspect of research that is too often absent from the autobiographical interview research literature, even more so in the L2 literature. However ethnographers and scholars in the health sciences have long recognized that prolonged and close fieldwork can have an intense and long-lasting impact on the researcher (Arksey & Knight, 1999; Atkinson *et al.*, 2003; Dickson-Swift *et al.*, 2007; Dunn, 1991; Johnson & Clarke, 2003; Kleinman & Copp, 1993; Lillrank, 2012). In research contexts where it takes a long time to build relationships and establish trust, and where researchers are embedded and highly involved with a particular community or community members, the potential for the research to have a negative impact on the researcher is even more likely.

Along with the institutional activities of observing, asking questions and responding to participants' responses, researchers also engage in (and withhold, as shown in previous chapters) displays of understanding and empathy that show research participants how they understand and acknowledge their experiences and personal responses to them. However, an often unforeseen consequence of this empathic listening and relational work is that of 'emotional contagion' (Hatfield *et al.*, 1994; Planalp, 1999; cf. Wetherell, 2012, for a related critique), whereby listeners not only identify with their interactants, they also run the risk of 'picking up' or becoming 'infected' with speakers' emotional states. Intimacy and interpersonal sharing therefore facilitate emotional contagion. In the case of more 'positive' emotions or their associated actions (e.g. joy, humor, laughter), there is likely little threat to interlocutors' sense of well-being. However, when interviewees produce accounts of *anger* and/or express *anger* (or *sadness, fear,* etc.), for example, interviewers in turn may find themselves affiliating with the teller by similarly directing their own anger toward the people and events in the storyworld. They may also respond by 'feeling' or experiencing anger in the interactional world of the telling.

I have even witnessed emotional contagion spread vicariously in data sessions, a common disciplinary activity where novice and experienced researchers share data and hone their analytical skills. On several occasions when participants brought in recorded data that were highly emotional, I observed that the nonverbal and verbal cues of the listeners (i.e. session participants) frequently mirrored – to varying degrees – the emotions (e.g. *anger, happiness*) displayed or indexed by the speakers in these data.[9] If data were humorous, participants in the data sessions responded with laughter and appeared relaxed. If the data involved speakers showing frustration or discomfort, participants could also be seen to reflect those emotions. Following several conference talks where I presented some analyses of particularly emotion-filled segments, I have been approached by some audience members who reported that they found themselves crying or feeling upset in response to the data.

Emotional Danger

Adding to the emotional labor of the interview, the research activities of repeatedly listening to, transcribing and analyzing the recorded data further expose researchers to personal distress and even *emotional danger*. Lee-Treeweek and Linkogle (2013: 13) define 'emotional danger as the experience of severe threat due to negative "feeling states" induced by the research process'. The repeated vicarious exposure to emotionality and talk of difficulty and traumatic events can result in secondary traumatic stress that leaves the researcher feeling emotionally and physically affected (e.g. agitated, exhausted, emotionally drained; Arksey & Knight, 1999; Chrestman, 1999; Christophe & Rimé, 1997; Dunn, 1991; Lee-Treweek & Linkogle, 2000; Stamm, 1995). Dunn (1991: 390), writing about the 'health hazards' of qualitative research, dramatically describes the personal impact of her interviews with battered women:

> Conducting the interviews for this study was an emotionally-draining experience. I would often become choked with emotions during the tearful interviews. These same emotional responses were repeated numerous times in the course of reviewing and transcribing the tapes and analyzing the data. I experienced anger and powerlessness, which resulted in sleep disorders and other somatic complaints that were similar to those voiced by the informants.

I distinctly recall that when I first began conducting interviews with research participants discussed in this book (as well as others not discussed here), many of them began by detailing their experiences with war, escape and survival in the refugee camps. These vivid and dramatic tellings were filled with talk of death, fear and other experiences involving discrimination and cruelty. After conducting several of these interviews in person and then repeatedly listening to the recordings, I discovered myself dwelling on these stories and even having difficulty sleeping as I replayed imagined versions of my participants' stories and experiences in my head. I found myself thinking about what I would do if I were in those situations. But that did not make any sense. These were not *my* experiences, so why should they affect me? It was only later by consulting the research literature and comparing my reactions with those of other researchers that I recognized that due to the intimate nature of the relationships we build with our research participants, we often cannot help but identify with them and their experiences. In other words, the personal empathy and sensitivity that enables us to successfully cultivate rapport with our research participants and carry out thoughtful analyses is also that which may threaten our own personal well-being. Even now, when reviewing data from my L2 interview participants about discrimination, isolation, abuse, anger and other emotional matters, I find myself ruminating on some of those stories and feeling agitated, even with the separation of time and physical distance from the initial contexts of the tellings.

Despite the existence of published accounts from the field about the hazards and difficulties of research, few are included in research methods courses (as informal queries to colleagues confirm). As a result of the lack of attention to these matters, I suggest that researchers remain inadequately prepared to manage the potential psychological impact of and challenges involved in conducting interviews and related qualitative research – particularly research that involves sensitive topics and close interaction with members from stigmatized communities and participants with traumatic histories. For this reason, some scholars (primarily in the disciplines of health care, psychology and feminist studies) advocate extending ethical considerations to include the researcher's own self-care:

> ... qualitative researchers need to be encouraged to think through issues relating to developing rapport, developing attachments to participants, dealing with vulnerability, listening to untold stories, and mental and physical exhaustion. Researchers and research supervisors should also ensure that researchers are well armed with appropriate contact details of possible sources of professional advice and support for those participants who may need ongoing therapeutic support. (Dickson-Swift *et al.*, 2007: 344)

Dickson-Swift *et al.* (2007: 345) also point out that 'debriefing, counseling, scheduling of rest breaks' and developing 'protocols focusing on both physical and emotional safety' are important strategies for reducing the emotional danger of research on the researcher's well-being. Because researchers in L2 studies and applied linguistics are largely interested in people and problems and in the 'real world', and because they recognize that 'we live amid a world of pain' (Poster, 1989: 3; also Pennycook, 2001: 5), it is inevitable that our research will produce conditions that create or topicalize personal distress and therefore require some level of emotional work or emotion management. As a result, the pressing question is not just what we will do when that happens, but rather how we will prepare ourselves *before* that happens.

Summary

In this chapter I considered some of the ways that interviewers and interviewees manage their own and each other's emotionality. Looking back on my novice researcher self, I recognize now how little conscious consideration I had given to the management of potentially sensitive or distressing topics. However, my present conviction is that preparing for such eventualities is part of researchers' ethical and moral responsibilities to their research participants, and to themselves. Even though we prefer to see ourselves as researchers rather than *emotional brokers* (i.e. counselors or therapists), as active investigators of human life and experience we nevertheless engage in professional practices that overlap in many ways (at least superficially) with psychotherapeutic interaction. As a result, we are frequently put in the position of having to do emotional work – for ourselves and for our research participants. It is ethically imperative that we anticipate these eventualities and prepare in advance a list of mental health professionals and social agencies that we can consult and refer our participants and ourselves to when circumstances warrant such intervention (Dickson-Swift *et al.*, 2007; Weiss, 1994).

Dunn (1991: 389), citing Van Maanen's (1988) ethnographic work, urges qualitative researchers to cultivate even greater recognition of the emotionality of research and advocate analytical transparency by incorporating their own emotional reactions into their published studies.

> Therefore, reports of qualitative studies should include not only the researcher's observations but the researcher's experiences because these experiences can affect the data analysis (Van Maanen, 1988). Personal involvement with subjects may produce pain and stress within the researcher as informants relate their lived experiences. The researcher must identify these physical and emotional reactions and acknowledge the possibility that such reactions may influence the interpretation of qualitative data (Van Maanen, 1988).

Atkinson (2015: 166) argues that this does *not* mean that researchers should elevate the emotional at the expense of anything else. Emotions, whether those of research participants or researchers, are no less and no more than any other forms of expression and thus require the same kind of 'methodical and sustained analysis'. However, as I pointed out in Chapter 1, an ever-present concern for scholars who do give space to such matters in their work is that they may find themselves in a Catch-22 situation in their academic career path (Gilbert, 2001). By focusing on emotions and possibly confirming emotionalist and other stigmatized stereotypes, scholars 'may end up positioned below rational cognitive actors in the hierarchy constructed on the basis of dominant conceptions' (Gilbert, 2001: 133) or accused of falling to the 'Romantic fallacy', where they emphasize the personal and experiential over systemic attention to social action and organization (Atkinson, 2015). I do not have ready answers for these dilemmas, since no professional context is precisely the same and researchers must make their own determinations regarding how best to manage and make visible their own emotional work and its consequences throughout the processes of conducting and disseminating research.

It is my contention that autobiographical interview research and narrative inquiry would benefit greatly from greater transparency and attention to the actual (rather than 'ideal') practices of research and the dilemmas, failures and 'messiness' that we invariably encounter. Dickson-Swift *et al.* (2007: 347) articulate these personal and professional challenges faced by qualitative researchers in the field of health research, and they go on to question whether researchers in other disciplines face similar issues:

> While the current research clearly demonstrated that there are a number of issues faced by qualitative researchers undertaking health research on sensitive topics, we do not know whether researchers from other disciplines such as sociology, anthropology, psychology, nursing and social work face similar issues to those reported here. Further empirical work with researchers from a range of backgrounds would extend the findings discussed here.

The findings of the present project unequivocally affirm that autobiographical interview researchers and L2 scholars do indeed face similar issues as those faced by qualitative researchers in other disciplines. In addition to increased transparency within our disciplinary borders, perhaps more transdisciplinary dialogue and cross-fertilization would improve the conditions of research as well as the conditions for researchers and research participants.

Notes

(1) In the Prologue, I commented that I found some aspects of researcher reflexivity 'unnatural' because it was contrary to my *personal* nature. Here I refer to turning a blind eye to the troubling aspects of research as *professionally* 'unnatural' because it reflects a severely limited portion of the human socio-affective experience.

(2) For an important discussion on informed consent, see Hammersley (2014a,b), Smith (2014), Taylor (2014).
(3) Talk of identity fragmentation and dilemmas was found throughout the interview corpus. Interestingly, these matters were often described in relation to the metaphors of 'water' and 'wind':

> **Kim:** it's you say (.) you pick your destiny (.) I mean you pick your- (.) I mean you make your decision. drifting along with the current (.) or you fight back.
> **John:** °so, (.) I guess° (.) <u>so</u> (.) <u>like</u> (.) so to me I'm like a sailboat? (.) I <u>sail</u> wherever that (.) the wind blow me to?
> **Trang:** le'ssay you have to bend yourse- y'have to bend. [...] like a tree in order like a wind okay e-example like a wind okay (.) blowing the tree. .hh (0.7) a tree alway go f- (0.9) any side that the wind blow the tree go (a b- a) go with (1.0) °right?° (1.0) and then (0.5) go back (.) the way it is.

(4) It is interesting to note that the first two songs from the 1970s reflect the music that was available to John at the time he escaped Vietnam, so the songs were also reinforcing the particular time frame of his stories (i.e. as temporal 'background' music). *Have I Told You Lately That I Love You* is from a later time frame and coincided with tellings of later events.
(5) John and other Asian men commented that it was much easier for 'girly' or 'feminine' gay men in their ethnic communities because they never had to 'come out'.
(6) There may likely be some cultural components to the ways that speakers manage their emotional histories and emotionality in the present (see also Chapter 8). Tom Vendetti's (2003) powerful documentary *Years of Darkness* tells the story of the mental and emotional health challenges of Sam Khong, a Cambodian man residing in Hawai'i. As part of his mental health treatment, Sam returned to Cambodia after 29 years to seek out his remaining family members and explore the ties to his past. His story closely parallels Trang's experience in many significant ways and offers rich insights into the long-term experiences and mental health challenges of Southeast Asian immigrants living in the US and Canada.
(7) Many immigrants from Cambodia and Vietnam were sponsored by various church and charity groups. After arriving, and to this day, many still attend church while also following their own Buddhist or other spiritual practices. Several immigrants I met said that church was a good way for them to develop community relationships, practice English (many churches offer English as a second language classes) and maintain their heritage language skills, regardless of their actual religious beliefs. Some even saw it as a kind of 'game', where they listened to the sermons and went to bible classes while using those opportunities primarily for linguistic rather than spiritual development.
(8) This is another reason why longitudinal interviews are useful, because they can enable the researcher to establish a baseline of speakers' talk for comparison.
(9) See also comments on the connections between interactional displays of emotion and emotion regulation in Peräkylä and Sorjonen (2012) and Ruusuvuori (2013).

8 Being 'Negative'

> *Anomie and alienation, regardless of the way they are brought about, are not only antithetical to the maintenance of a rule-based society, but they also play an important negative role in morale, personal motivation, identity, and social commitment. Other words for these states of mind are 'powerlessness', 'meaninglessness', 'norm-lessness', 'isolation', and 'estrangement from the self', all of which have negative emotional consequences.*
> (Lazarus, 1999: 39)

> *Because when you go home ... you feel ... you feel ...'You know I'm not ... I'm not happy the way I live ... I'm not happy at all.' Here, yes ... here's ... here's rich country ... here's North America. Supposed to be whatever they think. But you know it's very hard here. You feel very ... you feel left out. Each every day you go to work, you feel left out because you don't belong. Because everyone communicate with English.*
> (Trang, study participant)

In Chapter 1, I specified that though the central project of this book is the discursive construction and management of emotionality in L2 autobiographical interview research, I was not seeking to ascribe special status to stories of hardship over stories of success or to elevate 'negative' emotions over 'positive' ones. Nevertheless, based on the preceding chapters it is apparent that much of the autobiographical interview material I have discussed routinely involved actions that 'expected' and supported talk of personal troubles and transgressive events. In this chapter, I take up this phenomenon in more detail by examining factors that may explain the apparent expectation in some interview interaction of the production of 'negatively'-valenced talk.[1] I begin by considering not just negative emotionality but interviewees' active resistance to talking about positive or 'happy' emotions and experiences.

As a point of clarification, by 'negativity', I am referring to the so-called 'negative' (i.e. *sadness, anger, depression*) and 'positive' (i.e. *happiness, laughter, contentment*) binary. This is admittedly a simplistic dualism, but it will suit my purposes here. I am not expressing a value judgment regarding particular emotions (i.e. 'positive' emotions are good, 'negative' emotions are bad). In fact, there may be times when it is normatively 'good' to be *sad* and 'bad' to be *happy* (e.g. at a funeral). Through an analysis of data excerpts from my L2 interview corpus, I consider how interviewees resist and transform talk of positive emotionality in ways that minimize happy and relatively trouble-free perspectives and emphasize negative, trouble-filled or neutral experiences. In the second half of the chapter, I draw on various lines of interdisciplinary emotion research to discuss other factors that potentially contribute to the negative tilt found in some autobiographical talk and interviews.

Resisting 'Positive' Emotionality

In the preceding chapters I have described that L2 autobiographical interviews can be found to generate complaints and stories of mistreatment and other experiences that are intense, memorable and that have resulted in adverse socio-psychological consequences (e.g. *stress, sadness, disappointment, anger, fear, estrangement, isolation*) for the teller. In Chapters 4–6, I showed that this preference toward talk of negative experience and emotionality is at least partly traceable to the scope of the responses the interviewer's questions invite and make relevant. For example, though *feeling questions* and other explicitly emotion-indexing questions allow for a range of responses (e.g. negative, positive, neutral), *emotion-implicative questions* and *reformulations* (e.g. utterances that use descriptions such as 'hard', 'problem', 'tough', 'happy', 'great', 'best' and so on) greatly narrow the range of potential responses. They thus force interviewees to either take up those descriptions to follow the conversational preference for agreement or work up an account to justify disagreement with the interviewer.[2]

In pointing out some of the ways that the interviewers may prompt and co-construct talk of an emotional nature, I am not suggesting that they only pursue and validate negative emotions and experiences. In my own L2 interview corpus, though troubles tellings and complaints were common, there were also humorous tellings, most often where speakers displayed resistance to their troubles (Jefferson, 1984) by reframing them in less serious terms. There were also explicit interviewer requests for positive (e.g. 'happy') experiences. A curious finding is that these 'positive' emotionality pursuits most often led to elicitation failures. To illustrate interviewee resistance to positive emotionality, I analyze here a few cases of interviewer prompts that failed to elicit positive talk.

'Happiest memory'

Excerpt 8.1 took place in my first recorded interview with Bona, an immigrant man from Cambodia. Bona and I previously met through Jack, a mutual Cambodian acquaintance and study participant, at a community social gathering. Leading up to this sequence, Bona came to Jack's apartment so that I could interview him. Jack was in the kitchen cleaning and cooking while Bona and I talked in the living room. After Bona and I made some small talk and got comfortable, he then responded to my prompts by talking about his family, friends, immigration experiences and his recent move for work. This excerpt shows how the interviewer initiates an explicit and 'positive' emotion-related topic by asking Bona about his 'happiest' memory:

(Excerpt 8.1). Bona: 'Happiest memory'

```
01   →   M:   so- (1.4) what's yer- what's your happiest
02   →        memory?
03            (0.5)
04       B:   happiest memory?
05            (1.0)
06            I don't know.
07            (2.0)
08            happiest memory what is that?
09            (1.0)
10            never heard of that. ha ha ha
11       M:   never heard of it?
12            (0.8)
13       B:   never heard of that.
14       M:   heh heh heh=
15       B:   =hh hm hm hm ((muffled laughter))
16            (1.7)
17   →   M:   would you say you're a happy person?
18            (1.8)
19       B:   ah::: (2.2) below that
```

In this segment, the interviewer asks Bona, by means of an extreme case formulation (Pomerantz, 1986), to provide a story of his *'happiest' memory* (lines 1–2). As a declarative question (contrast with *'Do you have* a happiest memory?'), it presumes Bona has a 'happiest' story to tell. After a brief pause, Bona responds dryly with a partial repetition (Sacks, 1992) of the interviewer's utterance (line 4: 'happiest memory?'). Partial repetition or try-marked utterances with rising intonation have been found to be common in other-initiated repair (Sacks & Schegloff, 1979; Schegloff *et al.*, 1977) as well as dispreferred actions such as disagreements (e.g. Koshik, 2005; Pomerantz, 1984; Sidnell & Stivers, 2013). Among the possible (and overlapping) functions of Bona's partial repetition are to: (a) locate a source of trouble in the interviewer's question, (b) request confirmation, (c) resist providing 'happy' talk, or (d) acknowledge and align with the topic by displaying a memory search. The partial repetition is followed by a longer one-second gap of silence (line 5), and then Bona in a prosodically flat tone rejects the interviewer's story request by claiming a lack of knowledge (line 6: 'I don't know'). After a longer two-second gap of silence and still no response or clarification forthcoming from the interviewer, Bona then self-repairs his own response by indicating that the trouble source lay with the meaning of the phrase 'happiest memory', not a mishearing or failed understanding. With an extreme case formulation (line 10: '<u>never</u> heard of <u>that</u>') and prosodic stress on *never* and *that*, Bona intensifies his resistance through his epistemic assertion that he does not know what 'happiest memory' is.

Based on Bona's high competence in conversational English, it is unlikely that his claim not to know 'happiest memory' is to be taken at face value. Indeed, his subsequent laughter in line 10 confirms that his response is to be treated as humorous and even sarcastic. Laughter often accompanies a closing of a sequence (Glenn, 1992; Holt, 2010; Liddicoat, 2011) and can signal that interactants are orienting to particular matters as delicate (Haakana, 1999, 2010). Bona's laughter in line 10 can therefore be hearable as resistance toward this line of talk and a bid to shut it down. He then repeats the punch line of his joke (another closing move) and the interviewer joins in with affiliative laughter, immediately followed by more laughter from Bona. With this line of questioning effectively terminated, the interviewer then reformulates his question from an open-ended request for Bona's 'happiest experience' to a *yes-no* question asking Bona to conduct a self-analysis of his psychological well-being (line 17: 'Would you say you're a happy person?'). Bona's utterance ('ah:::'), marked by a sound stretch and surrounding pauses, displays both hesitancy as well as a cognitive search in response to the interviewer's question. Instead of responding with 'yes' or 'no' (e.g. 'Yes, I am', 'No, I'm not') type-conforming response (Raymond, 2003; Schegloff, 2007) – which may potentially lead to a sequence requiring Bona to account for his answers – this line of questioning also gets closed down by Bona with a statement (line 19: 'below that') that again rejects the possibility of characterizing him as 'happy'.

As this sequence shows, despite the interviewer's repeated requests for 'happy' talk, the interviewee resists this particular categorization and positive valorization. Yet, even though he avoids identifying with the positive or 'happy' label, he skillfully does it in a way that resists overtly identifying as 'unhappy' or 'negative' (i.e. 'below that' is ambiguous and avoids taking an explicitly negative stance). As a result, he is able to characterize his psychological status for the interviewer while avoiding the appearance of taking life too seriously (or too lightly).

'Are you happy here?'

Another example of resistance to 'happy' talk comes from an interview with Kiet (K), an adult immigrant man from Vietnam (Excerpt 8.2). This interview took place in a metropolitan city in California, where Kiet and his family ran a successful nail salon. In this interview, Kiet talked about his life in Vietnam and compared it to life in the US. He spoke often of his desire to go back to Vietnam because life in the United States was 'too hard' (due to his limited formal English skills, lack of education and permanent status as an immigrant and cultural outsider). The following data fragment begins with the interviewer asking Kiet to comment on his happiness.

(8.2). Kiet: 'You happy here?'

```
01  →   M:    are you happy in XX ((city name))?
02              (1.0)
03  →         you happy here?
04      K:    good choi' (.) (this is) my family he:re? (.)
05            my mom, (.) you know I'm gay li:fe. I don't
06            have family, so (0.8) I (thinks) I live with
07            my (parent).
08              (1.0)
09            sometime I so upset I want move.
10              (0.7)
11            I had before few people (0.5) they want invite
12            me go live uh-out state?
13      M:    uhuh
14      K:    and live with them. they have a house already
15            [have] business nail salon (.)
16      M:    [yeah]
17      K:    take care of me
18      M:    why not?
19      K:    I just work.=I can't.
              ((K talks about being tied down by family and
              business and thus unable to move.))
```

In line 1, the interviewer explicitly invokes an affective frame by first asking Kiet if he is 'happy' in the city where he lives. After a one-second pause and no uptake by Kiet, he immediately reformulates it to 'happy here'. The place formulation (Schegloff, 1972) in line 1 restricts Kiet's response to a particular location. The revised question in line 3 ('happy here') is ambiguous and thus offers a wider range of responses ('here' can potentially refer to his city as well as California, the US, North America, and so on). It may be that the reformulation is a strategic move on the part of the interviewer to elicit talk from the interviewee, as it follows the lack of response from Kiet in line 2. Both utterances in lines 1 and 3 are positive polarity questions that project an affirming answer as a type-conforming response. Instead of providing a *yes-no* response, Kiet lexically ties his answer ('here') to the interviewer's question (indicating its relevance) and frames living in that place not as a matter of happiness (thus rejecting 'happy' talk), but as a decision based on his duty to his family (e.g. his family is there; he is a single, gay man). Kiet then produces an emotional story preface (line 9: 'sometimes I so upset I want to move') that leads into talk about people who have invited him to move away and be a part of their nail salon businesses. However, despite his desire to relocate and be independent, family obligations prevent him from doing so.

This excerpt is filled with a number of category contrasts invoking tensions related to, for example, *emotions* (happy-upset), *place* (here-out of state), *people* (family, mom, parent-friends), and *institutions* (family nail business-other nail business). Rather than free-flowing components of memory recall, these category-bound tensions are produced in direct response to the interviewer's questions in lines 1–3. As a display of intersubjectivity toward the interviewer, Kiet ties his response to the interviewer's question by framing it in terms of emotionality (e.g. 'unhappy'). Rejecting the interviewer's focus on 'happy' talk, Kiet speaks of being 'unhappy' or 'upset', thereby progressing the interview toward talk of difficult experiences and negative emotionality.

Throughout this corpus, as Excerpts 8.1 and 8.2 illustrate, interviewer moves to elicit talk of happy experiences were frequently met with failure. Interviewees regularly avoided characterizing their own emotional states, experiences, etc. in happy/positive terms by responding with non-type-conforming responses. Non-type-conforming responses to *yes-no* questions have been shown to be a device by which interviewees resist the institutional agenda or presuppositions behind the question (Raymond, 2003; Stivers, 2008). Although I offer these data as further evidence that both interviewee and interviewer may orient to a preference *toward* talk of negative emotions and experiences in research interviews, it may more accurately be the case that they are orienting *away from* positive or 'happy' talk. Though the discursive outcome may be the same (i.e. 'negative' emotionality and troubles tellings), the antecedent cause may be different. This may be an important distinction worth investigating in future research.

Thus far, I have identified that this negative preference is due at least partly to interviewer questioning patterns and responses as well as the shared interactional history between interviewer and interviewee. In my data, participants regularly produced complaints and troubles tellings. This may have been because I showed an explicit interest in their emotions, because I structured the interview in an open-ended and non-threatening manner, and because they were invited to speak 'as immigrants' to non-immigrants (i.e. the interviewer and a future audience). In the following section, I step beyond the boundaries of conversation analysis (CA) to consider how these discursive practices intersect with other contributing factors that potentially influence the emotional valence of autobiographical material.

Explaining 'Negativity'

Researcher bias

Even a cursory review of the interdisciplinary research literature on qualitative interviewing, personal narratives and emotion/affect reveals a strong tendency of researchers as well as research participants to focus on 'negative' (e.g. *anger, fear*) rather than 'positive' emotions (e.g. *joy, happiness*). In psychology, where the investigation of affective matters has been most prominent, there is growing criticism of research practices that attend primarily to negative emotions and people's coping strategies while failing to also adequately investigate positive emotions (e.g. Folkman, 2011). Explaining researchers' interest in negativity in psychology, Robbins (2006: 174) notes, 'Positive experiences such as joy are viewed as mere coping mechanisms and negative experiences are believed to be authentic.' This negative orientation is not limited to psychology but permeates the broad interdisciplinary field(s) of research on emotion/affect, including applied linguistics and multilingualism studies (e.g. Dewaele, 2010; Pavlenko, 2005; Wierzbicka, 1999). In the field of second language acquisition, studies of individual differences such as language anxiety and motivation/demotivation have been long-standing topics of interest (e.g. Dörnyei & Schmidt, 2001; Dörnyei & Ushioda, 2009; Gardner, 1985; Horwitz & Young, 1991; Tsui, 1996) and may just as likely be contributors to the negativity orientation in L2 research as they are indicative of it. However, recent L2 scholarship shows a growing interest in drawing from positive psychology and investigating positive affect (see contributions in Dörnyei *et al.*, 2014; Gabryś-Barker & Bielska, 2013). In the near future, we may witness a 'positive' affective turn as scholars identify and explore the role of *happiness* and other positive dimensions that promote as well as result from language learning, language use and social participation.

Though the emphasis on negativity may appear to be a signature of my own data corpus, the work of many other applied linguists can similarly be found to contain talk of 'anger', 'sadness', 'fear', 'shame' and other 'negative' emotions (e.g. Baynham & De Fina, 2005; Block, 2007; Kamada, 2010; Kinginger, 2004; Menard-Warwick, 2009; Miller, 2011; Norton, 2000; Norton Peirce, 1995; Sandhu, 2014; Vitanova, 2004). In the previous chapter I noted that applied linguists, whose raison d'être is addressing language-related *problems* in the real world (Davies, 2007; Kaplan, 2010), are some of the most prolific producers of interviews and narrative research. It is little wonder, then, that their research questions and findings regularly attend to identity conflict and talk of problems and negative affect. Miller's (2014: 137) findings on immigrant learners of English are representative of many of the negative accounts found across much L2 language and identity research involving personal narratives and interviews:

... in my analysis of their production of evaluative stance toward their capacity to learn English, I showed that the majority of the interviewees consistently produced negative evaluations. Many of them disparaged their language proficiency as still limited and problematic. These negative stance acts were typically embedded in accounts that also highlighted constraints to their capacity to learn English well.

Perhaps much of the contemporary emphasis on negativity may be attributable also to the social turn (Block, 2003) in L2 studies and researcher interest in revealing the personal understandings and dramatic aspects of human experience and communication. Within L1 and L2 autobiographical interview research, as illustrated throughout these chapters, negative emotionality is also closely implicated in the representation of experience and speakers' claims of authenticity and their work to assemble factual or believable accounts for the researcher.

Tell-ability and share-ability of troubles talk

Although the researcher's agenda and actions are certainly implicated in the foregrounding of negative emotionality, they are not the only contributing factors. Negative emotionality may also be attributable to the basic norms of conversational reporting and storytelling (but see Rintell, 1990, for a counter perspective on social conventions that may inhibit the sharing of strong or negative emotions). As a pervasive feature of conversation, negative emotions feature prominently in persuasive discourse, complaints, troubles tellings and other talk where individuals produce autobiographical tellings and solicit sympathy from listeners (see also discussions in Buttny, 1993; Haakana, 2007).

The literature on personal narratives has given some attention to the representation of negative or problematic experiences. According to many narrative scholars (e.g. Becker, 1997; Labov, 1972; Ochs & Capps, 1996, 2001), events are made tellable by virtue of being unusual, deviant or otherwise problematic.

> Narrators attempt to identify life problems, how and why they emerge, and their impact on the future. As such, narrative allows narrators to work through deviations from the expected within a conventional structure. (Ochs & Capps, 1996: 27)

> ... unusual or exceptional circumstances stimulate the production of narration because it allows for the sketching of a world within a context where the encountered exception makes sense. Within the framework of a story, exceptions can be made comprehensible. In addition, emotional circumstances generally involve unfamiliar or atypical objects or events that are likely to shatter collective representations and shared

knowledge ... Conversation can transform and absorb unfamiliar elements into social representation. (Rimé, 2009: 81)

There is much research evidence to support the conclusion that moral breaches and transgressive events in human social life naturally result in the production of talk highlighting negative emotions and events (e.g. Buttny, 1993, 2004; Drew, 1998; Pastor & De Fina, 2005). These stories may be story fragments or what Gabriel (2000: 26) refers to as 'proto-stories' that then become resources for further sharing and development:

> These are fragments of stories, similar to Boje's terse stories, sometimes highly charged emotionally and symbolically. Yet their plot is very rudimentary. Under certain conditions of repetition, embellishment, and cross-fertilization, such narratives may yield fully-fledged stories.

Because I am interested in interactional tellings, I am uncomfortable with structuralist or other etic designations of stories as 'rudimentary', 'fully-fledged', 'small', 'big' and so on. However, I do find the possibility that stories may both change and consolidate over time and become affectively charged and shared is important to recognize and explore.

A related perspective concerns what have been called 'resilience' or 'redemption' narratives (McAdams, 2008; see also Campbell, 1968, on 'the hero's journey' narrative and Wildschut et al., 2011, on 'nostalgic' narratives), where speakers start their stories with talk of past suffering and negative emotionality but then bring them to a positive resolution by describing how they ultimately triumphed over adversity:

> The results suggest that it is not so much that happy people tell happy stories about their lives. Instead, happy people tend to tell life stories filled with episodes in which suffering is redeemed by positive outcomes. (McAdams, 2005: 247)

This view aligns with Gergen and Gergen's (1988: 52) general observation that positive emotions are favored for narrative endings but emotional scenarios 'commencing with an expression of what may be termed a positive emotion (an emotion that is valued, sought, or prized) are more truncated or less extended than those commencing with a negative emotion'. Accounts highlighting the individual's past or ongoing efforts to work through traumatic events can (but do not necessarily) lay out a cohesive and understandable biography for the story recipient.

Negatively-valenced stories, it seems, are highly tell-worthy. Perhaps because of this, as many scholars suggest, they *must* be told – and they must even be told in a particular temporal order (though what shape that order will take may vary across speakers, cultures and languages) to reproduce the teller's psychological and social journey for the story recipient:

> When one looks to the social practices by which social life is accomplished, one finds – with surprising frequency – people telling stories to each other, as a means of giving cognitive and emotional coherence to experience, constructing and negotiating social identity. (Bauman, 1986: 113)

Storytelling is thus seen as a means for organizing, representing, coming to terms with and ultimately sharing the transgressive aspects of social life as well as one's responses to them. Supporting this view, psychological research shows traumatic experiences engender emotional thoughts and the desire to share those experiences with others immediately and across time (Zech *et al.*, 2004). In sum, it appears that humans, as social creatures, have a driving need to tell their personal stories and for others to know and share in them.

Intense emotions

In settings where speakers produce stories with a negative tilt, they may also produce material that is *intensely* negative. As Labov (1984) explains, intensity is a key resource for communicating emotion (see also Prior, 2016). Based on my L2 data as well the various L1 and L2 studies cited throughout these chapters, it is clear that the interviewees' stories often circulate around *strong* emotions and highly transgressive or unexpected events.

Considering that autobiographical interview research frequently focuses on groups and individuals perceived as marginalized, it is perhaps unsurprising that the questions, topics, settings and participants tend to generate talk involving negative accounts and emotionality. It is also possible that the ordinary activity of assembling first-person accounts predisposes speakers toward talk of extraordinary or problematic events. The primary goal of the institutional activity of interviewing is the elicitation of autobiographical experience and personal perspectives; therefore, it may be that talk of troubles, negative emotions and the like are made exceptionally salient. To be tell-worthy and listen-worthy, particularly in and *for* research interviews, first-person accounts must be interesting and interactionally relevant. Because the autobiographical interview context likely amplifies normal conversational and storytelling norms (though I am cautious in this claim), it may naturally result in a large number of questions and responses oriented to the interviewees' own psychological perspectives on problematic life events and correspondingly strong negative emotions.

> In short, when people have to recognize that they are tacitly constructing their social worlds, and in an arbitrary and conventional way, rather

than simply reacting to a world that is objectively there, *they show intense negative emotions* ... One could well say that everyday life reality-construction is an emotional process, and that emotions that uphold reality come forth in intense from when the social reality is broken. (Collins, 1990: 29, emphasis added)

For recipients of this negatively valenced and intensely emotional autobiographical material, there may be a strong emotional or empathic response that extends beyond the immediate context of the telling (see Chapter 7 on *emotional contagion*). This has been shown to be true even in the context of third-person narrative production. For example, Curci and Bellelli (2004) conducted a diary and questionnaire study where young adults ($M = 20.65$) and their parents ($M = 49.18$) were asked to recall an emotional episode that had previously been told to them by a relative or acquaintance. A key finding of that study was that '[n]egative episodes were generally found to elicit a more intense emotional reaction than positive episodes' (Curci & Bellelli, 2004: 896). As Rimé (2009: 71) asserts, 'data indeed show that being exposed to an emotional narrative is in itself an emotion-eliciting situation'. This suggests that a central function of negatively valenced stories is to create greater intersubjectivity and emotive involvement between tellers and recipients.

Managing negativity and trauma

Based on the *positive-negative* emotion binary, it is widely believed that negative emotions lead to negative health outcomes (e.g. stress, depression, illness) and positive emotions facilitate wellness and positive health outcomes (Lazarus, 1999; Selye, 1974). Neurological studies lend support for this view by showing that negative emotions, anxiety and associated stressors induce physiological arousal and prepare the body for a fight-or-flight response. In contrast, positive emotions quiet and reverse this process (Frederickson & Levenson, 1998; Tugade, 2011). As a result, the interactional sharing of stories of troubles and hardship, as a cathartic and confessional activity, is assumed to enable individuals to cope with and lessen the undesirable effects of distress:

> Narrative helps to make sense of suffering. I have suggested that narrative ameliorates disruption: it enables the narrator to mend the disruption by weaving it into the fabric of life, to put experience into perspective. (Becker, 1997: 166)

One critical function of autobiographical memory is to use past experiences in ways that allow us to cope with aversive experiences, resolve negative affect, and draw on past emotions in the service of understanding the present and future ... [A]dults who are able to narrate the emotional events of their lives in more self-reflective ways show better physical and psychological health ... indicating that autobiographical narratives play a critical role in regulating emotion. (Fivush *et al.*, 2010: 46)

A review of the narrative literature suggests this sense-making and storytelling function of talk is likely what draws scholars to the investigation of emotion and autobiographical experience: it is immediate, highly relatable, visceral, authentic and often 'therapeutic'.

So accepted is the therapeutic benefit of storying and sharing experience that there are various branches of health care and psychotherapeutic intervention built on the perspective that putting emotional and traumatic memories into narrative can facilitate personal change and healing (e.g. Brown & Augusta-Scott, 2007; Gaydos, 2005; Madigan, 2011; Reyes *et al.*, 2007; White & Epston, 1990). Nevertheless, the evidence is mixed regarding the actual psychological outcomes of expressing or repressing negative emotion (Nyklíček *et al.*, 2011; Zech *et al.*, 2004). Research on individuals diagnosed with PTSD (post-traumatic stress disorder) indicates memories of traumatic memories may be more vivid and involve more lexical representation of negative emotions (Foa & Kozak, 1986). Research by Bohanek *et al.* (2005) further finds that long-term recall of negative emotions about intensely negative events is stronger than for positive emotions about intensely positive events.[3] Conversely, scholarship on emotion regulation suggests that some people display a 'repressive coping style' (Cutler *et al.*, 1996; Weinberger, 1990; Westen & Blagov, 2007) that deactivates emotional arousal and expression. Even though such individuals may have experienced severe distress in the past, they now deny or 'forget' those memories. Furthermore, experimental research by Pennebaker and Francis (1996) suggests that when individuals write about traumatic experiences over time, the greater use of positive rather than negative emotion words correlates with improved mental health.

'Talking' cure or 'social' cure?

Evidence also indicates, at least for some survivors of stressful events, that 'emotional ventilation' may increase psychological distress rather than reduce it (Nyklíček *et al.*, 2011; Sijbrandij *et al.*, 2006). This appears to counter the fact that individuals frequently report the personal benefits of putting their traumatic experiences into stories. How can we explain this seeming discrepancy? It may very well be that in some circumstances the act of organizing and sharing stories of difficulty and negative experiences is indeed therapeutic by allowing the speaker to make visible and thereby consciously process those emotions and events. This may explain why these negative accounts are produced so frequently in autobiographical interviews as well as why they get repeated and condensed or consolidated over time.[4] However, some researchers suggest that the benefit for the teller is not emotional recovery (i.e. the 'talking cure') as we might assume, but reduced isolation and increased social affiliation. This makes intuitive sense if we also recognize that storytellers tend to be selective in choosing story recipients as well as the specific stories and details they provide:

> The reviewed evidence suggested that one does not share with any available person but that sharing partners were chosen according to the relevant information they could provide about coping with emotions, or according to the warmth and emotional support that they would provide to the sharer ... [S]ocial sharing may well provide help in meeting two fundamental human needs: affiliation and social consensus. We have shown that agreement as well as empathy with the listener led to more affective closeness, to a partial restoration of a belief in a just world, and to a decrease of loneliness. (Zech *et al.*, 2004: 180)

Just as I have shown throughout these chapters that story recipients play a key role in the interactional construction of stories, there is ample evidence to demonstrate that recipients and their responses influence the perceived and real-world benefits for the tellers who story their emotional and traumatic experiences. In longitudinal and ethnographic interviews, such as the present L2 corpus, the increased comfort of the interviewees with the interviewer over time may explain the escalating emotionality of the narratives that they collaboratively produce. It is also significant to note that a number of L2 studies suggest, at least indirectly, that the quality of L2 users' social relationships is an important contextual factor that significantly impacts how they perceive and regulate their emotions and affective experiences in and outside the classroom (e.g. Bown & White, 2010; Kinginger, 2004; Menard-Warwick, 2009; Miller, 2014; Pavlenko & Blackledge, 2004).

Emotionality and complexity

The matter of the length and complexity (e.g. rhetorical, syntactic) of emotional narratives is inconclusive, though the oral and written representation of negative experiences appears to be less grammatically complex than for positive experiences (Davitz, 1969; Rintell, 1990). In a written narrative study[5] of women's (M = 19.22) memories of positive and negative emotional events, Bohanek *et al.* (2005) found that 'negative' narratives were longer but less complex and less coherent than 'positive' narratives. To explain the differences, the researchers surmised that the women were still working through their experiences. This lends support to the earlier-cited research on 'proto-stories' and how they may develop over time. Some studies also suggest that less coherent narratives are often associated with recent trauma and mental health issues; whereas more well-organized and complex narratives, as noted earlier, correlate with greater well-being and the processing of traumatic experience (Alvarez-Conrad *et al.*, 2001; Bohanek *et al.*, 2005). In another study, Rees *et al.* (2013) elicited written narratives from 680 young adult (17–25 years) United Kingdom medical school students about their most memorable professional dilemmas. An interesting finding was that over 90% of the narratives incorporated negative emotion talk. The authors note that 'Just under half of the narratives had occurred over 6 months previously, suggesting that these negative experiences were well rehearsed in that they had been thought about and talked about, and were therefore better remembered' (Rees *et al.*, 2013: 89–90).

I observed in Chapter 3 that *repeated* narratives were found throughout my L2 corpus (as well in some of the narrative literature). In a previous study (Prior, 2011a), I found that later tellings may be more complex, more emotional and more detailed than previous versions. Because negative experiences tend to be repeatedly storied, and thereby rehearsed and condensed, they can become readily available resources, allowing speakers to (re)package their experience for intimates as well as the interviewer. Due to the interconnectedness of emotional experience and its representation, more work is certainly warranted to further investigate the matter of narrative complexity. For researchers interested in L2 development, for example, there may be some important interactions between emotionality and the complexity of talk that impacts its production.

Cultural and social factors

There are undoubtedly also cultural components that promote talk of negative emotion/experience and minimize talk of positive emotion/experience. A number of scholars (e.g. Averill, 1980; Ellis, 1991; Gaylin, 1979; Schrauf & Sanchez, 2004) have noted the preponderance of negative rather than positive emotion talk in English. In Western contexts, socialization into and through talk of negative emotion/experience has been shown to begin in early childhood.[6] Conversations between children and caregivers in the US frequently center on talk of negative emotion, leading to more linguistically sophisticated input, moral and ideological development, and problem-solving and social coping skills (Dunn & Brown, 1991; Fivush, 1994; Gross, 2014a; Quas & Fivush, 2009; Saarni, 1999). Although much attention has been given to the ways in which young children are socialized into culturally appropriate ways of displaying, recognizing and talking about emotions, less understood is how these socialization processes operate for older children and adults – particularly for multilingual, transcultural, migratory and other groups and individuals. Moreover, due to differing levels of socialization and exposure to L2 norms, the development of emotional arousal and personal associations with particular emotions varies widely for multilinguals (e.g. Dewaele, 2004, 2008, 2010; Dewaele & Pavlenko, 2002; Marian & Kaushanskaya, 2004, 2008; Pavlenko, 2005, 2006).

The literature on how various ethnic/cultural groups, immigrants, refugees and those who have experienced trauma, discrimination and other life stressors use emotion talk also shows mixed findings. Some research on adult immigrants suggests that the L2 may facilitate talk of emotional matters precisely because it is *less* emotional (i.e. allowing psychological detachment and distance) than the L1 (Dewaele, 2004, 2006; Marian & Kaushanskaya, 2004, 2008; Pavlenko, 2005). Marian and Kaushanskaya (2004), in an interview-based study of emotion representation in immigration narratives by Russian bilinguals, found that speakers used more emotion words in the L2, and negative emotion words were more prevalent than positive emotion words (a pattern confirmed by other studies, e.g. Bown & White, 2010; Hanauer, 2010).

Indo-Chinese

Because most of the focal and other research participants in my interview corpus were from Vietnam and Cambodia, there may be some cultural-specific explanations for the prevalence of negative emotionality in their talk. The findings, however, are mixed. Some health researchers have noted that Indochinese immigrants and other Asian groups tend to suppress talk of feelings in general and negative emotions in particular (e.g. Enelow *et al.*, 1996; Tran *et al.*, 2003). Based on ethnographic and interview-based research with survivors of the infamous Cambodian genocide at the hands of the Khmer Rouge, Hinton (1998, 2007; see also Blair, 2000; Carlson & Rosser-Hogan, 1991) observes that Cambodians frequently manage negative emotions by minimizing or hiding them:

> Cambodians often do hide negative feelings in order to avoid losing face or making someone else lose face. If, for example, a person becomes angry at another individual, he or she will sometimes not let the other person know. As one informant told me: 'Cambodians put their anger in their head and don't let it out'. (1998: 104)

> Cambodians only talk about such sad stories once in a while ... If a person starts to get upset and begins to cry ... the person should stop speaking about the matter that is making them suffer. They should think about something else. (2007: 441)

Despite the existence of cultural norms that discourage the overt expression of negative emotions, Hinton (2007) also found cases of intense physical (e.g. crying, shaking) and verbal expressions of emotionality (e.g. talk of *fear, hate, suffering, anger*) in his interviews with Cambodian survivors about their wartime experiences. Therefore, while there may be cultural norms that encourage the suppression of negative emotions, features of the interview context that promote story production may also encourage and facilitate emotional expression.

Similar contrasts between the suppression and representation of emotion have been found in interview-based research involving Vietnamese interviewees. In focus group interviews with older Vietnamese immigrants in Australia about their emotional well-being and family relationships, Vo-Thanh-Xuan and Liamputtong (2003) discovered that many elderly Vietnamese declined to participate in their group interviews because of an unwillingness to discuss negatively-valenced matters. McKelvey (1999), a child psychiatrist, carried out oral interviews (through an interpreter, which creates its own challenges for analysis) with Amerasian children from Vietnam who had faced discrimination and abandonment because of negative social attitudes toward their biracial heritage. McKelvey observed that while some dealt with their anger and sadness by hiding negative emotions and transforming them into positive emotions (e.g. concern for others), many interviewees also talked openly about their negative feelings and experiences.

Kamm (1996), in a journalistic study of post-war, present-day Vietnam, found that many interviewees did not hide talk of anger and other emotions.[7] Groleau and Kirmayer (2004: 120), in an investigation of the illness narratives of Vietnamese immigrants in Canada, observed that participants who spoke of negative emotions made use of a cultural model and malady called *uất ức* [to be indignant or angry because of injustice][8]:

> Participants in this study described *uất ức* as a complex negative emotion composed of several different emotions including anger, sadness, indignation, bitterness, stress, hate, and frustration. A young women suffering from *uất ức* told the interviewer that it is 'a mental depression more sophisticated than what Westerners call depression because it is a social disease of indignation'. Vietnamese know who suffers from *uất ức* only by knowing the personal story of that person. For example, one participant explained that a lot of Vietnamese who were held in war camps and tortured suffer from *uất ức* because they were, as one participant said, 'treated like animals and couldn't say a thing about it; they couldn't denounce their captors'.

The Vietnamese-speaking participants in the present study did not talk explicitly about *uất ức*, but much of their talk described negative emotions (e.g. *anger, sadness*) resulting from injustice and breaches of moral conduct in the past and present. They also used their stories to 'talk back' to people in the storyworld in ways that they could not at the time of the represented events. Despite over 30 years of post-war immigration from Southeast Asia and beyond, and much present-day interest by researchers in contemporary transcultural flows, scholarly studies of immigrant groups and individuals and their indigenous, hybrid, shifting and even enduring ways of constructing and managing emotions remain scarce.[9] Much more research is needed if we are to understand the various modes and methods speakers use to manage *talk about* emotions (i.e. emotion as topic) and manage *talk by means of* emotions (i.e. emotion as resource) in daily life.

Summary

This chapter has considered some of the explanations for the overwhelming discursive and embodied production of negative emotionality in the autobiographical tellings and other talk produced in the research interviews discussed in these chapters. Based on the findings of the previous chapters on the present corpus and other published studies, it is clear that institutional features of the activity of interviewing greatly shape the content and manner of talk that interviewees and interviewers produce. The questions, responses, story invitations and generated stories displayed an orientation toward talk of problems, conflict, anger, sadness and other types of negative experience and emotional expression. Not only did interviewees tend to frame their experiences in negative and emotional terms, they were also found to resist inquiries into 'happy' or positive experiences. A review of the literature suggests a number of other intersecting contributors to this negative tilt, including storytelling conventions, trauma, memory, therapeutic benefits, culture and researchers' interest in investigating and addressing real-world problems and concerns that negatively impact human life, social participation, language use and personal well-being.

Again, more research is needed in this area if we are to better comprehend not just how and why 'negative emotionality' is prevalent but also what discursive, interactional, interpersonal and intrapersonal forms and functions it has in the tellings and in the contexts in which it is produced and made available for response and commentary. Attending to the seemingly 'negative' side of human emotional life and its discursive construction and management, I suggest, can ultimately lead to positive insights and productive outcomes.

Notes

(1) Speakers may also give an account for agreement. However, in keeping with work on dispreference (see Mori, 1999; Schegloff, 2007), it is more often the case that speakers provide accounts (or at least longer utterances) when disagreeing.
(2) It is important to note that several researchers have criticized such biographic episodes (or 'big stories') as artificial and relatively rare in everyday life (e.g. Atkinson, 2015; Bamberg & Georgakopoulou, 2008). Nevertheless, I disagree with notions that so-called 'big stories' only *represent* speakers' worlds and identities and 'small stories' (i.e. conversational stories and story fragments), as 'real' interaction, enable speakers to *construct* their identities (Bamberg & Georgakopoulou, 2008; cf. Talmy & Prior, 2015). In my view, this assumes a rather shortsighted view of speakers' interactional resources and competences.

(3) 'Negativity bias' appears to be a part of the neurological processing of stimuli. As 'negative events in a context evoke stronger and more rapid physiological, cognitive, emotional, and social responses than neutral or positive events' (Cacioppo et al., 2002: 508; Taylor, 1991), negative experiences are more vivid and easily recalled, we seek to avoid things that are unpleasant, our taste buds respond more strongly to bitter tastes, negative information is weighed more heavily when making judgments and so on. There is also evidence pointing to the predominance of negative emotions in the working emotional vocabulary of speakers of English (Ben-Ze'ev, 2000; Schrauf & Sanchez, 2004).

(4) It is important to recognize that stories have trajectories. I found that many immigrants re-told stories or versions of events that they have produced multiple times for various governmental agencies and other gatekeepers (see, e.g. Blommaert, 2001a, 2001b).

(5) For more on negative emotionality in written L1 and L2 narratives, see also Chamcharatsri (2013) on *fear*. It is interesting to note contrasting findings for other genres. Hanauer (2010), in an analysis of a corpus of L2 poetry, found the percentage of positive emotion words was significantly higher than for negative emotion words (4.39% versus 2.76%).

(6) For discussions of socialization in and through emotion talk in non-Anglo cultural contexts, see Cervantes, 2002; Cole et al., 2006; Lutz, 1988; Schieffelin, 1990; Schieffelin & Ochs, 1986.

(7) Supporting the perspective that emotions take 'intensional objects' (Edwards, 1997), many of the participants in Kamm's study directed their anger against governments and the military, rather than individuals.

(8) I am grateful to Dr Hanh Nguyen (personal communication), for pointing out that *uất ức* is often treated as a result of having to suppress one's anger at injustice and unfair treatment (i.e. one is angry but is not able to act on that anger).

(9) Notable exceptions include Pavlenko's work on emotions and multilingualism (2005, 2006). A related area in need of investigation includes the construction and reception of emotion by lingua franca speakers (i.e. speakers who interact in a language that is shared but not necessarily native). A rare mention of this comes from Russell (1995), who cites the code-switching patterns of Wolof speakers as an important part of emotion discourse and multilingualism.

9 Reflecting Back, Moving Forward

> *Ultimately, we need to recognize and incorporate the emotional nature of qualitative research in our training and education of those new to this research tradition. Doing so will prepare researchers better for their first encounters in the field and move them along the journey that is qualitative research.*
> (Gilbert, 2001: 13)

> *I do not think effective ethnographic research can be done without emotional engagement, and the pursuit of a methodology that ignores what we learn from our emotions is undermining the validity of the resulting information.*
> (Gearing, 1995: 209)

The preceding chapters have covered a great deal of affective ground within the interactional landscape of autobiographical interview research. The perspective that I have sought to develop in this book is that *emotionality* – emotions as social actions rather than 'thing-like entities' (Sarbin, 2001: 217) – offers a theoretical and analytical lens through which to examine human experience and its emergent discursive representation. I have argued that this emotionality is as much a part of the activity of research as it is a product of the life histories of those whom we research. But this story is far from complete – in fact, it is just beginning. It should be evident, as I promised in the Introduction, that this investigation has opened up just as many questions as it answered while making visible the inherent tensions and 'messiness' surrounding qualitative interviewing. Even this concluding chapter offers no neat resolution or denouement to bring this book to a satisfying sense of closure.

As I take stock of the discussions, analyses, findings, questions and other issues raised in these chapters, I find myself returning to the matter of *versions* introduced in Chapter 2. I am reminded of Riessman's (2008: 4) observation, 'Just as interview participants tell stories, investigators construct stories from their data.' This book is therefore no less constructed or versioned than any other story. In answer to the question, 'Which story do you prefer?' (Martel, 2001: 307), this is the version I would have written when I first 'collected' these data (based on my notes and earlier writings):

> Building on previous autobiographical L2 (second language) interview research, this book has incorporated personal narratives as well as observational methods to investigate the shared and unique experiences and trajectories of immigrants to North America. It confirms and extends previous findings by offering evidence of the ways that these research participants experienced and continue to face social and linguistic discrimination, challenges surrounding acculturation and language use, marginalizing and delegitimizing power structures, sociopolitical barriers to participation and belonging, and various identity and psychological struggles. As this investigation as shown, sociolinguistic life is fundamentally emotional. These data and the repeated themes they raise also offer new insight into the often intensely felt socio-affective components and outcomes of experience (e.g. anger, sadness, fear) that continue to shape these individuals' interpretations of their present-day realities and imagined futures. In other words, narratives constitute 'emotional acts' as well as 'identity acts'. This study therefore concludes that qualitative interviewing and narrative inquiry are powerful tools that enable the researcher and research participants to collaboratively reveal and make sense of the hidden and often fragmented aspects of selfhood.

However meaningful the above statements may appear, they are more representative of the kinds of thematic summaries and glosses that are common in much autobiographical interview research, which I have sought to counter vigorously with this book. For the sake of our field(s) and the quality of our research, we cannot let analyses that only highlight the thematic, the experiential, the personal and the emotional be 'good enough'. Our research participants deserve better; so do we, as narrative researchers, and so do the disciplinary areas of study within which we work (Atkinson, 2015; Pavlenko, 2007; Richards, 2009).

Taking up repeated calls that question the uncritical celebration of autobiographical inquiry, narrative sensemaking, and the emotional content and impact of our research at the expense of rigor and accountability, I have aimed to conduct a critical and reflexive examination of the institutional and interpersonal frames of the research process itself. To carry out this investigation, I have explored the 'whats' and the 'hows' (Holstein & Gubrium, 1995) of the discursive construction and management of *emotionality* in autobiographical research interviews. I have sought to engage with this research as a fundamentally social interactional practice by examining the emotion-indexing topics that interviewee *and* interviewer take up, the discursive and extra-discursive resources they employ, and the ways in which they actively 'bracket in' and 'bracket out' (Wooffitt, 1992) various aspects of the affective material they collaboratively *generate* (rather than recall or reveal) in the situated encounter constituting the 'research interview'. I gave consideration also to the 'whos' (i.e. the individuals engaged and described in the talk) and the 'wheres' (i.e. the interactional junctures and contexts of activity) to better contextualize and make visible the dynamic processes of emotion management and its consequences.

Based on the discussions and findings across these chapters, it is clear that recognizing the presence of emotions in our research activities and products is the easy task. Defining, operationalizing, analyzing and managing emotionality, and ultimately deciding whether, when and how to address it in our scholarship are just some of the many challenges researchers continue to encounter. There is no shortage of both folk and academic theories explaining the mechanisms that underlie the production and reception of emotions in social life. Often these various theories are at odds due to conflicting views regarding the ontological origins of the phenomena (e.g. psychological, physiological, social, internal, external, innate, learned) as well as their relevance to particular research questions and contexts. Of course, these observations are just as applicable to *narrative, identity, desire, motivation* and other related objects upon which we often fix our scholarly attention.

Theory and model building are often considered fundamental aspects of research in L2 studies, indeed across the social sciences (Chalhoub-Deville *et al.*, 2006; McCarthy, 2001; McGroarty, 1998; Shoemaker *et al.*, 2004). However, building theories and models need not be the only goals of research. In this book I have aimed to encourage a greater recognition that the assumptions underlying our theories and methods, as well as the practices they engender, can also be worthy objects of study. These kinds of 'social studies of interview studies' (Prior, 2014; Rapley, 2012; Roulston, 2012) are long overdue in the field. To my knowledge, this book is the first, at least in the interdisciplinary domain of L2 studies, to investigate the autobiographical research interview, or qualitative research interview more broadly, as a collaborative, interactional site for generating and managing emotionality, rather than gaining unmediated access to speakers' authentic voices and affective worlds. I hope it will soon be joined by others representing a wider range of research methods, topics and contexts.

In the following sections, I review some of the key findings and contributions of this project and then offer suggestions for some ways in which this area of scholarly inquiry might further be developed in L2 studies.

Contributions to Research

Getting discursive

In this book I have advanced a discursive constructionist (DC) approach to investigate emotion management in L2 autobiographical interview research. This approach is informed largely by the empirical methods and findings of conversation analysis (CA) and discursive psychology (DP). Defining characteristics of this approach are its 'ethnomethodological spirit' (Antaki & Widdicombe, 1998: 1–2), which treats emotion and other social life as interactional business; its 'ethnographic mentality' (Hammersley & Atkinson, 2007: 30), which shapes how the researcher looks, listens and thinks about the phenomena of interest; and its inclusion of extra-discursive knowledge and background material to better contextualize and explain 'curious' and ambiguous sequences. It draws also on insights from work on narrative as well as other lines of social interactional inquiry. I have argued that because it considers the 'visible' and even 'invisible' contexts, this approach offers an analytically grounded and reflexive analysis of research practices and products. However, it is not enough to 'make the invisible visible' (Hine, 2000: 54); we must also be able to account for its relevance to the participants in their context(s).

It is not my aim to insist that researchers must adopt this particular DC approach. However, I do contend that the approaches we take must be intentionally selected rather than determined by convenience or accident. Throughout these chapters I have sought to show that an action-oriented DC approach has much to offer because it facilitates transparency, reflexivity and a close and defensible analysis, thereby making visible speakers' various interactional and linguistic resources and competences. I also suggest that if we are to advance disciplinary knowledge and theory of human social and emotional life that goes beyond thematic summarizing and quotation, we must take more seriously our obligation to rigorously inspect and reflect on our own research practices (Richards, 2009; Roulston, 2010). Whatever our implicit or explicit stance toward emotionality and other related matters, the ways in which we inspect (or ignore) our *actual* (rather than idealized) research practices have important consequences for our methods, our data histories, our analyses and findings, our participants and even our own professional trajectories.

Getting 'real'

This book is also to my knowledge the first DC study to analyze the accounts and other talk of immigrant and transcultural men. It has brought focused attention to the ways that they make visible and manage emotionality in relation to their sociolinguistic histories (and futures) and their identity struggles (e.g. ethnicity, sexuality, L2 user, immigrant), as well as their relationships with the researcher, with L1 speakers, with North American society, and even with each other. There is no doubt that these speakers' troubles tellings, humorous stories and anecdotes are intrinsically interesting and accessible due to their emotional and moral content as well as their dramatic or performative features. Nevertheless, throughout these chapters I have rejected the conclusion that interviewees produce intense and affect-laden talk *simply because* they have had numerous difficult and emotionally impactful experiences as L2 users, immigrants and so on. Instead, my stance is fundamentally discursive. I have shown that specific features of the dialogic activity of the interview itself also play important roles in eliciting, foregrounding and maintaining a focus on emotionality and empathy-worthy tellings. Such features include the interview format; the institutional agenda; the identities/categories under which participants are recruited; the topics, identities and experiences that are made relevant; the ways in which those topics, identities and experiences are (not) taken up and (not) responded to; and the activity of organizing autobiographical experience.

Of course, this is not to deny the 'reality' (however defined) of speakers' versions of experience; neither does it suggest that we celebrate narratives and other talk as 'the baseline of the Real' (Freeman, 2006: 133). I take no ontological position beyond that these stories were collaboratively co-constructed with me in research interviews. That is, because I am interested in speakers' rhetorical and interactional competences as well as the experiences that those competences allowed participants to story, these versions are precisely 'truthful enough'. Although I could not have said this when I initially began this study, I realize now that these narratives may be what some might call mistaken, partial, half-truths and even deceptions. A DC approach is not concerned with uncovering hidden 'truths'; it attends to ways in which 'truth', 'morality', emotion and much more are interactionally managed. As Silverman (2011: 199) comments, 'This means that we need not hear interview responses simply as true or false reports on reality. Instead, we can treat such responses as displays of perspectives and moral forms which draw upon available cultural resources.' In other words, it means treating research participants as competent social beings.

Getting reflexive

With the goal of making our research practices transparent and accountable, giving attention to researcher positionality and identifying the various power and identity struggles in the research process certainly offer important insights. However, I have aimed to show reflexivity requires more of us than simply glossing 'positions' or producing thematic summaries. I commented in the Prologue that researcher reflexivity can be viewed (and experienced) as an 'unnatural' and even 'violent act'. As a mode of 'reflective practice', interrogating our own actions and beliefs forces us to expose our failures as well as our successes. We may find our practices betray our naïve assumptions and the superficiality of our claims regarding the 'rigor' and 'relevance' of our professional inquiry. Yet, reflecting on interview and other research dilemmas can be, as Rapley (2012: 548) points out, 'a therapeutic intervention for researchers' (see also Prior, 2014). It may therefore offer us a much-needed antidote to combat our own complacency and our taken-for-granted beliefs and practices.

I have also sought to show that reflexivity is part of a larger ethical and moral project. As conscientious researchers, we recognize that we have a responsibility to our participants, the field, our institutions and ourselves to conduct and represent our research in accordance with institutional policies and other regulations. To the best of our ability, we seek to minimize risk, ensure confidentiality and maintain professional standards. Reflexivity, as an ethical and practical matter, is also a professional obligation that goes beyond legislated protocols. Not all contingencies can be anticipated, and not all ethics are necessarily ethical for those involved in the research. What is needed 'is a contextualized and flexible approach to ethical decision making, relying more on the researchers' professional reflexivity and integrity in maintaining high standards' (Dörnyei, 2007: 72; also Hammersley, 2014a; Richards, 2009).

As the preceding suggests, reflexivity involves reflective practice, corrective or therapeutic intervention, moral and ethical considerations and professional standards of conduct. Nevertheless, I have argued that the kind of reflexivity advocated here demands more. A superficial reflexivity that privileges the researcher's self-reflection runs the risk of failing to recognize that the research objects, subjects and contexts are not just waiting to be studied; instead, they are generated and co-constructed through the very act of conducting and writing up research. At the heart of a DC approach lies a deeper form of reflexivity:

> Reflexivity is the condition whereby any social research inevitably helps to constitute the phenomenon under investigation. Social research is, therefore, necessarily reactive. Because our research topics consist of human conduct, and because those phenomena are produced by social actors, we are inevitably and inextricably implicated in what we study. (Atkinson, 2015: 26)

I have described that in a DC approach, reflexivity refers to the observable fact that human activity is made recognizable because it is 'doubly contextual' (Heritage, 1984: 242). Interviews are not 'interviews' because we label them so: they become built and recognizable as 'interviews' because participants engage in actions that are normatively associated with that activity. In other words, interviewer and interviewee do not *come* to an interview – they *construct* (and *deconstruct*) it through the activities of recording, asking and answering questions, inviting and producing tellings, offering and withholding responses, summarizing and repeating and so on. In this recursive relationship, their actions build the context and the context also shapes and reinforces their actions. This is ultimately an 'emic' perspective because it seeks to understand the context on its own terms (including through interactants' own terms and labels) and through the close analysis of the actions of those involved. Reflexivity that concentrates only on a one-sided inspection of the researcher's self-reflection ignores the collaboratively built nature of research. Conversely, because of the 'ethnographic mentality' of the DC approach advocated here, I also argue that only focusing on actions and what is made explicitly visible in a particular interaction can potentially lead to misrepresentation as well as underrepresentation of the various complexities and competences within a given interactional context.

Getting personal

A related issue I brought up in this book was that of the stigmatized and even 'erotic' aspects of our research and dilemmatic relationships with participants. A discussion of these matters has largely been taboo in L2 research. Yet, for a field of scholars who conduct research in various multilingual and multicultural contexts, and who have been eager to explore gender and sexuality in relation to L2 identities and pedagogy (e.g. Kappra & Vandrick, 2006; King, 2008; Menard-Warwick, 2009; Nelson, 2009; Norton, 2000), we have been curiously silent on the existence and influence of such matters within our research activities. I find it incomprehensible for us to remain content to proceed as if gender and sexuality only apply to the individual lives of our research participants and not to researchers and their research relationships. Because autobiographical, ethnographic and related person-centered (and longitudinal) research often involves a high level of trust and intimacy, I have maintained that it is shortsighted and even irresponsible to ignore the personal subtexts that permeate our research. Nevertheless, it appears researcher discomfort and professional fears continue to preclude us from addressing such things.

My point is not that we must hypersexualize every encounter or suspect every word or gesture carries a sexual or double meaning; rather, we should be willing to recognize our research participants and ourselves as social beings and whole persons who have 'intentions, agency, affect, and above all histories' (Pavlenko & Lantolf, 2000: 155) – and I would add, *genders, sexualities* and *desires*. Let me be clear that this is not to say that these or other concerns are *necessarily* relevant or active for interactants. It is true that some settings may make certain identity categories *potentially* 'omni-relevant' (Sacks, 1992): e.g. 'doctor' and 'patient' in a healthcare setting, 'teacher' and 'student' in an educational environment, or 'interviewer' and 'interviewee' in a research study. But because there is 'no omni-relevant categorization device across settings' (Schegloff, 2007: 39), a DC perspective insists that relevance is an emergent outcome of interactants' collaborative efforts. In the present project, sexuality, for example, was shown to be relevant; in other data and research contexts, it may not be. Claims of relevance are therefore dependent on the research data at hand and therefore must be empirically warranted – otherwise research runs the risk of trading in emic analysis for preconceived etic notions and endless speculation.

In a previous published study of the narratives of a man who immigrated to the United States from Vietnam (Prior, 2011c), I gave much attention to his identity dilemmas and the ways that he mediated his perceived incompatible 'gay' and 'Asian' identities by foregrounding his Chinese ethnicity as a kind of 'identity anchor'. However, I said nothing about my own identity or what the interviewee and I knew about each other's identities or histories. Nor did I comment on the fact that his interviews should be contextualized as interactions between two gay men. To correct such errors, in this book I have aimed to make clear the background that shaped my interest in this study and that informed my interactions with the participants. I have also sought to give attention, *when warranted* (and this cannot be overemphasized), to issues involving sexual orientation, gender, masculinity and related concerns of these men and the researcher. For instance, I noted a few occasions where my personal discomfort with the possible sexual subtext of a speaker's talk prompted me to reframe the topic and the affective tone of the talk. I also point out that Kim, the only woman in these data, also brought up concerns that connected English ability, gender, ethnicity, hypersexualization and negative and prejudicial attitudes of 'Americans' (i.e. described as Caucasian, monolingual, native English-speakers).

Nevertheless, while attending to these matters as they became relevant in the data, I have endeavored to avoid stigmatizing participants (or myself) by representing a skewed perspective or sensationalizing one aspect of their identities over another. I am not suggesting that every researcher must reveal themselves as heterosexual, non-heteronormative, and so on in their research. However, if a research participant is speaking about an identity category shared with the interviewer, and we take the stance that interviews are collaboratively-built interactions, then it seems irresponsible not to include those matters in the analysis – *especially* if the participants make those identities relevant or the research data come about because of those identities (see discussions in Potter & Hepburn, 2005, 2012; Prior, 2014; Talmy & Richards, 2011).

Getting extra-discursive

Another contribution of this study is its use of ethnographic insights and extra-discursive information to complement conversation analysis (CA). Following other social interactional scholars (e.g. Goodwin, 2000; Maynard, 2003; Mondada, 2013a, 2013b), I find such contextual information is often essential for making us aware of certain issues and for explaining 'curious' or ambiguous phenomena, especially in longitudinal studies like this one. Thus, sequential analysis and ethnography are not incompatible and may prove essential in providing sufficient context for understanding and analyzing our data and pointing to phenomena for investigation (Atkinson *et al.*, 2011; Talmy, 2009). This is particularly relevant for researchers and readers who may be cultural or linguistic novices in a particular community of study – and when working with participants who may be unfamiliar with the practices of research interviewing and the expectations of *this* interviewer in *this* research setting.

Analysis of these data also emphasizes the crucial contributions that contextual and baseline data offer when examining individual episodes or even series of episodes over time. As productive as it may be to draw conclusions based on a specific interaction, we must not lose sight of the fact that interviews, like any social interactions, are always part of larger, extended sequences, contexts and interpersonal relationships. In social research, like all of human life, nothing exists in isolation. Even the act of research is creating the data we are examining. We are, in essence, *generating* as well as collecting 'cultural artifacts' (Moerman, 1988: 2). My use of extra-situational material and observations, along with interaction analysis, differentiates this work from canonical or 'basic' CA. However, as I have noted, an ethnographic mentality and discursive constructionist perspective can enable us to more carefully explicate our research interactions beyond the superficial.

Contributions to the Study of Emotion

Getting emotional

It is clear that the investigation of and close engagement with emotionality in L2 (and L1) autobiographical interview research is an inherently interesting yet highly challenging and even challenged enterprise. Decisions to address or avoid emotionality are inevitable in the course of all scholarly inquiry. As with any discipline or area of study, one encounters the familiar binary tropes. On the one side of the emotion continuum, there are those scholars seen as taking an 'anti-emotionalist' or 'objective' stance where they intentionally or unwittingly gloss over or even altogether avoid addressing the presence and role of emotionality in their research (see discussions in Couper-Kuhlen, 2009; Gilbert, 2001). When emotion does become and object of attention, it is frequently decontextualized from the interactional circumstances of its production and attributed primarily to intra-psychological or physiological processes (Gross, 2014a; Hatfield *et al.*, 1994; Imai, 2010; Lutz & Abu-Lughod, 1990; Nyklíček *et al.*, 2011).

At the other end of the continuum are researchers accused of taking an 'emotionalist', 'romantic' or 'subjective' stance (Atkinson, 2015; Silverman, 2011) that uncritically elevates and even celebrates emotionality as proof of the authenticity of speakers' self-reports and as privileged insight into the deeply personal and authentic parts of human experience without establishing its relevance. Though these are admittedly crude characterizations of scholarly treatments of emotion, they nonetheless capture some of the tensions that play out in the field of research.

Rather than seeking to develop yet another theory of emotion or narrative, this book has sought to contribute to previous autobiographical and narrative scholarship while advancing contemporary understandings of the interactional forms and functions of emotionality as well as the methods by which we as researchers/interactants generate and analyze our research data. This study confirms the centrality of emotionality in L2 users' *talk of their experiences* and in the *talk eliciting and responding to those experiences*. It demonstrates that emotionality operates as a fundamental organizational device as well as a topic and resource that progresses the interview talk and interaction.

To bring into focus the interactional aspects of speakers' affective work, I have made a conceptual distinction between *emotion* and *emotionality*. Attending to emotionality, I have argued, enables us to extract ourselves from endless debates regarding how to objectively define or measure emotions as, for example, intra-psychological objects or static mood or feeling states. Instead, it recognizes that whatever else emotions may or may not be, they are recurrent, socially embedded and socially evaluated topics and resources in speakers' communicative repertoires. Seen in this light, emotionality intersects with our actions, our histories, our stories, our identities, our relationships, our goals, our psychologies and even our biologies – and in the ways we discursively represent those intersections. Across these chapters, I have also discussed how researcher and research participants actively display, orient to, respond to and otherwise manage their own emotionality as well as the emotionality of their interlocutors. At times, speakers were found to erupt in anger, recount sadness, make humorous jokes and even resist displaying or responding to particular emotions. However, this emotionality was never random. It was designed in ways that 'made sense' or were eventually shown to be relevant in particular interactional contexts. Although 'negative' emotionality was found to be prevalent, it was shown to align with speakers' personal accounts and represent them as human beings with fears, concerns, joys and hopes.

My aim in this book has not been to argue that researchers must focus on *emotions, narratives, interviews* – or any other particular analytical object over another (recognizing, of course, that research always entails the intentional selection of phenomena, sites, questions, methods and so on). On the contrary, I insist that emotions, narratives and interviews are *not* special and therefore should *not* be celebrated any more or any less than any other human social concerns or activities. I also argue that we should be committed to representing social members (including research participants and researchers) and their lives, competences, practices, successes, failures and so on, 'in their full complexity' (Atkinson, 2015: 173). Thus focused attention on these matters can bring added breadth and depth to our scholarly knowledge by revealing and accounting for that complexity, at least in part if not in full.

In this book, I have chosen to inspect the management of emotionality in L2 autobiographical interview research. I contend that this is a much-needed project and offers an important contribution to research practice and knowledge. It focuses on a necessarily restricted range of phenomena that fall within the complexity of human life and scholarship that I seek to represent and explicate. Thus, this investigation adds to the larger human story of emotionality and L2 autobiographical interview research.

Contributions to Discursive Practices

Because this project is interested in 'interactional realities', not just 'lived realities' (Kasper & Prior, 2015), it has given close attention to some of the key devices responsible for soliciting and generating emotionality in speakers' talk: *telling and remembering sequences* that launch personal accounts, *researcher questioning* sequences that elicit tellings and talk of feelings, and *(re) formulations* that offer particular lexical descriptions of events. I briefly comment on some of these findings below.

Telling and remembering

Too much of our research still assigns special status to narratives without considering the discursive and interpersonal work that goes into the surrounding material and activities of remembering, assembling, producing and responding to speakers' stories and related meta-commentary. Although previous researchers (primarily interested in L1 speakers and contexts) have examined story prefaces and related story-launching devices, only a handful have treated emotionality as an object of inquiry in speakers' stories (e.g. Drew, 1998; Couper-Kuhlen, 2012; Günthner, 1997a; Selting, 2010). Analysis of the story prefaces in this corpus showed that speakers did not always label the emotionality of the projected material (e.g. 'mad', 'sad', 'funny'); they often used implicit and implicative features of talk (e.g. vocal and paravocal) to make emotionality hearably relevant. Analysis further showed that story telling sequences are bounded and highly coordinated. This study also addresses Georgakopoulou's (2007) criticism of CA for failing to look beyond story openings and endings. I suggest more work examining a wider range of tellings and extended sequences may help us better understand how the material that gets projected, produced, touched-off and repeated function as interactional devices.

Questioning sequences

There has been much research on questioning sequences in institutional settings (e.g. doctor–patient interaction, counseling sessions, news interviews, classrooms, courtrooms), but the analysis of questioning sequences in qualitative research interviews has yet to be systematically taken up. Examining two interview question types (*feeling questions* and *emotion-implicative questions*), I showed how they steer the interviewee to talk about feelings and emotion-related matters. While *feeling* questions ('How did that feel?') explicitly request talk of feelings, *emotion implicative* questions are subtler. They make emotionality relevant by using evaluative terms such as 'good', 'bad', 'easy' and 'hard' – thus inviting interviewees to respond from a particular affective stance. Attending to the actions of questioning also gives insight into the ways the participants respond or withhold their responses. A particular 'therapeutic' insight I found regarding my own practices is that I often withheld empathic or affiliative responses during speakers' highly emotional or uncomfortable talk. In many cases, interviewees intensified the emotionality of their talk to pursue an affiliative and empathic response from the interviewer.

Reformulations

As I have noted, this study of emotionality indicates some points of convergence between qualitative interviews and psychotherapy, particularly in the use of reformulations and their discursive scaling ('hard', 'very tough') in interaction. Despite a growing body of research on reformulations in psychotherapeutic settings, little investigation has been done on their use in other contexts. An important finding on reformulations in this corpus is that though they can display empathy and affiliation, they also are key devices by which speakers signal epistemic authority and ownership over their descriptions of events. At times, this was found to result in an invisible struggle over the formulation of feelings, knowledge and events. Thus, the ways particular reformulations get produced and confirmed shape what version of events gets treated as relevant.

These chapters have departed from contemporary CA scholarship by concentrating on qualitative interview data and highlighting interactants' discursive and rhetorical work, but they largely maintain their analytical footing along canonical lines by seeking to first explicate what interviewees and interviewers understand themselves to be doing (Schegloff, 1998). Just as previous social interactional scholarship on gender (e.g. Land & Kitzinger, 2005; Speer, 2005) has demonstrated its fruitful application to a variety of concerns and disciplines, including feminist and other critical purposes, there is nothing intrinsically unique about the present approach to the topic of emotionality that precludes its application to other 'psychological' or sociological topics (e.g. cognition, motivation, identity, power, desire) and applied concerns (Antaki, 2011).

Moving Ahead

Emotion resources

Some further questions these chapters raise concern the semiotic resources speakers use to *do* emotionality. How do individuals come to have (or not have) particular affective resources (e.g. vocabulary, tellings; e.g. Blommaert, 2001a)? What, if any, are some of their general and specialized forms and functions?

After carrying out many of the interviews and other data collection for the present study, I discovered that several of the research participants had previously been in counseling (psychological or spiritual) and/or had told some of their stories to therapists, lawyers, government officials and other professionals and gatekeepers. This undoubtedly contributed to the organization, production and even rehearsal of some of their tellings, and it suggests the importance of taking into account the entextualization[1] processes by which experiences become storied data and interactional resources. Another question that this project raises is how the interviews and the activities of talking about and managing emotionality (i.e. their retrospective organization and present production) can influence future language use and social participation.[2] Again, this suggests the urgent need and potential benefits of more longitudinal and ethnographic research on *emotion* and *emotional socialization*.

Discussing the treatment and analysis of interview data, Rapley (2001: 318) has argued that the discursive resources are part of the wider cultural context; nevertheless, the local context of their production must be given analytical primacy:

> Interviewees' talk speaks to *and* emerges from the wider strategies and repertoires available to, and used by, *all* people. A focus on interview-talk as locally accomplished does not deny that interviewees' talk is reflexively situated in the wider cultural arena (Silverman, 1993). The ways of speaking that are available to talk (and texts) that are engaged in talk about drugs, or other topics, can be highlighted as well as both speakers' negotiations with the broader (moral) social context (emphasis in original).

As the main thrust of this book is that interviews and emotions should be approached interactionally, I concur with Rapley's insistence that data must always be analyzed and presented in the contexts in which they occurred. However, from my perspective as an L2 researcher, I am less comfortable with the implicit assumption that strategies, repertoires, etc., are readily available to and used by *all* people. Certainly, there are semiotic resources that are shared – otherwise, communication would be impossible. But multilinguals and monolinguals, L1 speakers and L2 speakers, adults and children and so on, may not have equal access to the same resources (but this is an empirical question rather than a conclusion). Again, a language (and emotion) socialization perspective may be useful in exploring the differential availability and deployment of particular affective resources in interaction.

Emotional Well-Being and Regulation

In Chapter 1, I cited an additional motivation for this study was an interest in the linkages among discursive practices, transculturalism and well-being or mental health – particularly in light of the backgrounds of the research participants (e.g. as L2 users, immigrants, former refugees, linguistic and ethnic minorities). It is not a stretch to link autobiographical stories of participants' sociolinguistic experiences with mental health, even within the study of L2 use. Block (2007; see also Berry & Kim, 1988), discussing immigration and transnationalism, hints at their potential links with psychological matters:

> Thus migration today opens up new and different adaptations options for migrants. Whereas in the past, immigration, with the connotation of 'staying for life', was the dominant option, today migrants can live, as it were, straddling *geographical, social* and *psychological borders*. (Block, 2007: 33, emphasis added)

Block's observation that 'staying for life' may no longer be the default option for contemporary immigrants is salient for understanding my study participants (including those not represented in this book). In fact, almost all of them, as well as many of their friends and family members, stated that they would like to return to their home country or move to Europe in the future. As they often commented, fitting into North American society is tiring and stressful – and largely impossible. Lo and Reyes (2004: 117), considering matters of identity and assimilation, find that racial and linguistic positioning of Asian immigrants and those of Asian descent in the US ultimately erases their membership in American society. Maalouf (2000: 38), also writing on modern migration and belonging, powerfully articulates these emotional dilemmas faced by immigrants:

> If only one affiliation matters, if a choice absolutely has to be made, a migrant finds himself split and torn, condemned to betray either his country of origin or his country of adoption, and whichever course he follows the consequent betrayal is bound to cause him lasting bitterness and anger.

As I pointed out in Chapter 8, evidence suggests that the ways in which individuals talk about and are able to regulate their negative emotions have important implications for their mental health, sense of well-being and ability to interact with their social environment (Gross, 2014a; Lazarus, 1999; Nyklíček *et al.*, 2004). To link L2 research with mental health topics, other promising areas of inquiry would include extending contemporary CA research on psychotherapeutic talk (e.g. Peräkylä *et al.*, 2008; Peräkylä & Sorjonen, 2012) to include attention to L2 users/multilingual persons, the management of stress by students and teachers (for an example, see Hepburn & Brown, 2001) and how emotional talk and writing may be used, learned, encouraged, resisted, avoided and so on, in the language classroom and other contexts (e.g. Benesch, 2011; Chamcharatsri, 2013; Hanauer, 2010).

The content of these L2 interviews included much talk of negative emotions, complaints, trauma, stress, discrimination and dilemmas tied to gender, class, sexuality and social belonging (and unbelonging). These topics are not necessarily unique to these speakers or this corpus. Although seldom the objects of research interest, similar concerns can also be found in many L2 studies involving interviews and narratives, as intra-psychological and social processes of *being* and *becoming* are made relevant by both researchers and research participants. For example, Menard-Warwick's (2009) study of Jorge, a Zapotec immigrant from Mexico, found that his identity and socioeconomic struggles were accompanied also by psychological struggles. Menard-Warwick (2009: 63) even describes Jorge's self-analysis where he recounted feeling 'psychologically abused' by his boss:

> He'd psychologically give you situations in the head (él psicológicamente te daba situaciones en la cabeza), for example, many other companies ask for references, no? So one of the things he'd say to me is that 'if you leave the carwash, [...] when they ask me for a reference, I'll tell them you're a very bad person [...] and wherever you go (dondequiera que vayas), you're not going to be able to work'.

Though previous scholarship has recognized the presence of emotion within speakers' autobiographical histories, little attention has been given to the ways in which the research process is itself a site where such psychological matters get actively generated and managed. Because ways of constructing, organizing and making sense of personhood may change across time and place (see discussions in Baynham & De Fina, 2005; Langman, 2004; Pavlenko & Blackledge, 2004), greater attention to how multilingual and transcultural individuals manage the shifting processes of self-identification, self-presentation and even self-preservation[3] may help to explain differential representations of agency and success over both the short term and long term. Therefore, autobiographical interview research can create a space for making these representations visible and analyzable.

Doing 'therapy'

There is a sense in which autobiographical interviews can be considered 'doubly therapeutic'. On the one hand, as described in the previous chapter, the act of organizing and producing stories of personal experience may be considered *discursively therapeutic* by enabling speakers to make visible and work through particularly traumatic or difficult experiences and their personal consequences (i.e. the 'talking cure'); on the other hand, the interview activity is *superficially therapeutic* because it involves actions (e.g. questions, responses, emotionality, emotional labor, reformulations) that overlap in many respects with and even seemingly reproduce 'psychotherapeutic' or counseling interaction. This is not to claim, however, that autobiographical interviewing necessarily results in emotional confessions, deep insights or improved mental health and well-being – though interviewees may indeed report these benefits (e.g. Prior, 2011b). As Chapter 8 shows, research indicates that the benefits may often be social (e.g. affiliation and decreased loneliness) rather than attributable to explicitly interventional or intra-psychological changes.

Getting longitudinal

In these chapters, how individuals described and even re-categorized talk of negative emotions and experiences varied. Because the data were collected over months and years, I had the opportunity to observe changes in the ways speakers organized and talked about their experiences over time. For example, some initially described themselves as victims and then later used the storytelling space to challenge or fight back against those who wronged them. Some made use of multiple tellings to reframe their stories over time – to later treat events as humorous rather than tragic or depressing. Others used their stories to make visible and create a cohesive presentation of self across time. Due to the time commitment involved and the amount of data produced, longitudinal interview and discourse-based studies remain exceptions to the norm. However, if we wish to study change *and* consistency, then more extended studies are sorely needed. We must also recognize that researchers are also a part of the longitudinal process: their relationships with interviewees, their own perspectives on the research, their analytical approaches and their embeddedness in the research context are all subject to longitudinal sameness and change. Moreover, researchers may even become a part of the stories that research participants tell.

A closer examination of the longitudinal processes by which speakers produce their accounts can not only deepen our understanding of L2 learning and use as a multi-faceted and reflexive process of interaction and meaning-making – it can also contribute to the body of knowledge on motivational trajectories, multilingualism and language as a contextualized and developmental process by examining how L2 users themselves conceptualize and organize their accumulated experiences over time. Furthermore, it can reveal the general, specific and unique semiotic and interactional resources that speakers make use of in the midst of navigating the various social arenas in which they live and interact.

Summary

Based on the discussions and analyses throughout these chapters, I summarize below some of the key observations and implications of this project for narrative and autobiographical interview research practices and emotion-related research. This is not meant to be a comprehensive list, but it does make visible some of the methodological and ethical realities and responsibilities that I argue researchers would do well to more closely acknowledge and address:

- Qualitative research interviews are analyzable as 'naturalistic' events. Though they contain features of both casual conversation and institutional talk, they must be analyzed *as interviews* and not privileged sites of data collection or automatically rejected as artificial environments.
- Reflexivity, if it is to be taken seriously, must be made a part of the *entire* research process, from the initial stages of identifying topics and questions to the writing up and dissemination of the findings. It must also go beyond the researchers 'self-reflection' to include a reflexive analysis of the larger interactional, relational and sequential contexts.
- Researchers' and research participants' contributions (e.g. questions, responses) shape the interactional trajectory of research and therefore influence the generation, selection, deletion, analysis, and ultimately, the representation of the data. Therefore, these matters must be acknowledged and incorporated in our analyses.
- Consequently, the narratives and other materials that interview interactants collaboratively generate are active representations, constructions, versions and accounts rather than passive or objective reports.
- Researchers and research participants may even resist and challenge one another's contributions, the interactional material and the research context. Because conflict and tension is a part of the research context – indeed, all human interaction – it should be included in the analyses and reports, not rejected as a methodological inconvenience.
- Emotionality functions as a topic or object of talk as well as an important interactional and interpersonal resource.
- Researchers and research participants closely attend to and manage their own emotionality as well as the emotionality of their interlocutor(s).
- The 'negative' emotionality frequently found in some autobiographical interview research should be examined also as an outcome of the activities of interviewing and storytelling, not just a consequence of speakers' personal biographies and 'psychologies'.
- Autobiographical research interviews may take on the shape of 'therapeutic' and 'psychological' contexts. Though researchers are not counselors or quasi-therapists, they are – like those whom they study – social, empathic beings. They must therefore be prepared for emotionality that is positive, negative and intense. Accordingly, they must plan for professional and personal support to help them and research participants better manage issues that may potentially affect their mental health and personal well-being.

Final Words

I will conclude with a data excerpt (Excerpt 9.1) that I believe represents the essence of the dynamic interface between emotionality and autobiographical interview research that I have sought to explore in this book. This comes from an extended interview sequence with Trang, an immigrant from Cambodia and Vietnam.

(Excerpt 9.1). Trang: 'I'm trying to be myself and tell the story' (simplified excerpt)

T: Being with-with people sometime I-I try to be somebody else. I-I'm trying to be s- … I'm trying to be z- … either I please them I try to please them trying to please them not … upset … or-or I feel upset because they act certain way make me upset? so that's why I rather be-be alone so I don't have to face all those … those … unpleasant … p-feeling?

M: So who are you trying to be now?

T: I'm trying to be … hahaha … myself and tell the story.

The emotionality of Excerpt 9.1 is made plain though the speaker's lexical descriptions (e.g. 'feel upset', 'unpleasant feeling'), dilemmatic aspects of identity presentation (e.g. 'I try to be somebody else'), talk of isolation ('I rather be alone'), prosodic cut-offs and pauses, serious tone and topic and even laughter. The interactional nature of this talk is also made evident through the *question-response* turn design and the rising, response-soliciting intonation ('feeling?'). What is also evident is that both interviewer and interviewee recognize that identity ('So who are you trying to be now?') and autobiographical experience ('I'm trying to be … hahaha … myself and tell the story') are also discursive constructions.

Based on the inspection of research data such as these, researchers have long observed that our participants produce highly emotional and detailed accounts to explain the personal histories and responses to them that have shaped their present-day realities. We have given much attention to the various topics and concerns that research participants raise and how they weave language and identity together in the 'there-and-then' storyworld as well as in the 'here-and-now' of the telling. We are also becoming increasingly aware that research participants, too, recognize that they are not just *reporting* events and perceptions but are in the moment *generating* and *managing* versions as well as the emotionality of their personal histories for the researcher, themselves and the larger research project. As we begin to appreciate that the various activities and relationships that make up our research are integral to the construction and reception of this autobiographical and emotional material, it is time for us to put our claims of reflexivity to the test by examining how this work gets done – and redone. Ultimately, this demands a commitment by researchers to produce studies investigating their *research practices*, not just summaries of the stories and other material that they generate.

Finally, I acknowledge that this book is but one contribution toward a closer engagement with emotionality and the practices of narrative and autobiographical interview research. Like all theoretical and practical research and knowledge representation, it is necessarily partial and continually unfolding (Denzin & Lincoln, 2011; Given, 2008):

> There is a sense in which research is never finished. Reflection will enable you as a researcher to see both the possibilities and the liabilities of your ever-developing reflexive and interpretive account of your research. (Burgess *et al.*, 2006: 89)

For some, this work may be overly micro-analytic and lacking in 'critical' commentary – as I have been cautious in making claims about the particular social conditions driving the form and content of the autobiographical talk of the study participants. Nevertheless, I have offered evidence that participants faced repeated discrimination and perceived marginalization based on language, ethnicity, gender, sexuality, educational background and national origin.[4] For others, because this study involves interaction in which the researcher/analyst is a participant, it runs the risk of being labeled as overly emotionalist. However, I have aimed to demonstrate that qualitative researchers should confidently reclaim the 'emotionalist' label by attending to speakers' affective work while maintaining reflexivity and analytical rigor. Whatever intellectual or emotional reactions this book sparks, I hope that it will inspire other researchers by contributing to a more serious, empirical, defensible and engaged conversation on the dynamic activity of investigating and representing human emotional life.

Notes

(1) On entextualization, see Bauman (2004), Bauman and Briggs (1990), Silverstein and Urban (1996); also Blommaert (2001a) on 'text trajectories'.
(2) I discuss the transformative dimensions of narrative-based research in Prior (2011b).
(3) I am grateful to an anonymous author who cites my 2011a article as 'Self-*Preservation* in L2 Interview Talk' rather than 'Self-*Presentation*'. Upon reflection, I cannot help but think this may also be an apt characterization of speakers' ongoing psychological and emotional work.
(4) To protect participants' identities, I have intentionally withheld details on their sociolinguistic and life outcomes. For some it has been tragic, while others have found stability and better life opportunities.

References

Ahmed, S. (2010) *The Promise of Happiness*. Durham, NC: Duke University Press.
Akbari, R. (2007) Reflections on reflective teaching: A critical appraisal of reflective practices in L2 teacher education. *System* 35 (2), 192–207.
Alvarez-Conrad, J., Zoellner, L.A. and Foa, E.B. (2001) Linguistic predictors of trauma pathology and physical health. *Applied Cognitive Psychology* 15, 159–170.
Andrews, F.M. and Withey, S.B. (1976) *Social Indicators of Well-being: The Development and Measurement of Perceptual Indicators*. New York: Plenum.
Andrews, M., Squire, C. and Tamboukou, M. (eds) (2013) *Doing Narrative Research* (2nd edn). London: SAGE.
Antaki, C. (1994) *Explaining and Arguing: Social Organization of Accounts*. London: SAGE.
Antaki, C. (2008) Formulations in psychotherapy. In A. Peräkylä, C. Antaki, S. Vehviläinen and I. Leudar (eds) *Conversation Analysis and Psychotherapy* (pp. 26–42). New York: Cambridge University Press.
Antaki, C. (ed.) (2011) *Applied Conversation Analysis: Intervention and Change in Institutional Talk*. New York: Palgrave MacMillan.
Antaki, C., Barnes, R. and Leudar, I. (2005) Diagnostic formulations in psychotherapy. *Discourse Studies* 7 (6), 627–647.
Antaki, C., Barnes, R. and Leudar, I. (2007) Members' and analysts' analytic categories: Researching psychotherapy. In A. Hepburn and S. Wiggins (eds) *Discursive Research in Practice* (pp. 166–181). New York: Cambridge University.
Antaki, C., Billig, M.G., Edwards, D. and Potter, J.A. (2003) Discourse analysis means doing analysis: A critique of six analytic shortcomings. *Discourse Analysis Online* 1 (1). See www.shu.ac.uk/daol/articles/v1/n1/a1/antaki2002002-paper.html
Antaki, C. and Widdicombe, S. (1998) Identity as an achievement and as a tool. In C. Antaki and S. Widdicombe (eds) *Identities in Talk* (pp. 1–14). London: SAGE.
Arksey, H. and Knight, P. (1999) *Interviewing for Social Scientists: An Introductory Resource with Examples*. London: SAGE.
Arndt, H. and Janney, R.W. (1987) *InterGrammar: Toward an Integrative Model of Verbal, Prosodic, and Kinesic Choices in Speech*. Berlin: Mouton de Gruyter.
Arnold, J. (ed.) (1999) *Affect in Language Learning*. New York: Cambridge.
Atkinson, D., Talmy, S. and Okada, H. (2011) Ethnography and discourse analysis. In K. Hyland and B. Paltridge (eds) *Bloomsbury Companion to Discourse Analysis* (pp. 85–100). London: Continuum.
Atkinson, J.M. and Drew, P. (1979) *Order in the Court: The Organization of Verbal Behavior in Judicial Settings*. London: Macmillan.
Atkinson, J.M. and Heritage, J. (eds) (1984) *Structures of Social Action: Studies in Conversation Analysis*. New York: Cambridge.
Atkinson, P. (1988) Ethnomethodology: A critical review. *Annual Review of Sociology* 14, 441–465.

Atkinson, P. (1997) Narrative turn or blind alley. *Qualitative Health Research* 7 (3), 325–344.
Atkinson, P. (2015) *For Ethnography*. London: SAGE.
Atkinson, P., Coffey, A. and Delamont, S. (2003) *Key Themes in Qualitative Research*. Walnut Creek, CA: AltaMira Press.
Atkinson, P. and Delamont, S. (2006) Rescuing narrative from qualitative research. *Narrative Inquiry* 16 (1), 164–172.
Atkinson, P. and Silverman, D. (1997) Kundera's *Immortality*: The interview society and the invention of the self. *Qualitative Inquiry* 3 (3), 304–325.
Atkinson, R. (1998) *The Life Story Interview*. London: SAGE.
Augoustinos, M. and Tileaga, C. (2012) Twenty five years of discursive psychology. *British Journal of Social Psychology* 51 (3), 405–412.
Austin, J.L. (1962) *How to Do Things with Words*. London: Oxford University Press.
Averill, J.R. (1980) A constructivist view of emotion. In R. Plutchik and H. Kellerman (eds) *Emotion: Theory, Research and Experience: Vol. I. Theories of Emotion* (pp. 305–339). New York: Academic Press.
Baker, C.D. (2003) Ethnomethodological analyses of interviews. In J. Holstein and J. Gubrium (eds) *Inside Interviewing: New Lenses, New Concerns* (pp. 395–412). London: SAGE.
Baker, C.D. (2004) Membership categorization and interview accounts. In D. Silverman (ed.) *Qualitative Research: Theory, Method and Practice* (2nd edn) (pp. 162–76). London: SAGE.
Bamberg, M.G. (1997) Language, concepts and emotions. The role of language in the construction of emotions. *Language Sciences* 19, 309–340.
Bamberg, M.G. (2004) Talk, small stories, and adolescent identities. *Human Development* 47, 366–369.
Bamberg, M.G. and Georgakopoulou, A. (2008) Small stories as a new perspective in narrative and identity analysis. *Text and Talk* 28, 377–396.
Baquedano-López, P. (2004) Literacy practices across learning contexts. In A. Duranti (ed.) *A Companion to Linguistic Anthropology* (pp. 245–268). Malden, MA: Blackwell.
Barkhuizen, G. (ed.) (2011) Narrative research in TESOL [Special issue]. *TESOL Quarterly* 45.
Barkhuizen, G. (ed.) (2013) *Narrative Research in Applied Linguistics*. Cambridge: Cambridge University Press.
Barkhuizen, G., Benson, P. and Chik, A. (2014) *Narrative Inquiry in Language Teaching and Research*. New York: Routledge.
Bauman, R. (1986) *Story, Performance, and Event: Contextual Studies of Oral Narrative*. Cambridge: Cambridge University Press.
Bauman, R. (2004) *A World of Others' Words: Cross-cultural Perspectives on Intertextuality*. Malden, MA: Blackwell.
Bauman, R. and Briggs, C. (1990) Poetics and performance as critical perspectives on language and social life. *Annual Review of Anthropology* 19, 59–88.
Baynham, M. and De Fina, A. (eds) (2005) *Dislocations/Relocations: Narratives of Displacement*. Northampton, MA: St. Jerome Publishing.
Beach, W.A. (1995) Conversation analysis: 'Okay' as a clue for understanding consequentiality. In S.J. Sigman (ed.) *The Consequentiality of Communication* (pp. 121–162). Mahwah, NJ: Erlbaum.
Becker, G. (1997) *Disrupted Lives: How People Create Meaning in a Chaotic World*. Berkeley: University of California Press.
Ben-Ze'ev, A. (2000) *The Subtlety of Emotions*. Cambridge, MA: MIT Press.
Benesch, S. (2011) *Considering Emotions in Critical English Language Teaching*. New York: Routledge.
Benson, P. and Nunan, D. (eds) (2005) *Learners' Stories: Difference and Diversity in Language Learning*. New York: Cambridge.

Benwell, B. and Stokoe, E. (2006) *Discourse and Identity*. Edinburgh: Edinburgh University Press.
Bercelli, F., Rossano, F. and Viaro, M. (2008) Clients' responses to therapists' re-interpretations. In A. Peräkylä, C. Antaki, S. Vehviläinen and I. Leudar (eds) *Conversation Analysis and Psychotherapy* (pp. 43–61). New York: Cambridge University Press.
Berger, P.L. and Luckmann, T. (1966) *The Social Construction of Reality: A Treatise in the Sociology of Knowledge*. New York: Anchor Books.
Bergmann, J.R. (2004) *Ethnomethodology*. In U. Flick, E.v. Kardorff and I. Steinke (eds) *A Companion to Qualitative Research* (pp. 72–80). London: SAGE.
Berry, J.W. and Kim, U. (1988) Acculturation and mental health. In J.W. Berry, P.R. Dasen and N. Sartorius (eds) *Health and Cross-cultural Psychology* (pp. 207–233). London: SAGE.
Besnier, N. (1990) Language and affect. *Annual Review of Anthropology* 19, 419–451.
Besnier, N. (2009) *Gossip and the Everyday Production of Politics*. Honolulu: University of Hawai'i Press.
Billig, M. (1996) *Arguing and Thinking: A Rhetorical Approach to Social Psychology* (2nd edn). New York: Cambridge University Press.
Billig, M. (1999a) Conversation analysis and the claims of naivety. *Discourse & Society* 10 (4), 572–576.
Billig, M. (1999b) Whose terms? Whose ordinariness? Rhetoric and ideology in conversation analysis. *Discourse & Society* 10 (4), 543–558.
Billig, M., Condor, S., Edwards, D., Gane, M., Middleton, D. and Radley, A.R. (1988) *Ideological Dilemmas: A Social Psychology of Everyday Thinking*. London: SAGE.
Bilmes, J. (1986) *Discourse and Behavior*. New York: Plenum Press.
Bilmes, J. (2011) Occasioned semantics: A systematic approach to meaning in talk. *Human Studies* 34, 129–153.
Binnick, R.I. (ed.) (2012) *The Oxford Handbook of Tense and Aspect*. New York: Oxford University Press.
Blackman, S.J. (2007) 'Hidden ethnography': Crossing emotional borders in qualitative accounts of young people's lives. *Sociology* 41 (4), 699–716.
Blair, R.G. (2000) Risk factors associated with PTSD and major depression among Cambodian refugees. *Health and Social Work* 25, 23–30.
Block, D. (2003) *The Social Turn in Second Language Acquisition*. Washington, DC: Georgetown University Press.
Block, D. (2007) *Second Language Identities*. New York: Continuum.
Block, D. (2008) *Multilingual Identities in a Global City: London Stories*. Basingstoke: Palgrave Macmillan.
Blommaert, J. (2001a) Context is/as critique. *Critique of Anthropology* 21 (1), 13–32.
Blommaert, J. (2001b) Investigating narrative inequality: African asylum seekers' stories in Belgium. *Discourse & Society* 12 (4), 413–449.
Blommaert, J. (2006) Applied ethnopoetics. *Narrative Inquiry* 16 (1), 181–190.
Blommaert, J. and Jie, D. (2010) *Ethnographic Fieldwork: A Beginner's Guide*. Bristol: Multilingual Matters.
Boden, D. and Zimmerman, D.H. (1991) *Talk and Social Structure: Studies in Ethnomethodology and Conversation Analysis*. Berkeley: University of California Press.
Bohanek, J.G., Fivush, R. and Walker, E. (2005) Memories of positive and negative emotional events. *Applied Cognitive Psychology* 19, 51–66.
Bohannan, P. and van der Elst, D. (1988) *Asking and Listening: Ethnography as Personal Adaptation*. Long Grove, IL: Waveland Press, Inc.
Boler, M. (1999) *Feeling Power: Emotions and Education*. New York: Routledge.
Bolton, S.C. (2005) *Emotion Management in the Workplace*. New York: Palgrave MacMillan.

Borg, S. (2015) *Teacher Cognition and Language Education: Research and Practice.* New York: Bloomsbury.
Bourdieu, P. (1991) *Language and Symbolic Power*, J.B. Thompson (ed.). Cambridge, MA: Harvard University Press.
Bousfield, D. (2008) *Impoliteness in Interaction.* Philadelphia, PA: John Benjamins.
Bown, J. and White, C. (2010) A social and cognitive approach to affect in SLA. *IRAL* 48, 331–353.
Briggs, C.L. (1986) *Learning How to Ask: A Sociolinguistic Appraisal of the Role of the Interview in Social Science Research.* New York: Cambridge.
Briggs, C.L. (2007) Anthropology, interviewing, and communicability in contemporary society. *Current Anthropology* 48 (4), 551–580.
Brouwer, C.E. (2012) Conversation analysis methodology in second language studies. *The Encyclopedia of Applied Linguistics*, 5 November 2012. DOI: 10.1002/9781405198431.wbeal0219
Brown, C. and Augusta-Scott, T. (eds) (2007) *Narrative Therapy: Making Meaning, Making Lives.* London: SAGE.
Brown, J.D. (2005) *Using Surveys in Language Programs.* New York: Cambridge.
Bucholtz, M. (2003) Sociolinguistic nostalgia and the authentication of identity. *Journal of Sociolinguistics* 7 (3), 398–416.
Burgess, H., Sieminski, S. and Arthur, L. (2006) *Achieving Your Doctorate in Education.* London: SAGE.
Burr, V. (2004) *Social Constructionism* (2nd edn). London: Routledge.
Buttny, R. (1993) *Social Accountability in Communication.* London: SAGE.
Buttny, R. (2004) *Talking Problems: Studies of Discursive Construction.* Albany, NY: SUNY Press.
Buttny, R. (2012) Protean experience in discursive analysis. *Discourse & Society* 23 (5), 602–608.
Button, G. (1990) On member's time. *Réseaux* 8 (1), 161–182.
Button, G., Coulter J., Lee, J. and Sharrock, W. (1995) *Computers, Minds and Conduct.* Cambridge: Polity Press.
Byrne, B. (2004) Qualitative interviewing. In C. Seale (ed.) *Researching Society and Culture* (pp. 179–192). London: SAGE.
Cacioppo, J.T., Gardner, W.L. and Berntson, G.G. (2002) The affect system has parallel and integrative processing components: Form follows function. In J.T. Cacioppo, G.G. Berntson, R. Adolphs, C.S. Carter, R.J. Davidson, M.K. McClintock, B.S. McEwen, M.J. Meaney, D.L. Schacter, E.M. Sternberg, S.S. Suomi and S.E. Taylor (eds) *Foundations in Social Neuroscience* (pp. 493–522). Cambridge, MA: MIT Press.
Cameron, D. and Kulick, D. (2003) *Language and Sexuality.* New York: Cambridge University Press.
Campbell, J. (1968) *The Hero With a Thousand Faces.* Princeton, NJ: Princeton University Press.
Canagarajah, S. (1996) From critical research practice to critical research reporting. *TESOL Quarterly* 30 (2), 321–331. doi: 10.2307/3588146.
Candland, D.K. (2003) *Emotion.* Lincoln, NE: Wadsworth Publishing Company.
Capps, L. and Ochs, E. (1995) *Constructing Panic: The Discourse of Agoraphobia.* Cambridge, MA: Harvard University Press.
Carlson, E.B. and Rosser-Hogan, R. (1991) Trauma experiences, posttraumatic stress, dissociation, and depression in Cambodian refugees. *American Journal of Psychiatry* 148 (11), 1548–1551.
Carter, S.K. and Bolden, C.L. (2012) Culture work in the research interview. In J.F. Gubrium, J. Holstein, A.B. Marvasti and K.D. McKinney (eds) *The SAGE Handbook of Interview Research: The Complexity of the Craft* (2nd edn) (pp. 255–268). London: SAGE.

Cervantes, C.A. (2002) Explanatory emotion talk in Mexican immigrant and Mexican American families. *Hispanic Journal of Behavioral Sciences* 24 (2), 138–163.

Chafe, W. (2007) *The Importance of Not being Earnest: The Feeling behind Laughter and Humor.* Philadelphia, PA: John Benjamins.

Chalhoub-Deville, M., Chapelle, C. and Duff, P. (2006) *Inference and Generalizability in Applied Linguistics: Multiple Perspectives.* Philadelphia, PA: John Benjamins.

Chamcharatsri, P.B. (2013) Emotionality and second language writers: Expressing fear through narrative in Thai and in English. *L2 Journal* 5 (1), 59–75.

Chase, S.E. (2008) Narrative inquiry: Multiple lenses, approaches, voices. In N. Denzin and Y. Lincoln (eds) *Collecting and Interpreting Qualitative Materials* (pp. 57–94). London: SAGE.

Chaudron, C., Nguyen, H. and Prior, M.T. (2006) *Vietnamese Elicited Imitation Test.* Honolulu: University of Hawai'i Press.

Chrestman, K.R. (1999) Secondary exposure to trauma and self-reported distress among therapists. In B.H. Stamm (ed.) *Secondary Traumatic Stress: Self-care Issues for Clinicians, Researchers, and Educators* (2nd edn) (pp. 29–36). Lutherville, MD: Sidran Press.

Christianson, S. (1992) *The Handbook of Emotion and Memory.* Hillsdale, NJ: Lawrence Erlbaum Associates.

Christophe, V. and Rimé, B. (1997) Exposure to social sharing of emotion: Emotional impact, listener responses and secondary social sharing. *European Journal of Social Psychology* 27, 37–54.

Clarke, S. and Hoggett, P. (2009) *Researching Beneath the Surface: Psycho-social Research Methods in Practice.* London: Karnac.

Clayman, S.E. and Heritage, J. (2002) *The News Interview: Journalists and Public Figures on the Air.* New York: Cambridge University Press.

Clayman, S.E. and Maynard, D.W. (1995) Ethnomethodology and conversation analysis. In P. ten Have and G. Psathas (eds) *Situated Order: Studies in the Social Organization of Talk and Embodied Activities* (pp. 1–30). Washington, DC: University Press of America.

Clift, R. (2006) Indexing stance: Reported speech as an interactional evidential. *Journal of Sociolinguistics* 10 (5), 569–595.

Clough, P.T. and Halley, J.O.M. (2007) *The Affective Turn: Theorizing the Social.* Durham, NC: Duke University Press.

Coffey, A. (2004) Autobiography. In M.S. Lewis-Beck, A.E. Bryman and T.F. Liao (eds) *The SAGE Encyclopedia of Social Science Research Methods* (pp. 45–46). London: SAGE.

Cole, P.M., Tamang, B.L. and Shrestha, S. (2006) Cultural variations in the socialization of young children's anger and shame. *Child Development* 77 (5), 1237–1251.

Collins, R. (1990) Stratification, emotional energy, and the transient emotions. In T.D. Kemper (ed.) *Research Agendas in the Sociology of Emotions* (pp. 27–57). Albany, NY: SUNY Press.

Coulter, J. (1985) Two concepts of the mental. In K.J. Gergen and K.E. Davis (eds) *The Social Construction of the Person* (pp. 129–144). London: Springer-Verlag.

Coulter, J. (1986) Affect and social context: Emotion definition as a social task. In R. Harre (ed.) *The Social Construction of Emotions* (pp. 120–134). Oxford: Blackwell.

Coulter, J. (2005) Language without mind. In te Molder and J. Potter (eds) *Conversation and Cognition* (pp. 79–92). New York: Cambridge.

Couper-Kuhlen, E. (2009) A sequential approach to affect: The case of 'disappointment'. In M. Haakana, M. Laakso and J. Lindström (eds) *Talk in Interaction: Comparative Dimensions* (pp. 94–123). Helsinki: Finnish Literature Society (SKS).

Couper-Kuhlen, E. (2012) Exploring affiliation in the reception of conversational complaint stories. In A. Peräkylä and M.-L. Sorjonen (eds) *Emotion in Interaction* (pp. 113–146). New York: Oxford University Press.

Coupland, N. (2003) Sociolinguistic authenticities. *Journal of Sociolinguistics* 7 (3), 417–431.
Crane, T. (2003) *The Mechanical Mind: A Philosophical Introduction to Minds, Machines and Mental Representations* (2nd edn). New York: Routledge.
Cresswell, J. (2012) Including social discourses and experience in research on refugees, race, and ethnicity. *Discourse & Society* 23 (5), 553–575.
Cresswell, J. and Smith, L. (2012) Embodying discourse analysis: Lessons learned about epistemic and ontological psychologies. *Discourse & Society* 23 (5), 619–625.
Crookes, G. (2013) *Critical ELT in Action: Foundations, Promises, Praxis*. New York: Routledge.
Crystal, D. (2011) *Dictionary of Linguistics and Phonetics* (6th edn). Malden, MA: Blackwell Publishing.
Cuff, E.C. and Francis, D.W. (1978) Some features of 'invited stories' about marriage breakdown. *International Journal of the Sociology of Language* 18, 111–133.
Cupples, J. (2002) The field as a landscape of desire: Sex and sexuality in geographical fieldwork. *Area* 34 (4), 382–390.
Curci, A. and Bellelli, G. (2004) Cognitive and social consequences of exposure to emotional narratives: Two studies on secondary social sharing of emotions. *Cognition and Emotion* 18 (7), 881–900.
Cutler, S.E., Larsen, R.J. and Bunce, S.C. (1996) Repressive coping style and the experience and recall of emotion: A naturalistic study of daily affect. *Journal of Personality* 64, 379–405.
Danchev, D. and Ross, A. (2014) *Research Ethics for Counselors, Nurses and Social Workers*. London: SAGE.
Davies, A. (2007) *An Introduction to Applied Linguistics: From Practice to Theory* (2nd edn). Edinburgh: Edinburgh University Press.
Davies, B. and Harré, R. (1990) Positioning: The discursive production of selves. *Journal for the Theory of Social Behaviour* 20, 43–63.
Davis, H. (2001) The management of self: Practical and emotional implications of ethnographic work in a public hospital setting. In K.R. Gilbert (ed.) *The Emotional Nature of Qualitative Research* (pp. 37–61). New York: CRC Press.
Davis, K. (1986) The process of problem (re)formulation in psychotherapy. *Sociology of Health & Illness* 8, 44–74.
Davitz, J.R. (1969) *The Language of Emotions*. New York: McGraw Hill.
Day, D. (1998) Being ascribed, and resisting, membership of an ethnic group. In C. Antaki and S. Widdicombe (eds) *Identities in Talk* (pp. 151–190). London: SAGE.
DeBonis, S. (1995) *Children of the Enemy: Oral Histories of Vietnamese Amerasians and their Mothers*. Jefferson, NC: McFarland.
De Fina, A. (2003) *Identity in Narrative: A Study in Immigrant Discourse*. Philadelphia, PA: John Benjamins.
De Fina, A. and Georgakopoulou, A. (2012) *Analyzing Narrative: Discourse and Sociolinguistic Perspectives*. Cambridge: Cambridge University Press.
De Fina, A., Schiffrin, D. and Bamberg, M. (eds) (2006) *Discourse and Identity*. New York: Cambridge University Press.
deMarrais, K. and Tisdale, K. (2002) What happens when researchers inquire into difficult emotions? Reflections on studying women's anger through qualitative interviews. *Educational Psychologist* 37, 115–123.
Demuth, C. (2012) On living social discourse, embodiment and culture: The potential of a broadened conception of discursive psychology. *Discourse & Society* 23 (5), 589–595.
Denzin, N.K. (1984) *On Understanding Emotion*. San Francisco: Jossey-Bass.
Denzin, N.K. (1992) The many faces of emotionality: Reading *Persona*. In C. Ellis and M.G. Flaherty (eds) *Investigating Subjectivity: Research on Lived Experience* (pp. 17–30). London: SAGE.

Denzin, N.K. (2001) The reflexive interview and a performative social science. *Qualitative Research* 1 (1), 23–46.
Denzin, N.K. and Lincoln, Y.S. (2011) *The SAGE Handbook of Qualitative Research* (4th edn). London: SAGE.
Dewaele, J.-M. (2004) The emotional force of swearwords and taboo words in the speech of multilinguals. *Journal of Multilingual and Multicultural Development* 25, 204–222.
Dewaele, J.-M. (2005) Investigating the psychological and emotional dimensions in instructed language learning: Obstacles and possibilities. *Modern Language Journal* 89 (3), 367–380.
Dewaele, J.-M. (2006) Expressing anger in multiple languages. In A. Pavlenko (ed.) *Bilingual Minds: Emotional Experience, Expression, and Representation* (pp. 118–151). Clevedon: Multilingual Matters.
Dewaele, J.-M. (2008) Dynamic emotion concepts of learners and L2 users: A second language acquisition perspective. *Bilingualism: Language and Cognition* 11 (2), 173–175.
Dewaele, J.-M. (2010) *Emotions in Multiple Languages*. Basingstoke: Palgrave Macmillan.
Dewaele, J.-M. (2013) Emotions. In P. Robinson (ed.) *The Routledge Encyclopedia of Second Language Acquisition* (pp. 208–210). New York: Routledge.
Dewaele, J.-M. and Pavlenko, A. (2002) Emotion vocabulary in interlanguage. *Language Learning* 52, 265–324.
Dickson-Swift, V., James, E.L., Kippen, S. and Liamputtong, P. (2007) Doing sensitive research: What challenges do qualitative researchers face? *Qualitative Research* 7 (3), 327–353.
Dörnyei, Z. (2007) *Research Methods in Applied Linguistics: Quantitative, Qualitative and Mixed Methodologies*. Oxford: Oxford University Press.
Dörnyei, Z. (2009) *The Psychology of Second Language Acquisition*. New York: Oxford University Press.
Dörnyei, Z. and Kubanyiova, M. (2014) *Motivating Learners, Motivating Teachers: Building Vision in the Language Classroom*. Cambridge: Cambridge University Press.
Dörnyei, Z., MacIntyre, P. and Henry, A. (eds) (2014) *Motivational Dynamics in Language Learning*. Bristol: Multilingual Matters.
Dörnyei, Z. and Schmidt, R. (eds) (2001) *Motivation and Second Language Acquisition*. Honolulu, HI: Second Language Teaching and Curriculum Center, University of Hawai'i at Mānoa.
Dörnyei, Z. and Ushioda, E. (2009) *Motivation, Language Identity and the L2 Self*. Bristol: Multilingual Matters.
Dörnyei, Z. and Ushioda, E. (2011) *Teaching and Researching Motivation* (2nd edn). New York: Routledge.
Drew, P. (1997) 'Open' class repair initiators in response to sequential sources of troubles in conversation. *Journal of Pragmatics* 28, 69–101.
Drew, P. (1998) Complaints about transgressions and misconduct. *Research on Language and Social Interaction* 31 (3–4), 295–325.
Drew, P. (2003) Comparative analysis of talk-in-interaction in different institutional settings: A sketch. In P.J. Glenn, C.D. LeBaron and J. Mandelbaum (eds) *Studies in Language and Social Interaction: In Honor of Robert Hopper* (pp. 293–308). Mahwah, NJ: Erlbaum.
Drew, P. and Heritage, J. (1992) *Talk at Work: Interaction in Institutional Settings*. London: Cambridge University Press.
Du Bois, J.W. (2007) The stance triangle. In R. Englebretson (ed.) *Stancetaking in Discourse: Subjectivity, Evaluation, Interaction* (pp. 139–182). Amsterdam: Benjamins.
Duff, P. (2008) *Case Study Research in Applied Linguistics*. Mahwah, NJ: Erlbaum.
Dunn, J. and Brown, J. (1991) Becoming American or English? Talking about the social world in England and the U.S. In M. Bornstein (ed.) *Cross Cultural Approaches to Parenting* (pp. 155–172). Hillsdale, NJ: Erlbaum.

Dunn, L. (1991) 'Research Alert! Qualitative research may be hazardous to your health!' *Qualitative Health Research* 1, 388–92.
Eades, D. (2008) *Courtroom Talk and Neocolonial Control*. Berlin: Mouton de Gruyter.
Eckert, P. (2003) Sociolinguistics and authenticity: An elephant in the room. *Journal of Sociolinguistics* 7 (3), 392–431.
Edley, N. (2001a) Analysing masculinity: Interpretive repertoires, ideological dilemmas and subject positions. In M. Wetherell, S. Taylor and S. J. Yates (eds) *Discourse as Data: A Guide for Analysis* (pp. 189–228). London: SAGE.
Edley, N. (2001b) Conversation analysis, discursive psychology and the study of ideology: A response to Susan Speer. *Feminism & Psychology* 11 (1), 136–140.
Edley, N. and Wetherell, M. (1997) Jockeying for position: The construction of masculine identities. *Discourse & Society* 8 (2), 203–217.
Edley, N. and Wetherell, M. (1999) Imagined futures: Young men's talk about fatherhood and domestic life. *British Journal of Social Psychology* 38, 181–194.
Edley, N. and Wetherell, M. (2001) Jekyll and Hyde: Men's constructions of feminism and feminists. *Feminism and Psychology* 11 (4), 439–457.
Edwards, D. (1997) *Discourse and Cognition*. London: SAGE.
Edwards, D. (1999) Emotion discourse. *Culture and Psychology* 5 (3), 271–291.
Edwards, D. (2000) Extreme case formulations: Softeners, investment, and doing nonliteral. *Research on Language and Social Interaction* 33 (4), 347–373.
Edwards, D. (2005) Discursive psychology. In K. Fitch and R. Sanders (eds) *Handbook of Language and Social Interaction* (pp. 257–273). Mahwah, NJ: Erlbaum.
Edwards, D. (2006) Discourse, cognition and social practices: The rich surface of language and social interaction. *Discourse Studies* 8 (1), 41–49.
Edwards, D. (2007) Managing subjectivity in talk. In A. Hepburn and S. Wiggins (eds) *Discourse Research in Practice* (pp. 31–49). New York: Cambridge.
Edwards, D., Ashmore, M. and Potter, J. (1995) Death and furniture: The rhetoric, politics and theology of bottom line arguments against relativism. *History of the Human Sciences* 8 (2), 25–49.
Edwards, D. and Potter, J. (1992) *Discursive Psychology*. London: SAGE.
Edwards, D. and Potter, J. (2005) Discursive psychology, mental states and descriptions. In H. te Molder and J. Potter (eds) *Conversation and Cognition* (pp. 241–259). New York: Cambridge University Press.
Edwards, D. and Stokoe, E. (2004) Discursive psychology, focus group interviews, and participants' categories. *British Journal of Developmental Psychology* 22, 499–507.
Ehrenreich, B. and Hochschild, A.R. (2003) *Global Woman: Nannies, Maids, and Sex Workers in the New Economy*. New York: Metropolitan Books.
Eisenberg, N., Cumberland, A. and Spinrad, T.L. (1998) Parental socialization of emotion. *Psychological Inquiry* 9, 241–273.
Ekman, P. (1985) *Telling Lies: Clues to Deceit in the Marketplace, Politics, and Marriage*. New York: Norton.
Ekman, P. (2003) *Emotions Inside Out: 130 Years after Darwin's the Expression of the Emotions in Man and Animals*. New York: New York Academy of Sciences.
Ekman, P. and Friesen, W.V. (2003) *Unmasking the Face: A Guide to Recognizing Emotions from Facial Clues*. Cambridge, MA: Malor Books.
Ellis, C. (1991) Sociological introspection and emotional experience. *Symbolic Interaction* 14 (1), 23–50.
Ellis, C. and Berger, L. (2003) Their story/my story/our story: Including the researcher's experience in interview research. In J.F. Gubrium and J.A. Holstein (eds) *Postmodern Interviewing* (pp. 157–186). London: SAGE.
Emerson, R.M., Fretz, R.I. and Shaw, L.L. (2011) *Writing Ethnographic Field Notes*. Chicago, IL: University of Chicago Press.

Enelow, A.J., Forde, D.L. and Brummel-Smith, K. (1996) *Interviewing and Patient Care* (4th edn). New York: Oxford University Press.
Enfield, N.J. (2007) Meanings of the unmarked: How 'default' person reference does more than just refer. In N.J. Enfield and T. Stivers (eds) *Person Reference in Interaction: Linguistic, Cultural and Social Perspectives* (pp. 97–120). New York: Cambridge University Press.
Enfield, N.J. and Stivers, T. (eds) (2007) *Person Reference in Interaction: Linguistic, Cultural, and Social Perspectives*. New York: Cambridge University Press.
Englebretson, R. (ed.) (2007) *Stancetaking in Discourse: Subjectivity, Evaluation, Interaction*. Amsterdam: John Benjamins.
Etherington, K. (2004) *Becoming a Reflexive Researcher: Using Ourselves in Research*. Philadelphia, PA: Jessica Kingsley Publishers.
Faragher, R.V. and Heimann, F.F. (1954) Price controls, antitrust laws, and minimum price laws – The relation between emergency and normal economic controls. *Law and Contemporary Problems* 19 (4), 648–684.
Fine, M. and Weis, L. (1998) Writing the 'wrongs' of fieldwork: Confronting our own research/writing dilemmas in urban ethnographies. In G. Shacklock and J. Smyth (eds) *Being Reflexive in Critical and Social Education Research* (pp. 13–35). Bristol, PA: Falmer Press.
Fink, A. (2008) *How to Conduct Surveys: A Step-by-Step Guide*. London: SAGE.
Fink, A., Bourque, L. and Fielder, E.P. (2003) *How to Conduct Telephone Surveys*. London: SAGE.
Fitzgerald, R. and Housley, W. (eds) (2015) *Advances in Membership Categorisation Analysis*. London: SAGE.
Fivush, R. (1994) Constructing narrative, emotion and self in parent-child conversations about the past. In U. Neisser and R. Fivush (eds) *The Remembering Self: Accuracy and Construction in the Life Narrative* (pp. 136–157). New York: Cambridge University Press.
Fivush, R., Bohanek, J.G. and Zaman, W. (2010) Personal and intergenerational narratives in relation to adolescents' well-being. In T. Habermas (ed.) The development of autobiographical reasoning in adolescence and beyond. *New Directions for Child and Adolescent Development* 131, 45–57.
Flick, U. (2004) Triangulation in qualitative research. In U. Flick, E. von Kardoff and I. Steinke (eds) *A Companion to Qualitative Research* (pp. 178–183). London: SAGE.
Foa, E.B. and Kozak, M.J. (1986) Emotional processing of fear: Exposure to corrective information. *Psychological Bulletin* 99, 20–35.
Foley, L. (2012) Constructing the respondent. In J.F. Gubrium, J.A. Holstein, A.B. Marvasti and K.D. McKinney (eds) *The SAGE Handbook of Interview Research: The Complexity of the Craft* (2nd edn) (pp. 305–317). London: SAGE.
Folkman, S. (2011) *The Oxford Handbook of Stress, Health, and Coping*. Oxford: Oxford University Press.
Francis, D.J. and Hester, S. (2004) *An Invitation to Ethnomethodology: Language, Society and Interaction*. London: SAGE.
Frankel, R.M. (1984) From sentence to sentence: Understanding the medical encounter through microinteractional analysis. *Discourse Processes* 7, 135–170.
Frederickson, B.L. and Levenson, R.W. (1998) Positive emotions speed recovery for the cardiovascular sequelae of negative emotions. *Cognition & Emotion* 12, 191–220.
Freed, A.F. and Ehrlich, S. (eds) (2010) *'Why Do You Ask?': The Function of Questions in Institutional Discourse*. New York: Oxford University Press.
Freeman, M. (2006) Life 'on holiday'?: In defense of big stories. *Narrative Inquiry* 16 (1), 131–138.
Fussell, S.R. (2002) *The Verbal Communication of Emotions: Interdisciplinary Perspectives*. Mahwah, NJ: Lawrence Erlbaum Associates.
Gabriel, Y. (2000) *Storytelling in Organizations: Facts, Fictions, and Fantasies*. New York: Oxford University Press.

Gabryś-Barker, D. and Bielska, J. (eds) (2013) *The Affective Dimension in Second Language Acquisition*. Bristol: Multilingual Matters.
Galasiński, D. (2004) *Men and the Language of Emotions*. Houndmills: Palgrave Macmillan.
Gale, J. (1991) *Conversation Analysis of Therapeutic Discourse: Pursuit of a Therapeutic Agenda*. Norwood, NJ: Ablex.
Galletta, A. and Cross, W.E. (2013) *Mastering the Semi-structured Interview and Beyond: From Research Design to Analysis and Publication*. New York: New York University Press.
Gardner, R.C. (1985) *Social Psychology and Second Language Learning: The Roles of Attitudes and Motivation*. London: Edward Arnold.
Gardner, R.C. (2004) On delaying the answer: Question sequences extended after the question. In R. Gardner and J. Wagner (eds) *Second Language Conversations* (pp. 246–266). New York: Continuum.
Garfinkel, H. (1967) *Studies in Ethnomethodology*. Englewood Cliffs, NJ: Prentice-Hall.
Garfinkel, H. and Sacks, H. (1970) On formal structures of practical actions. In J.D. McKinney and E.A. Tiryakian (eds) *Theoretical Sociology* (pp. 337–366). New York: Appleton-Century Crofts.
Garrett, P.B. and Baquedano-Lopez, P. (2002) Language socialization: Reproduction and continuity, transformation and change. *Annual Review of Anthropology* 31, 339–361.
Garrett, P.B. and Young, R. (2009) Theorizing affect in foreign language learning: An analysis of one learner's responses to a communicative Portuguese course. *The Modern Language Journal* 93 (2), 209–226.
Gaydos, H.L. (2005) Understanding personal narratives: An approach to practice. *Journal of Advanced Nursing* 49 (3), 254–259.
Gaylin, W. (1979) *Feelings: Our Vital Signs*. New York: Harper & Row.
Gearing, J. (1995) Fear and loving in the West Indies: Research from the heart (as well as the head). In D. Kulick and M. Willson (eds) *Taboo: Sex, Identity and Erotic Subjectivity in Anthropological Fieldwork* (pp. 186–218). London: Routledge.
Georgakopoulou, A. (2007) *Small Stories, Interaction and Identities*. Philadelphia, PA: John Benjamins.
Gergen, K.J. and Gergen, M.M. (1988) Narrative and the self as relationship. In L. Berkowitz (ed.) *Advances in Experimental Social Psychology*, V. 21 (pp. 17–56). New York: Academic Press.
Gilbert, G.N. and Mulkay, M. (1984) *Opening Pandora's Box: A Sociological Analysis of Scientists' Discourse*. New York: Cambridge.
Gilbert, K.R. (2001) *The Emotional Nature of Qualitative Research*. Boca Raton, FL: CRC Press.
Given, L.M. (ed.) (2008) *The SAGE Encyclopedia of Qualitative Research Methods*. London: SAGE.
Glenn, P.J. (1992) Current speaker initiation of two-party shared laughter. *Research on Language & Social Interaction* 25, 139–162.
Glenn, P.J. (2003) *Laughter in Interaction*. New York: Cambridge.
Goffman, E. (1956) *The Presentation of Self in Everyday Life*. Edinburgh: University of Edinburgh, Social Sciences Research Centre.
Goffman, E. (1963) *Stigma: Notes on the Management of Spoiled Identity*. New York: Simon & Schuster.
Goffman, E. (1978) Response cries. *Language* 54, 787–815.
Goffman, E. (1981) *Forms of Talk*. Philadelphia: University of Pennsylvania Press.
Goldstein, T. (1996) *Two Languages at Work: Bilingual Life on the Production Floor*. New York: Mouton De Gruyter.
Golombek, P. and Doran, M. (2014) Unifying cognition, emotion, and activity in language teacher professional development. *Teaching and Teacher Education* 39, 102–111.
Golombek, P. and Jordan, S.R. (2005) Becoming 'black lambs' not 'parrots': A poststructuralist orientation to intelligibility and identity. *TESOL Quarterly* 39 (3), 513–533.

Goodwin, C. (2000) Action and embodiment within situated human interaction. *Journal of Pragmatics* 32, 1489–1522.
Goodwin, C. (2007) Participation, stance and affect in the organization of activities. *Discourse & Society* 18 (1), 53–73.
Goodwin, J. (2012) *SAGE Secondary Data Analysis*. London: SAGE.
Goodwin, M.H. and Goodwin, C. (2001) Emotion within situated activity. In A. Duranti (ed.) *Linguistic Anthropology: A Reader* (pp. 239–257). Malden, MA: Blackwell.
Goss, C., Rossi, A. and Moretti, F. (2010) Assessment stage: Data gathering and structuring the interview. In M. Rimondini (ed.) *Communication in Cognitive Behavioral Therapy* (pp. 25–52). London: Springer.
Greatbatch, D. (1988) A turn-taking system for British news interviews. *Language in Society* 17 (3), 401–430.
Greatbatch, D. (1992) The management of disagreement between news interviewees. In P. Drew and J. Heritage (eds) *Talk at Work* (pp. 268–301). New York: Cambridge University Press.
Greco, M. and Stenner, P. (eds) (2008) *Emotions: A Social Science Reader*. New York: Routledge.
Grice, H.P. (1975) Logic and conversation. In P. Cole and J.L. Morgan (eds) *Syntax and Semantics: Vol. 3, Speech Acts* (pp. 41–58). New York: Academic Press.
Groleau, D. and Kirmayer, L.J. (2004) Sociosomatic theory in Vietnamese immigrants' narratives of distress. *Anthropology & Medicine* 11 (2), 117–133.
Gross, J.J. (ed.) (2014a) *Handbook of Emotion Regulation* (2nd edn). New York: Guilford Press.
Gross, J.J. (2014b) Emotion regulation: Conceptual and empirical foundations. In J.J. Gross (ed.) *Handbook of Emotion Regulation* (2nd edn) (pp. 3–20). New York: Guilford Press.
Gubrium, J.E. and Holstein, J.A. (eds) (2002) *Handbook of Interview Research: Context and Method*. London: SAGE.
Gubrium, J.F. and Holstein, J.A. (2009) *Analyzing Narrative Reality*. London: SAGE.
Gubrium, J.F. and Holstein, J. (2012) Narrative practice and the transformation of interview subjectivity. In J.F. Gubrium, J. Holstein, A.B. Marvasti and K.D. McKinney (eds) *The SAGE Handbook of Interview Research: The Complexity of the Craft* (2nd edn) (pp. 27–43). London: SAGE.
Gubrium, J.F., Holstein, J., Marvasti, A.B. and McKinney, K.D. (eds) (2012) *The SAGE Handbook of Interview Research: The Complexity of the Craft* (2nd edn). London: SAGE.
Günthner, S. (1997a) Complaint stories. Constructing emotional reciprocity among women. In H. Kotthoff and R. Wodak (eds) *Communicating Gender in Context* (pp. 179–218). Amsterdam: John Benjamins.
Günthner, S. (1997b) The contextualization of affect in reported dialogues. In S. Niemeier and R. Dirven (eds) *The Language of Emotions: Conceptualization, Expression, and Theoretical Foundation* (pp. 247–277). Oxford: Blackwell.
Haakana, M. (1999) Laughing matters: A conversation analytical study of laughter in doctor patient interaction. Doctoral dissertation, University of Helsinki, Department of Finnish Language.
Haakana, M. (2007) Reported thought in complaint stories. In E. Holt and R. Clift (eds) *Reporting Talk: Reported Speech in Interaction* (pp. 150–178). New York: Cambridge.
Haakana, M. (2010) Laughter and smiling: Notes on co-occurrences. *Journal of Pragmatics* 42 (6), 1499–1512.
Halkowski, T. (2006) Realizing the illness: Patients' narratives of symptom discovery. In J. Heritage and D.W. Maynard (eds) *Communication in Medical Care: Interaction between Primary Care Physicians and Patients* (pp. 86–114). Cambridge: Cambridge University Press.
Hall, C., Sarangi, S. and Slembrouck, S. (1997) Narrative transformation in child abuse reporting. *Child Abuse Review* 6, 272–282.

Hammersley, M. (2003) Conversation Analysis and discourse analysis: Methods or paradigms. *Discourse & Society* 14 (6), 751-781.
Hammersley, M. (2014a) On the ethics of interviewing for discourse analysis. *Qualitative Research* 14 (5), 529-541.
Hammersley, M. (2014b) The ethics of interviewing for discourse analysis: A reply to Taylor and Smith. *Qualitative Research* 14 (6), 763-766.
Hammersley, M. and Atkinson, P. (2007) *Ethnography: Principles in Practice*. New York: Routledge.
Hanauer, D.I. (2010) *Poetry as Research: Exploring Second Language Poetry Writing*. Philadelphia, PA: John Benjamins Publishing.
Harré, R. (1986) *The Social Construction of Emotions*. Oxford: Blackwell.
Harré, R. and Langenhove, L.V. (1999) *Positioning Theory: Moral Contexts of Intentional Action*. Malden, MA: Blackwell Publishers.
Harré, R. and Stearns, P.N. (eds) (1995) *Discursive Psychology in Practice*. London: SAGE.
Harris, S. (1991) Evasive action: How politicians respond to questions in political interviews. In P. Scannell (ed.) *Broadcast Talk* (pp. 76-99). London: SAGE.
Hatch, E.M. (1992) *Discourse and Language Education*. New York: Cambridge University Press.
Hatfield, E., Cacioppo, J.T. and Rapson, R.L. (1994) *Emotional Contagion*. New York: Cambridge University Press.
He, A.W. (1998) *Reconstructing Institutions: Language Use in Academic Counseling Encounters*. Greenwich, CT: Ablex Publishing Corporation.
Heath, C. (1992) The delivery and reception of diagnosis in the general practice consultation. In P. Drew and J. Heritage (eds) *Talk at Work* (pp. 235-267). New York: Cambridge University Press.
Heigham, J. and Croker, R.A. (eds) (2009) *Qualitative Research in Applied Linguistics: A Practical Introduction*. New York: Palgrave Macmillan.
Hepburn, A. and Brown, S.D. (2001) Teacher stress and the management of accountability. *Human Relations* 54 (6), 691-715.
Hepburn, A. and Wiggins, S. (2007) Discursive research: Themes and debates. In A. Hepburn and S. Wiggins (eds) *Discursive Research in Practice: New Approaches to Psychology and Interaction* (pp. 1-28). New York: Cambridge.
Heritage, J. (1984) *Garfinkel and Ethnomethodology*. New York: Polity Press.
Heritage, J. (1985) Analyzing news interviews: Aspects of the production of talk for an overhearing audience. In T.A. van Dijk (ed.) *Handbook of Discourse Analysis* (Vol. 3, pp. 95-117). London: Academic Press.
Heritage, J. (1998) Oh-prefaced responses to inquiry. *Language in Society* 27 (3), 291-334.
Heritage, J. (2005a) Cognition in discourse. In H. te Molder and J. Potter (eds) *Conversation and Cognition* (pp. 184-202). New York: Cambridge University Press.
Heritage, J. (2005b) Conversation analysis and institutional talk. In K.L. Fitch and R.E. Sanders (eds) *Handbook of Language and Social Interaction* (pp. 103-146). Mahwah, NJ: Erlbaum.
Heritage, J. (2010) Questioning in medicine. In A.F. Freed and S. Ehrlich (eds) *'Why Do You Ask?': The Function of Questions in Institutional Discourse* (pp. 42-68). Oxford: Oxford University Press.
Heritage, J. (2011) Territories of knowledge, territories of experience: Empathic moments in interaction. In T. Stivers, L. Mondada and J. Steensig (eds) *The Morality of Knowledge in Conversation* (pp. 42-68). New York: Cambridge University Press.
Heritage, J. and Clayman, S.E. (2010) *Talk in Action: Interactions, Identities, and Institutions*. Malden, MA: Wiley-Blackwell.
Heritage, J. and Greatbatch, D. (1989) On the institutional character of institutional talk: The case of news interviews. In P.A. Forstorp (ed.) *Discourse in Professional and Everyday Culture* (pp. 47-98). Linkoping, Sweden: University of Linkoping.

Heritage, J. and Raymond, G. (2005) The terms of agreement: Indexing epistemic authority and subordination in talk-in-interaction. *Social Psychology Quarterly* 68 (1), 15–38.

Heritage, J. and Robinson, J.D. (2006a) Accounting for the visit: Giving reasons for seeking medical care. In J. Heritage and D.W. Maynard (eds) *Communication in Medical Care: Interaction between Primary Care Physicians and Patients* (pp. 48–85). Cambridge: Cambridge University Press.

Heritage, J. and Robinson, J.D. (2006b) The structure of patients' presenting concerns: Physicians' opening questions. *Health Communication* 19 (2), 89–102.

Heritage, J. and Watson, D. (1979) Formulations as conversational objectives. In G. Psathas (ed.) *Everyday Language: Studies in Ethnomethodology* (pp. 123–162). New York: Irvington Press.

Heritage, J. and Watson, D. (1980) Aspects of the properties of formulations. *Semiotica* 30 (3–4), 245–262.

Herr, K. and Anderson, G.L. (2005) *The Action Research Dissertation: A Guide for Students and Faculty.* London: SAGE.

Hesse-Biber, S.N. and Leavy, P. (2008) *Handbook of Emergent Methods.* New York: Guilford Press.

Hester, S. and Eglin, P. (eds) (1997) *Culture in Action: Studies in Membership Categorization Analysis.* Washington, DC: International Institute for Ethnomethodology and Conversation Analysis & University Press of America.

Hibberd, F.J. (2005) *Unfolding Social Constructionism.* London: Springer.

Hine, C. (2000) Virtual ethnography. London: SAGE.

Hinton, A.L. (1998) Why did you kill?: The Cambodian genocide and the dark side of face and honor. *The Journal of Asian Studies* 57 (1), 93–122.

Hinton, A.L. (2007) Terror and trauma in the Cambodian genocide. In L.J. Kirmayer, R. Lemelson and M. Barad (eds) *Understanding Trauma; Integrating Biological, Clinical, and Cultural Perspectives* (pp. 433–450). New York: Cambridge.

Hochschild, A.R. (1979) Emotion work, feeling rules, and social structure. *American Journal of Sociology* 85 (3), 551–575.

Hochschild, A.R. (1983) *The Managed Heart: Commercialization of Human Feeling.* Berkeley: University of California Press.

Hochschild, A.R. (2003) *The Managed Heart: Commercialization of Human Feeling* (2nd edn). Berkeley: University of California Press.

Holliday, A. (2007) *Doing and Writing Qualitative Research* (2nd edn). London: SAGE.

Holstein, J.A. and Gubrium, J.F. (1995) *The Active Interview.* London: SAGE.

Holstein, J.A. and Gubrium, J.F. (eds) (2003) *Inside Interviewing: New Lenses, New Concerns.* London: SAGE.

Holstein, J.A. and Gubrium, J.F. (eds) (2008) *Handbook of Constructionist Research.* New York: Guilford Press.

Holstein, J.A. and Gubrium, J.F. (2011) The constructionist analytics of interpretive practice. In J.A. Holstein and J.F. Gubrium (eds) *The Sage Handbook of Qualitative Research* (pp. 341–357). London: SAGE.

Holt, E. (1999) Reported speech and recipients' reactions in interaction. In J. Verschueren (ed.) *Pragmatics in 1998: Selected Papers from the 6th International Pragmatics Conference* (pp. 261–275). Antwerp: International Pragmatics Association.

Holt, E. (2010) The last laugh: Shared laughter and topic termination. *Journal of Pragmatics* 42 (6), 1513–1525.

Holt, E. and Clift, R. (eds) (2007) *Reporting Talk: Reported Speech in Interaction.* Cambridge: Cambridge University Press.

Hook, D. (2001) Discourse, knowledge and materiality: Foucault and discourse analysis. *Theory & Psychology* 11, 521–547.

Hook, D. (2007) *Foucault, Psychology and the Analytics of Power.* New York: Palgrave.

Horwitz, E.K. and Young, D.J. (1991) *Language Anxiety: From Theory and Research to Classroom Implications*. Englewood Cliffs, NJ: Prentice Hall.
Horwitz, E.K., Horwitz, M.B. and Cope, J.A. (1986) Foreign language classroom anxiety. *Modern Language Journal* 70 (2), 125–132.
Housley, W. and Fitzgerald, R. (2000) Conversation analysis, practitioner based research, reflexivity and reflective practice: Some exploratory remarks. *Ethnographic Studies Issues* 5, 27–41.
Housley, W. and Fitzgerald, R. (2002) The reconsidered model of membership categorization. *Qualitative Research* 2 (1), 59–74.
Hutchby, I. (2005) Conversation analysis and the study of broadcast talk. In K.L. Fitch and R.E. Sanders (eds) *Handbook of Language and Social Interaction* (pp. 437–460). Mahwah, NJ: Erlbaum.
Hutchby, I. and Wooffitt, R. (2008) *Conversation Analysis*. Oxford: Polity Press.
Imai, Y. (2010) Emotions in SLA: New insights from collaborative learning for an EFL classroom. *The Modern Language Journal* 94 (2), 272–292.
Irvine, F., Roberts, G. and Bradbury-Jones, C. (2008) The researcher as insider versus the researcher as outsider: Enhancing rigour through language and cultural sensitivity. In P. Liamputtong (ed.) *Doing Cross-cultural Research: Ethical and Methodological Perspectives* (pp. 35–48). Dordrecht, The Netherlands: Springer.
Jaffe, A. (2009) *Stance: Sociolinguistic Perspectives*. New York: Oxford University Press.
Jaggar, A.M. (1992) Love and knowledge: Emotions in feminist epistemology. In A.M. Jaggar and S.R. Bordo (eds) *Gender/Body/Knowledge* (pp. 145–171). New Brunswick, NJ: Rutgers University Press.
Jayyusi, L. (1984) *Categorization and the Moral Order*. Boston, MA: Routledge & Kegan Paul.
Jayyusi, L. (1991) Values and moral judgement. In G. Button (ed.) *Ethnomethodology and the Human Sciences* (pp. 227–251). New York: Cambridge University Press.
Jefferson, G. (1978) Sequential aspects of storytelling. In J. Schenkein (ed.) *Studies in the Organization of Conversational Interaction* (pp. 219–248). New York: Academic.
Jefferson, G. (1984) On the organization of laughter in talk about troubles. In J.M. Atkinson and J. Heritage (eds) *Structures of Social Action: Studies in Conversation Analysis* (pp. 346–369). New York: Cambridge.
Jefferson, G. (1988) On the sequential organization of troubles-talk in ordinary conversation. *Social Problems* 35 (4), 418–441.
Jefferson, G. (2004) Glossary of transcript symbols with an introduction. In G.H. Lerner (ed.) *Conversation Analysis: Studies from the First Generation* (pp. 13–23). Philadelphia, PA: John Benjamins.
Jefferson, G., Sacks, H. and Schegloff, E.A. (1976) Some notes on laughing together. *Pragmatics Microfiche* 1 (8), A2–D9.
Jefferson, G., Drew, P., Heritage, J., Lerner, G. and Pomerantz, A. (eds) (2015) *Talking about Troubles in Conversation*. New York: Oxford University Press.
Johnson, B. and Clarke, J. (2003) Collecting sensitive data: The impact on researchers. *Qualitative Health Research* 13, 421–434.
Jones, S.R., Torres, V. and Arminio, J.L. (2006) *Negotiating the Complexities of Qualitative Research in Higher Education: Fundamental Elements and Issues*. New York: Routledge.
Jørgensen, M.W. and Phillips, L.J. (2002) *Discourse Analysis as Theory and Method*. London: SAGE.
Kalaja, P., Menezes, V. and Barcelos, A.F. (2008) *Narratives of Learning and Teaching EFL*. New York: Palgrave MacMillan.
Kamada, L.D. (2010) *Hybrid Identities and Adolescent Girls Being 'Half' in Japan*. Bristol: Multilingual Matters.

Kamm, H. (1996) *Dragon Ascending: Vietnam and the Vietnamese.* New York: Arcade Publishing.
Kanagy, R. (ed.) (1999) Language socialization and affect in first and second language acquisition [Special Issue]. *Journal of Pragmatics* 31 (11).
Kanno, Y. (2003) *Negotiating Bilingual and Bicultural Identities: Japanese Returnees Betwixt Two Worlds.* Mahwah, NJ: Erlbaum.
Kanno, Y. and Norton, B. (2003) Imagined communities and educational possibilities: Introduction. *Journal of Language, Identity, and Education* 2 (4), 241–249.
Kaplan, R. (ed.) (2010) *The Oxford Handbook of Applied Linguistics.* New York: Oxford University Press.
Kappra, R. and Vandrick, S. (2006) Silenced voices speak: Queer ESL students recount their experiences. *The CATESOL Journal* 18 (1), 138–150.
Kärkkäinen, E. (2003) *Epistemic Stance in English Conversation: A Description of its Interactional Functions, With a Focus on I Think.* Philadelphia, PA: John Benjamins.
Kasper, G. (2009) Locating cognition in second language interaction and earning: Inside the skull or in public view? *IRAL* 47 (1), 11–36.
Kasper, G. and Prior, M.T. (2015) Analyzing story telling in TESOL interview research. *TESOL Quarterly* 49 (2), 226–255.
Kasper, G. and Ross, S.J. (2007) Multiple questions in oral proficiency interviews. *Journal of Pragmatics* 39, 2045–2070.
Kasper, G. and Wagner, J. (2011) A conversation-analytic approach to second language acquisition. In D. Atkinson (ed.) *Alternative Approaches to Second Language Acquisition* (pp. 117–142). New York: Routledge.
Kasper, G. and Wagner, J. (2014) Conversation analysis in applied linguistics. *Annual Review of Applied Linguistics* 34, 171–212.
Kenny, A. (2003) *Action, Emotion and Will* (2nd edn). New York: Routledge.
Kindlon, D. and Thompson, M. (2000) *Raising Cain: Protecting the Emotional Life of Boys.* New York: Ballantine Books.
King, B. (2008) 'Being gay guy, that is the advantage': Queer Korean language learning and identity construction. *Journal of Language, Identity, and Education* 7, 230–252.
King, N. (2010) Research ethics in qualitative research. In M.A. Forrester (ed.) *Doing Qualitative Research in Psychology: A Practical Guide* (pp. 98–118). London: SAGE.
King, N. and Horrocks, C. (2010) *Interviews in Qualitative Research.* London: SAGE.
Kinginger, C. (2004) Alice doesn't live here anymore: Foreign language learning and renegotiated identity. In A. Pavlenko and A. Blackledge (eds) *Negotiation of Identities in Multilingual Contexts* (pp. 219–242). Clevedon: Multilingual Matters.
Kirsch, G.E. (1999) *Ethical Dilemmas in Feminist Research: The Politics of Location, Interpretation, and Publication.* Albany, NY: State University of New York Press.
Kitzinger, C. (2000) Doing feminist conversation analysis. *Feminism & Psychology* 10 (2), 163–193.
Kitzinger, C. (2005) 'Speaking as a heterosexual': (How) does sexuality matter for talk-in-interaction? *Research on Language and Social Interaction* 38 (3), 221–265.
Kitzinger, C. (2013) Conversation analysis and gender and sexuality. In C.A. Chapelle (ed.) *The Encyclopedia of Applied Linguistics* (pp. 996–1000). Malden, MA: Blackwell Publishing.
Kleinman, S. and Copp, M.A. (1993) *Emotions and Fieldwork.* London: SAGE.
Kong, T.S.K., Mahoney, D. and Plummer, K. (2002) Queering the interview. In J. Gubrium and J. Holstein (eds) *Handbook of Interview Research* (pp. 239–258). London: SAGE.
Korobov, N. and Bamberg, M. (2004) Positioning a 'mature' self in interactive practices: How adolescent males negotiate 'physical attraction' in group talk. *British Journal of Developmental Psychology* 22, 471–492.
Koshik, I. (2002) Designedly incomplete utterances: A pedagogical practice for eliciting knowledge displays in error correction sequences. *Research on Language and Social Interaction* 35 (3), 277–309.

Koshik, I. (2005) *Beyond Rhetorical Questions: Assertive Questions in Everyday Interaction*. Philadelphia, PA: John Benjamins.

Kottler, J. (2015) *Stories We've Heard, Stories We've Told: Life-changing Narratives in Therapy and Everyday Life*. New York: Oxford University Press.

Koven, M. (2002) An analysis of speaker role inhabitance in narratives of personal experience. *Journal of Pragmatics* 34, 167–217.

Koven, M. (2004) Getting 'emotional' in two languages: Bilinguals' verbal performance of affect in narratives of personal experience. *Text* 24 (4), 471–515.

Kramsch, C.J. (2009) *The Multilingual Subject*. New York: Oxford University Press.

Kramsch, C.J. and Whiteside, A. (2007) Three fundamental concepts in second language acquisition and their relevance in multilingual contexts. *The Modern Language Journal* 91, 907–922.

Kuebli, J., Butler, S. and Fivush, R. (1995) Mother–child talk about past events: Relations of maternal language and child gender over time. *Cognition and Emotion* 9, 265–293.

Kulick, D. and Willson, M. (1995) *Taboo: Sex, Identity and Erotic Subjectivity in Anthropological Fieldwork*. London: Routledge.

Kupferberg, I. and Green, D. (2005) *Troubled Talk: Metaphorical Negotiation in Problem Discourse*. Berlin: Mouton de Gruyter.

Kvale, S. and Brinkmann, S. (2009) *InterViews: Learning the Craft of Qualitative Research Interviewing* (2nd edn). London: SAGE.

Labov, W. (1972) *Language in the Inner City: Studies in the Black English Vernacular*. Philadelphia: University of Pennsylvania Press.

Labov, W. (1984) Intensity. In D. Schiffrin (ed.) *Georgetown University Round Table on Languages and Linguistics* (pp. 43–70). Washington, DC: Georgetown University Press.

Labov, W. and Fanshel, D. (1977) *Therapeutic Discourse: Psychotherapy as Conversation*. New York: Academic Press.

Labov, W. and Waletzky. J. (1967, 1997) Narrative analysis. In J. Helm (ed.) *Essays on the Verbal and Visual Arts* (pp. 12–44). Seattle: University of Washington Press.

Land, G.H. and Kitzinger, C. (2005) Speaking as a lesbian: Correcting the heterosexist presumption. *Research on Language and Social Interaction* 38 (4), 371–416.

Langman, J. (2004) (Re)constructing gender in a new voice: An introduction. *Journal of Language, Identity, and Education* 3 (4), 235–243.

Larraín, A. and Haye, A. (2012) Discursive analysis of experience: Alterity, positioning, and tension. *Discourse & Society* 23 (5), 596–601.

LaSala, M.C., Jenkins, D.A., Wheller, D.P. and Fredriksen-Goldsen, K.I. (2008) LGBT faculty, research, and researchers: Risks and rewards. *Journal of Gay & Lesbian Social Services* 20 (3), 253–267.

Lazaraton, A. (2002) *A Qualitative Approach to the Validation of Oral Language Tests*. New York: Cambridge.

Lazarus, R.S. (1999) *Stress and Emotion*. London: Springer.

Lee-Treeweek, G. and Linkogle, S. (2000) *Danger in the Field: Ethics and Risk in Social Research*. New York: Routledge.

Lerner, G.H. (1992) Assisted storytelling: Deploying shared knowledge as a practical matter. *Qualitative Sociology* 15 (13), 247–271.

Lerner, G. (1996) On the 'semi-permeable' character of grammatical units in conversation: Conditional entry into the turn space of another speaker. In E. Ochs, E.A. Schegloff and S.A. Thompson (eds) *Interaction and Grammar* (pp. 238–276). New York: Cambridge University Press.

Lerner, G.H. (ed.) (2004) *Conversation Analysis: Studies from the First Generation*. Philadelphia, PA: John Benjamins.

Lerner, G. (2013) On the place of hesitating in delicate formulations: A turn-constructional infrastructure for collaborative indiscretion. In M. Hayashi, G. Raymond and J. Sidnell (eds) *Conversational Repair and Human Understanding* (pp. 95–134). New York: Cambridge University Press.

Letherby, G. (2000) Dangerous liaisons: Auto/biography in research and research writing. In G. Lee-Treweek and S. Linkogle (eds) *Danger in the Field: Ethics and Risk in Social Research* (pp. 91–113). New York: Routledge.

Levinson, S. (2006) Cognition at the heart of human interaction. *Discourse & Society* 8 (1), 85–93.

Lewis, P.J. and Adeney, R. (2014) Narrative research. In J. Mills and M. Birks (eds) *Qualitative Methodology: A Practical Guide* (pp. 161–180). London: SAGE.

Liamputtong, P. (2010) *Performing Qualitative Cross-cultural Research*. New York: Cambridge University Press.

Liddicoat, A.J. (2011) *An Introduction to Conversation Analysis* (2nd edn). New York: Continuum.

Lillrank, A. (2012) Managing the interviewer self. In J.F. Gubrium, J. Holstein, A.B. Marvasti and K.D. McKinney (eds) *The SAGE Handbook of Interview Research: The Complexity of the Craft* (2nd edn) (pp. 281–294). London: SAGE.

Lindström, J. and Lindholm, C. (2009) 'May I ask': Question frames in institutional interaction. In M. Haakana, M. Laakso and J. Lindström (eds) *Talk in Interaction: Comparative Dimensions* (pp. 180–205). Helsinki: Finnish Literature Society (SKS).

Linnekin, J. (1997) Consuming cultures: Tourism and the commoditization of cultural identity in the Island Pacific. In M. Picard and R.E. Wood (eds) *Tourism, Ethnicity, and the State in Asian and Pacific Societies* (pp. 215–250). Honolulu: University of Hawai'i Press.

Lo, A. and Reyes, A. (2004) Language, identity and relationality in Asian Pacific America: An introduction. *Pragmatics* 14 (2–3), 115–125.

Lutz, C. (1988) *Unnatural Emotions: Everyday Sentiments on a Micronesian Atoll and their Challenge to Western Theory*. Chicago: University of Chicago Press.

Lutz, C. and Abu-Lughod, L. (1990) *Language and the Politics of Emotion*. New York: Cambridge.

Lynch, M. and Bogen, D. (1996) *The Spectacle of History: Speech, Text, and Memory at the Iran-Contra Hearings*. Durham, NC: Duke University Press.

Lynch, M. and Bogen, D. (2005) 'My memory has been shredded': A non-cognitivist investigation of 'mental' phenomena. In H. t. Molder and J. Potter (eds) *Conversation and Cognition* (pp. 226–240). New York: Cambridge.

Maalouf, A. (2000) *In the Name of Identity: Violence and the Need to Belong*. New York: Penguin Books.

Madigan, S. (2011) *Narrative Therapy*. Washington, DC: American Psychological Association.

Mandelbaum, J. (2013) Storytelling in conversation. In J. Sidnell and T. Stivers (eds) *The Handbook of Conversation Analysis* (pp. 492–507). Malden, MA: Blackwell Publishing Ltd.

Mantero, M. (ed.) (2007) *Identity and Second Language Learning: Culture, Inquiry, and Dialogic Activity in Educational Contexts*. Charlotte, NC: Information Age Publishers.

Marian, V. and Kaushanskaya, M. (2004) Self-construal and emotion in bicultural bilinguals. *Journal of Memory and Language* 51, 190–201.

Marian, V. and Kaushanskaya, M. (2008) Words, feelings, and bilingualism: Cross-linguistic differences in emotionality of autobiographical memories. *The Mental Lexicon* 3 (1), 72–90.

Markee, N. (2000) *Conversation Analysis*. Mahwah, NJ: Erlbaum.

Marshall, C. and Rossman, G.B. (2006) *Designing Qualitative Research* (4th edn). London: SAGE.

Martel, Y. (2001) *The Life of Pi*. Orlando, FL: Harcourt.
Maryns, K. and Blommaert, J. (2001) Stylistic and thematic shifting as a narrative resource: Assessing asylum seekers' repertoires. *Multilingua* 20 (1), 61–84.
Massumi, B. (2002) *Parables for the Virtual: Movement, Affect, Sensation*. Durham, NC: Duke University Press.
Matusov, E. and von Duyke, K. (2012) Broader outside social discourses, embodiment, and technism in James Cresswell's critique of discourse analysis methodology. *Discourse & Society* 23 (5), 609–618.
Maynard, D.W. (1988) Language, interaction, and social problems. *Social Problems* 35, 311–334.
Maynard, D.W. (1991) Perspective-display sequences in conversation. *Western Journal of Speech Communication* 53, 91–113.
Maynard, D.W. (2003) *Bad News, Good News: Conversational Order in Everyday Talk and Clinical Settings*. Chicago: University of Chicago Press.
Maynard, D.W. and Clayman, S.E. (1991) The diversity of ethnomethodology. *Annual Review of Sociology* 17, 385–418.
Maynard, D.W. and Clayman, S.E. (2003) Ethnomethodology and conversation analysis. In L. Reynolds and N. Herman-Kinney (eds) *Handbook of Symbolic Interactionism* (pp. 173–202). Walnut Creek, CA: AltaMira Press.
Maynard, D.W. and Freese. J. (2012) Good news, bad news, and affect: Practical and temporal 'emotion work' in everyday life. In A. Peräkylä and M.-L. Sorjonen (eds) *Emotion in Interaction* (pp. 92–112). New York: Cambridge University Press.
McAdams, D.P. (2005) Studying lives in time: A narrative approach. In R. Levy, P. Ghisletta, J.-M. Le Goff, D. Spini and E. Widmer (eds) *Towards an Interdisciplinary Perspective. Advances in Life Course Research* (Vol. 10, pp. 237–258). San Diego, CA: Elsevier.
McAdams, D.P. (2008) American identity: The redemptive self. *The General Psychologist* 43, 20–27.
McCarthy, M. (2001) *Issues in Applied Linguistics*. New York: Cambridge University Press.
McGroarty, M. (1998) Constructive and constructivist challenges for applied linguistics. *Language Learning* 48 (4), 591–622.
McHoul, A.W. and Rapley, M. (2001) *How to Analyse Talk in Institutional Settings: A Casebook of Methods*. New York: Continuum.
McKelvey, R.S. (1999) *The Dust of Life: America's Children Abandoned in Vietnam*. Seattle: University of Washington Press.
McNaron, T.A.H. (1997) *Poisoned Ivy: Lesbian and Gay Academics Confronting Homophobia*. Philadelphia, PA: Temple University Press.
Medawar, P. (1996) Is the scientific paper a fraud? In *The Strange Case of the Spotted Mice and Other Classic Essays on Science* (pp. 33–39). New York: Oxford University Press.
Mehra, B. (2001) Research or personal quest: Dilemmas in studying my own kind. In B.M. Merchant and A.I. Willis (eds) *Multiple and Intersecting Identities in Qualitative Research* (pp. 69–82). Mahwah, NJ: Erlbaum.
Melrose, S. (2010) Naturalistic generalization. In A.J. Mills, G. Durepos and E. Wiebe (eds) *Encyclopedia of Case Study Research* (Vol. 2, pp. 599–601). London: SAGE.
Menard-Warwick, J. (2009) *Gendered Identities and Immigrant Language Learning*. Bristol: Multilingual Matters.
Merchant, B.M. and Willis, A.I. (eds) *Multiple and Intersecting Identities in Qualitative Research*. Mahwah, NJ: Erlbaum.
Merleau-Ponty, M. (2013) *Phenomenology of Perception*. New York: Routledge.
Messerschmidt, D.A. (1981) *Anthropologists at Home in North America: Methods and Issues in the Study of One's Own Society*. New York: Cambridge.
Miller, E.R. (2011) Positioning self, reporting experience: The construction of agency and indeterminacy in interview accounts. *Applied Linguistics* 32 (1), 43–59.

Miller, E.R. (2014) *The Language of Adult Immigrants*. Clevedon: Multilingual Matters.
Miller, G. and Silverman, D. (1995) Troubles talk and counseling discourse: A comparative study. *The Sociological Quarterly* 36 (4), 725–747.
Miller, J. (2003) *Audible Difference: ESL and Social Identity in Schools*. Clevedon: Multilingual Matters.
Milroy, L. (1987) *Language and Social Networks*. New York: Oxford University Press.
Mintz, B. and Rothblum, E. (1997) *Lesbians in Academia: Degrees of Freedom*. New York: Routledge.
Mishler, E.G. (1986) The analysis of interview narratives. In T. Sarbin (ed.) *Narrative Psychology: The Storied Nature of Human Conduct* (pp. 233–255). New York: Praeger.
Mishler, E.G. (1991) *Research Interviewing: Context and Narrative*. Cambridge, MA: Harvard University Press.
Moerman, M. (1988) *Talking Culture: Ethnography and Conversation Analysis*. Philadelphia: University of Pennsylvania Press.
Mondada, L. (2013a) Conversation analysis and institutional interaction. In C.A. Chapelle (ed.) *The Encyclopedia of Applied Linguistics* (pp. 1005–1011). Oxford: Wiley-Blackwell.
Mondada, L. (2013b) The conversation analytic approach to data collection. In J. Sidnell and T. Stivers (eds) *The Handbook of Conversation Analysis* (pp. 32–56). Oxford: Wiley-Blackwell.
Mori, J. (1999) *Negotiating Agreement and Disagreement in Japanese: Connective Expressions and Turn Construction*. Philadelphia, PA: John Benjamins.
Motha, S. (2006) Racializing ESOL teacher identities in U.S. K-12 public schools. *TESOL Quarterly* 41 (3), 495–518.
Motha, S. (2014) *Race, Empire, and English Language Teaching: Creating Responsible and Ethical Anti-racist Practice*. New York: Teachers College, Columbia University.
Motha, S. and Lin, A. (2013) 'Non-coercive rearrangements': Theorizing desire in TESOL. *TESOL Quarterly* 48 (2), 331–359.
Murray, G., Gao, X. and Lamb, T. (eds) (2011) *Identity, Motivation and Autonomy in Language Learning*. Bristol: Multilingual Matters.
Nairn, K., Munro, J. and Smith, A.B. (2005) A counter-narrative of a 'failed' interview. *Qualitative Research* 5 (2), 221–244.
Nelson, C. (2009) *Sexual Identities in English Language Education: Classroom Conversation*. New York: Routledge.
Norrick, N.R. (1998) Retelling stories in spontaneous conversion. *Discourse Processes* 25 (1), 75–97.
Norrick, N.R. (2000) *Conversational Narrative: Storytelling in Everyday Talk*. Philadelphia, PA: John Benjamins.
Norrick, N.R. (2005) Contextualizing and recontextualizing interlaced stories in conversation. In J. Thornborrow and J. Coates (eds) *The Sociolinguistics of Narrative* (pp. 107–127). Philadelphia, PA: John Benjamins.
Norton, B. (2000) *Identity and Language Learning: Gender, Ethnicity and Educational Change*. Harlow: Pearson Education Limited.
Norton, B. (2013) *Identity and Language Learning: Extending the Conversation*. Bristol: Multilingual Matters.
Norton, B. and Early, M. (2011) Research identity, narrative inquiry, and language teaching research. *TESOL Quarterly* 45 (3), 415–439.
Norton Peirce, B. (1995) Social identity, investment, and language learning. *TESOL Quarterly* 29 (1), 9–31.
Nyklíček, I., Temoshok, L. and Vingerhoets, A. (2004) *Emotional Expression and Health: Advances in Theory, Assessment and Clinical Applications*. New York: Brunner-Routledge.

Nyklíček, I., Vingerhoets, A. and Zeelenberg, M. (2011) *Emotion Regulation and Well-being*. New York: Springer.
O'Donoghue, J. (2006) *Technology Supported Learning and Teaching: A Staff Perspective*. Hershey, PA: Information Science Publishing.
Ochs, E. (1979) Transcription as theory. In E. Ochs and B. Schieffelin (eds) *Developmental Pragmatics* (pp. 43–72). New York: Academic Press.
Ochs, E. (1996) Linguistic resources for socializing humanity. In J. Gumperz and S. Levison (eds) *Rethinking Linguistic Relativity* (pp. 407–438). New York: Cambridge University Press.
Ochs, E. and Capps, L. (1996) Narrating the self. *Annual Review of Anthropology* 25, 19–43.
Ochs, E. and Capps, L. (2001) *Living Narrative: Creating Lives in Everyday Storytelling*. Cambridge, MA: Harvard University Press.
Ochs, E. and Schieffelin, B.B. (1989) Language has a heart. *Text* 9 (1), 7–25.
Olesen V. (2011) Feminist qualitative research in the millennium's first decade: Developments, challenges, prospects. In N.K. Denzin and Y.S. Lincoln (eds) *The SAGE Handbook of Qualitative Research* (4th edn) (pp. 129–146). London: SAGE.
Ong, A. (2003) *Buddha is Hiding: Refugees, Citizenship, and the New America*. Berkeley, CA: University of California Press.
O'Reilly, K. (2012) *Ethnographic Methods* (2nd edn). New York: Routledge.
Ovando, C.J. and Locke, S. (2011) Finding and reading road signs in ethnographic research: Studying the language and stories of the unwelcome stranger. In K.A. Davis (ed.) *Critical Qualitative Research in Second Language Studies: Agency and Advocacy* (pp. 233–249). Charlotte, NC: Information Age.
Oxford, R.L. (2011) *Teaching and Researching Language Learning Strategies*. New York: Taylor & Francis.
Parker, I. (1992) *Discourse Dynamics: Critical Analysis for Social and Individual Psychology*. New York: Routledge.
Parker, I. (2007) *Revolution in Psychology: Alienation to Emancipation*. Ann Arbor, MI: Pluto Press.
Parrott, W.G. (ed.) (2001) *Emotions in Social Psychology: Essential Readings*. Philadelphia, PA: Psychology Press.
Pastor, A.R. and De Fina, A. (2005) Contesting social place: Narratives of language conflict. In M. Baynham and A. De Fina (eds) *Dislocations/Relocations: Narratives of Displacement* (pp. 36–60). Manchester: St. Jerome Publishing.
Patton, M.Q. (1990) *Qualitative Evaluation and Research Methods*. London: SAGE.
Pavlenko, A. (2001) 'How am I to become a woman in an American vein?': Transformations of gender performance in second language learning. In A. Pavlenko, A. Blackledge, I. Piller and M. Teutsch-Dwyer (eds) *Second Language Learning, Multilingualism, and Gender* (pp. 133–174). Berlin: Mouton De Gruyter.
Pavlenko, A. (2005) *Emotions and Multilingualism*. New York: Cambridge.
Pavlenko, A. (ed.) (2006) *Bilingual Minds: Emotional Experience, Expression and Representation*. Clevedon: Multilingual Matters.
Pavlenko, A. (2007) Autobiographical narratives as data in applied linguistics. *Applied Linguistics* 28 (2), 163–188.
Pavlenko, A. (2013) From 'affective factors' to 'language desire' and 'commodification of affect'. In D. Gabryś-Barker and J. Bielska (eds) *The Affective Dimension in Second Language Acquisition* (p. 3). Bristol: Multilingual Matters.
Pavlenko, A. and Blackledge, A. (eds) (2004) *Negotiation of Identities in Multilingual Contexts*. Clevedon: Multilingual Matters.
Pavlenko, A. and Lantolf, J. (2000) Second language learning as participation and the (re)construction of selves. In J. Lantolf (ed.) *Sociocultural Theory and Second Language Learning* (pp. 155–177). New York: Oxford University Press.

Pawelczyk, J. (2011) *Talk as Therapy: Psychotherapy in a Linguistic Perspective*. Berlin: Walter De Gruyter.
Pennebaker, J.W. and Francis, M.E. (1996) Cognitive, emotional, and language processes in disclosure. *Cognition & Emotion* 10, 601–626.
Pennycook, A. (2001) *Critical Applied Linguistics: A Critical Introduction*. Mahwah, NJ: Lawrence Erlbaum.
Peräkylä, A. (2005) Patients' responses to interpretations: A dialogue between conversation analysis and psychoanalytic theory. *Communication & Medicine* 2 (2), 163–176.
Peräkylä, A., Antaki, C., Vehviläinen, S. and Leudar, I. (eds) (2008) *Conversation Analysis and Psychotherapy*. New York: Cambridge.
Peräkylä, A. and Sorjonen, M. (eds) (2012) *Emotion in Interaction*. Oxford: Oxford University Press.
Philippot, P. and Feldman, R.S. (eds) (2004) *The Regulation of Emotion*. Mahwah, NJ: Lawrence Erlbaum.
Pini, B. and Pease, B. (eds) (2013) *Men, Masculinities, and Methodologies*. New York: Palgrave MacMillan.
Planalp, S. (1999) *Communicating Emotion: Social, Moral, and Cultural Processes*. New York: Cambridge University Press.
Pomerantz, A.M. (1980) Telling my side: 'Limited access' as a 'fishing device'. *Sociological Inquiry* 50, 186–198.
Pomerantz, A.M. (1984) Agreeing and disagreeing with assessments: Some features of preferred/dispreferred turn shapes. In J.M. Atkinson and J. Heritage (eds) *Structures of Social Action: Studies in Conversation Analysis* (pp. 57–101). New York: Cambridge University Press.
Pomerantz, A.M. (1986) Extreme-case formulations: A way of legitimizing claims, *Human Studies* 9 (2–3), 219–229.
Portes, A. and Rumbaut, R.G. (2014) *Immigrant America* (4th edn). Oakland, CA: University of California Press.
Poster, M. (1989) *Critical Theory and Poststructuralism: In Search of a Context*. Ithaca, NY: Cornell University Press.
Potter, J. (1996) *Representing Reality: Discourse, Rhetoric and Social Construction*. London: SAGE.
Potter, J. (1998) Beyond cognitivism. *ROLSI* 32, 119–128.
Potter, J. (2002) Two kinds of natural. *Discourse Studies* 4 (4), 539–542.
Potter, J. (2003) Discursive psychology: Between method and paradigm. *Discourse & Society* 14 (6), 783–794.
Potter, J. (2006) Cognition and conversation. *Discourse Studies* 8 (1), 131–140.
Potter, J. (2010a) Contemporary discursive psychology: Issues, prospects, and Corcoran's awkward ontology. *British Journal of Social Psychology* 49, 657–678.
Potter, J. (2010b) Discursive psychology and the study of naturally occurring talk. In D. Silverman (ed.) *Qualitative Analysis: Issues of Theory and Method* (3rd edn) (pp. 187–207). London: SAGE.
Potter, J. (2012a) Conversation analysis and emotion and cognition in interaction. *The Encyclopedia of Applied Linguistics*, 5 November 2012. DOI: 10.1002/9781405198431. wbeal1316
Potter, J. (2012b) Discourse analysis and discursive psychology. In H. Cooper (ed.) *APA Handbook of Research Methods in Psychology: Vol. 2. Quantitative, Qualitative, Neuropsychological, and Biological* (pp. 111–130). Washington, DC: American Psychological Association Press.
Potter, J. (2012c) How to study experience. *Discourse & Society* 23 (5), 576–588.
Potter, J. and Edwards, D. (2013) Conversation analysis and psychology. In J. Sidnell and T. Sitvers (eds) *The Handbook of Conversation Analysis* (pp. 701–725). Malden, MA: Blackwell Publishing Ltd.

Potter, J. and Hepburn, A. (2005) Qualitative interviews in psychology: Problems and possibilities. *Qualitative Research in Psychology* 2, 281–307.
Potter, J. and Hepburn, A. (2007) Discursive psychology: Mind and reality in practice. In A. Weatherall, B.M. Watson and C. Gallois (eds) *Language, Discourse and Social Psychology* (pp. 160–181). New York: Palgrave MacMillan.
Potter, J. and Hepburn, A. (2008) Discursive constructionism. In J.A. Holstein and J.F. Gubrium (eds) *Handbook of Constructionist Research* (pp. 275–293). New York: Guildford.
Potter, J. and Hepburn, A. (2012) Eight challenges for interview researchers. In J.F. Gubrium, J. Holstein, A.B. Marvasti and K.D. McKinney (eds) *The SAGE Handbook of Interview Research: The Complexity of the Craft* (2nd edn) (pp. 555–570). London: SAGE.
Potter, J. and Wetherell, M. (1987) *Discourse and Social Psychology: Beyond Attitudes and Behaviour.* London: SAGE.
Prior, M.T. (2011a) Self-presentation in L2 interview talk: Narrative versions, accountability, and emotionality. *Applied Linguistics* 32 (1), 60–76.
Prior, M.T. (2011b) 'I'm two pieces inside of me': Negotiating hybridity and belonging through L2 narratives. In C. Higgins (ed.) *Negotiating the Self in Another Language: Identity Formation and Cross-cultural Adaptation in a Globalized World* (pp. 27–47). New York: De Gruyter Mouton.
Prior, M.T. (2011c) Blood talk: A discursive perspective on transcultural identity and mental health. In P. McPherron and V. Ramanathan (eds) *Language, Body, and Health* (pp. 221–244). New York: De Gruyter Mouton.
Prior, M.T. (2014) Re-examining alignment in a 'failed' L2 autobiographical research interview. *Qualitative Inquiry* 20 (4), 495–508.
Prior, M.T. (2016) Formulating and scaling emotionality in L2 research interviews. In M.T. Prior and G. Kasper (eds) *Talking Emotion in Multilingual Settings*. Philadelphia, PA: John Benjamins.
Prior, M.T. and Kasper, G. (eds) (2016). *Emotion in Multilingual Interaction*. Amsterdam: Benjamins.
Psathas, G. (1995) *Conversation Analysis: The Study of Talk-in-interaction.* London: SAGE.
Psathas, G. and Anderson, T. (1990) The 'practices' of transcription in conversation analysis. *Semiotica* 78, 75–99.
Quas, J.A. and Fivush, R. (2009) *Emotion and Memory in Development: Biological, Cognitive, and Social Considerations.* New York: Oxford University Press.
Quirk, R., Greenbaum, S. Leech, G. and Svartvik, J. (1985) *A Comprehensive Grammar of the English Language.* New York: Longman.
Rae, J. (2008) Lexical substitution as a therapeutic resource. In A. Peräkylä, C. Antaki, S. Vehviläinen and I. Leudar (eds) *Conversation Analysis and Psychotherapy* (pp. 62–79). New York: Cambridge University Press.
Ramanathan, V. (2002) *The Politics of TESOL Education: Writing, Knowledge, Critical Pedagogy.* New York: Routledge Falmer.
Ramanathan, V. (2005) *The English-Vernacular Divide: Postcolonial Language Politics and Practice.* Clevedon: Multilingual Matters.
Ramanathan, V. (2010) *Bodies and Language: Health, Ailments, and Disabilities.* Bristol: Multilingual Matters.
Ramanathan, V. and Atkinson, D. (1999) Ethnographic approaches and methods in L2 writing research: A critical guide and review. *Applied Linguistics* 20 (1), 44–70.
Rapley, T.J. (2001) The art(fulness) of open-ended interviewing: Some considerations on analysing interviews. *Qualitative Research* 1 (3), 303–323.
Rapley, T.J. (2007) *Doing Conversation, Discourse and Document Analysis.* London: SAGE.
Rapley, T.J. (2012) The (extra)ordinary practices of qualitative interviewing. In J.F. Gubrium, J. Holstein, A.B. Marvasti and K.D. McKinney (eds) *The SAGE Handbook*

of Interview Research: The Complexity of the Craft (2nd edn) (pp. 541–554). London: SAGE.
Raymond, G. (2003) Grammar and social organization: Yes/no interrogatives and the structure of responding. *American Sociological Review* 68, 939–967.
Raymond, G. and Heritage, J. (2006) The epistemics of social relations: Owning grandchildren. *Language in Society* 35 (5), 677–705.
Rees, C.E., Monrouxe, L.V. and McDonald, L.A. (2013) Narrative, emotion and action: Analyzing 'most memorable' dilemmas. *Medical Education* 47 (1), 80–96.
Reinharz, S. and Chase, S.E. (2002) Interviewing women. In J.E. Gubrium and J.A. Holstein (eds) *Handbook of Interview Research: Context and Method* (pp. 221–239). London: SAGE.
Reyes, G., Elhai, J.D. and Ford, J.D. (eds) (2007) *The Encyclopedia of Psychological Trauma*. Hoboken, NJ: John Wiley & Sons.
Richards, K. (2003) *Qualitative Inquiry in TESOL*. New York: Palgrave Macmillan.
Richards, K. (2009) Interviews. In J. Heigham and R.A. Croker (eds) *Qualitative Research in Applied Linguistics: A Practical Introduction* (pp. 182–199). New York: Palgrave Macmillan.
Riessman, C.K. (1993) *Narrative Analysis*. London: SAGE.
Riessman, C.K. (2008) *Narrative Methods for the Human Sciences*. London: SAGE.
Rimé, B. (2009) Emotion elicits the social sharing of emotion: Theory and empirical review. *Emotion Review* 1 (1), 60–85.
Rintell, E.M. (1984) But how did you feel about that? The learner's perception of emotion in speech. *Applied Linguistics* 5 (3), 255–264.
Rintell, E.M. (1990) That's incredible: Stories of emotion told by second language learners and native speakers. In R. Scarcella, E. Anderson and S. Krashen (eds) *Developing Communicative Competence in a Second Language* (pp. 75–94). Boston, MA: Heinle & Heinle.
Robbins, B. (2006) An empirical, phenomenological study: Being joyful. In C.T. Fischer (ed.) *Qualitative Research Methods for Psychologists: Introduction through Empirical Studies* (pp. 173–212). Amsterdam: Elsevier.
Roberts, C. (2001) Critical social theory: Good to think with or something more? In N. Coupland, S. Sarangi and C. Candlin (eds) *Sociolinguistics and Social Theory* (pp. 323–333). London: Longman Pearson Education.
Rorty, A. (1980) *Explaining Emotions*. Berkeley: University of California Press.
Röttger-Rössler, B. and Markowitsch, H.J. (2009) *Emotions as Bio-cultural Processes*. London: Springer.
Roulston, K. (2010) *Reflective Interviewing: A Guide to Theory and Practice*. London: SAGE.
Roulston, K. (2011) Working through challenges in doing interview research. *International Journal of Qualitative Methods* 10 (4), 348–366.
Roulston, K. (2012) The pedagogy of interviewing. In J.F. Gubrium, J. Holstein, A.B. Marvasti and K.D. McKinney (eds) *The SAGE Handbook of Interview Research: The Complexity of the Craft* (2nd edn) (pp. 61–74). London: SAGE.
Roulston, K. (2014) Interactional problems in research interviews. *Qualitative Research* 14 (3), 277–293.
Rubin, H.R. and Rubin, I.S. (2005) *Qualitative Interviewing: The Art of Hearing Data* (2nd edn). London: SAGE.
Russell, J.A. (1995) *Everyday Conceptions of Emotion: An Introduction to the Psychology, Anthropology, and Linguistics of Emotion*. Boston, MA: Kluwer Academic Publishers.
Ruusuvuori, J. (2007) Managing affect: Integration of empathy and problem-solving in health care encounters. *Discourse Studies* 9 (5), 597–622.
Ruusuvuori, J. (2013) Emotion, affect, and conversation. In J. Sidnell and T. Sitvers (eds) *The Handbook of Conversation Analysis* (pp. 330–349). Malden, MA: Blackwell Publishing.

Ryave, A.L. (1978) On the achievement of a series of stories. In J. Schenkein (ed.) *Studies in the Organization of Conversational Interaction* (pp. 113–132). New York: Academic Press.

Saarni, C. (1999) *The Development of Emotional Competence*. New York: Guilford Press.

Sacks, H. (1992) *Lectures on Conversation*. Cambridge, MA: Blackwell.

Sacks, H. and Schegloff, E.A. (1979) Two preferences in the organization of reference to persons in conversation and their interaction. In G. Psathas (ed.) *Everyday Language: Studies in Ethnomethodology* (pp. 15–21). New York: Irvington.

Sacks, H., Schegloff, E.A. and Jefferson, G. (1974) A simplest systematics for the organization of turn-taking for conversation. *Language* 50 (4), 696–735.

Sandhu, P. (2014) The interactional and narrative construction of normative and resistant discourses about Hindi and English. *Applied Linguistics* 35 (1), 29–47.

Sandlund, E. (2004) *Feeling by Doing: The Social Organization of Everyday Emotions in Academic Talk-in-interaction*. Karlstad: Karlstad University Studies.

Sarbin, T.R. (2001) Embodiment and the narrative structure of emotional life. *Narrative Inquiry* 11 (1), 217–225.

Schank, R.C. and Abelson, R.P. (1995) Knowledge and memory: The real story. In R.S. Wyer, Jr. (ed.) *Knowledge and Memory: The Real Story* (pp. 1–85). Hillsdale, NJ: Lawrence Erlbaum.

Schegloff, E.A. (1968) Sequencing in conversational openings. *American Anthropologist* 70, 1075–1095.

Schegloff, E.A. (1972) Notes on a conversational practice: Formulating place. In D. Sudnow (ed.) *Studies in Social Interaction* (pp. 75–119). New York: Free Press.

Schegloff, E.A. (1980) Preliminaries to preliminaries: Can I ask you a question? *Sociological Inquiry* 50, 114.

Schegloff, E.A. (1982) Discourse as an interactional achievement: Some uses of 'Uh huh' and other things that come between sentences. In D. Tannen (ed.) *Georgetown University Roundtable on Languages and Linguistics, 1981: Analyzing Discourse: Text and Talk* (pp. 71–93). Washington, DC: Georgetown University Press.

Schegloff, E.A. (1987a) Analyzing single episodes of interaction: An exercise in conversation analysis. *Social Psychology Quarterly* 50 (2), 101–114.

Schegloff, E.A. (1987b) Recycled turn beginnings: A precise repair mechanism in conversation's turn-taking organization. In G. Button and J.R.E. Lee (eds) *Talk and Social Organisation* (pp. 70–85). Clevedon: Multilingual Matters.

Schegloff, E.A. (1988) On an actual virtual servo-mechanism for guessing bad news: A single case conjecture. *Social Problems* 35 (4), 442–457.

Schegloff, E.A. (1992) On talk and its institutional occasions. In P. Drew and J. Heritage (eds) *Talk at Work* (pp. 101–134). New York: Cambridge

Schegloff, E.A. (1995) Discourse as an interactional achievement III: The omnirelevance of action. *Research on Language and Social Interaction* 28 (3), 185–211.

Schegloff, E.A. (1996) Turn organization: One intersection of grammar and interaction. In E. Ochs, E.A. Schegloff and S.A. Thompson (eds) *Interaction and Grammar* (pp. 52–133). New York: Cambridge University Press.

Schegloff, E.A. (1997) Whose text? Whose context? *Discourse & Society* 8 (2), 165–187.

Schegloff, E.A. (1998) Reply to Wetherell. *Discourse and Society* 9, 413–416.

Schegloff, E.A. (1999) 'Schegloff's texts' as 'Billig's data': A critical reply. *Discourse and Society* 10, 558–572.

Schegloff, E.A. (2000) On granularity. *Annual Review of Sociology* 26, 715–720.

Schegloff, E.A. (2007) *Sequence Organization in Interaction: A Primer in Conversation Analysis*. New York: Cambridge University Press.

Schegloff, E.A. (2009) One perspective on conversation analysis: Comparative perspectives. In J. Sidnell (ed.) *Conversation Analysis: Comparative Perspectives* (pp. 357–406). New York: Cambridge.

Schegloff, E.A., Jefferson, G. and Sacks, H. (1977) The preference for self correction in the organization of repair in conversation. *Language* 53, 361–82.

Schegloff, E.A. and Lerner, G.H. (2009) Beginning to respond: Well-prefaced responses to Wh-questions. *Research on Language and Social Interaction* 42 (2), 91–115.

Schieffelin, B.B. (1990) *The Give and Take of Everyday Life: Language Socialization of Kaluli Children*. New York: Cambridge University Press.

Schieffelin, B.B. and Ochs, E. (eds) (1986) *Language Socialization across Cultures*. Cambridge: Cambridge University Press.

Schiffrin, D. (2006) *In Other Words: Variation in Reference and Narrative*. New York: Cambridge University Press.

Schiffrin, D., De Fina, A. and Nylund, A. (eds) (2010) *Telling Stories: Language, Narrative, and Social Life*. Washington, DC: Georgetown University Press.

Schmitt, C.S. and Clark, C. (2006) Sympathy. In J.E. Stets and J.H. Turner (eds) *Handbook of the Sociology of Emotions* (pp. 467–492). New York: Springer.

Schrauf, R.W. and Sanchez, J. (2004) The preponderance of negative emotion words across generations and across cultures. *Journal of Multilingual and Multicultural Development* 25 (2–3), 266–284.

Schumann, J.H. (1997) *The Neurobiology of Affect in Language*. Malden, MA: Blackwell Publishers.

Schwalbe, M.L. and Wolkomir, M. (2001) Interviewing men. In J.F. Gubrium and J.A. Holstein (eds) *The SAGE Handbook of Interview Research* (2nd edn) (pp. 203–220). London: SAGE.

Schwartz, H. (1976) On recognizing mistakes: A case of practical reasoning in psychotherapy. *Philosophy of the Social Sciences* 6, 56–63.

Scott, M.B. and Lyman, S.L. (1968) Accounts. *American Sociological Review* 33 (1), 44–62.

Scovel, T. (1978) The effect of affect on foreign language learning: A review of the anxiety research. *Language Learning* 28 (1), 129–142.

Searle, J.B. (1983) *Intentionality: An Essay in the Philosophy of Mind*. Cambridge: Cambridge University Press.

Seedhouse, P. (2004) *The Interactional Architecture of the Language Classroom: A Conversation Analysis Perspective*. Malden, MA: Blackwell.

Seidman, I. (2013) *Interviewing as Qualitative Research: A Guide for Researchers in Education and the Social Sciences* (4th edn). New York: Teachers College Press.

Selting, M. (1994) Emphatic speech style – with special focus on the prosodic signaling of heightened emotive involvement in conversation. *Journal of Pragmatics* 22 (3–4), 375–408.

Selting, M. (1996) Prosody as an activity-type distinctive cue in conversation: The case of so-called 'astonished' questions in repair initiation. In E. Couper-Kuhlen and M. Selting (eds) *Prosody in Conversation: Interactional Studies* (pp. 231–270). New York: Cambridge University Press.

Selting, M. (2010) Affectivity in conversational storytelling: An analysis of displays of anger or indignation in complaint stories. *Pragmatics* 20, 229–277.

Selye, H. (1974) *Stress Without Distress*. Philadelphia, PA: J. B. Lippincott.

Shoemaker, P.J., Tankard, J.W. and Lasorsa, D.L. (2004) *How to Build Social Science Theories*. London: SAGE

Sidnell, J. (2004) There's risks in everything: Extreme case formulations and accountability in inquiry testimony. *Discourse & Society* 15 (6), 745–766.

Sidnell, J. (2010a) *Conversation Analysis: An Introduction*. Malden, MA: Wiley-Blackwell.

Sidnell, J. (2010b) The design and positioning of questions in inquiry testimony. In A.F. Freed and S. Ehrlich (eds) *'Why Do You Ask?' The Function of Questions in Institutional Discourse* (pp. 20–41). New York: Oxford University Press.

Sidnell, J. and Stivers, T. (eds) (2013) *The Handbook of Conversation Analysis*. Chichester: Wiley-Blackwell.
Sijbrandij, M., Olff, M., Reitsma, J.B., Carlier, I.V.E. and Gersons, B.P.R. (2006) Emotional or educational debriefing after psychological trauma: Randomised controlled trial. *The British Journal of Psychiatry* 189, 150–155.
Silverman, D. (1987) *Communication and Medical Practice*. London: SAGE.
Silverman, D. (1998) *Harvey Sacks: Social Science and Conversation Analysis*. New York: Oxford University Press.
Silverman, D. (2001) *Interpreting qualitative Data: Methods of Analysing Talk, Text and Interaction* (2nd edn). London: SAGE.
Silverman, D. (2010) *Doing Qualitative Research* (3rd edn). London: SAGE.
Silverman, D. (2011) *Interpreting Qualitative Data* (4th edn). London: SAGE.
Silverstein, M. and Urban, G. (eds) (1996) *Natural Histories of Discourse*. Chicago: University of Chicago Press.
Simpson, J. (ed.) (2011) *The Routledge Handbook of Applied Linguistics*. New York: Routledge.
Sirgy, M.J. and Samli, A.C. (eds) (1995) *New Dimensions in Marketing and Quality-of-Life Research* (2nd edn). Westport, CT: Greenwood Press.
Smith, R. (2014) The ethics of interviewing for discourse analysis: Responses to Martyn Hammersley. *Qualitative Research* 14 (5), 545–548.
Snow, C.E., van Eeden, R. and Muysken, P. (1981) The interactional origins of foreigner talk: Municipal employees and foreign workers. *International Journal of the Sociology of Language* 28, 81–92.
Sparkes, A.C. and Smith, B.M. (2008) Narrative constructionist inquiry. In J. Holstein and J. Gubrium (eds) *Handbook of Constructionist Research* (pp. 295–314). New York: Guilford Publications.
Speer, S.A. (2001a) Participants' orientations, ideology and the ontological status of hegemonic masculinity: A rejoinder to Nigel Edley. *Feminism & Psychology* 11 (1), 141–144.
Speer, S.A. (2001b) Reconsidering the concept of hegemonic masculinity: Discursive psychology, conversation analysis and participants' orientations. *Feminism & Psychology* 11 (1), 107–135.
Speer, S.A. (2002) 'Natural' and 'contrived' data: A sustainable distinction? *Discourse Studies* 4 (4), 511–525.
Speer, S.A. (2005) *Gender Talk: Feminism, Discourse, and Conversation Analysis*. London: Routledge.
Speer, S.A. and Stokoe, E. (eds) (2011) *Conversation and Gender*. New York: Cambridge University Press.
Spradley, J.P. (1979) *The Ethnographic Interview*. New York: Holt, Rinehart, & Winston.
Stamm, B.H. (ed.) (1995) *Secondary Traumatic Stress: Self-care Issues for Clinicians, Researchers, and Educators*. Lutherville, MD: Sidran Press.
Stanley, L. and Wise, S. (1983) *Breaking Out: Feminist Consciousness and Feminist Research*. London: Routledge & Kegan Paul.
Steensig, J. and Drew, P. (2008) Introduction: Questioning and affiliation/disaffiliation in interaction [special issue]. *Discourse Studies* 10 (1), 5–15.
Stevens, A. (2012) *The Talking Cure: Psychotherapy, Past, Present, and Future (Vol. 1)*. Toronto, Ontario: Inner City.
Stivers, T. (2008) Stance, alignment, and affiliation during storytelling: When nodding is a token of affiliation. *Research on Language and Social Interaction* 41 (1), 31–57.
Stivers, T., Mondada, L. and Steensig, J. (eds) (2011) *The Morality of Knowledge in Conversation* (pp. 82–106). Cambridge: Cambridge University Press.
Stokoe, E. (2012) Moving forward with membership categorization analysis: Methods for systematic analysis. *Discourse Studies* 14 (3), 277–303.

Stokoe, E. and Edwards, D. (2006) Story formulations in talk-in-interaction. *Narrative Inquiry* 16 (1), 56–65.

Stokoe, E. and Edwards, D. (2007) 'Black this, black that': Racial insults and reported speech in neighbour complaints and police interrogations. *Discourse & Society* 18 (3), 337–372.

Stokoe, E. and Edwards, D. (2009) Accomplishing social action with identity categories: Mediating neighbor complaints. In M. Wetherell (ed.) *Theorizing Identities and Social Action* (pp. 95–115). New York: Palgrave MacMillan.

Stokoe, E. and Edwards, D. (2010) 'I advise you not to answer that question': Conversation analysis, legal interaction and the analysis of lawyers' turns in police interrogations of suspects. In A. Johnson and M. Coulthard (eds) *Routledge Handbook of Forensic Linguistics* (pp. 155–168). London: Routledge.

Stokoe, E., Hepburn, A. and Antaki, C. (2012) Beware the 'Loughborough School' of social psychology? Interaction and the politics of intervention. *British Journal of Social Psychology* 53 (3), 486–496.

Stokoe, E. and Smithson, J. (2001) Making gender relevant: Conversation analysis and gender categories in interaction. *Discourse & Society* 12 (2), 217–244.

Streeck, J. and Mehus, S. (2005) Microethnography: The study of practices. In K.L. Fitch and R.E. Sanders (eds) *Handbook of Language and Social Interaction* (pp. 381–404). Mahwah, NJ: Lawrence Erlbaum Associates.

Stritikus, T. (2002) *Immigrant Children and the Politics of English-only: Views from the Classroom*. New York: LFB Scholarly Publishing.

Sullivan, G. and Jackson, P.A. (eds) (2007) *Gay and Lesbian Asia: Culture, Identity, Community*. New York: Routledge.

Swain, M., Kinnear, P. and Steinman, L. (2011) *Sociocultural Theory in Second Language Education: An Introduction through Narratives* (1st edn). Bristol: Multilingual Matters.

Takahashi, K. (2013) *Language Learning, Gender and Desire: Japanese Women on the Move*. Bristol: Multilingual Matters.

Talmy, S. (2004) Forever FOB: The cultural production of ESL in a high school. *Pragmatics* 14 (2–3), 149–172.

Talmy, S. (2008) The cultural productions of the ESL student at Tradewinds High: Contingency, multidirectionality, and identity in L2 socialization. *Applied Linguistics* 29, 619–644.

Talmy, S. (2009) Resisting ESL: Categories and sequence in a critically 'motivated' analysis of classroom interaction. In G. Kasper and H.t. Nguyen (eds) *Talk-in-interaction: Multilingual Perspectives*. Honolulu, HI: University of Hawai'i, National Foreign Language Resource Center.

Talmy, S. (2010a) Becoming 'local' in ESL: Racism as resource in a Hawai'i public high school. *Journal of Language, Identity, and Education* 9, 36–57.

Talmy, S. (2010b) Qualitative interviews in applied linguistics: From research instrument to social practice. *ARAL* 30, 128–148.

Talmy, S. (2011) The interview as collaborative achievement: Interaction, identity, and ideology in a speech event. *Applied Linguistics* 32 (1), 25–42.

Talmy, S. and Prior, M.T. (2015) *Taking Stock of Small Stories*. Paper presented at the American Association for Applied Linguistics/Canadian Association of Applied Linguistics Annual Conference, Toronto, Ontario, Canada, March.

Talmy, S. and Richards, K. (eds) (2011) Qualitative interviews in applied linguistics: Discursive perspectives [Special issue]. *Applied Linguistics* 32 (1).

Tannen, D. (1989) *Talking Voices: Repetition, Dialogue, and Imagery in Conversational Discourse*. New York: Cambridge University Press.

Taylor, S.E. (1991) Asymmetrical effects of positive and negative events: The mobilization-minimization hypothesis. *Psychological Bulletin* 110 (1), 67–85.

Taylor, S. (2006) Narrative as construction and discursive resource. *Narrative Inquiry* 16 (1), 94–102.
Taylor, S. (2014) The ethics of interviewing for discourse analysis: Responses to Martyn Hammersley. *Qualitative Research* 14 (5), 542–545.
te Molder, H. and Potter, J. (eds) (2005) *Conversation and Cognition*. New York: Cambridge.
ten Have, P. (2002) The notion of member is the heart of the matter: On the role of membership knowledge in ethnomethodological inquiry. *Forum Qualitative Sozialforschung/ Forum: Qualitative Social Research* 3 (3). See www.qualitative-research.net/index.php/fqs/article/view/834
ten Have, P. (2007) *Doing Conversation Analysis: A Practical Guide* (2nd edn). London: SAGE.
Thornborrow, J. (2001) 'Has it ever happened to you?' Talk show stories as mediated performance. In A. Toslon (ed.) *Television Talk Shows: Discourse, Performance, Spectacle*. Mahwah, NJ: Erlbaum.
Thornborrow, J. (2010) Questions and institutionality in public participation broadcasting. In A.F. Freed and S. Ehrlich (eds) *'Why Do You Ask?': The Function of Questions in Institutional Discourse* (pp. 279–296). New York: Oxford University Press.
Thornborrow, J. and Coates, J. (eds) (2005) *The Sociolinguistics of Narrative*. Philadelphia, PA: John Benjamins.
Toerien, M. and Kitzinger, C. (2007) Emotional labor in action: Navigating multiple involvements in the beauty salon. *Sociology* 41 (4), 645–662.
Tran, T.V., Ngo, D. and Conway, K. (2003) A cross-cultural measure of depressive symptoms among Vietnamese Americans. *Social Work Research* 27 (1), 56–64.
Trask, H.-K. (2000) Settlers of color and 'immigrant' hegemony: 'Locals' in Hawai'i. *Amerasia Journal* 26 (2), 1–24.
Trimble, J.E. and Fisher, C.B. (eds) (2006) *The Handbook of Ethical Research with Ethnocultural Populations and Communities*. London: SAGE.
Tsui, A.B. (1996) Reticence and anxiety in second language learning. In K.M. Bailey and D. Nunan (eds) *Voices From the Language Classroom* (pp. 145–167). New York: Cambridge University Press.
Tsui, A.B. (2013) A functional description of questions. In M. Coulthard (ed.) *Advances in Spoken Discourse Analysis* (pp. 89–110). London: Routledge.
Tugade, M.M. (2011) Positive emotions, coping: Examining dual-process models of resilience. In S. Folkman (ed.) *Oxford Handbook of Stress, Health, and Coping* (pp. 186–199). New York: Oxford University Press.
Turner, J.H. and Stets, J.E. (2005) *The Sociology of Emotions*. New York: Cambridge.
Van Maanen, J. (1988) *Tales of the Field: On Writing Ethnography*. Chicago: The University of Chicago Press.
van den Berg, H., Wetherell, M. and Houtkoop-Steenstra, H. (2003) *Analyzing Race Talk: Multidisciplinary Perspectives on the Research Interview*. New York: Cambridge University Press.
Vandrick, S. (2009) *Interrogating Privilege: Reflections of a Second Language Educator*. Ann Arbor: University of Michigan Press.
Vendetti, T. (Producer, Director, Cinematographer, Editor) (2003) *Years of Darkness: A Spiritual Journey to Recovery* [Documentary]. Maui: USA: Public Broadcasting Service.
Vitanova, G. (2004) Gender enactments in immigrants' discursive practices: Bringing Bakhtin to the dialogue. *Journal of Language, Identity, and Education* 3 (4), 261–277.
Vitanova, G. (2013) Narratives as zones of dialogic constructions: A Bakhtinian approach to data in qualitative research. *Critical Inquiry in Language Studies* 10 (3), 242–261.
Vo-Thanh-Xuan, J. and Liamputtong, P. (2003) What it takes to be a grandparent in a new country: The lived experience and emotional well-being of Australian-Vietnamese grandparents. *Australian Journal of Social Issues* 38 (2), 209–228.

Voloder, J. and Kirpitchenko, L. (eds) (2014) *Insider Research on Migration and Mobility: International Perspectives on Researcher Positioning.* Burlington, VT: Ashgate.

Walby, K. (2010) Interviews as encounters: Issues of sexuality and reflexivity when men interview men about commercial same sex relations. *Qualitative Research* 10 (6), 639–657.

Walford, G. (1991) Reflexive accounts of doing educational research. In G. Walford (ed.) *Doing Educational Research* (pp. 1–17). New York: Routledge.

Wang, J. and Yan, Y. (2012) The interview question. In J.F. Gubrium, J.A. Holstein, A.B. Marvasti and K.D. McKinney (eds) *The SAGE Handbook of Interview Research: The Complexity of the Craft* (2nd edn) (pp. 231–242). London: SAGE.

Warriner, D.S. (2004) 'The days now is very hard for my family': The negotiation and construction of gendered work identities among newly arrived women refugees. *Journal of Language, Identity, and Education* 3 (4), 279–294.

Warriner, D.S. (2013) 'It's better life here than there': Elasticity and ambivalence in narratives of personal experience. *International Multilingual Research Journal* 7 (1), 15–32.

Wästerfors, D., Åkerström, M. and Jacobsson, K. (2014) Reanalysis of qualitative data. In U. Flick (ed.) *The SAGE Handbook of Qualitative Data Analysis* (pp. 467–480). London: SAGE.

Watson, G. and Seiler, R.M. (eds) (1992) *Text in Context: Contributions to Ethnomethodology.* London: SAGE.

Watson-Gegeo, K.A. (1988) Ethnography in ESL: Defining the essentials. *TESOL Quarterly* 22 (4), 575–592.

Weatherall, A. (2002) *Gender, Language and Discourse.* London: Routledge.

Weinberger, D.A. (1990) The construct validity of the repressive coping style. In J.L. Singer (ed.) *Repression and Dissociation: Implications for Personality Theory, Psychopathology, and Health* (pp. 337–386). Chicago: University of Chicago Press.

Weiss, R.S. (1994) *Learning from Strangers: The Art and Method of Qualitative Interview Studies.* New York: Free Press.

Wengraf, T. (2001) *Qualitative Research Interviewing: Biographic Narrative and Semi-structured Methods.* London: SAGE.

Westen, D. and Blagov, P.S. (2007) A clinical-empirical model of emotion regulation: From defense and motivated reasoning to emotional constraint satisfaction. In J.J. Gross (ed.) *Handbook of Emotion Regulation* (pp. 373–392). New York: Guilford Press.

Wetherell, M. (1998) Positioning and interpretative repertoires: Conversation analysis and post-structuralism in dialogue. *Discourse and Society* 9, 387–412.

Wetherell, M. (2003) Racism and the analysis of cultural resources in interviews. In H. van den Berg, M. Wetherell and H. Houtkoop-Steenstra (eds) *Analyzing Race Talk: Multidisciplinary Perspectives on the Research Interview* (pp. 11–30). New York: Cambridge University Press.

Wetherell, M. (2007) A step too far: Discursive psychology, linguistic anthropology and questions of identity. *Journal of Sociolinguistics* 11 (5), 661–681.

Wetherell, M. (2012) *Affect and Emotion: A New Social Science Understanding.* London: SAGE.

Wetherell, M. and Edley, N. (1999) Negotiating hegemonic masculinity: Imaginary positions and psycho-discursive practices. *Psychology* 9 (3), 335–356.

Wetherell, M. and Potter, J. (1992) *Mapping the Language of Racism: Discourse and the Legitimation of Exploitation.* New York: Columbia University Press.

Whalen, J. and Zimmerman, D. (1998) Observations on the display and management of emotions in naturally occurring activities: The case of 'hysteria' in calls to 9-1-1. *Social Psychology Quarterly* 61, 141–159.

White, M. and Epston, D. (1990) *Narrative Means to Therapeutic Ends.* New York: W.W. Norton & Company.

Widdicombe, S. and Wooffitt, R. (1995) *The Language of Youth Subcultures: Social Identity in Action*. Englewood Cliffs, NJ: Prentice Hall.
Wierzbicka, A. (1999) *Emotions across Languages and Cultures: Diversity and Universals*. New York: Cambridge.
Wiggins, S. and Potter, J. (2008) Discursive psychology. In C. Willig and W. Hollway (eds) *Handbook of Qualitative Research in Psychology* (pp. 72–89). London: SAGE.
Wilce, J.M. (2009) *Language and Emotion*. New York: Cambridge.
Wildschut, T., Sedikides, C. and Cordaro, F. (2011) Self-regulatory interplay between negative and positive emotions: The case of loneliness and nostalgia. In I. Nyklíček, A. Vingerhoets and M. Zeelenberg (eds) *Emotion Regulation and Well-being* (pp. 67–83). London: Springer.
Wilkinson, S. and Kitzinger, C. (2006) Surprise as an interactional achievement: Reaction tokens in conversation. *Social Psychology Quarterly* 69 (2), 150–182.
Wilkinson, S. and Kitzinger, C. (2008) Using conversation analysis in feminist and critical research. *Social and Personality Psychology Compass* 2 (2), 555–573.
Williams, S.J. and Bendelow, G. (1998) Introduction: Emotions in social life: Mapping the sociological terrain. In G. Bendelow and S.J. Williams (eds) *Emotions in Social Life Critical Themes and Contemporary Issues* (pp. xv–xxx). London: Routledge.
Willig, C. (2013) *Introducing Qualitative Research in Psychology* (3rd edn). Berkshire, England: McGraw-Hill.
Willig, C. and Stainton-Rogers, W. (2008) *The SAGE Handbook of Qualitative Research in Psychology*. London: SAGE.
Wolcott, H.F. (2008) *Ethnography: A Way of Seeing*. New York; Lanham, MD: AltaMira Press.
Wooffitt, R. (1992) *Telling Tales of the Unexpected: The Organization of Factual Discourse*. Savage, MD: Barnes & Noble Books.
Wooffitt, R. (2005) *Conversation Analysis and Discourse Analysis: A Comparative and Critical Introduction*. London: SAGE.
Yoshino, K. (2011) *Covering: The Hidden Assault On Our Civil Rights*. New York: Random House.
Zech, E., Rimé, B. and Nils, F. (2004) Social sharing of emotion, emotional recovery, and interpersonal aspects. In P. Philippot (ed.) *The Regulation of Emotion* (pp. 157–185). Mahwah, NJ: Lawrence Erlbaum.
Ziff, P. (1960) *Semantic Analysis*. London: Cornell University Press.
Zimmerman, D.H. (1988) On conversation: The conversation analytic perspective. In J.A. Anderson (ed.) *Communication Yearbook 11* (pp. 406–432). London: SAGE.
Zimmerman, D.H. (1998) Identity, context and interaction. In C. Antaki and S. Widdicombe (eds) *Identities in Talk* (pp. 87–106). London: SAGE.
Zuengler, J. and Miller, E. (2006) Cognitive and sociocultural perspectives: Two parallel SLA worlds? *TESOL Quarterly* 40 (1), 35–58.

Author Index

Abelson, R.P., 54, 59–60
Abu-Lughod, L., 10, 32, 205
Adeney, R., 86
Ahmed, S., 35
Akbari, R. 3
Alvarez-Conrad, J., 192
Anderson, G.L., 8
Anderson, T., 22
Andrews, F.M., 107
Andrews, M., 55
Antaki, C., 23, 41–42, 46–47, 55–56, 91, 136–138, 154, 200, 208
Arksey, H., 156, 173–174
Arndt, H., 154
Arnold, J., 3
Atkinson, D., 35, 47–48, 173, 204
Atkinson, J.M., 22, 90–91
Atkinson, P., x, 4, 6, 9–11, 21, 27, 29, 36, 40, 45, 47–49, 86, 88–90, 156–157, 176–177, 195, 198, 200, 202, 205–206
Atkinson, R., 1, 106, 134
Augoustinos, M., 38
Augusta-Scott, T., 190
Austin, J.L., 33
Averill, J.R., 192

Baker, C.D., 37, 58, 126
Bamberg, M.G., 38–39, 41, 55, 195
Baquedano-Lopez, P., 3
Barkhuizen, G., 3, 5–6, 10, 55,
Bauman, R., 36, 188, 215
Baynham, M., 3, 5, 26, 55, 133, 165, 185, 211
Beach, W.A., 70,
Becker, G., 36, 57, 186, 189
Bellelli, G., 189
Ben-Ze'ev, A., 196
Bendelow, G., 4
Benesch, S., 3, 35, 157, 210

Benson, P., 3, 5, 133
Benwell, B.E., 36, 49, 50
Bercelli, F., 117, 138, 153–154
Berger, L., 85
Berger, P.L., 49
Bergmann, J.R., 40
Berry, J.W., 210
Besnier, N., 1, 10, 27, 31, 36, 61
Bielska, J., 3, 185
Billig, M., 37, 45, 53, 138
Bilmes, J., 36, 45, 134, 153
Binnick, R.I., 121
Blackledge, A., 6, 191, 211
Blackman, S.J., 4, 13
Blagov, P.S., 190
Blair, R.G., 193
Block, D., 3, 5, 133, 185–186, 210
Blommaert, J., 7, 36, 45, 91, 101, 160, 165, 196, 208, 215
Boden, D., 94
Bogen, D., 37, 81, 93–95, 153
Bohanek, J.G., 190–192,
Bohannan, P., 36
Bolden, C.L., 89
Boler, M., 4, 32
Bolton, S.C., 157
Borg, S., 3
Bourdieu, P., xi, 58,
Bousfield, D., 45,
Bown, J., 191, 193
Briggs, C.L., xiii, 6, 10, 12, 36, 48, 55, 88–89, 156, 215
Brinkmann, S., 13, 106, 156
Brouwer, C.E., 42
Brown, C., 190
Brown, J., 192
Brown, J.D., 107
Brown, S.D., 210
Bucholtz, M., 7–8, 23
Burgess, H., 215

Burr, V., 49
Buttny, R., 10, 33, 36, 40–41, 50, 53, 56–57, 61, 94, 186–187
Button, G., 52, 153
Byrne, B., 15

Cacioppo, J.T., 196
Cameron, D., 14
Campbell, J., 187
Canagarajah, S., 8
Candland, D.K., 31
Capps, L., 10, 20, 29, 55–59, 61, 81, 186
Carlson, E.B., 193
Carter, S.K., 89
Cervantes, C.A., 196
Chafe, W., 121
Chalhoub-Deville, M., 199
Chamcharatsri, P.B., 3, 196, 210
Chase, S.E., 13, 93
Chaudron, C., xii
Chrestman, K.R., 174
Christianson, S., 81
Christophe, V., 174
Clark, C., 5
Clarke, J., 173
Clarke, S., 3
Clayman, S.E., 3, 37, 87, 91–92, 108, 111, 122
Clift, R. 36, 41, 57, 60, 65, 105
Clough, P.T., 3
Coates, J., 58, 61, 157, 169
Coffey, A., 1
Cole, P.M., 196
Collins, R., 189
Copp, M.A., 173
Coulter, J., 35, 40, 81
Couper-Kuhlen, E., 205, 207
Coupland, N. 57
Crane, T. 52,
Cresswell, J., 53
Croker, R.A., 4
Crookes, G., 3
Cross, W.E., 49
Crystal, D., 92
Cuff, E.C., 61, 93–94
Cupples, J., 13
Curci, A., 189
Cutler, S.E., 190

Danchev, D., x
Davies, A., 185
Davies, B., 57

Davis, H., 169
Davis, K., 138
Davitz, J.R., 191
Day, D., 126
De Fina, A., 3, 5–6, 10–11, 26–27, 36, 55, 133, 165, 185, 187, 211
DeBonis, S., 82
Delamont, S., 9–10, 49
deMarrais, K., 93
Demuth, C., 53
Denzin, N.K., 6–8, 31, 49, 53, 55, 156, 215
Dewaele, J.-M., 1, 3, 16, 32, 84, 185, 192, 193
Dickson-Swift, V., 173, 175–177
Doran, M., 3
Dörnyei, Z., 3–4, 185, 202
Drew, P., 41, 56–57, 63, 90-91, 94, 118, 129, 137, 154, 166, 187, 207
Du Bois, J.W., 35, 57
Duff, P., 7
Dunn, J., 192
Dunn, L., 173–174, 176

Eades, D., 91
Early, M., 8
Eckert, P., 7, 45, 87
Edley, N., 38–39, 53
Edwards, D., 21, 35–39, 41, 52, 91, 94, 102, 138, 153–154, 166, 196
Eglin, P., 36–37
Ehrenreich, B., 68
Ehrlich, S., 63, 90–92
Eisenberg, N., 32
Ekman, P., 32, 81
Ellis, C., 85, 192
Emerson, R.M., 60
Enelow, A.J., 193
Enfield, N.J., 45, 153
Englebretson, R., 57
Epston, D., 190
Etherington, K., 7

Fanshel, D., 36, 86
Faragher, R.V., 172
Feldman, R.S., 157
Fine, M., x
Fink, A., 107
Fisher, C.B., 88
Fitzgerald, R., ix
Fivush, R., 190, 192
Flick, U., 53
Foa, E.B., 190

Foley, L., 86
Folkman, S., 185
Francis, D.J., 91
Francis, D.W., 61, 93–94
Francis, M.E., 190
Frankel, R.M., 90–91
Frederickson, B.L., 189
Freed, A.F., 63, 90–92
Freeman, M., 55, 201
Freese, J., 50
Friesen, W.V., 32
Fussell, S.R., 32

Gabriel, Y., 187
Gabryś-Barker, D., 3, 185
Galasiński, D., 32
Galletta, A., 49
Gardner, R.C., 101, 127, 185
Garfinkel, H., 9, 36–37, 40, 56–57, 94, 134, 155
Garrett, P.B., 3
Gaydos, H.L., 190
Gaylin, W., 192
Gearing, J., 197
Georgakopoulou, A., 6, 10, 36, 55, 71, 133, 195, 207
Gergen, K.J., 187
Gergen, M.M., 187
Gilbert, G.N., 37, 38
Gilbert, K.R., 4, 10, 169, 177, 197, 205
Given, L.M., 15, 215
Glenn, P.J., 79, 121, 166, 182
Goffman, E., 11, 13, 35–37, 46, 142, 163
Goldstein, T., 11
Golombek, P., 3
Goodwin, C., 36, 40, 48, 57, 204
Goodwin, J. 114
Goodwin, M.H., 36, 40
Goss, C., 138
Greatbatch, D., 63, 91, 108
Greco, M., 3
Green, D., 36
Grice, H.P., 58, 82
Groleau, D., 194
Gross, J.J., 157, 192, 205, 210
Gubrium, J.F., 1, 6, 10, 15, 47–50, 54, 86–88, 91, 108, 110–111, 134, 149, 156, 198
Günthner, S., 57, 94, 207

Haakana, M., 182, 186
Halkowski, T., 63
Hall, C., 93,
Halley, J.O.M., 3

Hammersley, M., 6, 36–37, 39, 47, 178, 200, 202
Hanauer, D.I., 3, 193, 196, 210
Harré, R., 31, 33, 37–38, 49, 57
Harris, S., 91
Hatch, E.M., 105
Hatfield, E., 173, 205
Haye, A., 53
He, A.W. 63, 91
Heath, C., 94
Heigham, J., 4
Heimann, F.F., 172
Hepburn, A., 9, 10, 22–23, 36, 38–41, 49–50, 66, 156, 204, 210
Heritage, J., ix, 22, 36–37, 41–42, 63, 66, 70, 78, 86–87, 90–92, 94, 103–104, 111, 113, 116–117, 121–123, 129, 136–137, 140, 142–143, 150, 161–162, 173, 202
Herr, K., 8
Hesse-Biber, S.N., 7
Hester, S., 36–37, 91
Hibberd, F.J., 49
Hine, C., 200
Hinton, A.L., 193
Hochschild, A.R., 10, 32, 68, 157, 172
Hoggett, P., 3
Holliday, A., 8
Holstein, J.A., 6, 10, 15, 47, 49–50, 54, 86–88, 91, 110–111, 134, 149, 198
Holt, E., 36, 41, 60, 65, 121, 182
Hook, D., 38
Horrocks, C., 132
Horwitz, E.K., 3, 185
Housley, W., ix, 37
Hutchby, I., 10, 22, 36–37, 93–94, 109, 135, 137

Imai, Y., 205
Irvine, F., 48

Jackson, P.A., 168
Jaffe, A., 57
Jaggar, A.M., 4
Janney, R.W., 154
Jayyusi, L., 37, 126
Jefferson, G., 27, 37, 57, 63, 71, 79, 97, 116, 118, 143–144, 166, 180
Jie, D., 36
Johnson, B., 173
Jones, S.R., 7
Jordan, S.R., 3
Jørgensen, M.W., 38–39

Kalaja, P., 3, 5
Kamada, L.D., 185
Kamm, H., 194, 196
Kanagy, R., 3
Kanno, Y., 3, 5, 10
Kaplan, R., 185
Kappra, R., 203
Kärkkäinen, E., 57
Kasper, G., 36, 37, 40, 55, 68, 87, 92, 101, 144, 148, 170, 207
Kaushanskaya, M., 192–193
Kenny, A., 52
Kim, U., 210
Kindlon, D., 32
King, B., 203
King, N., 132, 158
Kinginger, C., 185, 191
Kirmayer, L.J., 194
Kirpitchenko, L., 88
Kirsch, G.E., 156
Kitzinger, C., 10, 36, 45–46, 53, 123, 142, 157, 169, 208
Kleinman, S., 173
Knight, P., 156, 173–174
Kong, T.S.K., 12–14
Korobov, N., 38
Koshik, I., 111, 135, 151, 181
Kottler, J., 59
Koven, M., 3, 5, 59, 71,
Kozak, M.J., 190
Kramsch, C.J., 31–32
Kubanyiova, M., 3
Kuebli, J., 32
Kulick, D., 13–14
Kupferberg, I., 36
Kvale, S., 13, 106, 156

Labov, W., 35–36, 58, 86, 93, 95, 104, 149, 186, 188
Land, G.H., 208
Langenhove, L.V., 57
Langman, J., 11, 211
Lantolf, J., 203
Larraín, A., 53
LaSala, M.C., 13
Lazaraton, A., 22
Lazarus, R.S., 179, 189, 210
Leavy, P., 7
Lee-Treeweek, G., 174
Lerner, G.H., 61, 71, 93, 111, 114, 125, 151
Letherby, G., 158
Levenson, R.W., 189

Levinson, S., 41
Lewis, P.J., 86
Liamputtong, P., 88, 194
Liddicoat, A.J., 36–37, 55, 61, 73, 93, 94, 121–123, 127, 182
Lillrank, A., 169, 173
Lin, A., 3
Lincoln, Y.S., 7–8, 49, 53, 55, 156, 215
Lindholm, C., 90
Lindström, J., 90
Linkogle, S., 174
Linnekin, J., xii
Lo, A., 11, 210
Locke, S., 86
Luckmann, T., 49
Lutz, C., 10, 32, 196, 205
Lyman, S.L., 56
Lynch, M., 37, 81, 93–95, 153

Maalouf, A., 210
Madigan, S., 190
Mandelbaum, J., 55
Mantero, M., 3
Marian, V., 192–193
Markee, N., 53
Markowitsch, H.J., 31
Marshall, C., 7
Martel, Y., 29, 198
Maryns, K., 101, 165
Massumi, B., 3
Matusov, E., 53
Maynard, D.W., 10, 22, 36–37, 47, 53, 58, 60, 79, 108–109, 204
Maynard, D.W., 50
McAdams, D.P., 187
McCarthy, M., 199
McGroarty, M., 199
McHoul, A.W., 35
McKelvey, R.S., 194
McNaron, T.A.H., 13
Medawar, P., 8
Mehra, B., 8, 88
Mehus, S., 47
Melrose, S., 64
Menard-Warwick, J., 3, 5, 7, 11, 133, 185, 191, 203, 211
Merchant, B.M., 88
Merleau-Ponty, M., ix
Messerschmidt, D.A., 88
Miller, E.R., 3, 128, 133, 152, 185, 191
Miller, G., 148
Miller, J., 6, 58
Milroy, L., 3, 95

Mintz, B., 13
Mishler, E.G., 6, 36, 48, 55, 88, 150, 156
Moerman, M., 47–48, 205
Mondada, L., 47, 204
Mori, J., 195
Motha, S., 3, 6
Mulkay, M., 37–38
Murray, G., 3

Nairn, K., 8
Nelson, C., 14, 45, 203
Norrick, N.R., 58–60, 94, 166
Norton Peirce, B., 133, 185
Norton, B., 3, 6, 8, 10–11, 129, 133, 152, 185, 203
Nunan, D., 3, 5, 133
Nyklíček, I., 190, 205, 210

O'Donoghue, J., 107
O'Reilly, K., 47
Ochs, E., 10, 20, 26, 29, 31, 55–59, 61, 81, 144, 186, 196
Olesen V., x, 88
Ong, A., xiii
Ovando, C.J., 86
Oxford, R.L., 3

Parker, I., 38
Parrott, W.G., 35
Pastor, A.R., 27, 187
Patton, M.Q., 108
Pavlenko, A., 3, 6, 11, 15–16, 26, 31–32, 55, 88, 185, 191–193, 196, 198, 203, 211
Pawelczyk, J., 36
Pease, B., 13
Pennebaker, J.W., 190
Pennycook, A., 176
Peräkylä, A., 36, 41, 130, 138, 178, 210
Philippot, P., 157
Phillips, L.J., 38–39
Pini, B., 13
Planalp, S., 5, 173
Pomerantz, A.M., 43, 75, 95, 116, 142, 149, 153, 181
Portes, A., xiii
Poster, M., 176
Potter, J., 9, 10, 15, 21–23, 36–41, 49–51, 66, 72, 94, 113, 138, 153, 156, 204
Prior, M.T., x, 2–4, 8, 10, 23–24, 35, 40, 47, 55, 57–61, 68, 71, 75, 87–89, 91, 94, 96, 98, 117, 126, 134, 144, 148–149, 166–167, 170, 188, 192, 195, 199, 201, 204, 207, 212, 215
Psathas, G., 22, 37

Quas, J.A., 192
Quirk, R., 121

Rae, J., 117, 138–139, 154
Ramanathan, V., 7, 24, 47
Rapley, T.J., 6, 8–11, 21–22, 24, 35, 40, 45, 155–156, 170, 199, 201, 209
Raymond, G., 78, 137, 142, 182, 184
Rees, C.E., 192
Reinharz, S., 13
Reyes, A., 11, 210
Reyes, G., 190
Richards, K., 4, 6, 10, 23, 55, 157, 198, 200, 202, 204
Riessman, C.K., 1, 6, 10, 15, 21, 29, 36, 55, 156, 197
Rimé, B., 174, 187, 189
Rintell, E.M., 3, 186, 191
Robbins, B., 185
Roberts, C., 7–8
Robinson, J.D., 63
Rorty, A., 35
Ross, A., x
Ross, S.J., 101
Rosser-Hogan, R., 193
Rossman, G.B., 7
Rothblum, E., 13
Röttger-Rössler, B., 31
Roulston, K., 2, 4, 6, 8, 10–11, 23–24, 47, 55, 88–89, 133, 156–157, 199–200
Rubin, H.R., 155
Rubin, I.S., 155
Rumbaut, R.G., xiii
Russell, J.A., 196
Ruusuvuori, J., 31, 33, 35, 165, 178
Ryave, A.L., 71

Saarni, C., 32, 192,
Sacks, H., 36–37, 42, 46, 55, 58, 61–62, 64, 71, 93–94, 111, 126–127, 131, 134, 153, 181, 203
Samli, A.C., 107
Sanchez, J., 192, 196
Sandhu, P., 185
Sandlund, E., 40
Sarbin, T.R., 1, 197
Schank, R.C., 54, 59–60

Schegloff, E.A., 36–37, 42, 44–46, 53, 58, 61, 91–92, 96, 111, 114, 125–127, 153, 181–183, 195, 203, 208
Schieffelin, B.B., 26, 31, 144, 196
Schiffrin, D., 55, 59
Schmidt, R., 185
Schmitt, C.S., 5
Schrauf, R.W., 192, 196
Schumann, J.H., 3, 31
Schwalbe, M.L., 107–108
Schwartz, H., 134
Scott, M.B., 56
Scovel, T., 3
Searle, J.B., 52
Seedhouse, P., 41, 90
Seidman, I., 85, 132, 134, 153,
Seiler, R.M., 45
Selting, M., 40–41, 63, 66, 144, 162, 207,
Selye, H., 189
Shoemaker, P.J., 199
Sidnell, J., 36–37, 41, 55, 58, 61–62, 71, 86, 92–94, 111, 136, 181
Sijbrandij, M., 190
Silverman, D., 4, 38, 40–41, 53, 71, 86, 90, 148, 156, 201, 205, 209
Silverstein, M., 215
Simpson, J., 4
Sirgy, M.J., 107
Smith, B.M., 10
Smith, L., 53
Smith, R., 178
Smithson, J., 45, 47
Snow, C.E., 105,
Sorjonen, M., 36, 178, 210
Sparkes, A.C., 10
Speer, S.A., 36, 38–39, 45, 46, 53, 94, 208
Spradley, J.P., 47, 89
Stainton-Rogers, W., 4
Stamm, B.H., 174
Stanley, L., 13
Stearns, P.N., 37–38
Steensig, J., 57, 90
Stenner, P., 3
Stets, J.E., 31
Stevens, A., 134
Stivers, T., 36–37, 41, 57, 140, 143, 153, 181, 184,
Stokoe, E., 21, 36, 37–39, 41, 45, 47, 49, 50, 91, 102, 153
Streeck, J., 47
Stritikus, T., 11

Sullivan, G., 168
Swain, M., 3, 6

Takahashi, K., 3
Talmy, S., xii, 6, 8–11, 22–23, 45–47, 53, 55, 108, 126, 131, 195, 204
Tannen, D., 83
Taylor, S., 58, 178
Taylor, S.E., 196
te Molder, H., 21, 36, 38, 40, 41
ten Have, P., 37, 46, 88
Thompson, M., 32
Thornborrow, J., 58, 61, 63, 157, 169
Tileaga, C., 38
Tisdale, K., 93
Toerien, M., 10, 46
Tran, T.V., 193
Trask, H.-K., xii
Trimble, J.E., 88
Tsui, A.B., 92, 185
Tugade, M.M., 189
Turner, J.H., 31

Urban, G., 215
Ushioda, E., 3, 185

van den Berg, H., 108
van der Elst, D., 36
Van Maanen, J., 176
Vandrick, S., x, 203
Vendetti, T., 178
Vitanova, G., 3, 6, 11, 132, 185
Vo-Thanh-Xuan, J., 194
Voloder, J., 88
von Duyke, K., 53

Wagner, J., 36–37
Walby, K., 14
Waletzky, J., 93, 95, 149
Walford, G., 8
Wang, J., 88–89
Warriner, D.S., 3, 11
Wästerfors, D., 114
Watson-Gegeo, K.A., 36
Watson, D., 129, 136, 150
Watson, G., 45
Weatherall, A., 39
Weinberger, D.A., 190
Weis, L., x
Weiss, R.S., 1, 134, 153–154, 156, 176
Wengraf, T., 156, 159
Westen, D., 190

Wetherell, M., 15, 27, 37–39, 53, 110, 114, 173
Whalen, J., 31
White, C., 191, 193
White, M., 190
Whiteside, A., 32
Widdicombe, S., 41–42, 72, 200
Wierzbicka, A., 31, 185
Wiggins, S., 36, 38–39, 41
Wilce, J.M., 10, 27, 31
Wildschut, T., 187
Wilkinson, S., 46, 53, 123, 142
Williams, S.J., 4
Willig, C., 4, 19
Willis, A.I., 88
Willson, M., 13
Wise, S., 13

Withey, S.B., 107
Wolcott, H.F., 36
Wolkomir, M., 107–108
Wooffitt, R., 10, 22, 36–39, 72, 81, 91, 93–94, 138, 153, 198

Yan, Y., 88–89
Yoshino, K., 13, 46
Young, D.J., 185
Young, R., 3

Zech, E., 188, 190
Ziff, P., 45
Zimmerman, D.H., 22, 31, 42, 89, 94, 127
Zuengler, J., 3

Subject Index

accounts (accountability, accounting) *see also* tellings, 1, 6–7, 9, 15, 17, 19–20, 23–24, 30, 35, 39–40, 44–46, 48, 50–51, 55–57, 60, 63–67, 72, 74–76, 78, 81, 83, 85, 89, 93–96, 102, 105, 108–109, 113, 116, 118–119, 121, 123, 125, 127, 129, 133–137, 143, 146, 151, 153, 161, 165–167, 170, 173, 175, 180, 182, 186–88, 191, 195, 198, 200–201, 206–207, 212–215

affect *see also* emotion, emotionality, xi, xii, 1–5, 11, 26–27, 29–32, 35, 40, 50, 54, 57, 61, 63, 72, 78, 83, 85, 90, 99–100, 109, 112, 114–118, 127, 130–131, 135, 139, 142–145, 155, 157, 159, 161, 165, 177, 183, 185, 187, 189, 191, 197–200, 203–204, 206, 208–209, 215

affective stance *see also* affiliation, stance, 57, 112, 127, 130, 135, 142, 208

affective turn, 157, 185

affiliation *see also* affective stance, alignment, empathy, 57, 123, 140, 143, 147, 150, 165, 169, 191, 208, 210, 212

African-Americans, 84, 168

agency, 1, 9, 11, 15, 19, 25, 27, 36, 38, 50, 52, 61, 74, 127, 144, 203, 211

alignment *see also* affiliation, 51, 57, 63, 70, 76, 82, 94, 95, 104, 118, 122, 123, 139, 181

Amerasians, 81–82, 84, 194

America (Americans) see also Canada, North America, United States, xi, xii, xiii, 15, 43, 66, 68, 75–76, 79–81, 83–84, 103, 120–122, 132, 167, 170–171, 179, 183, 198, 200, 204, 210

applied linguistics, 2–3, 9, 88, 176, 185

Asians, 12, 65, 67–68, 84, 89, 120–121, 126–127, 131, 166, 168, 178, 193, 204, 210

assessment, x, 43, 78, 81, 91, 114, 120, 130, 135, 139, 142, 145–146, 149, 154, 165

asylum (asylum seekers, refugees), xiii, 11, 13, 17–18, 30, 68, 71–73, 76, 89, 100–101, 103 131, 140, 143, 148, 163, 165, 169–170, 175, 193, 210

refugee camp, 17, 68, 71–73, 76, 103, 163, 165, 169, 175

autobiographic(al) (talk, tellings, interviews, and research) *see also* narrative, tellings, xiii, 1–2, 5–6, 8–10, 15, 20, 22–26, 29–30, 37, 52, 54–56, 58, 61, 70, 73, 80, 82–83, 85, 87, 90, 94–96, 100, 106, 109, 132, 134, 144, 154–155, 172–173, 177, 179–180, 184–186, 188–191, 195, 197–199, 201, 203, 205–207, 210–215

belonging (and unbelonging), x–xiii, 10, 17, 63, 75, 89, 103, 198, 210–211

California, 103, 182–183

Cambodians (Cambodia, Khmer), xii, 15–18, 27, 42, 44, 60, 74–75, 79–84, 97–98, 123, 131–132, 135, 160, 178, 180, 193,

Canada *see also* North America, x–xi, 2, 11–12, 15–18, 60, 69, 72, 75, 79, 100, 129, 140, 163–164, 178, 194

Caucasians, x–xii, 12, 32, 64–66, 68, 83, 110, 112, 166, 170, 204

Chinese, xi, 14, 102

class (social), xii, xiii, 8, 11, 13, 32, 46, 125, 211
co-construction (collaborative production), 2, 10, 15, 22, 26, 30, 34–35, 40, 42, 44, 54, 79, 83, 85, 90–91, 94, 106, 111–112, 115, 129, 131, 140, 150–151, 153, 162, 180, 198–199, 201–204, 213
cognitive (intra-psychological)
  displays, 26, 70, 74, 81, 103–105, 113, 182
  perspectives, 3–4, 31–32, 38, 41, 49–50, 52, 59, 66, 109, 158, 177, 188, 196
complaints see troubles tellings and transgression
conflict, x, 6, 20, 81, 139, 142, 149, 168, 173, 185, 195, 213
constraints (interactional and institutional), x, 16, 25, 31, 50, 54, 58, 91, 186
construction (constructionism) see also deconstruction, 39, 48–51,
context, 8, 13, 23, 35, 41–48, 53, 56, 58, 64, 68, 73–74, 79, 82, 84–85, 88–93, 95, 104–105, 108–109, 113, 115, 125, 127, 130–131, 135, 137, 157, 165, 169, 173, 177, 186, 188–189, 191–192, 194–196, 199–200, 202–207, 209, 212–213
conversation see also institutional settings, 14–16, 26, 37–39, 49, 55, 58, 61–62, 63, 70, 74, 89–94, 105, 113, 121–123, 127–128, 137, 150–151, 166, 180, 182, 186–188, 192, 196, 213
conversation analysis (CA) see also discursive psychology, EMCA, ethnomethodology, ix, 7, 10, 23, 25, 30, 36, 29, 40, 46, 92, 133, 184, 200, 204–205, 207
  'basic' (canonical) CA, ix, 39, 46, 48, 52, 205, 208
  critiques of, 7, 23, 45–46
  psychological topics, 40–41
counseling see also therapy, 81, 90, 138, 153, 165, 175, 207, 209, 212
culture, 32, 46, 48, 63, 79, 84, 87, 98, 110, 169–170, 188, 195
  insider and outsider knowledge, xi, 8, 16, 88–90, 133, 183

data
  ambiguity, 45, 47, 106, 112, 114, 116, 156, 182–183, 200, 204

content and thematic analysis, 9, 22, 52, 55, 64, 73, 102
cultural artifacts, 48, 205
curious patterns, xiii, 22, 47, 53, 56, 59, 72, 83, 200, 204
extra-discursive material, 10, 16, 47–48, 52–53, 58, 90, 152, 184, 198, 200, 204
generation versus collection, 2, 4, 15, 16, 23, 39, 47, 70, 72, 88, 105, 114, 118, 133, 156, 209, 213
inductive analysis, 37, 46
interaction analysis, 6, 10, 36, 46, 157, 205
motivated and unmotivated looking, 45–47
reanalysis, 98, 114, 144
relevance, 7, 11, 41–47, 54, 58–59, 61–62, 74, 82, 113, 125, 183, 199–201, 203, 205
thematic and content analysis, 9, 19, 22, 52, 55, 102, 198, 200–201
triangulation, 52–53
truth (authenticity, believability, validity), 4, 7, 16, 19–21, 23, 30, 35, 48, 50, 53, 55, 58, 65, 67–68, 80, 86–87, 95–96, 101, 105, 139, 180, 185–186, 190, 197, 199, 201, 205
deception (lies) see also truth, 19, 45, 54, 87, 117, 119, 201
designedly incomplete utterances, 111, 135, 151
desire, xii–xiii, 3, 10, 12–14, 183–184, 199, 203, 208
dilemmas, x, xiii, 1, 4, 13, 21, 94, 114, 152, 155–156, 162, 177–178, 192, 201, 203–204, 210–211, 214
discourse analysis (DA) 7, 10, 36–38, 45, 53
discourse markers and tokens, 44, 70–72, 74, 99, 101, 103–104, 112–113, 121–123, 129, 139, 149
discrimination (mistreatment) see also troubles tellings, transgression, xi, 10, 13, 19, 60, 64–67, 75–76, 79, 81–85, 109–110, 116, 125–126, 135, 169, 175, 193–194, 198, 211, 215,
discursive competence(s), xi, 8, 10, 15, 19, 31–32, 52, 61, 66, 83, 87–88, 90, 105, 157, 167, 182, 196, 200–201, 203, 206

Subject Index

discursive constructionism (DC) *see also* constructionism, xiii, 2, 10, 21, 25, 29, 30, 36, 48–49, 52, 54–55, 83, 92, 105, 131, 158, 161, 166, 179–180, 195, 198–203, 205, 214
discursive psychology (DP), 10, 23, 25, 30, 36–41, 47–49, 53, 58, 200
  origins, 37–41
  three main strands, 37–39
discursive scaling
  downgrading (de-escalation, minimization), 13, 43, 68, 100, 112, 121, 131, 142, 148, 154, 157, 161, 180, 192–193
  upgrading (escalation, intensification), 78, 102, 109, 121, 123, 127, 138, 142, 149, 153–154, 157, 159, 161, 182, 191, 208
distress, 134, 155–178, 189–190

education *see* school
elicitation (invitation, solicitation) of talk, 6, 10, 15–16, 25–26, 29, 30, 35, 43, 55–56, 58, 62, 63, 70, 72, 82, 85–131, 132–136, 142–143, 146, 148–150, 152, 154, 159, 161, 165–166, 170, 180, 183–184, 186, 188–189, 192, 201, 206–207, 214
EMCA *see also* conversation analysis (CA), ethnomethodology (EM), discursive psychology (DP), membership categorization analysis (MCA), 36–37, 41, 53
emotion(s) *see also* emotionality
  as social actions, 1
  defining, 1, 31
  emotion-implicative utterances *see also* questions, 75, 103, 105, 106, 109, 114, 118, 120, 129–131, 133, 142, 147, 180, 207
  emotion labels and emotion-implicative terms:
    anger (angry, mad) xii, xiii, 10, 31, 33, 35, 52, 57, 60, 64, 75–76, 78, 82, 93, 102, 115–116, 127, 159, 162–163, 165, 168, 169, 171–175, 179–180, 185, 193–195, 198, 206, 210
    anxiety, 133, 155, 160, 163, 165, 185, 189
    bad, 76, 80, 111, 120–121, 128–130, 147–148, 150–152, 170, 208, 211
    depression (depressing), 165–166, 168, 179, 189, 194, 212
    difficult, 147–149, 171, 173
    disappointment, 77, 180
    disconnected, 150–151
    disgust, 20, 31
    easy, 26, 122, 130–131, 208
    embarrassment, 24, 78, 108
    enjoyment, 67, 163, 168
    fear, xi, 13, 16, 26, 30, 35, 52, 68, 109, 133, 140–146, 163, 167, 173, 175, 180, 185, 193, 196, 198, 206
    frustration, xiii, 174, 194
    grief, 31
    guilt, x, 111, 114, 132–133, 159–160
    happiness (happy), 33, 60, 108, 159, 164–166, 179–185, 187, 195
    hard, 26, 120–122, 130, 139, 140–142, 147, 149, 153, 179–180, 183, 208
    hate, 76, 193–194
    joy, 31, 33, 52, 77, 173, 185, 206
    loneliness (isolation), 31, 150–151, 175, 179–180, 191, 212, 214
    lost, 150–151
    love, 31, 111, 114, 167, 171–172
    mood, 127
    nervous, 152
    painful, 10, 20, 34, 79, 139, 142
    panic, 133
    risk, 141, 143, 153,
    sad, sadness, xii, 19, 34, 35, 108, 116, 132, 146, 159, 160–163, 167, 169, 173, 179–180, 185, 193–195, 198, 206–207
    scared, scary, 26, 140–146
    shame, ashamed, x, xiii, 46, 64, 68–74, 75, 116, 150–151, 159, 167, 185
    sorrow, 148
    suffering, 29, 30, 187, 189, 193–194
    surprise, 31, 57, 96, 123
    tolerate, 127
    tough, 26, 141–142, 147–149, 180, 208
    upset, 33–35, 64–65, 158, 174, 183–184, 193, 214
    uptight, 163, 165
  interactional reading of, 32–35
  language choice and, 193
  management of *see also* emotional labor, 11, 109, 154–179, 195, 199, 209
  regulation of (see also well-being, mental health), 157, 178, 190–191, 209–210

emotion(s) (*Continued*)
  social norms and display rules, 32, 192, 196, 209
  universal aspects of, 31
emotional
  contagion, 26, 173–174, 189
  danger, 26, 174–177
  labor (emotion work) *see also* emotion management, 4, 10, 157–158, 174, 211
  objects (intensionality, sticky objects) *see also* directionality, 34–35, 52 196
emotionalism (emotionalist) *see also* romanticism, ix, 4–5, 177, 205, 215
emotionality, xiii, 2, 4–6, 9–11, 20, 22, 24–27, 29–37, 41, 48, 52, 54, 57, 63–64, 66, 70, 72, 74–77, 79, 82–83, 85, 92–93, 105–109, 113–115, 117, 119–120, 123–124, 127, 129–130, 132, 140, 150, 152–153, 155–158, 161–162, 165–166, 168–169, 173–174, 176, 178–180, 184, 186–188, 191–193, 195–201, 205–209, 211, 213–215
  negative *see also* emotion, affect, 2, 26, 79–81, 83–84, 113, 120–121, 123, 129, 135, 139, 141, 151, 161, 163, 165–166, 169, 172–174, 179–196, 204, 206, 210–213
  positive, 2, 26, 33, 116, 155, 173, 179–182, 184–185, 187, 189–196, 213
empathy (empathic responses) *see also* affiliation, 26, 32–33, 63, 66, 75, 82–83, 85, 116, 140, 142–143, 145–146, 159, 161–162, 169, 173, 175, 189, 191, 201, 208, 213
epistemics *see also* stance, 8, 16, 23, 26, 30, 34, 45, 49, 55, 57, 60, 71–72, 78, 83, 94–95, 104–105, 113, 121, 137, 142–144, 146, 148–149, 182, 208
ESL (English as a Second language), xi, 79, 81–82, 135, 148
ethnicity (race), xiii, 8, 13, 17–19, 32, 35, 42, 45, 63, 65, 68, 81, 83–84, 135, 168, 194, 110, 200, 204, 210
  ethnic conflict, 17, 79–80
  ethnic hierarchies, xi–ii, 10, 210
  ethnic hybridity, 75, 133, 135, 194
ethnography (ethnographic methods), 1, 2, 10, 13, 25, 30, 36, 47–48, 53, 60, 88–89, 169, 173, 176, 191, 193, 197, 200, 203–205, 209

emic perspectives, 9, 24, 45, 47, 53, 202, 203
ethnographic mentality, 25, 47–48, 200, 203, 205
ethnomethodology *see also* EMCA, 25, 36–38, 41, 50, 88, 94, 200

Filipinos (Philippines) *see also* Southeast Asians, xi, 14, 16, 17–18, 30, 68–69, 71–72, 83, 100, 103, 140
FOB (Fresh off the boat) *see also* discrimination, 76, 131
folk beliefs (folk ideologies), 35, 39, 43, 154, 199
formulation *see* (re)formulation
French, xi–xii, 79, 84

gender *see also* sexuality, xii, 8, 11, 13–14, 18–19, 25, 27, 32, 39, 45–46, 48, 67–68, 107, 167, 203–204, 208, 211, 215
  masculinity, 27, 108, 168, 178, 204, 207

haole see also Caucasians, x, 12, 83, 166
Hawai'i, xii, 12, 15, 17, 27, 68, 84, 105, 154, 164, 178
hesitation, 44, 72, 99–101, 104, 127, 129
humor (joking) *see also* laughter, 12, 77–79, 82, 84, 97, 98, 102, 120, 123, 144, 163, 166, 168, 170, 172–174, 180, 182, 200, 206–207, 212

identity
  categories, 43, 75, 83, 85, 89, 109, 114, 125, 126, 127, 163, 184, 201, 203, 204
  hidden, x, 13, 198
  liminality and marginalization, 10, 45, 86, 188, 198, 215
  minorities xiii, 4–5, 13, 79, 84–85, 110, 210
Indo-Chinese *see also* Cambodians, Vietnamese, 193
institutional settings and practices (institutionality), 2, 6, 10, 26, 35, 37–40, 45, 49, 55, 62, 63, 65, 71, 74–75, 85, 87, 90–95, 97, 105, 115, 129, 131, 134–137, 139, 150, 152–154, 156, 165, 179, 173, 184, 188, 195, 198, 201–202, 205, 207, 213
intensionality *see* emotional objects

Subject Index 257

intention (intentionality), 52, 53, 55, 88, 123, 159, 172, 200, 203, 205–206, 215
interpretive
  frames, 10–11, 35, 30, 43, 46, 56, 65, 71, 79, 95, 109, 112, 116, 130–131, 144–145, 168, 172, 180, 183–184, 195, 204, 212
  puzzles *see* 'curious' patterns
  repertoires, 38, 39
intersubjectivity, 31, 71, 112, 138–140, 150–151, 184, 189
interview(s) *see also* narrative, research, tellings
  absence/presence of interviewer in, 23, 130
  confessional nature of, 1, 4, 59, 134, 153, 189, 212
  critiques of, 6, 9–10
  discomfort in, 16, 162, 165, 169, 172, 174, 203–204
  establishing rapport, 13, 156, 175
  failures xiii, 2, 24, 88, 98, 156, 177, 180, 184, 201, 206
  flirtation in, 14, 123, 172
  language of, 15–16
  natural(istic) versus contrived, ix, 23, 38–40, 195, 213
  quasi-conversational, 62–63, 91
  self-report data, 39, 157, 205
  social studies of interview studies, 10, 199
  society, 86, 205
  therapeutic insights for researchers, 201–202, 208
  therapy-like nature of, 134, 140, 162, 165, 190, 195, 211–213

Japanese, xi–xii, 79–80, 84

Koreans, xi, 66–67, 83

Laotians (Lao), 120, 121, 170
laughter *see also* humor, 27, 31, 64, 69, 73, 78, 97, 110, 116, 120, 123, 127, 144–145, 158, 166, 168, 172–174, 179, 181, 182, 214

membership categorization analysis (MCA) *see also* EMCA, 25, 36–37, 39, 46, 203

memory (remembering), xiii, 1, 10, 20, 25–26, 38, 41, 54–84, 94, 96, 98, 101, 103–104, 109, 121, 140, 148, 153, 155, 159, 170–171, 180–182, 184, 189–192, 195, 207
  failure (forgetting), xiii, 58–59, 64, 66, 79–82, 159–160, 170, 190
mental health (well-being), 1, 11, 25–26, 134, 165, 175–176, 178, 182, 190, 192, 194–195, 209–210, 212–213
  post-traumatic stress disorder (PTSD), 190
  support, 175–176
meta-commentary, 10, 21, 26, 55, 106, 141, 207
metaphor, ix, 36, 39, 117, 150, 160, 178
microethnography, 47
micro-macro distinctions, 36, 38, 43, 46–47, 215
Micronesians, xii
migration (immigration), xii, 14–17, 30, 83, 89, 95, 100–103, 132, 135, 140, 144, 150, 163, 181, 192–194, 204, 210
  migrants (immigrants) *see also* asylum, refugees, xi, xii, xiii, 2, 11–13, 16, 24–25, 27, 42–44, 60, 68, 73–76, 79, 81, 83–85, 89, 96, 105, 120–121, 124, 126, 128–129, 131, 135–136, 147, 159, 163–164, 166, 169–170, 178, 182–184, 193–196, 198, 200–201, 210–211, 214
  transnational and transcultural, xi–xiii, 2, 24–25, 85, 192, 195, 200, 209–211
morality *see also* stance, x, 21, 30, 35, 57, 61, 66, 102, 115, 116, 126–127, 176, 187, 192, 194, 200–202, 209
music and songs, 84, 97–98, 166–168, 178

narrative(s) *see also* accounts, tellings, 1–10, 19–21, 23, 25, 36, 41, 47, 48, 50, 52, 55–56, 60–61, 68, 86, 88, 109, 128, 133, 149, 155, 166, 181, 185–187, 189, 192–194, 196, 198–201, 204, 206–207, 211, 213, 215
  complexity, 191–192
  entextualization, 91, 101, 209, 215
  hypothetical, 55, 142, 158
  interactional world ('here and now') *see also* storyworld, 22, 61, 66, 68, 82, 133, 142–145, 150, 155, 161, 172, 174, 194–196, 214

narrative(s) (*Continued*)
  listen-worthiness, 59, 106, 188
  narrative turn, 6
  personal transformation and catharsis in, ix, 134, 189–191, 211, 215
  storyworld ('there and then') *see also* interactional world, 22, 61, 65–66, 68, 82, 116, 133, 142–145, 155, 161, 172, 174, 194–196, 214
  talking back to people in, 10, 144, 194
  tellability (newsworthiness, tellworthiness), 26, 35, 54, 56, 58–59, 67, 79, 82, 93, 105, 135, 137, 109, 168, 186
  typologies, 2, 55, 187, 191
  versions, x, 11, 20–21, 26, 29–31, 50, 55, 58, 60, 61, 66, 80, 83, 89, 95, 100–101, 121, 165–166, 175, 192, 196–198, 201, 208, 213, 214
  written, 191–192, 196
nonverbal cues, 14, 22, 33, 36, 46, 56–57, 87, 158, 161, 174, 203, 207
norms, social and interactional, 32, 41, 48, 57–59, 63, 75, 90–91, 93, 116, 126, 129, 130–131, 179, 186, 188, 192–194, 202
North America *see also* United States (US), Canada xiii, 15, 80–81, 179, 183, 198, 200, 210

objectivity *see also* subjectivity, ix, 4, 7, 8, 23, 58, 66, 80, 81, 86, 102, 113, 116, 151, 189, 205–206, 213
  illusion of, 8

power (power relations), 4, 7, 8, 11, 13, 15–16, 25, 36, 38, 46, 60, 156, 174, 179, 198, 201, 208
preference norms *see also* norms, 121–122, 128–129, 131, 150, 180, 195
progressivity *see also* alignment, 26, 51, 56, 59, 62, 71, 114, 126–127, 184, 206,
projection of talk *see also* story prefaces, 125–126, 135, 138, 143, 158, 183
prosody, 20, 22, 27–28, 36, 41, 56, 64, 71–72, 74, 77–78, 104, 109, 113, 118, 121, 123, 129, 135, 142–143, 148–149, 153–154, 158, 161, 165, 172, 182, 214

psychotherapeutic interaction, 10, 21, 26, 36, 63, 117, 129, 132–134, 137–140, 142, 146, 148, 152–153, 154, 162, 165, 175–176, 190, 195, 201–202, 208–213

questions
  alternative (split), 111, 122, 129, 148,
  ancillary, 173
  declarative, 181
  defined, 92–93
  emotion-implicative, 26, 106, 118, 120–127, 130, 180, 207–208
  feeling, 26, 106–119, 128, 130, 180, 207–208
  polar, 101, 121, 123, 128, 130, 149, 173, 183

race *see* ethnicity
recipient design, 20, 25–26, 36–37, 42, 54–55, 58–59, 61–62, 72, 74, 80, 82, 86, 92, 94, 106, 114, 118, 138, 166, 184, 187–189, 191
reflexivity (reflexive practice), ix–viii, 2–4, 6–9, 14, 22–25, 30, 35, 39, 41, 48–49, 51, 153, 156, 177, 198, 200–203, 209, 212–215
(re)formulation(s), 26, 51, 72–73, 75, 95, 97–98, 106–107, 112–113, 116–119, 121, 125, 127, 129–130, 132–154, 180, 183–184, 207–208, 211
  emotion and feelings, 70, 132–154
  emotion-implicative, 180
  extreme case, 75, 95, 97–98, 116, 149, 153, 181–182
  gist, 125, 129, 136–138
  thought, 106–131
  upshot, 113, 116, 118, 129, 136–137, 141–142, 151
  various types, 153–154
relativism *see also* constructionism, 21, 51
relevance (EMCA perspectives on), 13, 16, 24, 27, 31, 35, 42, 44–48, 51, 54, 56, 59, 62–63, 68, 71, 73, 81–82, 85–86, 88, 90–91, 93, 103–105, 107, 110–112, 114, 121, 125, 129–131, 135–136, 153, 161, 163, 180, 188, 191, 201, 203–204, 206–208, 211
repair, 44, 66–67, 97, 101, 105, 112, 114, 116, 121, 123, 131, 136, 138–139, 142, 181–182

Subject Index 259

repetition *see also* retellings, 44, 56, 59–61, 65, 79, 104, 116, 121, 129, 137–138, 140, 142, 146, 148–149, 152, 165, 167–170, 172, 174–175, 181–182, 187, 191–192, 198, 202, 207, 215
represented talk and thought (reported speech, quotatives, enactment), 28, 66–67, 74, 77, 83, 127, 145
research *see also* interviews
   Anglocentrism and Western perspectives, 4, 27, 45, 107, 192, 194
   cross-fertilization, 177, 187
   ethical considerations, ix, 4, 8–9, 14, 21, 89, 156, 175–176, 202, 213
   feminist and critical perspectives, ix, 3, 5, 8, 38–39, 46, 53, 158, 175, 208
   dangers of, x, 173–177
   generalizability, 7, 47, 64
   informed consent, 15, 156, 178
   longitudinal, 11, 48, 60, 89, 151, 173, 178, 191, 203–204, 209, 212
   partial nature of, 215
   participant recruitment, xii, 4, 11–13, 43, 85, 109, 163, 201
   practices, 2–3, 6, 14, 24, 48, 52, 106, 200–201, 206, 213, 215
   qualitative, ix, 1, 2, 4, 6–9, 11, 13, 24, 29, 35, 47, 48, 55, 85–86, 88–89, 91, 93, 106–107, 133, 153, 155–156, 158, 174–177, 185, 197–199, 207–208, 213, 215
   researcher positionality *see also* reflexivity, ix–x, 7–9, 57, 173, 201
   rigor (scholarly), ix, 5, 24, 41, 42, 46, 156, 198, 200–201, 215
   scientific, 4, 6, 8, 38–39
   taboo and erotic aspects of, 13–14, 45, 203
   transparency, 14, 83, 114, 176–177, 200–201
resistance, 4, 5, 26, 32, 51, 66–67, 72, 81, 88, 90–91, 113, 116, 126–127, 129, 133, 144, 146–147, 158, 179–182, 184, 195, 206, 210, 213
response cries, 36, 66, 109, 142, 161
response pursuits, 44, 73–74, 115, 140, 143, 146–147, 149, 151, 153, 161, 165, 208
retellings *see also* repetition, 53, 59–61, 196, 212

rhetoric (rhetorical work), 21, 22, 25, 27, 38–39, 41, 51, 53, 57, 60, 75, 88, 105, 113, 138, 191, 201, 208
romanticism *see also* emotionalism, 4–5, 13–14, 177, 205

school(ing) and classrooms, xiii, 10, 14, 16, 18–20, 79, 81, 20–21, 60, 68–70, 72–74, 79–81, 84, 90–91, 103–104, 115, 120–122, 135, 147–149, 151, 163, 165, 167–171, 178, 183, 191, 207, 210, 215
second language (L2) studies, 2–4, 14, 19, 24, 176–177, 186, 188, 191, 199, 211
sensitive matters (delicates), 12, 45, 97, 100, 112–113, 125, 156, 175–177, 182
sexuality (sexual orientation), 12–15, 27, 39, 45–46, 167–168, 200, 203–204, 211, 215
   GLBTQ (gay, lesbian, gay, bisexual, transgender, questioning), 13, 167
   bisexual, 12–14, 167
   gay, x, xi, 12–14, 27, 46, 76, 84, 117, 162, 166–168, 178, 183–184, 204
   lesbian, 13–14, 167
   questioning, 13–14, 167
   transgender, 13, 167
   'coming out', 13, 27, 167–168
   heteronormativity (heterosexism, homophobia), 11, 13–14, 45, 46, 204
   hypersexuality (hypersexualization), 14, 68, 203, 204
   mahu (Hawaiian term), 27
   queer, 27, 76
   straight, x, 14, 27, 117, 162, 167
silence (gaps, pauses), 22, 27, 44–45, 66, 70–71, 73–75, 101–102, 104, 111–113, 117–118, 120, 121, 123, 125–127, 135, 141–144, 149, 151, 158, 161, 164–165, 167, 172, 181–183, 214
socioeconomic status *see* class
Southeast Asia(ns) *see also* Cambodians, Filipinos, Indo-Chinese, Vietnamese, 1–2, 121, 178
spirituality, x, xiii, 13, 17, 60, 178, 209
stake (stake inoculation, stake and interest), 66, 72, 113

stance, x, 9, 23, 26, 30–31, 44, 56–58, 61, 71–72, 82, 97, 104, 107–109, 112–113, 116, 125, 127, 130, 135, 140, 142–143, 165, 172, 186, 205, 208
sticky objects *see* emotional objects, intensionality
stigma (stigmatization) *see also* discrimination, 4, 10, 12–13, 46, 68, 73, 76, 121, 175, 177, 203–204
stories *see* accounts, narrative, tellings
story prefaces *see also* narrative, projection, tellings, 52, 54, 56, 61–64, 66, 68, 70–72, 74–75, 82–83, 92, 94–95, 104, 127, 179, 184, 207
subject-object relations *see* also subjectivity, objectivity, 56, 58, 82, 116
subjectivity see also objectivity, subject-object relations, 1, 6, 58, 72, 81, 86, 112–113, 116, 130, 142, 158, 205
swearing (profanity, 'bad' words), 76, 81–82, 84, 122–123, 169, 170–171, 173

tellings (storytellings) *see also* accounts, narrative, xiii, 1, 2, 9–10, 14–15, 17, 19–21, 23, 25–26, 29–30, 47, 52–106, 109–110, 115, 123, 127, 130, 144, 146–147, 150, 152, 155, 158–159, 161–163, 165–166, 168–170, 172–175, 178–180, 184, 186–190, 192–196, 200–204, 206–210, 212–215
 conventionality, 6, 25–26, 33, 54, 56, 58, 75, 90, 92, 186–187, 189, 195
 defined, 55
 embeddedness of, 9, 55–56, 77, 83, 102, 212

launching, 52, 56, 61–73, 82, 83, 85, 207
Thai (Thailand), xi, 17–18, 76, 163, 169
transcripts
 sharing and reanalysis of, 51, 114, 152
 status of, 22, 95
 transcription conventions and details, 27–28, 113, 130, 152, 154
transgressive events *see also* discrimination, trauma, troubles tellings, 35, 57, 61, 64, 67, 78–79, 103, 179, 187–188
trauma *see also* mental health, 20, 26, 57, 80–82, 109, 119, 168–169, 172, 174–175, 187–193, 195, 211
troubles tellings (troubles talk) *see also* transgression, 19, 25, 44, 57–58, 60, 63–66, 79, 83, 85, 96, 101, 109, 116, 118, 121, 123, 128, 144, 148, 169, 174, 179–182, 184, 186, 188–189, 200, 211
 resistance to troubles, 67, 116, 180

uất ức (Vietnamese), 194, 196
United States (US) *see also* America, North America, x–xiii, 2, 11–12, 15–17, 19–20, 32, 67–68, 76, 79, 83, 98–99, 128, 131, 147, 150–151, 168–169, 178, 183, 192, 204, 210

Vietnamese (Vietnam), xii, 12–18, 27, 44, 46, 60, 69, 74–76, 79–84, 103, 126, 131–132, 135, 163, 166, 194
violence
 physical, xii, 17, 35, 102, 169, 173
 scholarly, ix, 201
voice, viii, 8, 19, 49, 86, 199

war, xii, 17, 79–80, 95, 110, 175, 194
workplace, 64–68, 128–129, 137, 145, 157

For Product Safety Concerns and Information please contact our EU Authorised Representative:

Easy Access System Europe

Mustamäe tee 50

10621 Tallinn

Estonia

gpsr.requests@easproject.com

www.ingramcontent.com/pod-product-compliance
Lightning Source LLC
Chambersburg PA
CBHW070557300426
44113CB00010B/1286